ADVANCES IN

EXPERIMENTAL
SOCIAL PSYCHOLOGY

VOLUME 20

ADVANCES IN

Experimental

Social Psychology

EDITED BY

Leonard Berkowitz
DEPARTMENT OF PSYCHOLOGY
UNIVERSITY OF WISCONSIN—MADISON
MADISON, WISCONSIN

VOLUME 20

ACADEMIC PRESS, INC.
Harcourt Brace Jovanovich, Publishers
San Diego   New York   Berkeley   Boston
London   Sydney   Tokyo   Toronto

Academic Press, Inc.
San Diego, California 92101

United Kingdom Edition published by
ACADEMIC PRESS INC. (LONDON) LTD.
24-28 Oval Road, London NW1 7DX

Library of Congress Catalog Card Number: 64-23452

ISBN 0-12-015220-7 (a

PRINTED IN THE UNITED STATES OF AMERICA
87 88 89 90   9 8 7 6 5 4 3 2 1

CONTENTS

Attitudes, Traits, and Actions: Dispositional Prediction of Behavior in Personality and Social Psychology

Icek Ajzen

Prosocial Motivation: Is it Ever Truly Altruistic?

C. Daniel Batson

Dimensions of Group Process: Amount and Structure of Vocal Interaction

James M. Dabbs, Jr. and R. Barry Ruback

The Dynamics of Opinion Formation

Harold B. Gerard and Ruben Orive

Positive Affect, Cognitive Processes, and Social Behavior

Alice M. Isen

Between Hope and Fear: The Psychology of Risk

Lola L. Lopes

Toward an Integration of Cognitive and Motivational Perspectives on Social Inference: A Biased Hypothesis-Testing Model

Tom Pyszczynski and Jeff Greenberg

ATTITUDES, TRAITS, AND ACTIONS: DISPOSITIONAL PREDICTION OF BEHAVIOR IN PERSONALITY AND SOCIAL PSYCHOLOGY

Icek Ajzen

DEPARTMENT OF PSYCHOLOGY
UNIVERSITY OF MASSACHUSETTS
AMHERST, MASSACHUSETTS 01003

I. Introduction

It is common practice for psychologists and laypersons alike to explain human behavior by reference to stable underlying dispositions (cf. Campbell, 1963; Heider, 1958). When people are caught lying or cheating they are considered dishonest; when they perform poorly they are said to lack ability or motivation; when they help a person in need they are called altruistic or compassionate; and when they discriminate against members of a minority group they are termed prejudiced. In the domain of personality psychology the *trait* concept has carried the burden of dispositional explanation. A multitude of personality traits has been identified and new trait dimensions continue to join the growing list. In a similar fashion the concept of *attitude* has been the focus of attention in explanations of human behavior offered by social psychologists. Numerous attitudes have been assessed over the years and, as new social issues emerge, additional attitudinal domains are explored.

The historical and largely artificial boundaries between personality and social psychology have resulted in divergent research traditions that have tended to obscure the conceptual similarities and common vicissitudes of the two concepts (Ajzen, 1982; Blass, 1984; Sherman & Fazio, 1983). Although definitions vary, personality traits and attitudes are typically conceived of as relatively enduring dispositions that exert pervasive influence on a broad range of behaviors. Both concepts gained wide popularity in the 1930s with the development of reliable psychometric techniques for their assessment, followed by a veritable avalanche of basic and applied research. For almost three decades the explanato-

1

ry values and practical utilities of attitudes and traits went virtually unchallenged. Personality psychologists devoted considerable effort to the description of personality structures in terms of multidimensional trait configurations (e.g., Cattell, 1946; Eysenck, 1953; Jackson, 1976) while social psychologists—in addition to collecting descriptive data regarding attitudes toward various social issues—attended to questions of consistency among cognitive, affective, and conative components of attitudes (see Abelson, Aronson, McGuire, Newcomb, Rosenberg, & Tannenbaum, 1968) and to effective strategies of persuasion and attitude change (see McGuire, 1969; Petty & Cacioppo, 1981). At the same time the new techniques and insights were applied to personnel selection, product design and promotion, political behavior, family planning, and a host of other more or less worthy causes. Traits and attitudes seemed assured of a central, lasting role in the prediction and explanation of social behavior.

To be sure, confidence in the trait and attitude concepts was not universal, but the occasional publication of cautionary notes or negative research findings went largely unnoticed. By the 1960s, however, doubts were being voiced with increasing frequency (see, e.g., DeFleur & Westie, 1958; Deutscher, 1966; McGuire, 1969; Peterson, 1968; Vernon, 1964). Two different lines of research contributed to the concerns. Personality psychologists often reasoned as follows: personality traits, defined as relatively enduring behavioral dispositions, should affect behavior across a variety of different situations. Thus, dishonest individuals might be expected to cheat on their income taxes, to lie to their friends, to shoplift items in department stores, and so on. Yet empirical research failed to support strong cross-situational consistency in behavior. A second line of research examined the correlation between a personality trait or attitude measure and selected behaviors deemed relevant for the trait or attitude in question. Thus, scores obtained on a questionnaire measure of hostility, or on a scale measuring attitude toward blacks, might be compared to aggressive or cooperative behavior in a laboratory setting. Studies of this kind also revealed very little consistency.

The alarm in the domain of personality psychology was sounded by Mischel (1968) who, after reviewing the literature, reached the following conclusions: "In spite of methodological reservations, . . . it is evident that the behaviors which are often construed as stable personality trait indicators actually are highly specific and depend on the details of the evoking situations and the response mode employed to measure them" (p. 37). "With the possible exception of intelligence, highly generalized behavioral consistencies have not been demonstrated, and the concept of personality traits as broad response predispositions is thus untenable" (p. 146).

The greatest challenge to the utility of the attitude concept was posed by Wicker's (1969) review of the literature in which he summarized, "Taken as a whole, these studies suggest that it is considerably more likely that attitudes will be unrelated or only slightly related to overt behaviors than that attitudes will be closely related to actions. Product–moment correlation coefficients relating the two kinds of responses are rarely above .30, and often are near zero'' (p. 65). And, like Mischel in the personality domain, Wicker concluded, ''The present review provides little evidence to support the postulated existence of stable, underlying attitudes within the individual which influence both his verbal expressions and his actions'' (p. 75).

There is also an interesting parallel between Wicker's conclusion regarding the magnitude of typical attitude–behavior correlations and Mischel's (1968) view with respect to the predictive validity of personality traits. Mischel coined the term ''personality coefficient'' to describe ''. . . the correlation between .20 and .30 which is found persistently when virtually any personality dimension inferred from a questionnaire is related to almost any conceivable external criterion involving responses sampled in a *different* medium—that is, not by another questionnaire'' (p. 78). Thus, by the end of the 1960s, personality and social psychologists had lost their faith in the trait and attitude concepts, and had concluded that only a very small proportion of behavioral variance could be explained by reference to these dispositions.

II. Manifestation of Dispositions in Behavior

Attitudes and personality traits are latent, hypothetical dispositions that must be inferred from observable responses. The crisis of confidence arose because different behavioral manifestations of the same attitude or personality trait failed to exhibit correspondence. One type of inconsistency was observed when behavioral manifestations of a given disposition varied across situations; a second when measures of general personality traits or attitudes showed only low correlations with specific actions.

A. CONSISTENCY ACROSS OBSERVATIONS

Inconsistency of behavior from one occasion to another can be introduced by factors related to the person performing the behavior, that is, by personal factors other than the attitude or personality trait of interest; by factors related to the situation in which the behavior is performed (its context, the target at which it is directed, etc.), and by factors related to the action selected to represent the behavioral domain.

1. Temporal Stability: Consistency across Time and Context

Repeated observations of the same action inevitably involve different situations. Although it is possible in principle to conceive of observing a given behavior under idential conditions on two or more occasions, conditions are rarely, if ever, identical in practice. It follows that observation of a particular action on a single occasion is a poor indication of a person's standing on an assumed underlying dispositional dimension. The observation is "contaminated" by a variety of contextual and time-bound factors that influence the behavior but are independent of the disposition in question. Temporal instability of this kind has, of course, long been recognized as a major source of unreliability in psychological measurement. The usual remedy is to aggregate observations across occasions. So long as the other influences on behavior ("measurement error") are uncorrelated across occasions, the aggregate will provide an unbiased and relatively stable measure of the behavioral disposition. For example, students' behavior on any given occasion will probably not be a reliable indicator of their tendency to return books to the library on time, but their behavior aggregated over a 6- or 12-month period should be a relatively good reflection of the disposition in question. This idea is embedded in the Spearman–Brown prophecy formula, and its implications are usually well understood (see Mischel, 1968; Mischel & Peake, 1982a,b) if not always heeded in empirical research (cf. Epstein, 1980).

Epstein (1979) has published persuasive evidence for the importance of aggregation to achieve temporal stability of behavior. In one of his experiments (Study 4), college students recorded, among other things, some of their behaviors on each day of a 14-day period. The behaviors recorded were the number of telephone calls made, the number of letters written, the number of social contacts initiated, the number of hours slept, and the number of hours studied. Consistency of behavior on any 2 days chosen at random was relatively low, ranging from a reliability coefficient of .26 for the number of telephone calls made to .63 for the number of social contacts initiated. Behavioral stability increased dramatically when the behavioral indices were aggregated across more than one observation. Comparison of average behavioral scores on the 7 odd days with average behavioral scores on the 7 even days produced correlations of .81 and .94 for the number of phone calls and number of social contacts, respectively.

Note that the temporal stability demonstrated in this kind of research also provides evidence for a certain degree of consistency across situations since different occasions provide different contexts for the same action. For instance, telephone calls made on different occasions may involve different people (targets), they may originate at home or in a public place, and so on. Although the process of aggregation tends to remove the influence of factors unique to a given context, situations encountered on one set of occasions (e.g., the 7 even days of observation) will usually not be identical to the situations encountered on another set of occasions (e.g., the 7 odd days of observation).

2. Behavioral Consistency: Manifestations across Actions and Situations

As Mischel (1983; Mischel & Peake, 1982a) has taken pains to point out, however, the demonstration that high temporal stability can be established by aggregating observations across occasions is not at the heart of the consistency debate. Of greater interest than temporal stability of a given behavior is the degree of consistency among *different* actions assumed to reflect the same disposition. Stability of this kind has usually been termed "cross-situational consistency" since different actions, even if in the same behavioral domain, almost inevitably are performed in different contexts and at different points in time. Nevertheless, it is important to realize that returning books on time to the library, for example, differs from punctuality in handing in written assignments, not only in terms of the context of the behavior but also, and perhaps more importantly, in terms of the particular activity involved (cf. Jackson & Paunonen, 1985).

There is general agreement that little consistency can be expected between a single action performed on one occasion and a different single action performed on another occasion, even if both actions are taken from the same behavioral domain (cf. Epstein, 1983; Mischel & Peake, 1982a). Evidence for instability of this kind was presented as early as 1928 by Hartshorne and May who showed, for example, that dishonesty of a specific kind in a given context (e.g., copying from another student's test paper) was virtually unrelated to dishonesty of a different kind in a different context (e.g., telling a lie outside the classroom). In a similar fashion, Newcomb (1929) found little consistency among individual behaviors related to introversion–extraversion. Thirty behaviors of problem boys in the general domain of introversion–extraversion were observed and divided into 10 trait categories. The average correlation between any two behaviors within a given category was about .14. LaPiere's (1934) well-known investigation of racial discrimination can also be seen as supporting the same argument. One single action, accepting a Chinese couple as guests in a restaurant or hotel, was found to be inconsistent with another single action, refusal to accept Chinese guests expressed in response to a written inquiry.

Findings of this kind are, of course, hardly surprising if we recall that even the *same* action performed on different occasions shows very little temporal stability. That is, inconsistency between different actions may be due, at least in part, to unreliability of measurement (see Epstein, 1979, 1980, 1983). Of greater interest, therefore, is the relation between two single actions when each is reliably assessed, i.e., when each has a high degree of temporal stability. This can be achieved by aggregating observations of each action across occasions.

An early indication that behavioral consistency is low even under such favorable conditions was provided by Dudycha (1936), who reported correlations among several aggregated measures of behavior related to punctuality: time of arrival at 8 a.m. classes, at college commons, at appointments, at extracurricular activities, at vesper services, and at entertainments. A correlation of moderate magnitude ($r = .44$) was observed between punctuality at commons and at entertainments, but the other correlations were much lower; the average correlation was .19. In a second study, Dudycha (1939) examined the relation between the number of times college students returned books to the library on time and several aggregated measures of punctuality similar to those used in the earlier research. Only one of six comparisions was found to be significant.

An example in the attitudinal domain is provided by Minard's (1952) study of race relations among black and white coal miners. Through interviews and observations, Minard discovered a general pattern of integration in the mines but widespread segregation in the community. Black and white miners tended to interact freely and on good terms in the mines, but little contact was maintained or permitted after working hours. Specifically, about 60% of the white miners displayed this inconsistent pattern of behavior, while approximately 20% discriminated in both settings and another 20% discriminated in neither.

More recent research has also provided little evidence in support of behavioral consistency. For example, Funder, Block, and Block (1983) obtained two scaled resistance-to-temptation measures in children: resisting approach to a present and resisting attractive but "forbidden" toys. Although the scales' reliabilities were not reported, each was based on more than a single observation and was thus likely to have had at least some degree of reliability. The correlation between them, however, was only .20. Similarly, even after aggregating behavioral self-reports, Epstein (1979, Study 3) found only very low and mostly nonsignificant correlations between individual behaviors seemingly tapping the same underlying disposition. Thus, the correlation between number of telephone calls made over a period of time and number of letters written in the same interval was .33; and the correlation between number of absences from class and number of papers not submitted was below .30; neither correlation was statistically significant.

In a systematic reexamination of behavioral stability with reliable measures, Mischel and Peake (1982a,b) presented data in the domain of conscientiousness among college students. Nineteen kinds of actions were observed on repeated occasions, including class attendance, punctuality in handing in assignments, thoroughness of notes taken, and neatness of personal appearance. Mischel and Peake first showed again that the temporal stability of single observations was quite low (the average correlation between observations on two individual occasions was .29) and that it could be greatly increased (to .65 on average) by aggregating across observations. These gains in temporal stability were, however, not accompanied by equal gains in behavioral consistency. The average correlation among the 19 different kinds of actions representing conscientiousness was a mere .13.[1]

On the basis of these findings, Mischel and Peake (1982a) concluded that "Although aggregation over occasions has the desirable effect of enhancing reliability, it does not provide a simple solution to the consistency paradox" (p. 736). According to these theorists, behavior is situationally specific and can be fully understood only by examining the pattern of different responses a person displays across situations. We will return to the problem of behavioral consistency and how it might be increased after considering one additional source of evidence for inconsistency, namely, research on the relation between global measures of attitudes or personality traits and particular behaviors.

B. GENERAL DISPOSITIONS AND SPECIFIC ACTIONS

The research reviewed thus far examined the relation between two or more actions that were assumed to reflect the same underlying disposition. In contrast, the approach discussed below attempts to predict performance or nonperformance of a given behavior, or a narrow range of behaviors, from a global dispositional measure, typically obtained by means of a questionnaire.

1. Global Attitudes and Specific Actions

General attitudes have been assessed with respect to a variety of targets, including organizations and institutions (the church, public housing, student government, one's job or employer), minority groups (blacks, Jews, Catholics), and particular individuals with whom one might interact (a black person, a fellow student). Attitudes of this kind are then often used to predict one or more specific acts directed at the attitude object.

A good example is the experiment reported by Himmelstein and Moore (1963). A sample of white male college students first completed a scale assessing attitudes toward blacks and, some time later, reported for a psychology experiment. Upon arrival, the participant found another student (a confederate), either black or white, already seated in the room. While they were waiting for the experiment to begin, a (white) confederate entered the room holding in his hand a petition to extend the university's library hours on Saturday nights. The black or white confederate either signed or refused to sign the petition and, following this

---

[1]In a reanalysis of the Mischel and Peake data, Jackson and Paunonen (1985) managed to raise the average correlation between different actions to .40 for a carefully selected subsample of five conscientiousness behaviors. The five behaviors selected loaded highly on the first rotated factor in a factor analysis of all 19 behaviors.

manipulation, the naive participant was asked to sign. His conformity or lack of conformity with the response of the confederate served as the measure of behavior. A secondary analysis of the data resulted in a nonsignificant phi coefficient of .06 between attitude toward blacks and conformity with the black confederate.

In a review of attitude–behavior research, Ajzen and Fishbein (1977) discovered many studies of this kind: of the 109 investigations reviewed, 54 assessed general attitudes in attempts to predict specific actions. Of these studies, 25 obtained nonsignificant results and the remainder showed correlations rarely in excess of .40. These findings are consistent with Wicker's (1969) review of the literature. In fact, it was largely on the basis of this kind of research that Wicker reached his pessimistic conclusions regarding the predictive validity of attitudes.

2. Global Personality Traits and Specific Actions

Examination of the personality literature reveals a comparable pattern of results: correlations between global personality characteristics and narrowly defined behaviors relevant to the trait in question are often nonsignificant and rarely exceed the .30 level. Epstein's (1979) study on the stability of behavior again provides some data of interest. It will be recalled that the college students in Study 4 recorded, on each day of a 14-day period, how many hours they slept and studied, how often they made telephone calls, wrote letters, and initiated social contacts. Aggregated over occasions, each action was shown to have a high degree of temporal stability. Prior to recording their behaviors, the participants completed a battery of personality inventories that assessed, among other variables, such traits as anxiety, hostility, sociability, and extroversion. The resulting measures of these traits were correlated with indices of behavior based on the total 14-day period. The great majority of these correlations was not significant despite the high reliability of the behavioral measures. Only social contacts initiated and number of hours studied correlated significantly ($r = .31$ to .52) with some of the personality traits.

The search for explanations of narrowly defined behaviors in terms of general personality traits has, as a general rule, turned out to be a frustrating experience (cf. Mischel, 1984; Mischel & Peake, 1982a), and many an investigator has given up in despair. The following sample of research is designed to illustrate the phenomenon; it is by no means an exhaustive review. One example is given by the large number of investigations that have attempted to identify unique personality characteristics of group leaders. To be sure, leadership behavior is not a single act. It is usually assessed by observing a person's amount of influence in a group, by retrospective judgments of group members, or by nominations for leadership. A measure of leadership thus encompasses a range of different behaviors reflecting influence on others in a group setting. Nevertheless, the behaviors involved are much narrower in scope than the broad personality characteristics usually considered in this context.

In an extensive review of the literature, Mann (1959) summarized obtained relations between measures of leadership and various personality characteristics. His summary results included the following: the median correlation of leadership with adjustment across different investigations was about .25; with extraversion–introversion it was about .15; and no significant correlations were reported with masculinity–femininity. In a more recent review of the available research in this area, Gibb (1969) concluded that ". . . numerous studies of the personalities of leaders have failed to find any consistent pattern of traits which characterize leaders" (p. 227).

In a similar vein, Westoff, Potter, Sagi, and Mischler (1961) found virtually no significant correlations between general personality characteristics of married women and measures of family planning behavior. Desired family size and fertility planning success correlated .11 or less with manifest anxiety, nurturance, self-control, introspection, compulsiveness, cooperativeness, and need for achievement. On the basis of reported research findings, the authors reached the conclusion that ". . . there is little evidence at this juncture . . . that the area of personality has produced fruitful results" (pp. 318–319).

Overweight and control of body weight is another area of research in which the search for personality correlates of narrowly defined behaviors has proved rather futile.[2] Although it is well known that there are great individual differences in people's ability to control their body weight, "Prediction of individual differences in weight loss has not at all been successful. Clinical intuition, MMPI, MPI, weight prior to treatment, general anxiety, situation specific anxiety, PAS, EPQ, I–E scale, body image measures, and the 16 PF questionnaire have all failed to predict success in treatment" (Hall & Hall, 1974, p. 362). A set of somewhat different personality traits was assessed in a study by Schifter and Ajzen (1985). In this investigation, an attempt was made to predict weight loss among female college students from measures of self-knowledge, ego strength, health locus of control, action control, and general competence. Only self-knowledge was found to correlate significantly with amount of weight lost (r = .25); the other correlations between personality characteristics and weight loss ranged from .05 to .17. Looking more generally at the traits of obese individuals, Leon and Roth (1977) summarized their review of the research literature as follows: "The evidence strongly suggests that there are very few personality

---

[2]As in the case of leadership, reducing and maintaining weight involve a set of behaviors (dieting, exercising), not a single action (see Ajzen & Fishbein, 1980), but the range of behaviors involved in dieting and exercising is much more narrowly defined than is the range of behaviors encompassed by the personality traits used to predict weight control.

characteristics that obese persons share that can be considered causative in the development of obesity. Neither orality, externality, nor depression universally characterize the obese individual . . .'' (p. 136).

Other illustrations of the same phenomenon abound, but the main point to be made is clear: research in diverse domains paints a discouraging picture of our ability to predict specific or narrowly defined behaviors from knowledge of people's general personality characteristics. In light of this evidence, it is easy to see why some theorists have questioned the trait approach (e.g., Argyle & Little, 1972; Endler, 1975) and why Mischel (1968) considered a correlation of .20 to .30 to be the "personality coefficient's" upper limit.

To summarize briefly, years of research failed to demonstrate impressive consistency among different behavioral manifestations of the same disposition. People were found to display little consistency across actions and situations, and their measured attitudes and personality traits did not permit prediction of specific behaviors. The accumulation of research findings of this kind undermined confidence in the trait approach among personality psychologists and cast doubts on the practices of social psychologists who relied on the attitude concept in their attempts to predict and explain human behavior.

III. Proposed Solutions

Just as infatuation and disenchantment with the trait and attitude concepts followed parallel lines, so did the proposed remedies for observed inconsistencies that emerged in the 1970s. The two most popular solutions advanced by personality and social psychologists are aggregation of observations across actions and situations, and identification of factors that moderate the degree of consistency between behavioral dispositions and actions.

A. THE AGGREGATION SOLUTION

Much of the negative research evidence reviewed above was collected in studies that used single actions, or narrowly defined classes of actions, as their behavioral criteria. Thus, behavioral stability was usually examined by correlating one specific action (e.g., returning books to the library on time) with another specific action (e.g., being on time for appointments), and global measures of traits or attitudes (e.g., dominance, sociability, attitude toward blacks or toward the church) were used to predict narrow actions deemed relevant for the trait or directed at the attitude object (e.g., using birth control methods, writing letters, conforming with the petition-signing behavior of a black individual). The problem with this approach is that single behaviors may be invalid or poor indicators of an underlying disposition. To claim evidence for inconsistency, the indicators found to be inconsistent with one another must each be based on an appropriate sample of responses from which the latent disposition can be validly inferred. Only when this condition is met can lack of correspondence between observed behaviors be taken as evidence against the existence of a stable behavioral disposition.

Before continuing our discussion of valid dispositional inference, it is important to realize that attitudes and personality traits can express themselves, and can therefore be inferred, from verbal as well as nonverbal responses. This point has often been misunderstood. Many investigators have assumed that verbal responses reflect a person's attitude or personality trait, whereas nonverbal ("overt") actions are measures of behavior. In point of fact, however, both verbal and nonverbal responses are observable behaviors. Neither is more or less a measure of attitude or personality than the other; both types of behavior can reflect the same underlying disposition (cf. Upmeyer, 1981; Roth & Upmeyer, 1985). Moreover, the validity of overt behaviors as indicators of a latent disposition cannot be taken for granted any more so than can the validity of verbal responses to questionnaire items. Both types of behavior must be submitted to standard scaling procedures, and only some responses—verbal or nonverbal— will be found adequate for the assessment of a given attitude or personality trait (cf. Ajzen & Fishbein, 1980; Jackson & Paunonen, 1985). Strictly speaking, therefore, most tests of the "attitude–behavior" or "trait–behavior" relation are better conceptualized as tests of the relation between verbal and nonverbal indicators of the same underlying disposition. However, for the sake of simplicity, and in line with common practice, the present article will continue to refer to attitude–behavior and trait–behavior relations.

To ensure selection of appropriate responses for observation, it is necessary to clearly define the behavioral domain to which the disposition applies. Consider first the case of attitudes. Most contemporary social psychologists seem to agree that the characteristic attribute of attitude is its evaluative (pro–con, pleasant–unpleasant) dimension (see, e.g., Bem, 1970; Edwards, 1957; Hill, 1981; Osgood, Suci, & Tannenbaum, 1957; Oskamp, 1977). This view is strengthened by the fact that virtually all accepted attitude scaling techniques result in a single score that locates an individual on an evaluative dimension vis-a-vis the attitude object (cf. Fishbein & Ajzen, 1975; Green, 1954). Thus, attitudes are assumed to predispose various favorable or unfavorable responses to the object of the attitude. To illustrate, attending Sunday worship services, praying before meals, and watching religious television programs might be classified as indicating a favorable attitude toward religion, whereas refusal to perform these behaviors, or engaging in such activities as premarital sex, might be taken as indications of an unfavorable attitude. Attitudes toward religion are inferred from a representative sample of all possible favorable and unfavorable behaviors of this kind. The selection of an appropriate sample of behaviors from which to infer an underlying attitude is accomplished by means of one of the standard attitude scaling procedures, such as Likert's summated ratings method or Thurstone's equal-appearing interval scale (see Edwards, 1957; Fishbein & Ajzen, 1975). For practical reasons, the behaviors sampled are usually verbal responses to statements of belief concerning the attitude object.

The inference of a personality trait from observed behavior follows very similar lines. Consider, for example, the honest–dishonest dimension. A person's standing on this trait can be inferred from a variety of behaviors, such as stealing, returning a lost wallet to its owner, cheating on income taxes, and so on. However, only behaviors that are clearly part of the trait's universe of content can be used as indicators. In the case of attitudes, the relevant universe of content was defined by the requirements that the attitude object serve as the focus of each behavior and that each behavior express some degree of favorableness or unfavorableness toward the attitude object. No limitations were placed on the *contents* of the behaviors from which attitudes are inferred; the same behaviors directed at different targets could be used to infer different attitudes. In contrast, behaviors used to infer a personality trait belong to a common content category, and different types of behaviors must be used to infer such traits as honesty, friendliness, conscientiousness, and dominance. Again, various item analysis and scaling procedures, similar to attitude scaling methods, are used to construct behavioral inventories from which personality traits can be validly inferred (see Kleinmuntz, 1967; Loevinger, 1957; Jackson, 1971; Wiggins, 1973). As in the case of attitudes, and due again mainly to practical considerations, personality inventories usually rely on verbal self-reports of behavior or reports provided by others familiar with the individual, rather than on actual behavioral observations.

The above discussion makes clear that traits and attitudes, as usually defined, represent broad behavioral dispositions and can be validly inferred only from equally broad sets of responses. Observation of a single behavior (on repeated occasions) can provide information about a person's tendency to perform that particular behavior, but it usually cannot provide a valid basis for inferring a broad response disposition. As Campbell (1963, p. 162) has pointed out, "The unreliability and invalidity of overt behavior measures should . . . be remembered . . . , and in no case should a single overt behavior be regarded as the criterion of a disposition." Yet, single actions have often been treated as if they were measures of broad behavioral tendencies. Thus, administering an electric shock to another person in a presumed learning situation is assumed to represent "aggression," waiting patiently for a toy or candy is considered to be a measure of "resistance to temptation," joining a white rather than a black person for a coffee break is taken as evidence of "discriminatory behavior," and so on. Each of these actions may in fact represent an *instance* of the behavioral category in question, but it is too specific to be representative of the general behavioral domain from which it is sampled (see Ajzen, 1982; Ajzen & Fishbein, 1980;

Epstein, 1980, 1983; Fishbein & Ajzen, 1975; Rushton, Brainerd, & Pressley, 1983). Each action is multiply determined, reflecting to some extent the influence exerted by the disposition, but also, and perhaps to a much larger extent, the effects of various other determinants, both situational and personal.

The obvious solution would seem to lie in applying the principle of aggregation to eliminate the contaminating influences of variables other than the disposition of interest. That is, in addition to aggregating repeated observations of a given action to obtain a high degree of temporal stability, it is possible to aggregate different actions in a given behavioral domain, observed on various occasions and in diverse contexts. Based on a representative set of responses, such a multiple-act index should serve as a valid indicator of the underlying disposition.[3]

1. Consistency of Behavioral Aggregates

As we saw earlier, the question of behavioral consistency has to do with the relation between two behavioral manifestations of the same disposition. Since a single action is an incomplete, unrepresentative, and hence often a poor indicator of the general behavioral tendency, we can at most expect rather low levels of consistency among single actions, an expectation well borne out by empirical research. However, if the logic of aggregation can be applied to the problem of behavioral consistency, then two multiple-act indices, each broadly representative of the same stable disposition, should correlate highly with each other.

Evidence in support of this idea has long been available in the convergent validation of attitude scales and personality trait measures. Different multi-item measures of a given attitude or personality characteristic are routinely found to yield comparable results, with convergent validities typically in the .60 to .80 range (see e.g., Edwards & Kenney, 1946; Fishbein & Ajzen, 1974; Jaccard, 1974; Lord, O'Connor, & Seifert, 1977). This point is also illustrated by the well-known fact that although interitem correlations in standard attitude or personality scales are typically in the .20 to .30 range, their split-half reliabilities or alpha coefficients are usually .70 or higher.

Convergence of different scales designed to assess attitudes or personality traits demonstrates behavioral consistency at the aggregate level, but the responses that are aggregated are all obtained by means of questionnaires. Perhaps more convincing would be data showing consistency between aggregates based on nonverbal behaviors. Ironically, evidence of this kind was already reported by Hartshorne and May (1928; Hartshorne, May, & Maller, 1929; Hartshorne, May, & Shuttleworth, 1930) in their studies of deceit and character. In the

---

[3]Although self-reports are generally considered inferior to observations of actual behavior, they often have the advantage of reflecting a summary judgment based on a diverse set of specific actions performed in a variety of contexts; that is, self-reports can be viewed as intuitive behavioral aggregates (see also Epstein, 1983).

reports of their findings, Hartshorne and May focused on the rather low correlations between individual tests, and their research has therefore often been interpreted as demonstrating little behavioral consistency. However, they also found that multi-item tests measuring different kinds of cheating in the classroom were found to correlate quite highly with each other. (See Rushton *et al.*, 1983, for a summary and discussion of this research; and Olweus, 1980, for evidence of temporal and cross-situational consistency with respect to aggregate measures of aggressiveness.)

Strong evidence for consistency of behavioral aggregates was also reported in a more recent study by Small, Zeldin, and Savin-Williams (1983). These investigators joined four small groups of adolescents as counselors on a 30-day wilderness trip and recorded the youngsters' behaviors for 2 hours each day. The actions recorded fell into two broad categories: eight different kinds of dominance behaviors (e.g., verbal directive, physical assertiveness, verbal or physical threat) and five different kinds of prosocial behaviors (e.g., physical assistance, sharing, verbal support). Moreover, behavioral observations were obtained in three different contexts: setting up and dismantling the camp, activities surrounding meals (including preparation and clean-up), and free time. Multiple-act aggregates were computed for each type of behavior (dominance and prosocial) in each of the three settings, and the data were analyzed separately for each of the four groups. Cross-situational consistency of behavioral aggregates was found to be very high. For dominance behavior, correlations between different settings ranged from .33 to .95, with a mean of .73; and for prosocial behavior the range was .48 to .99, with a mean correlation of .79.

2. *Global Dispositions and Behavioral Aggregates*

The logic of aggregation also implies a strong association between multiple-act indices of behavior and standard measures of attitudes or personality traits. Several investigations have provided support for this expectation. In one of the first demonstrations of the aggregation effect, Fishbein and Ajzen (1974) assessed attitudes toward religion by means of four standard multi-item scales: Thurstone, Likert, Guttman, and the semantic differential. In addition, the college students who participated in the research were given a list of 100 behaviors dealing with matters of religion and were asked to check the behaviors they had performed. The list of behaviors included praying before or after meals, taking a religious course for credit, and dating a person against parents' wishes. By applying Likert, Thurstone, and Guttman scaling criteria to the behavioral self-reports, three multiple-act indices of religious behavior were constructed. Each of the 100 self-reports of religious behavior (representing 100 single-act criteria), the three scaled aggregates, as well as the sum over the total set of behaviors (representing four multiple-act criteria) were correlated with each of the four standard attitude scales. As is typically found to be the case, prediction of single actions from global attitudes was largely unsuccessful. Although a few attitude–behavior correlations were as high as .40, most were rather low and not significant. The average correlation between attitudes toward religion and single behaviors was about .14. In marked contrast, the same global measures of attitude correlated highly and significantly with the aggregate indices of religious behavior; these correlations ranged from .53 to .73, and the mean correlation was .63 (see also Sjöberg, 1982; Werner, 1978). In a conceptual replication of the Fishbein and Ajzen (1974) study, Jaccard (1974) reported very similar results for the relation between the personality trait of dominance and self-reports of dominant behavior.

It can be argued as before that the weakness of these investigations is their reliance on self-reports of behavior (cf. Schuman & Johnson, 1976). However, several studies have shown the same pattern of results for observations of nonverbal behavior. For example, Weigel and Newman (1976) used a multi-item Likert scale to measure attitudes toward environmental quality and, 3 to 8 months later, obtained 14 observations of behavior related to the environment. The behaviors involved signing and circulating three different petitions concerning environmental issues, participating in a litter pick-up program, and participating in a recycling program on eight separate occasions. In addition to these 14 single-act, single-observation criteria, Weigel and Newman constructed four behavioral aggregates: one based on petition-signing behaviors, one on litter pick-ups, one on recycling, and one overall index based on all 14 observations. Prediction of each single observation from the general attitude measure was quite weak; the average correlation was .29 and not significant. The temporal aggregates, based on multiple observations of single actions, showed a mean correlation of moderate magnitude with the general attitude ($r = .42$), while the multiple-act index over all 14 observations correlated .62 with the same attitude measure. Strong associations between general measures of attitude and an aggregate index of actual behavior directed at the object of the attitude were also reported by Bandura, Blanchard, and Ritter (1969).

McGowan and Gormly (1976) reported evidence for an increase in the predictive validity of verbal *personality* measures as a result of behavioral aggregation. Undergraduate fraternity members judged each fellow member as being or not being energetic or physically active. The proportion of positive ratings was taken as a measure of each participant's standing on this trait. Five behavioral self-reports (e.g., time spent on sports, longest distance ever walked, longest distance ever run) and five observations of actual behavior (e.g., speed of walking, rate of speed going upstairs, rate of head movements) were available. The correlations between the trait measure and the ten individual behaviors ranged from .13 to .64, with an average of .42. After aggregation, the five self-reports of behavior had a correlation of .65 with the energism trait and the sum of the five observed behaviors correlated .70 with the trait. Finally, the correlation between the trait measure and an aggregate of behavior based on all ten activities was .74.

B. AGGREGATION AND THE QUESTION OF CONSISTENCY

Lack of behavioral consistency is generally seen as an embarrassing problem for personality and social psychologists. A person's behavior on one occasion suggests a friendly disposition and on another an unfriendly disposition; one day it implies that the person is honest but on another that he is dishonest. In a similar fashion, carefully constructed verbal measures of friendliness, honesty, or attitudes toward cheating are unrelated to overt behavior in specific contexts. Findings of this kind have been interpreted as evidence against the existence of stable behavioral dispositions, but the data reviewed here concerning effects of aggregation over actions and contexts should lay this pessimistic conclusion to rest. Clearly, it is possible to obtain high behavioral (i.e., cross-situational) consistency as long as the behaviors compared, even if different from each other, are each representative of the broad underlying disposition.

The issues involved are closely related to the question of reliability and what we mean by it. Factors that influence a behavior under investigation, but that are of no particular interest to the investigator, are considered ''error,'' and are said to contribute to unreliability of measurement. To be sure, what is ''error'' in one investigation may be the focus of study in another. Variations in mood, ambient temperature, noise level, and other incidental factors can constitute legitimate and important topics of investigation (e.g., Dulany, 1968; Eagly, 1974; Isen & Levin, 1972). However, they are usually of little concern in attempts to predict behavior from attitudes or personality traits; here they are thought to introduce unreliability.

It is, of course, not inconceivable that we might be interested in understanding the unique set of circumstances that cause a given action in a specific context on a given occasion. If so, we may well find that temporary moods, unanticipated distractions, situational demands, and so on account for a large proportion of the behavioral variance. The typical finding of little or no consistency among individual behaviors observed on single occasions, and their low correlations with measures of general attitudes and personality traits, attest to the relative unimportance of stable dispositions in comparison to the effects of incidental factors that are unique to a given occasion. However, with such notable exceptions as voting in an election, we are rarely interested in explaining performance or nonperformance of a single action on a given occasion. Instead, we are usually concerned with relatively stable tendencies to perform (or not to perform) a given behavior: drinking alcohol, rather than drinking a glass of champagne at a New

Year's party in the company of friends; using birth control pills, rather than taking the pill on a given day; etc. Incidental factors uniquely associated with any given occasion are therefore often of little concern. Aggregation across a sufficient number of occasions serves the purpose of reducing to an acceptable minimum error variance produced by factors of this kind.

By the same token, variance associated with different actions that are assumed to reflect the same underlying disposition may also be considered a source of error. This is legitimate whenever we are interested in a general behavioral trend, rather than in understanding the factors that result in performance or nonperformance of a given action. Thus, we may want to study aggression rather than administration of electric shocks in a learning situation, or discrimination rather than conformity with a minority group member's judgments. This requires use of multiple-act aggregates that reflect the broad behavioral tendency in question. As expected, such broad response dispositions are found to be relatively stable across time and context, and they tend to correlate well with equally broad questionnaire measures of attitudes and personality traits.

The aggregation solution to the consistency problem was anticipated as early as 1931 by Thurstone, who pointed out that two persons may hold the same attitude toward some object but that "their overt actions (may) take quite different forms which have one thing in common, namely, that they are about equally favorable toward the object" (p. 262). It would have come as no surprise to Thurstone that verbal attitudes of a general nature are largely unrelated to specific actions, but that they are closely related to multiple-act indices of behavioral trends. As is true of verbal attitude and personality trait measures, aggregate measures of behavior provide *quantitative* indicators of the underlying response disposition. Although the intensity of a general attitude or personality trait cannot predict whether or not a particular behavior will be performed, it can predict the strength of the behavioral tendency, as reflected in the aggregate response measure.

It should be noted that not all behaviors can be aggregated with equal effectiveness into a multiple-act measure (see Epstein, 1983; Jackson & Paunonen, 1985). It is not sufficient that the behaviors to be combined into an index appear to reflect the same underlying disposition, i.e., that they have face validity. Like items on a personality or attitude scale, they must be shown, by means of acceptable psychometric procedures, to share common variance and thus to be indicative of the same underlying disposition. The importance of selecting appropriate behaviors for aggregation is demonstrated in a series of studies by Buss and Craik (1980, 1981, 1984). In one of their investigations, for example, respondents in a pilot study rated each of 100 behaviors in terms of how good an example of dominance they thought it was (Buss & Craik, 1980). The average rating served as a measure of the act's prototypicality in relation to the trait of dominance. On the basis of these scores, the behaviors were divided into four categories of 25 behaviors each, from the most to the least pro-totypically dominant acts. In the main study, respondents completed two person-ality scales assessing dominance and also provided a self-rating of dominance on a 7-point scale. In addition, they reported the frequency with which they had, in the past, performed each of the 100 dominance behaviors. Four multiple-act indices were constructed by summing over the self-reports in the four pro-totypicality categories. As is usually the case, correlations between the three standard measures of dominance and each of the 100 single behaviors were very low, averaging between .10 and .20, depending on the measure used to assess the dominance trait. The correlations with the multiple-act aggregate based on the least prototypically dominant acts, however, were not much better; they ranged from .05 to .33. Only when the behaviors aggregated were considered very good examples of the dominance trait, i.e., when they appeared clearly relevant to the disposition, did the correlations between assessed dominance and behavioral trends in the dominance domain attain appreciable magnitude, rang-ing from .25 to .67.

In short, evidence for consistency and for the existence of relatively stable response dispositions is obtained when behaviors are appropriately selected and aggregated into multiple-act measures of behavioral tendencies. Mischel and Peake (1982a), however, reject this approach on the grounds that "cross-situa-tional aggregation also often has the undesirable effect of canceling out some of the most valuable data about a person. It misses the point completely for the psychologist interested in the unique patterning of the individual by treating within-person variance, and indeed the context itself, as if it were 'error' " (p. 738). Although quite consistent with the view of aggregation described above, this criticism fails to appreciate the fact that, according to the aggregation expla-nation of inconsistency, broad response dispositions (traits, attitudes) are largely irrelevant to an understanding of specific actions performed in a given context. Lack of consistency between global dispositional measures and specific actions, or between different specific acts, does not constitute evidence that the concept of personality traits as broad response dispositions is untenable (Mischel, 1968) or that there are no stable attitudes within an individual that influence verbal expressions as well as actions (Wicker, 1969). Rather, such inconsistency re-flects poor operationalization of "behavior." To expect strong relations between global measures of personality or attitude and any particular action may have been rather naive. In fact, such an expectation contradicts our definitions of attitude and personality trait as general behavioral dispositions.

It should be clear at the same time, however, that aggregation has its limitations. Through aggregation across actions and contexts we can demonstrate cross-situational consistency of behavior, as well as consistency between verbal and behavioral indicators of an underlying disposition. But, obviously, aggrega-tion does not open the way for an understanding of the factors that influence performance or nonperformance of a given action. If we are interested in the determinants of cheating on exams, for example, it will serve no useful purpose to treat this behavior as an instance of dishonesty, to compute a broad multiple-act index of various actions in the honesty domain, and to correlate this index with a verbal measure of honesty. A different approach will be needed to deal with the determinants of individual actions. We thus turn to the second proposed solution of the consistency dilemma, namely, the role of moderating variables.

C. THE MODERATING-VARIABLES SOLUTION

In contrast to the aggregation perspective, the moderating-variables solution holds out hope for consistency at the level of individual behaviors. According to this approach, the extent to which a general disposition is reflected in overt action is contingent on the operation of other factors. We may thus expect strong relations between verbal and nonverbal measures of a disposition in some instances, but little relation in others. That is, the effect of attitudes or personality traits on behavior is assumed to interact with the effects of other variables. This *interactionist* or *contingent consistency* position has been adopted both in the domain of personality (e.g., Bowers, 1973; Ekehammer, 1974; Endler & Magnusson, 1976) and in the domain of social psychology (e.g., Fazio & Zanna, 1981; Snyder, 1982; Warner & DeFleur, 1969). (See also Sherman & Fazio, 1983, for a discussion of moderating variables in personality and social psychology.) The factors that are said to interact with attitudes or personality traits may be grouped into four broad categories: characteristics of the individual, secondary characteristics of the disposition, circumstances surrounding performance of the behavior, and the nature of the behavior selected to represent the underlying disposition.

1. Individual Differences as Moderators

The search for individual difference variables as moderators of the relation between dispositions and behavior is based on the assumption that consistency can be expected for some individuals but not for others. Efforts of many investigators have thus centered on identifying the characteristics of individuals that are likely to promote or undermine consistency.

  a. Behavior-Specific Individual Differences. Arguing that not all traits are equally relevant to all people, Bem and Allen (1974) hypothesized that "Individuals who identify themselves as consistent on a particular trait dimension will in fact be more consistent cross-situationally than those who identify themselves as highly variable" (p. 512). People who are found to behave consistently in one behavioral domain may be inconsistent in another. Thus we can expect to predict behavior only for "some of the people some of the time." To test these ideas, Bem and Allen examined behavior of college students in the domains of friendliness and conscientiousness. Participants rated the extent to which they thought they *varied* from one situation to another in how friendly and outgoing they were and in how conscientious they were. They were then divided, at the median, into consistent and inconsistent subgroups, separately for each behavioral domain. The participants' standing on the two trait dimensions was assessed by means of a simple 7-point scale and by means of a multi-item self-report behavioral inventory. With respect to each trait dimension, ratings were provided by the participants themselves, by their parents, and by their peers. In addition, several nonverbal measures of behavior were obtained: friendliness displayed in the course of a group discussion and spontaneously while sitting with a confederate in a waiting room, and conscientiousness expressed in the prompt return of course evaluations, completion of course readings, and neatness of personal appearance and of living quarters. Finally, participants also completed an inventory assessing introversion–extraversion, as a possible predictor of friendliness.

Differences in consistency were explored by comparing the correlations of the high and low variability subgroups. Results in the domain of friendliness supported Bem and Allen's hypothesis. Inter-rater reliability of friendliness was significantly higher for individuals who considered themselves low rather than high in variability on the trait in question. Also, there was evidence that the introversion–extraversion scale was a somewhat better predictor of a person's rated friendliness and actual behavior in this domain for low-variability ($r = .25$ to .77) than for high-variability individuals ($r = -.12$ to .65). Finally, the correlation between friendliness in a group discussion and spontaneous friendliness was stronger in the low- ($r = .73$) than in the high- ($r = .30$) variability group. The results with respect to conscientiousness, however, did not provide as clear a picture. An analysis identical to that performed with respect to friendliness revealed no differences between low- and high-consistency subgroups. Consequently, Bem and Allen decided to divide participants into consistent versus inconsistent subgroups on the basis of variability in responses to the multi-item self-report behavioral inventory. When this was done, the expected differences in inter-rater reliabilities again emerged, but the correlations among the three objective measures of behavior did not show the expected pattern. The range of correlations here was from $-.01$ to $-.11$ for respondents low in variability and from .18 to $-.61$ for highly variable respondents.

In a replication of the Bem and Allen (1974) study, Mischel and Peake (1982a) presented data on the correlations among their 19 behaviors in the conscientiousness domain described earlier, computed separately for individuals who had judged themselves low as opposed to high in variability. The expected differences between the subgroups again failed to materialize. The mean correlation was .15 in the low variability group and .10 in the high variability group. A thorough attempt by Chaplin and Goldberg (1984) to replicate the Bem and Allen (1974) findings also resulted in failure. These investigators considered eight personality traits: friendliness, conscientiousness, honesty, sensitivity, assertiveness, activity level, emotional stability, and cultural sophistication. Furthermore, they used three methods to divide respondents into low and high consistency subgroups: Bem and Allen's two methods, as well as a division on the basis of self-rated consistency with respect to various behaviors in each of the trait domains. And, like Bem and Allen, they compared the subgroups in terms of inter-rater reliability and correlations among nonverbal measures of specific actions in each domain. The results revealed few significant differences between high- and low-consistency subgroups, irrespective of the method used to partition the sample, and there was no systematic pattern to the differences that were observed.

   b. *Personality.* In contrast to the approach advocated by Bem and Allen, which looks for individual differences in consistency that are tied to a given behavioral domain, some researchers have theorized that it is possible to identify stable personality characteristics that predispose certain individuals to exhibit strong consistency between dispositions and behavior and others to exhibit little consistency of this kind, irrespective of the behavioral domain under consideration. A case in point is Snyder's (1974) concept of *self-monitoring.* People high on this dimension are said to be rather pragmatic, acting in accordance with the requirements of the situation. In contrast, low-self-monitoring individuals are assumed to act on the basis of principles, in accordance with their personal values, preferences, and convictions. It follows that we should find stronger attitude–behavior and trait–behavior relations among the latter than among the former. Although it did not obtain a measure of actual behavior, Snyder and Swann's (1976) study of mock jury judgments is often taken as support for the idea that self-monitoring moderates the relation between attitudes and actions. The self-monitoring tendencies of college students were assessed by means of Snyder's (1974) scale, and the sample was divided at the median score into subgroups high and low on this dimension. A standard scale measuring attitudes toward affirmative action was administered and, 2 weeks later, participants were asked to reach a verdict in a mock court case involving alleged sex discrimination. For the total sample of participants, the correlation between attitudes toward affirmative action and the mock jurors' verdicts was a modest .22. However, as expected, it was stronger for individuals low in self-monitoring ($r = .42$) than for high-self-monitoring individuals ($r = .03$). Becherer and Richard (1978) reported similar differences between high- and low-self-monitoring individuals in the prediction of preferences between private and national brands of products from the 18 personality variables of the California Psychological Inventory.

However, other studies, looking at behavior rather than judgments or preferences, have not always been able to replicate these findings. For example, Zuckerman and Reis (1978) used attitudes toward donating blood at an upcoming blood drive to predict actual blood donations. In a hierarchical multiple regression analysis, the attitude–behavior correlation was found to be .36, and the addition of a term representing the interaction between attitude and self-monitoring did not significantly increase the proportion of explained variance in behavior. Little evidence for the moderating effects of self-monitoring was also reported by Ajzen, Timko, and White (1982), who attempted to predict whether or not college students would vote in an upcoming presidential election on the bases of several dispositional measures: social responsibility, liberalism–conservatism, political involvement, attitudes toward voting in the election, and intentions to vote. They also tried to predict marijuana use among the same students from social responsibility, attitudes toward smoking marijuana, and intentions to smoke marijuana. Only the intention–behavior correlations were significantly affected by self-monitoring, with low-self-monitoring individuals displaying stronger correlations than high-self-monitoring individuals. Self-monitoring failed to have a consistent moderating effect on any of the attitude–behavior or trait–behavior correlations.

Finally, Snyder and Kendzierski (1982) attempted prediction of volunteering to take part in psychological research from general attitudes toward psychological research. Participants overhead two confederates express the opinion that volunteering was either a matter of personal choice or that it depends on one's attitude toward psychological research. In neither condition did self-monitoring tendency significantly affect the magnitude of the correlations between attitudes and behavior; these correlations were .50 and .70 for low- and high-self-monitoring individuals, respectively, in the attitude-relevant condition, and .20 and .30 in the personal choice condition.

A second general characteristic that is said to moderate the degree of consistency between dispositions and behavior is *private self-consciousness*. Due to their introspective nature, people high in private self-consciousness are assumed to behave more in accordance with their dispositions than people low on this dimension. Scheier, Buss, and Buss (1978) provided some empirical support for this hypothesis. Private self-consciousness was assessed by means of the Fenigstein, Scheier, and Buss (1975) scale, and participants were selected from the top and bottom thirds of the distribution. Aggressive behavior, as measured by the average shock intensity administered on 25 ''error'' trials of the Buss (1961) aggression paradigm, was predicted from participants' scores on a 43-item aggressiveness/hostility inventory. The trait–behavior correlation was .34 for the total sample, .09 for participants low in private self-consciousness, and .66 for participants high in private self-consciousness.

Underwood and Moore (1981) replicated these findings but also obtained some unexpected results. Same-sex pairs of college students talked freely to form an impression of the other person. At the conclusion, each person rated his or her partner on overall sociability and on seven items concerning the extent to which the partner had displayed specific behaviors reflective of sociability. The two sets of ratings were combined to obtain a general measure of sociability during interaction. In addition, each participant provided the same ratings for his or her own behavior. Two behavioral sociability scores were thus available, one based on peer ratings, the other on self-ratings. The dispositional predictor was a personality measure of sociability obtained prior to the interaction, and private self-consciousness was assessed as in the Scheier *et al.* (1978) study. The correlation between the questionnaire measure of sociability and peer ratings of sociability was .44 in the case of participants high in private self-consciousness and .03 for participants low on this dimension. However, when self-ratings of sociability during interaction served as the dependent variable, the pattern was reversed: $r = .27$ and .61, respectively. No convincing explanation for this reversal is readily available.

Instead of exploiting existing differences in private self-consciousness, Wicklund and his associates (Wicklund, 1975; Duval & Wicklund, 1972) have created *self-awareness* in the laboratory, typically by means of confronting the participant with a mirror. Like private self-consciousness, heightened self-awareness is expected to increase consistency between general dispositions and specific actions. To test this hypothesis, Carver (1975) performed two replications of a study in which attitudes toward punishment were assessed by means of several questions concerning (1) its perceived effectiveness, and (2) the participant's willingness to use punishment. At a later point in time, the participants had an opportunity to administer shocks of varying intensities on 35 "error" trials in the Buss (1961) aggression paradigm. Depending on experimental conditon, a mirror was either present or absent during shock administration. In the first study, the two attitude measures predicted mean shock levels with correlations of .57 and .58 when the mirror was present, but the correlations were close to zero when the mirror was absent. A significant interaction between attitude and presence of mirror was also found in the second study, but no correlations were reported.

Similar results were obtained by Pryor, Gibbons, Wicklund, Fazio, and Hood (1977) with respect to the relation between personality and overt behavior. A mirror was either present or absent during administration of a questionnaire designed to assess sociability. Several days later, the male participants were observed interacting with a female confederate who assumed a passive role. The behavioral measure of sociability was a combination of the number of words emitted by the participant and the confederate's rating of his sociability. There were again two replications of the study, with trait–behavior correlations .55 and .73 in the mirror condition and .03 and .28 in the no-mirror condition.

2. Secondary Characteristics of the Disposition

Moderating variables related to secondary characteristics of a disposition have been examined primarily with respect to attitudes. In addition to assessing the strength and direction of an attitude, it is also possible to measure its internal structure, a person's involvement in the attitude domain, the confidence with which the attitude is held, the way it was formed, and so on. Each of these factors may have an effect on the magnitude of the relation between the general attitude and a specific behavioral tendency.

a. Internal Structure. The multidimensional view of attitude holds that attitudes are composed of cognitive, affective, and conative response tendencies (see Krech, Crutchfield, & Ballachey, 1962; McGuire, 1969; Rosenberg & Hovland, 1960). One question of interest is the degree to which the different components of attitude are evaluatively consistent with each other. In a series of three studies, Norman (1975) examined the moderating effects of consistency between an attitude's affective and cognitive components. It was expected that attitude–behavior correlations would be stronger when the two components were consistent rather than inconsistent with each other. The affective component of undergraduates' attitudes toward acting as a subject in psychological research was measured by means of a 9-point favorability scale and, in the third study, also by means of a 16-item evaluative semantic differential. The cognitive component was indexed by an expectancy-value scale based on 12 beliefs regarding the consequences of participating in psychological research. The two measures were each rank-ordered and, following Rosenberg's (1968) suggestion, the absolute difference between the ranks was taken as an index of affective–cognitive inconsistency. A median split partitioned participants into low and high internal consistency subgroups. To obtain measures of behavior, participants in the first two studies were invited to sign up for an experiment (signing up as well as actual attendance were scored), and in the third study they were recruited for two additional sessions while already participating in an experiment. The results provided partial support for the hypothesis. Across all three studies, the average correlation between behavior and the *affective* measure of attitude was .54 when affect was relatively consistent with cognition and significantly lower (mean $r = -.08$) when affect and cognition were relatively inconsistent with each other. With respect to the correlations between behavior and the *cognitive* measure of attitude, a significant difference between the high and low affective–cognitive consistency subgroups was obtained only in the third study (mean $r = .47$ and .28, respectively).

However, Fazio and Zanna (1978a) failed to find any moderating effect of affective–cognitive consistency in a replication of Norman's experiments with only minor modifications. Their hierarchical regression analysis resulted in a significant main effect of attitude on behavior (r = .32), but the attitude by internal consistency interaction did not increase this correlation significantly.

A different approach to the question of an attitude's internal consistency was adopted by Schlegel and DiTecco (1982). By means of a hierarchical factor analysis of a 20-item attitude-toward-marijuana scale administered to high school students, nonusers or initial users were shown to have less differentiated (i.e., more internally consistent) attitudes toward marijuana than occasional or regular users. Attitudes toward smoking marijuana, assessed by means of an evaluative semantic differential, were employed to predict self-reports of actual marijuana use. These attitude–behavior correlations were found to be stronger among relatively undifferentiated participants (the average attitude–behavior correlation across different subpopulations was .36) than among participants whose attitude structure was relatively complex (mean correlation = .18).

   b. Information and Reflection. Another secondary characteristic of verbal attitudes that is said to affect their relation to overt behavior is the amount of information on which the attitude is based. Davidson, Yantis, Norwood, and Montano (1985) conducted three studies that compared intention–behavior correlations among participants with varying amounts of information relevant to the behavior. The first two studies dealt with behavior in the political domain: voting choice among different candidates in a mayoral election and voting for or against certain legislative initiatives in a referendum. In the third study, behavioral intentions and actions of elderly citizens were assessed with respect to obtaining an influenza vaccination. In each case, intention–behavior consistency was found to be significantly greater for respondents who were more informed about the issues involved, or who reported being more informed.

   Somewhat related to the question of amount of information available to individuals is the extent to which attitudes are expressed after sufficient reflection. It is usually assumed that people are more likely to act in accordance with their attitudes if they "think before they act" (Snyder, 1982). Snyder and Swann's (1976) research on mock juror judgments in a sex discrimination court case mentioned earlier provided support for this idea. Prior to delivering their verdicts, one-half of the participants were encouraged to reflect upon their attitudes toward affirmative action. In this condition, the correlation between general attitudes toward affirmative action and the specific verdict was .58, as opposed to a correlation of .07 in a control group without prior reflection.

   Cacioppo, Petty, Kao, and Rodriquez (1986) have argued that people high in need for cognition are more likely to process information carefully than are people with low standing on this dimension. In accordance with Petty and Cacioppo's (1986) elaboration likelihood model, high-need-for-cognition individuals are therefore expected to exhibit stronger attitude–behavior correlations than are individuals low in need for cognition. A study designed to test this hypothesis assessed need for cognition by means of a personality scale and examined correlations between preferential attitudes toward candidates in a presidential election and voting choice. Consistent with the hypothesis, these correlations were found to be .86 versus .41 for people high and low in need for cognition, respectively. However, an analysis of responses obtained by means of thought elicitation provided little evidence that this effect was indeed due to differences in cognitive elaboration.

The findings concerning the moderating effects of reflection are quite consistent with the research on such individual difference variables as self-consciousness and self-awareness, in that reflection on one's attitudes presumably brings about self-focused attention. However, a series of studies by Wilson, Dunn, Bybee, Hyman, and Rotondo (1984) arrived at contradictory conclusions. The first of three studies employed Regan and Fazio's (1977) intellectual puzzles task, the second dealt with vacation snapshots, and the third with the relationships of dating couples. One half of the participants in each study was asked to list reasons for their attitudes toward the behavioral target: why they found the different puzzles interesting or boring, why they enjoyed or did not enjoy watching the snapshots, and why the dating relationship was good or bad. The behavioral criteria in the three studies were amount of time spent working on each puzzle type, nonverbal expressions of enjoyment while watching the snapshots, and status of the dating relationship about 9 months later. In each case, the attitude–behavior correlation was stronger (ranging from .53 to .57 across studies) when respondents were *not* asked to list reasons for their attitudes than when they were asked to do so (range of correlations: −.05 to .17). Realizing that these findings are inconsistent with previous research, Wilson *et al.* (1984) argued that whereas self-focused attention involves merely *observing* one's thoughts and feelings, participants in their studies were asked to *analyze* those thoughts and feelings. According to the investigators, this difference may be sufficient to explain the contradictory findings.

   c. Involvement.   Sivacek and Crano (1982) theorized that people with strong vested interest in a behavior are more likely to act on their attitudes than are people with little vested interest in the behavior. In one of two experiments designed to test this hypothesis, college students completed a Likert scale that assessed their attitudes toward instituting a senior comprehensive exam at their university. Vested interest in the topic was measured by responses to two question concerning the likelihood that the respondent would have to take the exam (if instituted) and the extent to which instituting the exam would directly affect the respondent. On the basis of the sum of these two responses, the participants were divided into three vested interest groups. The behavior observed was whether or not participants signed a petition opposing the proposed exam, whether or not they volunteered to help distribute petitions, write letters to newspapers, etc., and the number of hours of help they pledged. In addition, an aggregate measure of behavior was obtained by constructing a Guttman scale on the basis of these three actions. For the total sample of respondents, attitude–behavior correlations ranged from .34 to .43 for the three individual actions, while a correlation of .60 was obtained in the prediction of the behavioral aggregate. This again demonstrates the importance of aggregation to achieve strong attitude–behavior correlations. As to the effect of vested interest, the correlations between attitudes and individual actions ranged from .24 to .42 in the low vested interest group and from .60 to .74 in the high vested interest group. Using the behavioral Guttman score, this comparison showed correlations of .53 and .82, respectively. The second experiment reported by Sivacek and Crano (1982) showed a similar effect of vested interest on the relation between attitudes toward raising the legal drinking age and willingness to help defeat a referendum on this issue.

Fazio and Zanna (1978a) used latitude of rejection to operationalize involvement in the topic of psychological research. The number of positions college students judged as objectionable on a 7-point *boring–interesting* scale was taken as an index of latitude of rejection. The greater this latitude, the more involved a person is assumed to be (cf. Sherif & Hovland, 1961). A combination of the affective and cognitive instruments developed by Norman (1975) and described earlier was used to measure attitudes toward serving as a subject in psychological research. Toward the end of the experimental session, participants were asked to join a subject pool from which volunteers would be drawn for psychological research. The behavioral criterion was the number of experiments in which a person volunteered to participate. A hierarchical regression analysis resulted in a significant main effect of attitude on behavior ($r = .32$) as well as a significant attitude by involvement interaction which increased the multiple correlation to .37. When the sample was divided into high, medium, and low thirds in terms of the involvement measure, the attitude–behavior correlations in the respective subsamples were .52, .26, and .19. Additional evidence for the moderating effect of involvement on the attitude–behavior relation can be found in an investigation of a campus housing shortage reported by Regan and Fazio (1977).

d. Confidence. Several studies have obtained support for the moderating role of confidence in expressed attitudes. Perhaps the first demonstration was provided by Warland and Sample (1973; Sample and Warland, 1973). Attitudes of college students toward student government were assessed by means of a 15-item Likert scale developed by Tittle and Hill (1967). After responding to all 15 items the participants were asked to read each item again and to rate, on a 5-point scale, how certain they were with respect to the response they had given to the item. Based on the sum of these certainty ratings, participants were divided into low- and high-confidence subgroups. Attitudes toward student government were used to predict participation in undergraduate student elections, ascertained from the voting list. The correlation between attitudes and voting was .26 for the total sample, .10 for respondents with low confidence in their attitudes, and .47 for respondents with high confidence.

A significant moderating effect of attitudinal confidence was also reported in the study by Fazio and Zanna (1978a) described above. In addition to expressing their positions, the participants rated, on a 9-point scale, how certain they felt about their attitudes toward volunteering to act as subjects. The interaction between confidence and attitude, entered on the second step of a hierarchical regression analysis, increased the prediction of behavior significantly, from .32 to .37. When the sample was split into three equal subgroups on the basis of the confidence ratings, the attitude–behavior correlation was found to be .08 for respondents with low confidence and about .40 for respondents with moderate or high confidence.

Fazio and Zanna (1978b) also demonstrated the moderating effect of confidence by means of an experimental manipulation. As a measure of attitude, college students rated the interest value of each of five types of puzzles. They were then provided with bogus physiological feedback about the confidence with which they held their attitudes toward the different puzzles. One half were told that they held their attitudes with a high degree of confidence, the other half that they held their attitudes with little confidence. Three measures of behavior were obtained during a 15-minute free-play situation: the order in which each puzzle type was attempted, the number of puzzles of each type attempted (out of the total available), and the amount of time spent on each type of puzzle. Within-subjects correlations (across puzzle types) were computed between attitudes and each measure of behavior. The average correlation (across the three behaviors and across participants) in the high-confidence condition ($r = .60$) was significantly greater than the average correlation ($r = .44$) in the low-confidence condition.[4]

e. Direct Experience. It has been suggested that prediction of behavior from attitudes improves to the extent that the attitude is based on direct experience (Fazio & Zanna, 1978a,b; Regan & Fazio, 1977; see Fazio and Zanna, 1981, for a summary). Fazio and his associates have demonstrated the moderating effect of direct experience in two settings. In the first (Regan & Fazio, 1977), the relation between attitudes and behavior was examined with respect to a set of five types of intellectual puzzles. In the indirect experience condition of the experiment, participants were given a description of each puzzle type and were shown previously solved examples of the puzzles. By way of contrast, in the direct experience condition, participants were given an opportunity actually to work on the same puzzles. As described earlier, expressed interest in each puzzle type served as a measure of attitude, and behavior (order and proportion of each

---

[4]The experiment also manipulated direct versus indirect prior experience with the puzzles. The correlations reported here are averaged across these conditions of the experiment.

puzzle type attempted) was assessed during a 15-minute free-play period. Correlations between attitudes and the two measures of behavior were .51 and .54 in the direct experience condition and .22 and .20 in the indirect experience condition.

A second study demonstrating the moderating effect of direct experience was reported by Fazio and Zanna (1978a). As we saw earlier, this study examined the relation between attitudes toward participating in psychological research and actual participation (by becoming a member of the subject pool and signing up for a certain number of experiments). Amount of direct experience in this situation was defined by the number of experiments in which a person had participated as a subject in the past. Addition of the attitude-by-direct-experience interaction term in the second step of a hierarchical regression analysis raised the prediction of behavior significantly from .32 for attitude alone to .40. The attitude–behavior correlation was .42 in the top third of prior experience subsample, .36 in the subsample with moderate prior experience, and −.03 for the least experienced participants.

Fazio and Zanna (1978a) also showed that the effect of direct experience on attitude–behavior consistency was mediated in large part by confidence. Attitudes based on direct experience (as opposed to attitudes based on indirect information) were shown to be held with greater confidence, and the interaction between attitude and direct experience was reduced to nonsignificance when the investigators statistically controlled for the interaction between attitude and degree of confidence (as well as latitude of rejection).

Although the results of experiments on the moderating effects of direct experience have generally been supportive of the major hypothesis, there are also some discordant notes. Thus, the Schlegel and DiTecco (1982) study described earlier obtained stronger attitude–behavior correlations among high school students with relatively little experience concerning the use of marijuana than among students with a great deal of direct experience.

f. An Integrative Framework: Accessibility. Recently work by Fazio and his associates (Fazio, 1986; Fazio & Williams, 1986; Fazio, Chen, McDonel, & Sherman, 1982; Sherman & Fazio, 1983) has advanced a process model of the way attitudes guide behavior. This model promises to provide an integrative framework for the multitude of moderating factors related to an attitude's secondary characteristics. According to the model, accessibility of attitude in memory is perhaps the prime moderator of the attitude–behavior relation. An attitude is thought to be highly accessible if there is a strong association between the attitude object and an evaluative response. This associative strength is defined operationally as the time it takes to react to questions about the attitude object. Attitude accessibility determines the extent to which an attitude is activated upon exposure to the attitude object, and hence the extent to which the attitude is likely to guide behavior in the presence of the object. It follows that attitude–behavior consistency should increase with attitude accessibility.

The results of prior research concerning the moderating effects of direct experience, involvement, and confidence have been reinterpreted in light of the accessibility hypothesis. Thus, it is now argued (e.g., Fazio, 1986; Fazio & Williams, 1986; Sherman & Fazio, 1983) that direct experience with an attitude object, involvement in the attitudinal domain, and confidence in an expressed attitude all increase the attitude's accessibility in memory. As a result, the attitude is more likely to be activated and to guide behavior under these conditions. In support of this claim, it has been found that, in comparison to second-hand information, direct experience with intellectual puzzles leads to the formation of attitudes that are more accessible from memory (Fazio, Chen, McDonel, & Sherman, 1982; Fazio, Powell, & Herr, 1983).

Fazio and Williams (1986) provided more direct evidence for the link between attitude accessibility and the attitude–behavior relation. Voters in the 1984 presidential election were interviewed several months prior to the election. Among other things, they were asked to express their attitudes toward the two major candidates, Reagan and Mondale, on a 5-point scale, and the latencies of their responses were recorded. On the basis of these response latencies, participants were divided into high- and low-accessibility subgroups.[5] Immediately following the election, participants were contacted by telephone and were asked to report whether they had voted in the elections and, if so, for whom they had voted. As in previous studies of voting behavior, the correlation between attitudes toward the candidates and voting choice was quite high. However, in accordance with expectations, this correlation was significantly stronger among voters who had relatively easy access to their attitudes ($r = .88$) than among voters whose attitudes were less accessible ($r = .72$).

3. Situational Factors as Moderators

While most efforts to identify moderating variables have been directed at individual differences, several potential candidates of a situational nature have also been investigated. The general idea here is that different indicators of the same disposition will be more consistent with each other in some situations than in others. One factor, the *competency requirements of the situation* (Mischel, 1984), is actually a combination of situational and personal variables. Mischel (1983, 1984) has argued that consistency of behavior across situations may often be reflective of rigidity, maladjustment, and an inability to cope adequately with the requirements of a given situation. He thus hypothesized that we will find greater consistency in behavior whenever the competency requirements of the situation exceed the level of competence possessed by the individual. Mischel (1984) reports the results of a study conducted by Wright (1983) that was de-

---

[5]Because of a substantial correlation ($r = .53$) between response latency and attitude extremity, respondents were split at the median of their reaction times separately at each of the five levels of attitude.

signed to test this hypothesis. Emotionally disturbed children in summer camps served as subjects. Behaviors reflecting aggressiveness and withdrawal were of particular interest. Judges rated the situations in which behaviors were observed in terms of their cognitive and self-regulatory requirements, and they also rated the competencies of each child to meet those requirements. Within each behavioral category, correlations were computed among the various specific behaviors involved. These correlations were reported for two replications of the study. When the children's competencies were up to the requirements of the situation, the mean correlations (across behaviors and replications) were .35 for aggression and .17 for withdrawal. In contrast, when the situational requirements exceeded the competencies of the children, the corresponding correlations were .67 and .53.

A more obvious situational moderator, *situational constraints,* was investigated by Monson, Hesley, and Chernick (1982). On the basis of self-ratings, extraverted and introverted college students were selected for participation in the study. The student's taped interaction with two confederates was rated for the amount spoken and the degree of extraversion displayed. To manipulate situational constraint, the two confederates either acted neutrally during the interaction, thus permitting expression of the student's personality trait, or they constrained the student's behavior by strongly encouraging or discouraging talking on his part. As might be expected, there was significantly less behavioral variance in the two high-constraint conditions than in the condition of low constraint. That is, students tended to talk when they were encouraged to do so and to be relatively quiet when they were discouraged from talking. There was much greater variability in behavior when the confederates acted neutrally. The correlations between extraversion–introversion and behavior showed a corresponding pattern: stronger correlations ($r = .56$ and $.63$ for the two measures of behavior) under low constraint than under high constraint ($r = .10$ and $.38$).

Warner and DeFleur (1969), however, reported findings that appear to be at variance with these correlations. A large sample of college students was divided at the median score on a Likert scale designed to assess attitudes toward blacks. The measure of behavior was each participant's signed indication of willingness or refusal to perform one of eight behaviors, ranging from making a small donation to a charity for black students to dating an attractive black student. These commitments were elicited by means of a letter sent to each participant. For half the sample, the letter assured anonymity of response whereas for the other half it indicated that the participant's response would be made public in campus newspapers. It stands to reason that the public condition involved greater social constraints than did the private condition. We might thus expect behavior to be more consistent with attitudes in the latter than in the former. Although the results of the study must be interpreted with caution because of a very low response rate, they showed exactly the opposite pattern. The effect of attitude on signed approval or disapproval of the requested behavior was greater in the public condition (a difference of 77.8% between respondents with positive and negative attitudes toward blacks) than in the private condition (a difference of 17.2%).

4. Behavioral Factors as Moderators

The final source of variance in behavioral consistency to be considered has to do with the particular action that is taken as an indicator of an underlying disposition. The predictive validity of an attitude or a personality trait may be greater for some behaviors than for others. The question is how we can identify behaviors that are *relevant* for a given disposition and distinguish them from behaviors that are less relevant. One possible approach, taken by Buss and Craik (1980, 1981), was described earlier. These investigators examined the relevance of a behavior to a given disposition (e.g., dominance) by asking a sample of judges to rate how good an example of the disposition it was. However, rather than looking at the correlations between the disposition and each individual behavior in light of these ratings, Buss and Craik divided the total set of behaviors into four relevance categories (from low to high) and showed that predictive validity increased with the rated relevance of the actions comprising a multiple-act index.

By way of contrast, Fishbein and Ajzen (1974) reported data on the prediction of individual behaviors varying in their rated relevance to a disposition. It will be recalled that in this study, attitudes toward religion were assessed by means of four standard scales and that the college students who participated in the study indicated whether or not they had performed each of 100 behaviors related to matters of religion. An independent group of judges rated, for each behavior, the likelihood that it would be performed by individuals with positive attitudes toward religion and the likelihood that it would be performed by individuals with negative attitudes toward religion. The absolute difference between these two conditional probabilities was used as a measure of the behavior's relevance to the attitude. This measure of relevance was then correlated with the correlation between each behavior and the attitude score. The results thus show the extent to which the correlation between general attitudes and a specific action can be predicted from the action's judged relevance. These predictions ranged from .40 to .47 across the four measures of attitude toward religion.

Sjöberg (1982) replicated the Fishbein and Ajzen (1974) procedures in the domain of attitudes and behaviors with respect to aid to developing countries. The prediction of attitude–behavior correlations from the behavior's judged relevance to the attitude was .28 and .36 for two measures of attitude. Sjöberg also demonstrated the utility of a somewhat simpler procedure to identify the relevance of a given behavior, namely, by using the correlation between the specific action and the total behavioral score. This index of a behavior's representativeness of the behavioral domain predicted attitude–behavior correlations ($r = $ .48 and .45 for the two measures of attitude).

D. MODERATING VARIABLES AND THE QUESTION
    OF CONSISTENCY

There is an intuitive appeal to the moderating-variables approach to the consistency problem. After all, it seems reasonable to argue that some conditions are more conducive than others to a strong association between general dispositions and specific actions. Empirical research to date, however, has produced rather mixed results. The various moderating variables that have been proposed, and the limited support for their operation, give us a general sense of some of the reasons for lack of consistency between different expressions of the same underlying disposition, but the picture that emerges is far from clear.

At least two factors greatly complicate the search for moderating variables. First, the number of variables that might moderate the relation between general dispositions and specific actions is potentially unlimited. A recent study by Drake and Sobrero (1985) illustrates some unconventional possibilities. Correlations between private self-consciousness and attributions of responsibility to the self, as well as correlations between attitudes toward affirmative action and a hiring decision, were found to be moderated by whether instructions over earphones were given to the left or to the right ear. These correlations were much stronger when instructions were given to the right ear (thereby presumably activating the left cerebral hemisphere) than when they were given to the left ear. Clearly, without a conceptual framework for guidance, any attempt to identify all important moderators is bound to be a frustrating experience. The steady accumulation of additional moderators over the past few years, and the frequent failure to replicate earlier findings regarding the effects of a given moderator, may be the harbingers of things to come.

One positive development in this regard is the work by Fazio and his associates (Fazio, 1986; Fazio et al., 1982, 1983) on the processes whereby attitudes guide behavior. Their focus on attitude accessibility has provided a common explanation for the moderating effects of such secondary characteristics of an attitude as direct experience with the attitude object, involvement, confidence, and so on.

The second complicating factor is the possibility, indeed the likelihood, that the moderating effects of one variable will be found to depend on still other moderators. That is, we can expect higher-order interactions to obscure any the moderating effects of one variable will be found to depend on still other moderators. That is, we can expect higher-order interactions to obscure any systematic lower-order interactions between dispositions and identified moderating factors. Several recent studies have already demonstrated this problem. Zanna, Olson, and Fazio (1980) showed that self-monitoring tendency affected attitude–behavior correlations as predicted only for certain individuals. These investigators used a self-report of religiosity to predict several measures of religious behavior: a multiple-act index based on 90 self-reported behaviors of a religious nature, an index based on the number of times participants had attended religious services and prayed in private, and an index based on the number of times they had been intoxicated with alcohol and had used illegal drugs. No significant differences were observed in the attitude–behavior correlations of low- and high-self-monitoring individuals. However, to complicate matters, the study demonstrated a significant second-order interaction such that attitude–behavior correlations depended on a particular combination of self-monitoring tendency and self-reported behavioral variability. Correlations were highest for low-self-monitoring individuals who reported that their religious behavior was relatively invariant across situations. All other combinations of self-monitoring and variability resulted in lower correlations of about equal magnitude.

Snyder and Kendzierski (1982) also reported second-order interactions involving the self-monitoring variable. This study again employed Snyder and Swann's (1976) hypothetical sex discrimination case. With neutral instructions to weigh all relevant evidence before rendering a verdict, the study failed to replicate the original findings; that is, there was no significant difference between low- and high-self-monitoring individuals in terms of the correlation between attitudes toward affirmative action and the nature of the verdict ($r = .18$ and $-.17$, respectively). The expected difference emerged, however, when attitudes were made salient or "available" by asking participants to think about their attitudes toward affirmative action before the court case was presented. In this condition of the experiment, the attitude–behavior correlation for low-self-monitoring individuals was .47, but for high self-monitors it was only .18. Finally, attitudes predicted verdicts about equally well for both types of participants ($r = .45$ and .60) in a third condition which encouraged participants to think about the implications of their verdicts prior to rendering them but after having read the court case.

Another example of qualifications that must be put on the effects of moderating variables is provided by two studies on the relationship between attitudes toward punishment and mean shock level administered in the Buss (1961) learning paradigm (Froming, Walker, & Lopyan, 1982). The moderating variable of interest in these studies was self-awareness. According to Duval and Wicklund (1972) it should make no difference how self-awareness is brought about, whether by means of a mirror, a TV camera, or an audience. Heightened self-awareness should improve dispositional prediction of behavior, no matter how it is created. However, Froming et al. showed that manipulation of self-awareness via a mirror and via presence of an audience can produce very different effects. Moreover, the moderating effects were also found to depend on the type of audience. At the beginning of the term, college students completed a 9-item attitude-toward-punishment scale, once expressing their own opinions and once expressing the views most people have on the issue. In the first study, the respondents selected for participation had more negative attitudes toward punishment than the attitudes they attributed to others, while the reverse was true in the second study. Shocks on 20 "error" trials were administered without a mirror (control condition), in the presence of a mirror, or in the presence of a two-person audience. In the first study, the audience was either said to merely observe the subject or to evaluate his effectiveness as a teacher; in the second study, the audience consisted either of advanced psychology students (experts) or of classmates. As in previous studies, presence of a mirror was found to produce behavior more in accordance with personal attitudes toward punishment, but presence of an evaluative or expert audience induced behavior in accordance not with personal attitudes but with perceived social norms. The nonevaluative and nonexpert audiences had no significant effects on attitude–behavior correspondence. The investigators explained the observed differences between mirror and effective-audience conditions by arguing that presence of a mirror produces *private* self-consciousness whereas an audience produces *public* self-consciousness.

Whatever interpretations we manage to offer for higher-order interactions, there is no question that they greatly complicate the picture. As Cronbach (1975) has noted, "Once we attend to interactions, we enter a hall of mirrors that extends to infinity. However far we carry our analysis—to third order or fifth order or any other, untested interactions of a still higher order can be envisioned" (p. 119). Beyond pointing to the futility of such an approach, this observation raises a troubling issue: whenever an investigation fails to support a hypothesized moderating effect of a given variable, rather than rejecting the hypothesis we can attribute the failure to as yet undiscovered additional factors upon which the effect of our moderating variable may be contingent in the sense of a higher-order interaction. Speaking out against the search for person–situation interactions, Nisbett (1977) stated the problem as follows: "There are serious inherent disadvantages to interaction hypotheses, notably the difficulty of disconfirming them, their illusory aura of precision, and the disadvantages of complex designs employed to test them" (p. 235).

However, let us assume for a moment that our research efforts did result in replicable identification of the many moderating factors and their higher-order interactions. Even in such an ideal world we would still be left with a serious problem as far as the prediction of specific actions from general dispositions is concerned. A successful moderating-variables approach leads ultimately to the unavoidable conclusion that general dispositions are, by and large, poor predictors of specific action; they can be expected to predict only some behaviors, for some individuals, in some situations. Although we may be able to create in the laboratory the unique set of circumstances required for consistency, it is unlikely that this particular combination of factors will be obtained under normal conditions. The general lack of consistency between global dispositional measures and specific actions documented in the first section of this article attests to the fact that, in most cases, the prevailing conditions are far from optimal.

IV. The Principle of Correspondence

If neither aggregation nor moderating variables holds the solution to the dispositional prediction of specific actions, perhaps it is time to abandon reliance on general response tendencies and to turn instead to dispositional variables that are more closely linked to the particular behavior in question. In their review of research on the attitude–behavior relation, Ajzen and Fishbein (1977) formulated a "principle of correspondence" that can point the way to a solution. Any dispositional measure, whether verbal or nonverbal, can be defined in terms of four elements: the action involved, the target at which the action is directed, the context in which it occurs, and the time of its occurrence. Two indicators of a disposition correspond to each other to the extent that their action, target, context, and time elements are assessed at identical levels of generality or specificity. The generality or specificity of each element depends on the measurement procedures employed. A single observation of an action is a highly specific behavioral indicator in that it involves a given response, directed at a particular target, performed in a given context at a given point in time. By aggregating actions across one or more elements, a behavioral indicator can be made arbitrarily general. In the same vein, attitude and personality trait measures can be analyzed according to the generality or specificity of the action, target, context, and time elements. Thus, global attitudes toward objects and generalized personality traits specify no particular action, i.e., they are very broadly defined in terms of the action element. According to the correspondence principle, consistency between two indicators of a given disposition is a function of the degree to which the indicators assess the disposition at the same level of generality or specificity. The more similar the action, target, context, and time elements of one indicator to the elements of the other, the stronger should be the statistical relation between them.

The principle of correspondence can be viewed as a special case of the contiguity hypothesis in Guttman's (1955, 1957, 1959) facet theory. Guttman proposed that any variable can be analyzed in terms of an underlying facet structure. The action, target, context, and time elements of behavioral dispositions are examples of facets, and their levels of generality constitute facet elements. Like the principle of correspondence, "The contiguity hypothesis of facet theory states that the correlation between two variables increases with the similarity between the facet elements defining them" (Guttman, 1957, p. 130; see also Foa, 1958; Olweus, 1980).

Lord, Lepper, and Mackie (1984) demonstrated the operation of the correspondence principle by experimentally manipulating the similarity between the target elements of attitudes and actions. In the first of two studies, college students at Princeton University reported their stereotypes of members of a certain "eating club" (fraternity or sorority) at the university by rating them on a set of 20 personality trait terms. At a later session, the participants expressed their attitudes toward members of the club and toward working with a member of the club on a joint project. They were then given paragraph descriptions of two persons they could work with, one description conforming closely to the individual's stereotype of club members, the other much less in accordance with the stereotype. Finally, the participants rated how much they would like to work with each of the two club members. The target element of this behavioral preference measure is the particular person described in the paragraph. This target is clearly more similar to the target of the attitude measures (members of the club in general) when the person described conforms to the respondent's stereotype of club members than when it does not. Consistent with the principle of correspondence, the correlations between the two attitude measures and the behavioral preference were stronger under high correspondence in target elements ($r = .49$ and $.69$) than under low correspondence ($r = .27$ and $.32$). Similar results were obtained in a second study dealing with the relation between attitudes toward homosexuals and willingness to visit a homosexual individual who was described in accordance with, or not in accordance with, the respondent's stereotype of homosexuals.

With respect to correspondence in action elements, we saw earlier how it is possible, by means of aggregation across actions and contexts, to obtain measures of nonverbal responses that correspond in their levels of generality to global attitude and personality trait measures. As suggested by the principle of correspondence, such multiple-act indices of behavior are indeed found to exhibit consistency with each other and to correlate well with questionnaire measures of general attitudes and personality traits.

A. ATTITUDES AND THE PRINCIPLE OF CORRESPONDENCE

The logic of correspondence in action elements can also be applied to the dispositional prediction of specific behaviors. Consider first the case of attitudes. It is important to realize that the object of an attitude is not necessarily a person, group, institution, or policy; it can also be a behavior. People hold attitudes not only toward religion but also toward praying in private, toward democracy as well as toward voting in a given election, toward doctors and also toward maintaining a medical regimen. In fact, standard scaling procedures have been used to assess attitudes toward such behaviors as smoking marijuana (Schlegel, 1975), using birth control methods (Kothandapani, 1971), drinking alcohol (Veevers, 1971), and so on.

According to the principle of correspondence, we should be able to predict individual behaviors (directed at a certain target) from measures of attitudes toward those behaviors. By and large, the literature lends support to this expectation (see Ajzen & Fishbein, 1977, for a review of the relevant literature). For example, Kothandapani (1971) assessed the attitudes of married women toward personal use of birth control methods by means of 12 standard scales. The self-reported use or nonuse of such methods served as the behavioral criterion. All 12 attitude–behavior correlations were found to be significant, with an average coefficient of .69. Similarly, Veevers (1971) used five different instruments to measure attitudes toward drinking alcoholic beverages. Self-reports of actual drinking among residents of two Alberta communities could be predicted from these attitudes with coefficients ranging from .46 to .72.

In two laboratory studies, Ajzen (1971; Ajzen & Fishbein, 1970) attempted to predict cooperative behavior in different Prisoner's Dilemma games. The participants were pairs of same-sex college students who played three Prisoner's Dilemma games that varied in their payoff matrices. Following a few practice trials, the players were asked to complete a questionnaire that included two semantic differential measures of attitude, each comprised of four or five bipolar evaluative scales. These scales were used to obtain measures of attitude toward choosing the cooperative strategy and of attitude toward the other player. The proportion of cooperative strategy choices following completion of the questionnaire served as the behavioral criterion. Looking at the three games played in the two experiments, actual choice of cooperative moves correlated .63, .70, and .65 with attitude toward choosing the cooperative strategy. By way of comparison, the correlations between attitude toward the other player (a global attitude) and cooperative game behavior were very low and not always significant (r = .26, .09, and .27, respectively).

As a final example, consider a study conducted during the 1974 general election in Great Britain (Fishbein, Thomas, & Jaccard, 1976). Voters were interviewed prior to the election and their attitudes toward voting for each candidate in their constituency were assessed by means of an evaluative sematic differential. The average correlation between these attitude measures and actual voting choice was .85. Parenthetically, more general attitudes toward the candidates themselves also predicted voting behavior, but here the average correlation was only .51, significantly lower than the correlation obtained by using attitudes toward the act of voting for or against the competing candidates.

B. PERSONALITY TRAITS AND THE PRINCIPLE
    OF CORRESPONDENCE

For reasons to be discussed below, the idea that dispositional measures can be closely tied to a particular behavior has found little expression in the personality domain. Nevertheless, it is important briefly to consider application of the correspondence principle to personality trait measures.

1. Beliefs as Personality Traits

Some personality dimensions may be considered dispositions to hold certain beliefs rather than dispositions to act in certain ways. Optimism, idealism, open-mindedness, etc. appear to fall into this category of traits. Perhaps the best-known case in point, however, is the concept of internal–external locus of control (Rotter, 1954, 1966). This concept refers to the generalized belief that one's outcomes are under the control of one's own behavior versus outcomes being under the control of such external factors as powerful others or chance. Much research over the past 20 years has attempted to relate locus of control to a broad range of specific actions (see Lefcourt, 1981a, 1982, 1983). In view of the poor predictive validity of various general personality traits documented in an earlier section of this article, it should come as no surprise that, by and large, the results have been disappointing. For example, early work with Rotter's (1966) I–E scale focused on achievement-related behavior. On the premise that internally oriented individuals are more likely to see a connection between their behavior and achievement than externally oriented individuals, it was hypothesized that the former would exert more effort and show greater persistence than the latter. However, investigations of the relation between locus-of-control beliefs and academic performance have often produced nonsignificant or inconclusive findings (see Warehime, 1972).

Another example is provided by the failure of general locus-of-control measures to predict social or political involvement. Believing that their actions can bring about desired goals, internals should be more likely to participate in the political process. However, as Levenson (1981, p. 49) stated in her review of this research, "Perhaps no area of study using the I–E construct has led to more confusing results than that of social and political activism." While some investigations obtained data in support of the hypothesis (e.g., Gore & Rotter, 1963), others found no differences between individuals with internal and external orientations (e.g., Evans & Alexander, 1970). Still other studies actually obtained results directly opposed to prediction, with externals showing greater involvement than internals (e.g., Sanger & Alker, 1972).

Results of this kind are quite consistent with the principle of correspondence. Generalized locus-of-control beliefs fail to correspond to specific behaviors in target, action, context, and time; they can thus not be expected to permit accurate prediction. Rotter (1966) was quite aware of the need for more specialized measures of perceived locus of control. Although his I–E scale assesses generalized expectancies, his initial efforts were designed to develop a set of scales or subscales that would measure control expectations with regard to a number of different goal areas, such as achievement, social recognition, and affection (see Lefcourt, 1981b).

More specialized locus-of-control scales have indeed been constructed in subsequent years, most notably the Intellectual Achievement Responsibility (IAR) scale (Crandall, Katkovsky, & Crandall, 1965) and the Health Locus of Control (HLC) scale (Wallston, Wallston, & DeVellis, 1978; Wallston, Wallston, Kaplan, & Maides, 1976). Although dealing with more circumscribed behavioral domains than the original I–E scale, these measures are still quite general and they thus fail to correspond closely to any particular action. As might therefore be expected, prediction of specific behavior from the IAR and HLC scales has met with only very qualified success (see Lefcourt, 1982; Wallston and Wallston, 1981, for relevant literature reviews). In the domain of achievement-related behavior, results tend to confirm a positive, if often weak, relation between internality and performance (see Bar-Tal & Bar-Zohar, 1977); however, the data also contain "paradoxical inconsistencies or failures at replication" (Lefcourt, 1982, p. 98). A pattern of weak and inconsistent results is also found in research that has used the HLC scale to predict such health-related behaviors as seeking information about illness, preventive health activities, smoking cessation, weight reduction, dental hygiene, and adherence to medical regimens. In their review of this research area, Wallston and Wallston (1981, p. 236) reached the following rather pessimistic conclusion: "Human behavior is complex and multidetermined. It is simplistic to believe that health locus of control beliefs will ever predict very much of the variance in health behavior by itself [sic]."

However, in terms of conceptualizing control beliefs that correspond more closely to a behavior of interest, one need not stop at the level of perceived achievement responsibility or health locus of control. Instead, one can consider perceived control over a given behavior or behavioral goal. Along those lines, Bandura (1977, 1982) has introduced the concept of perceived *self-efficacy*, which refers to the subjective probability that one is capable of executing a certain course of action. Bandura, Adams, and Beyer (1977) showed that such self-efficacy beliefs correlate strongly with coping behavior. Adult snake phobics received one of two treatments: participant modeling (going through a series of interactions with a snake, assisted by the therapist) or modeling only. Immediately following treatment, the participants rated the likelihood that they would be capable of performing each of 18 performance tasks involving a snake (self-efficacy beliefs). During the subsequent performance test, they were asked to actually perform the graded series of behaviors. The correlations between perceived self-efficacy and performance were .83 and .84 in the two treatment conditions, respectively.

Closely related to self-efficacy is Ajzen's (1985; Schifter & Ajzen, 1985) concept of *perceived behavioral control*. In a recent study (Ajzen & Timko, 1986) it was shown that perceived control over specific health-related behaviors was far superior to the more general health locus-of-control scale in predicting corresponding actions. College students reported the frequency with which they performed each of 24 health-related behaviors, such as staying out of smoke-filled rooms, taking vitamin supplements, performing cancer self-examinations, and getting periodic TB tests. Health locus of control was assessed by means of the Wallston *et al.* (1978) scale, while perceived control with respect to each behavior was indexed by asking respondents to rate, on a 7-point scale, how easy or difficult they considered performance of the behavior to be. Internal health locus of control correlated, on the average, .10 with the 24 individual behaviors. In contrast, the average correlation between perceived behavioral control and performance of the corresponding behavior was .77.

2. *Behavioral Tendencies as Personality Traits*

Most personality traits, however, cannot be conceptualized as generalized beliefs. Instead, traits such as honesty, friendliness, conscientiousness, etc. represent broad dispositions to behave in certain ways. When the principle of correspondence is applied to traits of this kind, the general trait dimension reduces to a single behavior. Thus, instead of assessing a person's general tendency to be punctual, we might consider his tendency to return books on time to the library. This response disposition, tied as it is to the specific behavior of interest, should be a good predictor of future punctuality in returning books to the library on time. In fact, evidence reviewed earlier provided strong support for this hypothesis: when aggregated across occasions to ensure reliability, individual behaviors are known to have considerable temporal stability (see Epstein, 1979). As has often been observed, the best predictor of future behavior is usually a measure of the same behavior taken earlier. The problem, of course, is that specific behavioral dispositions of this kind have little, if any, explanatory value. It is to this issue that we turn next.

C. THE PRINCIPLE OF CORRESPONDENCE AND THE PROBLEM OF CONSISTENCY

Personality traits, in and of themselves, have only limited explanatory power. It is not particularly illuminating to say that a person appears on time for appointments because she has a tendency to be punctual or that she smiles easily because she is friendly. The personality trait itself is inferred from behavior, observed or reported; what explanatory value it does have lies in the fact that it accounts for a specific behavioral tendency (e.g., showing up on time for appointments) in terms of a more general response disposition (e.g., punctuality). However, when—in line with the principle of correspondence—the "trait" used to predict a behavior is the tendency to perform that very behavior, its explanatory power is completely lost.[6]

---

[6]It should be clear, therefore, that it serves no useful purpose to include past behavior (a measure of a very specific behavioral disposition) in *causal* models of human action. Yet, this is precisely what some theorists have proposed (e.g., Bentler & Speckart, 1979, 1981; Bagozzi, 1981; Fredricks & Dossett, 1983; Speckart & Bentler, 1982).

In contrast to most personality traits, attitudes retain their explanatory value even when they are assessed with respect to a particular behavior. As is the case for attitudes toward objects, attitudes toward behaviors are typically traced back to underlying beliefs. Of course, the beliefs in question must be relevant to the behavior; they usually deal with its consequences, its advantages and disadvantages, and its costs and benefits (see Ajzen & Fishbein, 1980; Fishbein & Ajzen, 1975). By examining the underlying beliefs we gain an understanding of the informational basis for a person's attitude toward a behavior, just as we can explain a person's attitude toward an object by reference to his beliefs about the object. In fact, everything we know about measurement, formation, and change of attitudes directed at global objects, institutions, or events can be directly applied to attitudes toward behaviors. To explore this issue fully is beyond the scope of this article. However, a concrete example may help illustrate the point. With respect to beliefs relevant to women's attitudes toward use of birth control pills, Ajzen and Fishbein's (1980, pp. 141–142) discussion of the major research findings can be summarized as follows. The considerations that entered into women's decisions to use or not to use the pill revolved around questions of physiological side effects, morality, and effectiveness. Although most women believed that using the pill leads to minor side effects (such as weight gain), they differed in their beliefs about severe consequences. The more certain a woman was that using the pill would not lead to such negative outcomes as blood clots and birth defects, the more positive her attitude tended to be. Also associated with positive attitudes toward using the pill were beliefs that this was the best available method for preventing pregnancy and that it was not morally wrong to do so.

Our concern in this article, however, is not with understanding the determinants of attitudes but rather with the use of verbal attitudes to predict other, usually nonverbal, expressions of the same disposition. As we saw above, individual behaviors can usually be predicted with considerable accuracy from corresponding verbal attitudes, but some exceptions to this rule can also be found. For example, Ajzen *et al.* (1982) studied behavior in the political domain; the criterion in this study, however, was not voting choice, but whether college students did or did not vote in the 1980 presidential election in the United States. The correlation between attitudes toward voting in the election, assessed by means of an evaluative semantic differential, and voting behavior, although significant, was only .31. Similarly, Vinokur-Kaplan (1978) assessed attitudes toward having and toward not having another child among married couples who already had one or two children. An index based on the difference between these two attitudes was found to have a correlation of only .29 with actual childbirth assessed one year later. Finally, Ajzen and Madden (1987) obtained correlations of only .22 and .18 between two measures of attitude toward obtaining an "A" in a given course, administered in the latter part of the semester, and actual grade attained in the course. Some possible reasons for low correlations of this kind, and ways to improve prediction, are considered below.

V. Prediction of Specific Actions

Unlike multiple-act measures of behavioral tendencies, single actions—even if observed in the same situation on repeated occasions—do not have the benefit of aggregation across situations and behaviors. Although attitudes toward the behavior will often capture much of what is relevant in the tendency to perform the behavior of interest, other variables may also be consistently present and exert their influence independent of attitude. Consider, for example, the case of taking off one's jacket and tie at a formal dinner. Although an individual may have a positive (personal) attitude toward this behavior, perceived social pressures may work against enacting the personal disposition. Other instances of conflict between personal attitudes toward a certain behavior and perceived social norms can be found in many moral domains, such as engaging in premarital sex, stopping at the scene of an automobile accident, or paying one's income taxes. Social pressures may also have been responsible, at least in part, for the low attitude–behavior correlations in the examples cited above. However. it is possible that other factors were involved as well. For instance, having or not having another child may depend not only on a woman's personal preferences and on her husband's perceived expectations, but also on such factors as fecundity, miscarriage, accidental pregnancy, etc. In short, attitudes toward a behavior may fail to capture the influence of these other factors or may not capture their influence fully. Whenever this is the case, measures of other variables that exert a consistent effect on the behavior across different occasions will tend to improve behavioral prediction.

The idea that attitudes may be insufficient to predict specific actions, and that other variables may have to be considered in addition to attitudes, is of course not original. What is new here is that this claim is made with respect to attitudes toward the behavior itself. Although such behavior-specific attitudes are, in many instances, expected to permit quite accurate prediction, and although their predictive validity should be superior to that of global attitudes toward the target of the behavior, there will be cases where additional variables must be taken into account. The questions of interest have to do with the conditions under which this will be the case and with the nature of these other variables. As was true in relation to moderating variables, the number of additional behavioral predictors is, in principle, almost unlimited. It would be of little value to compile a never-ending list of such predictors, nor would it be very helpful to invoke different sets of predictors as we move from one behavior to another. What is needed instead is a systematic theoretical framework that includes a relatively small number of predictor variables and that specifies the ways in which they are expected to affect human behavior.

A THEORY OF PLANNED BEHAVIOR

A recent attempt to provide such a conceptual framework can be found in Ajzen's *theory of planned behavior* (Ajzen, 1985; Ajzen & Madden, 1986; Schifter & Ajzen, 1985), which is an extension of Fishbein and Ajzen's (1975; Ajzen & Fishbein, 1980) theory of reasoned action. As in the original model, a central factor in the theory of planned behavior is the individual's *intention* to perform a behavior. Intentions are assumed to capture the motivational factors that have an impact on a behavior; they are indications of how hard people are willing to try, of how much of an effort they are planning to exert, in order to perform the behavior. Of all behavioral dispositions, intentions are most closely linked to the corresponding actions. On the basis of considerations to be discussed below, people form intentions to engage in a certain behavior. These intentions remain behavioral dispositions until, at the appropriate time and opportunity, an attempt is made to translate the intention into action.

As mentioned above, intentions are assumed to mediate the effects of various motivational factors that impact behavior. Specifically, the theory postulates three conceptually independent determinants of intentions. The first is the *attitude* toward the behavior and refers to the degree to which the person has a favorable or unfavorable evaluation of the behavior in question. The second predictor is a social factor termed *subjective norm;* it refers to the perceived social pressure to perform or not to perform the behavior. The third and novel antecedent of intention, which was not part of the theory of reasoned action, is the degree of *perceived behavioral control.* This factor, discussed earlier, refers to the perceived ease or difficulty of performing the behavior and it is assumed to reflect past experience as well as anticipated impediments and obstacles. As a general rule, the more favorable the attitude and subjective norm with respect to a behavior, and the greater the perceived behavioral control, the stronger should be the individual's intention to perform the behavior under consideration.

Intention, in turn, is viewed as one immediate antecedent of actual behavior. That is, the stronger people's intentions to engage in a behavior or to achieve their behavioral goals, the more successful they are predicted to be. However, the degree of success will depend not only on one's desire or intention, but also on such partly nonmotivational factors as availability of requisite opportunities and resources (e.g., time, money, skills, cooperation of others, etc.; see Ajzen, 1985, for a review). Collectively, these factors represent people's *actual control* over the behavior. (See also the discussions of "facilitating factors" by Triandis,

1977, "the context of opportunity" by Sarver, 1983, "resources" by Liska, 1984, and "action control" by Kuhl, 1985.) To the extent that a person has the required opportunities and resources, and intends to perform the behavior, to that extent he or she should succeed in doing so.

At first glance, the problem of behavioral control may appear to apply to only a limited range of actions. Closer scrutiny reveals, however, that even very mundane activities, which can usually be executed (or not executed) at will, are sometimes subject to the influence of factors beyond one's control. Such a simple behavior as driving to the supermarket may be thwarted by mechanical trouble with the car. Control over behavior can thus best be viewed as a continuum. On one extreme are behaviors that encounter few if any problems of control. A good case in point is voting choice: once the voter has entered the voting booth, selection among the candidates can be done at will. On the other extreme are events, such as sneezing or lowering one's blood pressure, over which we have very little or no control. Most behaviors, of course, fall somewhere in between those extremes. People usually encounter few problems of control when trying to attend class lectures or read a book, but problems of control are more readily apparent when they try to overcome such powerful habits as smoking or drinking or when they set their sights on such difficult-to-attain goals as becoming a movie star. Viewed in this light it becomes clear that, strictly speaking, most intended behaviors are best considered *goals* whose attainment is subject to some degree of uncertainty. We can thus speak of behavior–goal units, and of intentions as plans of action in pursuit of behavioral goals (Ajzen, 1985).

Although it does not deal directly with the amount of control a person actually has in a given situation, the theory of planned behavior considers the possible effects of *perceived* behavioral control on achievement of behavioral goals. Whereas intentions reflect primarily an individual's willingness to try enacting a given behavior, perceived control is likely to take into account some of the realistic constraints that may exist. To the extent that perceptions of behavioral control correspond reasonably well to actual control, they should provide useful information over and above expressed intentions.[7] A structural model of the theory of planned behavior is shown in Fig. 1.

Of course, in many situations perceived behavioral control may not be particularly realistic. This is likely to be the case when the individual has relatively little information about the behavior, when requirements or available resources have changed, or when new and unfamiliar elements have entered into the situation. Under those conditions, a measure of perceived behavioral control may add little to accuracy of behavioral prediction. The broken arrow in Fig. 1

---

[7]This contrast between motivational factors on one hand and perceived control on the other is quite similar to Bandura's (1977, 1982) distinction between outcome beliefs and self-efficacy beliefs.

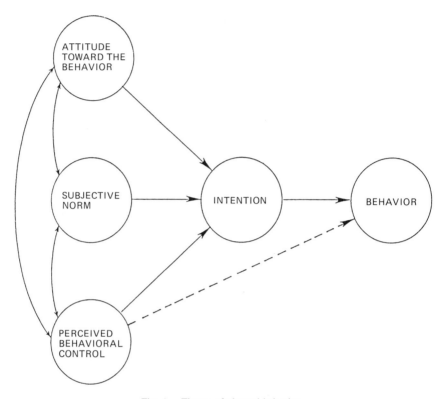

Fig. 1.   Theory of planned behavior.

indicates that the path from perceived behavioral control to behavior is expected
to emerge only when there is some agreement between perceptions of control and
the person's actual control over the behavior.

Finally, the theory deals with the antecedents of attitudes, subjective norms,
and perceived behavioral control, antecedents which in the final analysis determine intentions and actions. At the most basic level of explanation, the theory
postulates that behavior is a function of salient information, or beliefs, relevant
to the behavior. Three kinds of beliefs are distinguished: *behavioral beliefs,*
which are assumed to influence attitudes toward the behavior, *normative beliefs,*
which constitute the underlying determinants of subjective norms, and *control
beliefs,* which provide the basis for perceptions of behavioral control. As in
Ajzen and Fishbein's (1980; Fishbein & Ajzen, 1975) theory of reasoned action,
each behavioral belief links the behavior to a certain outcome or to some other
attribute such as the cost incurred by performing the behavior. The outcome's
subjective value then contributes to the attitude toward the behavior in direct

proportion to the strength of the belief, i.e., the subjective probability that performing the behavior will lead to the outcome under consideration. To obtain an estimate of attitude, belief strength is multiplied by outcome evaluation, and the resulting products are summed across all salient behavioral beliefs. Normative beliefs, on the other hand, are concerned with the likelihood that important referent individuals or groups would approve or disapprove of performing the behavior. The strength of each normative belief is multiplied by the person's motivation to comply with the referent in question, and an estimate of subjective norm is obtained by summing the resulting products across all salient referents.

According to the theory of planned behavior, among the beliefs that ultimately determine intention and action is a set that deals with the presence or absence of requisite resources and opportunities. These beliefs may be based in part on past experience with the behavior, but they will usually also be influenced by second-hand information about the behavior, by the experiences of acquaintances and friends, and by other factors that increase or reduce the perceived difficulty of performing the behavior in question. The more resources and opportunities individuals think they possess, and the fewer obstacles or impediments they anticipate, the greater should be their perceived control over the behavior. As in the case of normative beliefs, it is possible to separate out these control beliefs and treat them as partially independent determinants of behavior. Just as beliefs concerning consequences of a behavior are viewed as determining attitudes, and normative beliefs are viewed as determining subjective norms, so beliefs about resources and opportunities may be viewed as underlying perceived behavioral control.

Finally, it is worth noting that global attitudes and personality traits play no direct role in the theory of planned behavior. Variables of this kind are considered background factors that may influence some of the beliefs that ultimately result in behavioral performance, but as behavioral dispositions, they are too general to possess a great deal of predictive validity. It is possible to explore their effects within the theory's framework by examining their effects on behavioral, normative, and control beliefs and then tracing their impact on behavior through attitudes toward the behavior, subjective norms, perceived behavioral control and, finally, intentions (see Ajzen and Fishbein, 1980; Fishbein & Ajzen, 1981).

Empirical Support

Ajzen and Fishbein's (1980; Fishbein & Ajzen, 1975) theory of reasoned action can best be viewed as a special case of the theory of planned behavior. The original theory was designed to deal with behaviors over which people have a high degree of volitional control. A behavior may be said to be completely under a person's control if the person can decide at will to perform it or not to perform it. Conversely, the more that performance of the behavior is contingent on the presence of appropriate opportunities or on possession of adequate resources, the less the behavior is under purely volitional control. The theory of reasoned action assumed that most behaviors of interest in the domains of personality and social psychology fall into the volitional category (see Ajzen & Fishbein, 1980). The theory of planned behavior, however, explicitly recognizes the possibility that many behaviors may not be under complete control, and the concept of perceived behavioral control is added to handle behaviors of this kind. However, when perceived behavioral control approaches its maximum, i.e., when issues of control are not among an individual's important considerations, then the theory of planned behavior reduces to the theory of reasoned action. In those instances, neither intentions nor actions will be affected appreciably by beliefs about behavioral control, and the only remaining variables of interest are attitude toward the behavior and subjective norm.

    a. Support for the Theory of Reasoned Action. A great deal of research on the attitude–behavior relation has in recent years been conducted within the framework of the original theory of reasoned action. Considerable evidence in support of the theory has accumulated in a variety of experimental and naturalistic settings (see, e.g., Ajzen, 1971; Ajzen & Fishbein, 1980; Ajzen *et al.*, 1982; Manstead, Proffitt, & Smart, 1983; Smetana & Adler, 1980). The behaviors involved have ranged from very simple strategy choices in laboratory games to actions of appreciable personal or social significance, such as having an abortion, smoking marijuana, enlisting in the military, and choosing among candidates in an election. Since partial reviews of this literature are available elsewhere (e.g., Ajzen, 1985; Ajzen & Fishbein, 1973, 1980) no attempt will be made here to summarize the findings. Although the theory has come in for some criticism (e.g., Liska, 1984) and modifications of the theory have been proposed (e.g., Bentler & Speckart, 1979, 1981; Fredricks & Dossett, 1983), behavioral prediction on the basis of the theory is typically found to be quite successful so long as the behavior under study is of a clearly voluntary nature. In those cases, strong correlations are generally obtained between measures of intentions and observed or reported behavior. Furthermore, behavioral intentions are usually found to correlate well with attitudes toward the behavior and with subjective norms. In many studies (e.g., Ajzen, 1971; Manstead *et al.*, 1983) the attitudinal factor tends to have a stronger regression weight than the normative factor, but both are typically found to add significantly to the prediction of intentions; and in some cases (e.g., Smetana & Adler, 1980; Vinokur-Kaplan, 1978) subjective norms are found to carry more weight than attitudes. Finally, salient beliefs about the consequences of performing the behavior are generally found to correlate highly with attitudes toward the behavior, and subjective norms tend to be consistent with specific normative beliefs concerning the behavioral prescriptions of important referent individuals or groups (e.g., Fishbein & Ajzen, 1981).

    b. Perceived Behavioral Control and Intentions. Since the theory of reasoned action is a special case of the expanded theory of planned behavior, much of the empirical evidence that has accumulated in recent years with respect to the prediction of volitional behaviors is equally supportive of both models. The theory of planned behavior, however, goes beyond the theory of reasoned action in that it introduces the concept of perceived behavioral control and proposes a direct causal effect of perceived control on intention, an effect not mediated by attitude or subjective norm.[8] Evidence for this aspect of the theory is examined in this section.

Schifter and Ajzen (1985) applied the theory of planned behavior to the prediction of weight loss intentions, and actual weight reduction, among female college students. Attitudes toward losing weight during the next 6 weeks were assessed by means of several evaluative semantic differential scales. To measure subjective norms, participants were asked to indicate, again on 7-point scales, whether people who were important to them thought they should lose weight over the next 6 weeks and whether those people would approve or disapprove of their losing weight. As a measure of perceived behavioral control, participants indicated, on a scale from 0 to 100, the likelihood that if they tried they would manage to reduce weight over the next 6 weeks and their estimates that an attempt on their part to lose weight would be successful. The final measure of interest for present purposes dealt with intentions to lose weight over the next 6 weeks. Each woman indicated, on several 7-point scales, her intention to try to reduce weight and the intensity of her decision.

The first row in Table I shows the correlations of intentions to lose weight with attitudes, subjective norms, and perceived behavioral control. It can be seen that all three predictors correlated significantly with intention. A hierarchical regression analysis was performed on intentions to lose weight in which attitudes and subjective norms were entered on the first step and perceived behavioral control on the second. The results of the analysis confirmed the importance of perceived control as a third determinant of intentions to lose weight. Although the multiple correlation of intentions with attitudes and subjective norms alone was quite high ($r = .65$), it increased significantly, to .72, with the addition of perceived behavioral control. All three independent variables had significant regression coefficients, indicating that each made an independent contribution to the prediction of weight loss intentions.

The importance of perceived control over a behavioral goal was also demonstrated in a recent study on scholastic performance (Ajzen & Madden, 1987). In one part of the investigation, undergraduate college students enrolled in upper division courses expressed, at the beginning of the semester, their intentions to attempt getting an ''A'' in the course as well as their attitudes, subjective norms, and perceived control over this behavioral goal. Attitudes toward getting an

---

[8]According to the theory of reasoned action, any variable other than attitude and subjective norm can affect intention and behavior only indirectly, by influencing one of these two predictors or their relative weights.

TABLE I

Correlations of Intentions with Attitudes, Subjective Norms, and Perceived
Behavioral Control

Behavioral goal	Attitudes–intentions	Subjective norms–intentions	Perceived behavioral control–intentions
Losing weight	.62[a]	.44[a]	.36[a]
Getting an "A"	.48[a]	.11	.44[a]
Attending class	.51[a]	.35[a]	.57[a]

[a]Significant at $p < .05$.

"A," subjective norms, and perceived behavioral control were each assessed by means of several direct questions and on the basis of a set of relevant salient beliefs. The measure of intention was a set of three direct questions dealing with intentions to try getting an "A."

Before turning to the prediction of intentions, it is worth noting that the study provided support for the hypothesized relation between direct and belief-based measures of attitude, subjective norm, and perceived behavioral control. The correlations between the two types of measures ranged from .47 to .57 ($p < .01$).

The second row in Table I shows the correlations of intentions to get an "A" with the direct measures of attitudes, subjective norms, and perceived behavioral control. A hierarchical regression analysis revealed that attitudes and perceived behavioral control each had a significant effect on intention and that subjective norm did not make an independent contribution to the prediction. On the basis of attitude toward the behavior and subjective norm alone, the multiple correlation with intention was .48 ($p < .01$). The introduction of perceived behavioral control on the second step of the regression analysis raised the multiple correlation significantly, to the level of .65.

Losing weight and getting an "A" in a course are both behavioral goals over which people clearly have only limited volitional control. In addition to the desire to lose weight, people have to be familiar with an appropriate diet or exercise regimen, and they have to be capable of adhering to the diet or exercise program in the face of distractions and temptations. Similarly, getting an "A" in a course depends not only on strong motivation but also on intellectual ability, availability of sufficient time for study, resisting temptations to engage in activities more attractive than studying, etc. It is not surprising, therefore, that in light of these problems, perceived behavioral control is found to influence intentions to pursue or not to pursue the behavioral goal.

There is also evidence, however, that even when problems of volitional control are much less apparent, people's intentions are affected by their control beliefs. In the investigation by Ajzen and Madden (1987), records were kept of students' attendance of eight class lectures following administration of a questionnaire. The questionnaire contained measures of intention to attend classes regularly, attitudes toward this behavior, subjective norms, and perceived behavioral control. The latter three variables were again assessed by means of direct questions and, more indirectly, on the basis of sets of salient beliefs. The correlations between the belief indices and the direct measures were again significant, ranging from .47 to .54 ($p < .01$). As to the prediction of intentions from the direct measures, the third row of Table I shows that perceived behavioral control correlated significantly with intentions, as did attitudes and subjective norms. A hierarchical regression analysis showed that, on the basis of attitudes and subjective norms alone, the multiple correlation with intentions was .55 ($p < .01$). However, the addition of perceived behavioral control on the second step improved the prediction significantly, resulting in a multiple correlation of .68.

The findings presented above indicate that the original theory of reasoned action, with its implication that perceived behavioral control, like any other variable not included in the theory, can influence intention only indirectly via attitude or subjective norm, is not sufficient. The addition of perceived behavioral control as a direct determinant of intention improved prediction, and this effect was independent of attitudes and subjective norms.

   c. *Perceived Behavioral Control and Behavior.*   The theory of planned behavior also suggests the possibility that perceived behavioral control may be related to behavior not only indirectly, via its effect on intentions, but also directly, over and above the effect due to intentions. This possibility was explored in the studies described above in which attempts were made to predict attainment of three behavioral goals: attending lectures on a regular basis, getting an "A" in a course, and losing weight. Table II shows the correlations between

TABLE II

PREDICTION OF BEHAVIORAL ATTAINMENT FROM INTENTIONS AND PERCEIVED
BEHAVIORAL CONTROL

Behavioral goal	Intentions–behavioral attainment	Perceived behavioral control–behavioral attainment
Attending class	.36[a]	.28[a]
Losing weight	.25[a]	.41[a]
Getting an "A"		
Beginning of semester	.26[a]	.11
End of semester	.39[a]	.38[a]

[a]Significant at $p < .05$.

intentions and perceived behavioral control on one hand and attainment of the behavioral goal on the other.

With respect to regular class attendance, both intentions and perceived control correlated significantly with actual behavior. A hierarchical regression analysis, however, showed that addition of perceived behavioral control did not improve prediction of behavior significantly. This was expected since class attendance is a behavior over which students have considerable volitional control. The addition of a (subjective) measure of control thus added little information of value in the prediction of actual behavior.

In contrast, losing weight does pose problems of volitional control. As would therefore be expected, the results with respect to attainment of this goal showed the relevance of perceived behavioral control quite dramatically. As shown in the second row of Table II, both intentions and perceived control correlated significantly with goal attainment, but perceived control was the better predictor of the two. The addition of perceived behavioral control on the second step of a hierarchical regression analysis improved prediction significantly, raising the multiple correlation with goal attainment from .25 to .44.[9]

Perhaps the most interesting results, however, emerged in the study on getting an "A" in a course. The questionnaire assessing the different constructs of the theory of planned behavior was administered twice, once at the beginning of the semester and again toward the end. Perception of control over getting an "A" should, of course, become more accurate as the end of the semester approaches. As an addition to intentions, the later measure of perceived behavioral control should therefore contribute to the prediction of course grades more than the earlier measure. The data presented in the last two rows of Table II lend some support to this hypothesis. Although both, intentions and perceived control, gained in predictive accuracy, the more dramatic gain was observed with respect to the latter. Moreover, the hierarchical regression analysis showed that whereas with the data obtained early in the semester, only intention had a significant effect on behavior, with the later data, both intentions and perceived behavioral control had significant regression coefficients. Consequently, the addition of perceived behavioral control had no effect on the accuracy of behavioral prediction for the data obtained early in the semester, but it raised the correlation significantly from .39 to .45 for the data obtained toward the end of the semester.[10]

[9]There was also a marginally significant interaction between intention and perceived behavioral control. Addition of the interaction term raised the multiple correlation to .47.

[10]It is worth noting that the correlations in Table II are generally lower than those in Table I and that they are also lower than correlations typically obtained in past applications of the theory of reasoned action. The reason for the relatively weak predictions of the present behavioral criteria can probably be traced to the fact that we are dealing here with behavioral goals rather than with simple volitional acts. Inclusion of a measure reflecting perceptions of behavioral control tends to improve

VI. Discussion and Conclusions

The extensive literature reviewed and discussed in this article demonstrates that we have learned a great deal in recent years about the nature of behavioral dispositions. No longer do we hear calls for abandoning the trait approach in personality or for dispensing with the attitude construct. It is now generally understood that there is no magic about trait or attitude measures. We cannot construct a broad personality inventory or attitude scale and hope to use it as a basis for the prediction and explanation of any conceivable behavioral criterion. In fact, the very distinction between, on the one hand, attitudes and personality traits assessed by means of a questionnaire and, on the other hand, "overt" or objective behavior, must be discarded. Even so-called overt actions, observed and recorded by trained investigators, are of little interest in and of themselves. They only serve as indicators of people's response tendencies, that is, of their behavioral dispositions. As Campbell (1963) pointed out so eloquently, behavioral dispositions are residues of past experience that must be inferred from observable responses. Whether these responses are verbal or nonverbal, obtained by means of a questionnaire, observation of behavior, self-reports, or peer reports, is immaterial. Depending on circumstances, one means of data collection may produce more valid measures than another, but there is no difference in principle. Each of these methods can be used to infer the underlying disposition of interest.

It has also become very clear that reponse dispositions can be defined and measured at various levels of generality or specificity. Aggregation of responses across time, contexts, targets, or actions—or across a combination of these elements—permits inferences of dispositions at varying levels of generality. Inferred dispositions can range from the tendency to perform a single action (over time) to the tendency to engage in a broad range of actions, as reflected in a multiple-act aggregate. Even if they address the same content domain, two measures can be considered indicators of the *same* disposition only if they correspond in their levels of generality. And it is only in the presence of such correspondence that behavioral consistencies can be reliably demonstrated. The realization that measures of global attitudes and personality traits, obtained by means of responses to questionnaires, correspond only to general, broadly aggregated measures of other types of responses has helped clarify much of the initially baffling lack of predictve validity.

It is no longer very meaningful to ask whether attitudes and personality

---

prediction of goal attainment, but perceptions are not the same as actual control. Some of the unexplained variance in goal attainments may well be due to factors of control that are not sufficiently represented in perceptions.

traits predict behavior. Nor does the crucial issue have to do with the conditions under which attitudes and personality traits are related to behavior. Instead, the literature poses and provides answers to three interrelated questions. First, is there consistency between different observations of behavior? Second, do verbal responses predict "overt" behavior? And third, are general behavioral dispositions related to specific response tendencies?

A. BEHAVIORAL CONSISTENCY

The answer to the question of behavioral consistency across observations is closely tied to the issue of aggregation. Generally speaking, observations of single actions on individual occasions do not correlate well with each other. Too many factors unique to a given occasion prevent emergence of a clear response tendency. However, by aggregating observations of a given behavior across occasions, we obtain a stable measure of the disposition to perform the behavior in question. Temporal stability is in fact found to become quite high with aggregation over a sufficient number of observations.

There is also evidence for consistency between behavioral measures that aggregate across different actions, so long as each aggregate assesses the same broad underlying disposition. We can infer broad dispositions from representative samples of behaviors performed in a variety of situations, and multiple-act measures of this kind tend to correlate highly with each other.

B. GENERAL DISPOSITIONS AND SPECIFIC ACTIONS

As a general rule, broad response dispositions are poor predictors of specific actions. This is perhaps the most important lesson to be learned from the prolonged consistency controversy, but also perhaps the most difficult to accept. It would indeed be very convenient if we could measure general attitudes or personality traits and use the resulting scores to predict any behavior that appears relevant to the disposition in question. Unfortunately, both theory and empirical findings negate this possibility.

The alternative attempt to link broad behavioral dispositions to specific response tendencies by means of moderating variables has produced some interesting studies, but future progress along these lines faces serious difficulties. Perhaps the greatest shortcoming of the moderating-variables approach at this point is the lack of a conceptual framework, or even of a taxonomy, of the personal, situational, and behavioral factors that can be expected to interact with dispositions in the determination of specific actions (see Kenrick & Dantchik, 1983; Magnusson, 1981). An encouraging step in the direction of developing an integrative conceptual framework has been taken by Fazio (1986; Fazio et al., 1982, 1983) in his work on attitude accessibility. However, this framework is, at this stage, largely limited to the moderating effects of such variables as involvement with the attitude object, confidence in one's attitude, and direct experience in the attitudinal domain. Moreover, even if an acceptable framework were to emerge, there is no assurance that the moderating variables identified would indeed be found to affect accuracy of prediction in a consistent manner or that they would not interact with still other factors to produce a maze of difficult-to-reconcile effects. In any event, the multitude of conditions that moderating variables place on prediction of specific responses from broad dispositions severely limits the practical utility of this approach.

C. VERBAL AND NONVERBAL RESPONSES

What people say and what they do are not always the same (Deutscher, 1966, 1973). In part, this is a problem of measurement validity. The validity of verbal responses has often been questioned because of the possible presence of social desirability biases, acquiescence tendencies, strategic biases, etc. Somewhat less attention has been given to the measurement implications of the fact that observed actions may be equally biased to create favorable impressions, to avoid conflict, or to gain an advantage by means of ingratiation. The consequence of such biases is to invalidate the measures from which behavioral dispositions are inferred. If the biases associated with a verbal response differ greatly from the biases operating on the physical action, correlations between the two measures will necessarily deteriorate.

The potential for biased responding does not, however, doom efforts to predict nonverbal from verbal behaviors. Many situations provide little incentive for strong biases, and tendencies toward biased responding can be further reduced by careful application of appropriate measurement procedures. The question therefore remains, what is the relation between valid, relatively nonbiased verbal and nonverbal responses? The answer to this question is again related to the principle of correspondence, and it has nothing to do with the fact that one indicator of the disposition is verbal and the other nonverbal. Instead, the answer revolves around the generality or specificity of the measures involved. As noted above, verbal measures of broad attitudes or personality traits have been shown to predict equally broad, multiple-act measures of overt behavior. However, as a general rule, they do not predict specific responses, whether nonverbal or verbal. To predict single actions, we must turn to dispositional measures that deal specifically with those actions. The concept of intention appears to be a useful starting point. There is good evidence that many behaviors are sufficiently under volitional control to be predictable from people's intentions. The next step is the development of theories that specify the determinants of intentions and of corresponding actions. The theory of planned behavior described in this article represents one attempt to formulate a theory that accounts for the formation of intentions by reference to attitudes toward the behavior, subjective norms, and perceived behavioral control. The theory is designed to permit prediction and explanation of behavioral achievement by taking into account these motivational antecedents as well as other factors that may be only partly under volitional control.

ACKNOWLEDGMENTS

I would like to express my appreciation to Sy Epstein, Tony Manstead, and the editor, Leonard Berkowitz, for their helpful comments on an earlier draft of this article.

REFERENCES

Abelson, R. P., Aronson, E., McGuire, W. J., Newcomb, T. M., Rosenberg, M. J., & Tannebaum, P. H. (Eds.), (1968). *Theories of cognitive consistency: A sourcebook.* Chicago: Rand McNally.

Ajzen, I. (1971). Attitudinal vs. normative messages: An investigation of the differential effects of persuasive communications on behavior. *Sociometry,* **34,** 263–280.

Ajzen, I. (1982). On behaving in accordance with one's attitudes. In M. P. Zanna, E. T. Higgins, & C. P. Herman (Eds.), *Consistency in social behavior: The Ontario Symposium* (Vol. 2, pp. 3–15). Hillsdale, NJ: Erlbaum.

Ajzen, I. (1985). From intentions to actions: A theory of planned behavior. In J. Kuhl & J. Beckmann, (Eds.), *Action-control: From cognition to behavior* (pp. 11–39). Heidelberg: Springer.

Ajzen, I., & Fishbein, M. (1970). The prediction of behavior from attitudinal and normative variables. *Journal of Experimental Social Psychology,* **6,** 466–487.

Ajzen, I., & Fishbein, M. (1973). Attitudinal and normative variables as predictors of specific behaviors. *Journal of Personality and Social Psychology,* **27,** 41–57.

Ajzen, I., & Fishbein, M. (1977). Attitude-behavior relations: A theoretical analysis and review of empirical research. *Psychological Bulletin,* **84,** 888–918.

Ajzen, I., & Fishbein, M. (1980). *Understanding attitudes and predicting social behavior.* Englewood-Cliffs, NJ: Prentice-Hall.

Ajzen, I., & Madden, T. (1986). Prediction of goal-directed behavior: Attitudes, intentions, and perceived behavioral control. *Journal of Experimental Social Psychology,* **22,** 453–474.

Ajzen, I., & Timko, C. (1986). Correspondence between health attitudes and behavior. *Basic and Applied Social Psychology,* **7,** 259–276.

Ajzen, I., Timko, C., & White, J. B. (1982). Self-monitoring and the attitude-behavior relation. *Journal of Personality and Social Psychology,* **42,** 426–435.

Argyle, M., & Little, B. R. (1972). Do personality traits apply to social behavior? *Journal for the Theory of Social Behavior,* **2,** 1–35.

Bagozzi, R. P. (1981). Attitudes, intentions, and behavior: A test of some key hypotheses. *Journal of Personality and Social Psychology,* **41,** 607–627.

Bandura, A. (1977). Self-efficacy: Toward a unifying theory of behavioral change. *Psychological Review,* **84,** 191–215.

Bandura, A. (1982). Self-efficacy mechanism in human agency. *American Psychologist, 37,* 122–147.

Bandura, A., Adams, N. E., & Beyer, J. (1977). Cognitive processes mediating behavioral change. *Journal of Personality and Social Psychology, 35,* 125–139.

Bandura, A., Blanchard, E. B., & Ritter, B. (1969). Relative efficacy of desensitization and modeling approaches for inducing behavioral, affective, and attitudinal changes. *Journal of Personality and Social Psychology, 13,* 173–199.

Bar-Tal, D., & Bar-Zohar, Y. (1977). The relationship between perception of locus of control and academic achievement. *Contemporary Educational Psychology, 2,* 181–199.

Becherer, R. C., & Richard, L. M. (1978). Self-monitoring as a moderating variable in consumer behavior. *Journal of Consumer Research, 5,* 159–162.

Bem, D. J. (1970). *Beliefs, attitudes and human affairs.* Belmont, CA: Brooks/Cole.

Bem, D. J., & Allen, A. (1974). On predicting some of the people some of the time: The search for cross-situational consistencies in behavior. *Psychological Review, 81,* 506–520.

Bentler, P. M., & Speckart, G. (1979). Models of attitude-behavior relations. *Psychological Review, 86,* 452–464.

Bentler, P. M., & Speckart, G. (1981). Attitudes "cause" behavior: A structural equation analysis. *Journal of Personality and Social Psychology, 40,* 226–238.

Blass, T. (1984). Social psychology and personality: Toward a convergence. *Journal of Personality and Social Psychology, 47,* 1013–1027.

Bowers, K. S. (1973). Interactionism in psychology: An analysis and critique. *Psychological Review, 80,* 307–336.

Buss, A. H. (1961). *The psychology of aggression.* New York: Wiley.

Buss, D. M., & Craik, K. H. (1980). The frequency concept of disposition: Dominance and prototypically dominant acts. *Journal of Personality, 48,* 379–392.

Buss, D. M., & Craik, K. H. (1981). The act frequency analysis of interpersonal dispositions: Aloofness, gregariousness, dominance, and submissiveness. *Journal of Personality, 49,* 174–192.

Buss, D. M., & Craik, K. H. (1984). Acts, dispositions, and personality. In B. A. Maher & W. B. Maher (Eds.), *Progress in experimental personality research* (pp. 241–301). New York: Academic Press.

Cacioppo, J. T., Petty, R. E., Kao, C. F., & Rodriguez, R. (1986). Central and peripheral routes to persuasion: An individual difference perspective. *Journal of Personality and Social Psychology, 51,* 1032–1043.

Campbell, D. T. (1963). Social attitudes and other acquired behavioral dispositions. In S. Koch (Ed.), *Psychology: A study of a science.* (Vol. 6, pp. 94–172). New York: McGraw-Hill.

Carver, C. S. (1975). Physical aggression as a function of objective self-awareness and attitude toward punishment. *Journal of Experimental Social Psychology, 11,* 510–519.

Cattell, R. B. (1946). *Description and measurement of personality.* Yonkers-on-Hudson, NY: World.

Chaplin, W. F., & Goldberg, L. R. (1984). A failure to replicate the Bem and Allen study of individual differences in cross-situational consistency. *Journal of Personality and Social Psychology, 47,* 1074–1090.

Crandall, V. C., Katkovsky, W., & Crandall, V. J. (1965). Children's beliefs in their own control of reinforcement in intellectual-academic situations. *Child Development, 36,* 91–109.

Cronbach, L. J. (1975). Beyond the two disciplines of scientific psychology. *American Psychologist, 30,* 116–127.

Davidson, A. R., Yantis, S., Norwood, M., & Montano, D. E. (1985). Amount of information about the attitude object and attitude-behavior consistency. *Journal of Personality and Social Psychology, 49,* 1184–1198.

DeFleur, M. L., & Westie, F. R. (1958). Verbal attitudes and overt acts: An experiment on the salience of attitudes. *American Sociological Review*, **23**, 667–673.

Deutscher, I. (1966). Words and deeds. *Social Problems*, **13**, 235–254.

Deutscher, I. (1973). *What we say/what we do: Sentiments and acts*. Glenview, IL: Scott, Foresman.

Drake, R. A., & Sobrero, A. P. (1985). *Trait-behavior and attitude-behavior consistency: Lateral orientation effects*. Unpublished manuscript. University of Colorado.

Dudycha, G. J. (1936). An objective study of punctuality in relation to personality and achievement. *Archives of Psychology*, **29**, 1–53.

Dudycha, G. J. (1939). The dependability of college students. *Journal of Social Psychology*, **10**, 233–345.

Dulany, D. E. (1968). Awareness, rules, and propositional control: A confrontation with S-R behavior theory. In D. Horton & T. Dixon (Eds.), *Verbal behavior and S-R behavior theory* (pp. 340–387). Englewood-Cliffs, NJ: Prentice-Hall.

Duval, S., & Wicklund, R. A. (1972). *A theory of objective self-awareness*. New York: Academic Press.

Eagly, A. H. (1974). The comprehensibility of persuasive arguments as a determinant of opinion change. *Journal of Personality and Social Psychology*, **29**, 758–773.

Edwards, A. L. (1957). *Techniques of attitude scale construction*. New York: Appleton.

Edwards, A. L., & Kenney, K. C. (1946). A comparison of the Thurstone and Likert techniques of attitude scale construction. *Journal of Applied Psychology*, **30**, 72–83.

Ekehammer, B. (1974). Interactionism in personality from a historical perspective. *Psychological Bulletin*, **81**, 1026–1048.

Endler, N. S. (1975). The case for person-situation interactions. *Canadian Psychological Review*, **16**, 12–21.

Endler, N. S., & Magnusson, D. (1976). Toward an interactional theory of personality. *Psychological Bulletin*, **83**, 956–974.

Epstein, S. (1979). The stability of behavior: I. On predicting most of the people much of the time. *Journal of Personality and Social Psychology*, **37**, 1097–1126.

Epstein, S. (1980). The stability of behavior: II. Implications for psychological research. *American Psychologist*, **35**, 790–807.

Epstein, S. (1983). Aggregation and beyond: Some basic issues on the prediction of behavior. *Journal of Personality*, **51**, 360–392.

Evans, D. A., & Alexander, S. (1970). Some psychological correlates of civil rights activity. *Psychological Reports*, **26**, 899–906.

Eysenck, H. J. (1953). *The structure of human personality*. New York: Wiley.

Fazio, R. H. (1986). How do attitudes guide behavior? In R. M. Sorrentino & E. T. Higgins (Eds.), *The handbook of motivation and cognition: Foundations of social behavior* (pp. 204–243). New York: Guilford.

Fazio, R. H., Chen, J., McDonel, E. C., & Sherman, S. J. (1982). Attitude accessibility, attitude-behavior consistency, and the strength of the object-evaluation association. *Journal of Experimental Social Psychology*, **18**, 339–357.

Fazio, R. H., & Williams, C. J. (1986). Attitude accessibility as a moderator of the attitude–perception and attitude–behavior relations: An investigation of the 1984 presidential election. *Journal of Personality and Social Psychology*, **51**, 505–514.

Fazio, R. H., Powell, M. C., & Herr, P. M. (1983). Toward a process model of the attitude–behavior relation: Accessing one's attitude upon mere observation of the attitude object. *Journal of Personality and Social Psychology*, **44**, 723–735.

Fazio, R. H., & Zanna, M. (1978a). Attitudinal qualities relating to the strength of the attitude-behavior relationship. *Journal of Experimental Social Psychology*, **14**, 398–408.

Fazio, R. H., & Zanna, M. (1978b). On the predictive validity of attitudes: The roles of direct experience and confidence. *Journal of Personality*, **46**, 228–243.

Fazio, R. H., & Zanna, M. P. (1981). Direct experience and attitude-behavior consistency. In L. Berkowitz (Ed.), *Advances in experimental social psychology* (Vol. 14, pp. 161–202). New York: Academic Press.

Fenigstein, A., Scheier, M., & Buss, A. (1975). Public and private self-consciousness: Assessment and theory. *Journal of Consulting and Clinical Psychology,* **43**, 522–527.

Fishbein, M., & Ajzen, I. (1974). Attitudes toward objects as predictors of single and multiple behavioral criteria. *Psychological Review,* **81**, 59–74.

Fishbein, M., & Ajzen, I. (1975). *Belief, attitude, intention, and behavior: An introduction to theory and research.* Reading, MA: Addison-Wesley.

Fishbein, M., & Ajzen, I. (1981). Attitudes and voting behaviour: An application of the theory of reasoned action. In G. M. Stephenson & J. M. Davis (Eds.), *Progress in applied social psychology* (Vol. 1, pp. 253–313). London: Wiley.

Fishbein, M., Thomas, K., & Jaccard, J. J. (1976). Voting behavior in Britain: An attitudinal analysis. *Occasional Papers in Survey Research,* **7**, SSRC Survey Unit, London.

Foa, U. G. (1958). The contiguity principle in the structure of interpersonal relations. *Human Relations,* **11**, 229–238.

Fredricks, A. J., & Dossett, K. L. (1983). Attitude-behavior relations: A comparison of the Fishbein-Ajzen and the Bentler-Speckart models. *Journal of Personality and Social Psychology,* **45**, 501–512.

Froming, W. J., Walker, G. R., & Lopyan, K. J. (1982). Public and private self-awareness: When personal attitudes conflict with societal expectations. *Journal of Experimental Social Psychology,* **18**, 476–487.

Funder, D. C., Block, J. H., & Block, J. (1983). Delay of gratification: Some longitudinal personality correlates. *Journal of Personality and Social Psychology,* **44**, 1198–1213.

Gibb, C. A. (1969). Leadership. In G. Lindzey & E. Aronson (Eds.), *Handbook of social psychology* (2nd Ed., Vol. 4, pp. 205–282). Reading, MA: Addison-Wesley.

Gore, P. S., & Rotter, J. B. (1963). A personality correlate of social action. *Journal of Personality,* **31**, 58–64.

Green, B. F. (1954). Attitude measurement. In G. Lindzey (Ed.), *Handbook of social psychology* (Vol. 1, pp. 335–369). Reading, MA: Addison-Wesley.

Guttman, L. (1955). An outline of some new methodology for social research. *Public Opinion Quarterly,* **18**, 395–404.

Guttman, L. (1957). Introduction to facet design and analysis. *Proceedings of the Fifteenth International Congress of Psychology, Brussels* (pp. 130–132). Amsterdam: North-Holland Publishers.

Guttman, L. (1959). A structural theory for intergroup beliefs and action. *American Sociological Review,* **24**, 318–328.

Hall, S. M., & Hall, R. G. (1974). Outcome and methodological considerations in behavioral treatment of obesity. *Behavioral Therapy,* **5**, 352–364.

Hartshorne, H., & May, M. A. (1928). *Studies in the nature of character: Vol. 1. Studies in deceit.* New York: Macmillan.

Hartshorne, H., May, M. A., & Maller, J. B. (1929). *Studies in the nature of character: Vol 2. Studies in self-control.* New York: Macmillan.

Hartshorne, H., May, M. A., & Shuttleworth, F. K. (1930). *Studies in the nature of character: Vol. 3. Studies in the organization of character.* New York: Macmillan.

Heider, F. (1958). *The psychology of interpersonal relations.* New York: Wiley.

Hill, R. J. (1981). Attitudes and behavior. In M. Rosenberg & R. H. Turner (Eds.), *Social psychology: Sociological perspectives* (pp. 347–377). New York: Basic Books.

Himmelstein, P., & Moore, J. C. (1963). Racial attitudes and the action of Negro- and white-background figures as factors in petition signing. *Journal of Social Psychology,* **61**, 267–272.

Isen, A. M., & Levin, P. F. (1972). Effect of feeling good on helping: Cookies and kindness. *Journal of Personality and Social Psychology,* **21**, 384–388.

Jaccard, J. J. (1974). Predicting social behavior from personality traits. *Journal of Research in Personality*, **7**, 358–367.

Jackson, D. N. (1971). The dynamics of structured personality tests: 1971. *Psychological Review*, **78**, 229–248.

Jackson, D. N. (1976). *Jackson Personality Inventory Manual*. Port Huron, MI: Research Psychologists Press.

Jackson, D. N., & Paunonen, S. V. (1985). Construct validity and the predictability of behavior. *Journal of Personality and Social Psychology*, **49**, 554–570.

Kendrick, D. T., & Dantchik, A. (1983). Interactionism, idiographics, and the social psychological invasion of personality. *Journal of Personality*, **51**, 286–307.

Kleinmuntz, B. (1967). *Personality measurement: An introduction*. Homewood, IL: Dorsey.

Kothandapani, V. (1971). Validation of feeling, belief, and intention to act as three components of attitude and their contribution to prediction of contraceptive behavior. *Journal of Personality and Social Psychology*, **19**, 321–333.

Kretch, D., Crutchfield, R. S., & Ballachey, E. L. (1962). *Individual in society*. New York: McGraw-Hill.

Kuhl, J. (1985). Volitional aspect of achievement motivation and learned helplessness: Toward a comprehensive theory of action control. In B. A. Maher (Ed.), *Progress in experimental personality research* (Vol. 13, pp. 99–171). New York: Academic Press.

LaPiere, R. T. (1934). Attitudes vs. actions. *Social Forces*, **13**, 230–237.

Lefcourt, H. M. (1981a). (Ed.), *Research with the locus of control construct. Vol. 1: Assessment methods*. New York: Academic Press.

Lefcourt, H. M. (1981b). Overview. In H. M. Lefcourt (Ed.), *Research with the locus of control construct. Vol. 1: Assessment methods* (pp. 1–11). New York: Academic Press.

Lefcourt, H. M. (1982). *Locus of control: Current trends in theory and research* (2nd ed.). Hillsdale, NJ: Erlbaum.

Lefcourt, H. M. (1983). (Ed.), *Research with the locus of control construct. Vol. 2: Developments and social problems*. New York: Academic Press.

Leon, G. R., & Roth, L. (1977). Obesity: Psychological causes, correlations, and speculations. *Psychological Bulletin*, **84**, 117–139.

Levenson, H. (1981). Differentiating among internality, powerful others, and chance. In H. M. Lefcourt (Ed.), *Research with the locus of control construct. Vol. 1: Assessment methods* (pp. 15–63). New York: Academic Press.

Liska, A. E. (1984). A critical examination of the causal structure of the Fishbein/Ajzen attitude-behavior model. *Social Psychology Quarterly*, **47**, 61–74.

Loevinger, J. (1957). Objective tests as instruments of psychological theory. *Psychological Reports*, **3**, 635–694 (Monograph No. 9).

Lord, C. G., Lepper, M. R., & Mackie, D. (1984). Attitude prototypes as determinants of attitude-behavior consistency. *Journal of Personality and Social Psychology*, **46**, 1254–1266.

Lorr, M., O'Connor, J. P., & Seifert, R. F. (1977). A comparison of four personality inventories. *Journal of Personality Assessment*, **41**, 520–526.

Magnusson, D. (1981). (Ed.), *Toward a psychology of situations: An interactional perspective*. Hillsdale, NJ: Erlbaum.

Mann, R. D. (1959). A review of the relationships between personality and performance in small groups. *Psychological Bulletin*, **56**, 241–270.

Manstead, A. S. R., Proffitt, C., & Smart, J. L. (1983). Predicting and understanding mothers' infant-feeding intentions and behavior: Testing the theory of reasoned action. *Journal of Personality and Social Psychology*, **44**, 657–671.

McGowan, J., & Gormly, J. (1976). Validation of personality traits: A multicriteria approach. *Journal of Personality and Social Psychology*, **34**, 791–795.

McGuire, W. J. (1969). *The nature of attitudes and attitude change.* In G. Lindzey & E. Aronson (Eds.), *The handbook of social psychology* (2nd ed., Vol. 3, pp. 136–314). Reading, MA: Addison-Wesley.

Minard, R. D. (1952). Race relations in the Pocahontas coal field. *Journal of Social Issues,* **8,** 29–44.

Mischel, W. (1968). *Personality and assessment.* New York: Wiley.

Mischel, W. (1983). Alternatives in the pursuit of the predictability and consistency of persons: Stable data that yield unstable interpretations. *Journal of Personality,* **51,** 578–604.

Mischel, W. (1984). Convergences and challenges in the search for consistency. *American Psychologist,* **39,** 351–364.

Mischel, W., & Peake, P. K. (1982a). Beyond déjà vu in the search for cross-situational consistency. *Psychological Review,* **89,** 730–755.

Mischel, W., & Peake, P. K. (1982b). In search of consistency: Measure for measure. In M. P. Zanna, E. T. Higgins, & C. P. Herman (Eds.), *Consistency in social behavior: The Ontario Symposium* (Vol. 2, pp. 187–207). Hillsdale, NJ: Erlbaum.

Monson, T. C., Hesley, J. W., & Chernick, L. (1982). Specifying when personality traits can and cannot predict behavior: An alternative to abandoning the attempt to predict single-act criteria. *Journal of Personality and Social Psychology,* **43,** 385–399.

Newcomb, T. M. (1929). *Consistency of certain extrovert-introvert behavior patterns in 51 problem boys.* New York: Columbia University Teachers College, Bureau of Publications.

Nisbett, R. E. (1977). Interaction versus main effects as goals of personality research. In D. Magnusson & N. S. Endler (Eds.), *Personality at the crossroads: Current issues in interactional psychology* (pp. 235–241). New York: Wiley.

Norman, R. (1975). Affective-cognitive consistency, attitudes, conformity, and behavior. *Journal of Personality and Social Psychology,* **32,** 83–91.

Olweus, D. (1980). The consistency issue in personality psychology revisited—with special reference to aggression. *British Journal of Social and Clinical Psychology,* **19,** 377–390.

Osgood, C. E., Suci, G. J., & Tannenbaum, P. H. (1957). *The measurement of meaning.* Urbana, IL: University of Illinois Press.

Oskamp, S. (1977). *Attitudes and opinions.* Englewood-Cliffs, NJ: Prentice-Hall.

Ostrom, T. M. (1969). The relationship between the affective, behavioral, and cognitive components of attitude. *Journal of Experimental Social Psychology,* **5,** 12–30.

Peterson, D. R. (1968). *The clinical study of social behavior.* New York: Appleton.

Petty, R. E., & Cacioppo, J. T. (1981). *Attitudes and persuasion: Classic and contemporary approaches.* Dubuque, Iowa: Wm. C. Brown.

Petty, R. E., & Cacioppo, J. T. (1986). The Elaboration Likelihood Model of persuasion. In L. Berkowitz (Ed.), *Advances in experimental social psychology* (Vol. 19). Orlando, Fl.: Academic Press.

Pryor, J. B., Gibbons, F. X., Wicklund, R. A., Fazio, R. H., & Hood, R. (1977). Self-focused attention and self-report validity. *Journal of Personality,* **45,** 514–527.

Regan, D. T., & Fazio, R. H. (1977). On the consistency between attitudes and behavior: Look to the method of attitude formation. *Journal of Experimental Social Psychology,* **13,** 38–45.

Rosenberg, M. J. (1968). Hedonism, inauthenticity, and other goals toward expansion of a consistency theory. In R. P. Abelson, E. Aronson, W. J. McGuire, T. M. Newcomb, M. J. Rosenberg, & P. H. Tannenbaum (Eds.), *Theories of cognitive consistency: A sourcebook* (pp. 73–111). Chicago: Rand McNally.

Rosenberg, M. J., & Hovland, C. I. (1960). Cognitive, affective, and behavioral components of attitudes. In C. I. Hovland & M. J. Rosenberg (Eds.), *Attitude organization and change* (pp. 1–14). New Haven, CT: Yale University Press.

Roth, H. G., & Upmeyer, A. (1985). Matching attitudes towards cartoons across evaluative judgments and nonverbal evaluative behavior. *Psychological Research, 47,* 173–183.

Rotter, J. B. (1954). *Social learning and clinical psychology.* Englewood-Cliffs, NJ: Prentice-Hall.

Rotter, J. B. (1966). Generalized expectancies for internal versus external control of reinforcement. *Psychological Monographs, 80,* (1, Whole No. 609).

Rushton, J. P., Brainerd, C. J., & Pressley, M. (1983). Behavioral development and construct validity: The principle of aggregation. *Psychological Bulletin, 94,* 18–38.

Sample, J., & Warland, R. (1973). Attitude and prediction of behavior. *Social Forces, 51,* 292–303.

Sanger, S. P., & Alker, H. A. (1972). Dimensions of internal-external locus of control and the women's liberation movement. *Journal of Social Issues, 28,* 115–129.

Sarver, V. T., Jr. (1983). Ajzen and Fishbein's "theory of reasoned action": A critical assessment. *Journal for the Theory of Social Behavior, 13,* 155–163.

Scheier, M. F., Buss, A. H., & Buss, D. M. (1978). Self-consciousness, self-report of aggressiveness, and aggression. *Journal of Research in Personality, 12,* 133–140.

Schifter, D. B., & Ajzen, I. (1985). Intention, perceived control, and weight loss: An application of the theory of planned behavior. *Journal of Personality and Social Psychology, 49,* 843–851.

Schlegel, R. P. (1975). Multidimensional measurement of attitude towards smoking marijuana. *Canadian Journal of Behavioral Science, 7,* 387–396.

Schlegel, R. P., & DiTecco, D. (1982). Attitudinal structures and the attitude-behavior relation. In M. P. Zanna, E. T. Higgins, & C. P. Herman (Eds.), *Consistency in social behavior: The Ontario Symposium* (Vol. 2, pp. 17–49). Hillsdale, NJ: Erlbaum.

Schuman, H., & Johnson, M. P. (1976). Attitudes and behavior. *Annual Review of Sociology, 2,* 161–207.

Sherif, M., & Hovland, C. I. (1961). *Social judgment: Assimilation and contrast effects in communication and attitude change.* New Haven, CT: Yale University Press.

Sherman, S. J., & Fazio, R. H. (1983). Parallels between attitudes and traits as predictors of behavior. *Journal of Personality, 51,* 308–345.

Sivacek, J., & Crano, W. D. (1982). Vested interest as a moderator of attitude-behavior consistency. *Journal of Personality and Social Psychology, 43,* 210–221.

Sjöberg, L. (1982). Attitude-behavior correlation, social desirability and perceived diagnostic value. *British Journal of Social Psychology, 21,* 283–292.

Small, S. A., Zeldin, R. S., & Savin-Williams, R. C. (1983). In search of personality traits: A multimethod analysis of naturally occurring prosocial and dominance behavior. *Journal of Personality, 51,* 1–16.

Smetana, J. G., & Adler, N. E. (1980). Fishbein's value x expectancy model: An examination of some assumptions. *Personality and Social Psychology Bulletin, 6,* 89–96.

Snyder, M. (1974). The self-monitoring of expressive behavior. *Journal of Personality and Social Psychology, 30,* 526–537.

Snyder, M. (1982). When believing means doing: Creating links between attitudes and behavior. In M. P. Zanna, E. T. Higgins, & C. P. Herman (Eds.), *Consistency in social behavior: The Ontario Symposium* (Vol. 2, pp. 105–130). Hillsdale, NJ: Erlbaum.

Snyder, M., & Kendzierski, D. (1982). Acting on one's attitudes: Procedures for linking attitude and behavior. *Journal of Experimental Social Psychology, 18,* 165–183.

Snyder, M., & Swann, W. B., Jr. (1976). When actions reflect attitudes: The politics of impression management. *Journal of Personality and Social Psychology, 34,* 1034–1042.

Speckart, G., & Bentler, P. M. (1982). Application of attitude-behavior models to varied content domains. *Academic Psychology Bulletin, 4,* 453–465.

Thurstone, L. L. (1931). The measurement of attitudes. *Journal of Abnormal and Social Psychology, 26,* 249–269.

Tittle, C. R., & Hill, R. J. (1967). Attitude measurement and prediction of behavior: An evaluation of conditions and measurement techniques. *Sociometry, 30,* 199–213.

Triandis, H. C. (1977). *Interpersonal behavior*. Monterey, CA: Brooks/Cole.

Underwood, B., & Moore, B. S. (1981). Sources of behavioral consistency. *Journal of Personality and Social Psychology, 40*, 780–785.

Upmeyer, A. (1981). Perceptual and judgmental processes in social contexts. In L. Berkowitz (Ed.), *Advances in experimental social psychology* (Vol. 14, pp. 257–308). New York: Academic Press.

Veevers, J. E. (1971). Drinking attitudes and drinking behavior: An exploratory study. *Journal of Social Psychology, 85*, 103–109.

Vernon, P. E. (1964). *Personality assessment: A critical survey*. New York: Wiley.

Vinokur-Kaplan, D. (1978). To have—or not to have—another child: Family planning attitudes, intentions, and behavior. *Journal of Applied Social Psychology, 8*, 29–46.

Wallston, B. S., Wallston, K. A., Kaplan, G. D., & Maides, S. A. (1976). Development and validation of the health locus of control (HLC) scale. *Journal of Consulting and Clinical Psychology, 44*, 580–585.

Wallston, K. A., & Wallston, B. S. (1981). Health locus of control scales. In H. M. Lefcourt (Ed.), *Research with the locus of control construct. Vol. 1: Assessment methods* (pp. 189–243). New York: Academic Press.

Wallston, K. A., Wallston, B. S., & DeVellis, R. (1978). Development of the multidimensional health locus of control (MHLC) scales. *Health Education Monographs, 6*, 161–170.

Warehime, R. G. (1972). Generalized expectancy for locus of control and academic performance. *Psychological Reports, 30*, 314.

Warland, R. H., & Sample, J. (1973). Response certainty as a moderator variable in attitude measurement. *Rural Sociology, 38*, 174–186.

Warner, L. G., & DeFleur, M. L. (1969). Attitude as an interactional concept: Social constraint and social distance as intervening variables between attitudes and action. *American Sociological Review, 34*, 153–169.

Weigel, R. H., & Newman, L. S. (1976). Increasing attitude-behavior correspondence by broadening the scope of the behavioral measure. *Journal of Personality and Social Psychology, 33*, 793–802.

Werner, P. D. (1978). Personality and attitude-activism correspondence. *Journal of Personality and Social Psychology, 36*, 1375–1390.

Westoff, C., Potter, R., Sagi, P., & Mishler, E. (1961). *Family growth in metropolitan America*. Princeton, NJ: Princeton University Press.

Wicker, A. W. (1969). Attitudes versus actions: The relationship of verbal and overt behavioral responses to attitude objects. *Journal of Social Issues, 25*, 41–78.

Wicklund, R. A. (1975). Objective self awareness. In L. Berkowitz (Ed.), *Advances in experimental social psychology* (Vol. 8, pp. 233–275). New York: Academic Press.

Wiggins, J. S. (1973). *Personality and prediction: Principles of personality assessment*. Reading, MA: Addison-Wesley.

Wilson, T. D., Dunn, D. S., Bybee, J. A., Hyman, D. B., & Rotondo, J. A. (1984). Effects of analyzing reasons on attitude-behavior consistency. *Journal of Personality and Social Psychology, 47*, 5–16.

Wright, J. C. (1983). *The structure and perception of behavioral consistency*. Unpublished doctoral dissertation. Stanford University.

Zanna, M. P., Olson, J. M., & Fazio, R. H. (1980). Attitude-behavior consistency: An individual difference perspective. *Journal of Personality and Social Psychology, 38*, 432–440.

Zuckerman, M., & Reis, H. T. (1978). Comparison of three models for predicting altruistic behavior. *Journal of Personality and Social Psychology, 36*, 498–510.

PROSOCIAL MOTIVATION: IS IT EVER TRULY ALTRUISTIC?

C. Daniel Batson

DEPARTMENT OF PSYCHOLOGY
UNIVERSITY OF KANSAS
LAWRENCE, KANSAS 66045

I. Introduction

Imagine you are jogging down a quiet, country road. Rounding a corner, you come upon a horrible scene. A sports car is on its side, half in and half out of the ditch. On the pavement is the driver, a young woman. She is lying on her back, eyes closed, barely moving. Her face is bloody and bruised; her left leg, clearly broken, is twisted at a grotesque angle.

What do you do? The answer is likely obvious: You help. You rush to her side, or you race off to find a telephone and call the police or an ambulance. Few of us would not expect to help in this situation—the need is great and unambiguous; there is no one else to help; helping is not likely to bring personal danger; and so on. Helping in this situation is not only consistent with our expectations, it is consistent with a large body of research on situational factors that make helping more or less likely (see Krebs, 1970; Piliavin, Dovidio, Gaertner, & Clark, 1981, 1982; Staub, 1978, 1979, for reviews).

But *why* did you help? No doubt, you wanted to relieve her distress. But again, why? Was it in order to benefit her or was it, ultimately, in order to benefit yourself? More generally, when we help others, is our ultimate goal ever, in any degree, to benefit them, or is our ultimate goal always some form of self-benefit?

A. PROSOCIAL MOTIVATION AS SELF-SERVING: THE DOMINANT VIEW

Whether humans are ever, in any degree, altruistically motivated was a central question for many 19th and early 20th century social philosophers and

ADVANCES IN EXPERIMENTAL
SOCIAL PSYCHOLOGY, VOL. 20

social scientists (see, for example, Comte, 1851; Kropotkin, 1902; McDougall, 1908; Mill, 1863; Spencer, 1872). By around 1920, however, theories of motivation based on behaviorism or psychoanalysis were sufficiently sophisticated to provide an egoistic account of any behavior that might appear to be altruistically motivated. As a result, the question of the existence of altruism was shelved by mainstream psychologists; it was assumed either to be clearly answered in the negative or to be clearly unanswerable. Continued dominance of psychology by modern descendants of these early egoistic theories of motivation may explain why the recent upsurge of interest in and research on helping behavior (see Derlega & Grzelak, 1982; Dovidio, 1984; Krebs & Miller, 1985; Rushton & Sorrentino, 1981; Staub, 1978, 1979, for reviews) has not led to a parallel upsurge of interest in the classic question of whether at least some helping might be altruistically motivated. When asked why we act prosocially, all major psychological theories of motivation—Freudian, behavioral, and even humanistic or "third force" theories—are quite clear in their answer: everything we do, including all prosocial behavior, is ultimately done for our own benefit (see Hoffman, 1981b; Wallach & Wallach, 1983). When we help someone else, we do so only because it is an instrumental means to obtain some personal gain.

At times, the personal gain derived from helping is obvious—as when we get material rewards or public praise (or escape public censure). But psychologists have pointed out that even when we help in the absence of obvious external rewards, we may still benefit. We can receive self-rewards, congratulating ourselves for being kind and caring, or we can avoid self-censure, escaping guilt and shame (Bandura, 1977; Cialdini & Kenrick, 1976). In such cases the pat on the back may come from ourselves rather than from someone else, but it is a pat nonetheless. Alternatively, seeing someone in distress may cause us distress, and we may act to relieve the other's distress as an instrumental means to reach the ultimate goal of relieving our own distress.

Even heroes and martyrs can benefit from their acts of apparent selflessness. Consider the soldier who saves his comrades by diving on a grenade or the man who dies after relinquishing his place in a rescue craft. These persons may have acted to escape anticipated guilt and shame for letting others die. Or they may have acted to gain rewards—the admiration and praise of those left behind or the benefits expected in a life to come. Or they may simply have misjudged the consequences of their actions.

The view that all prosocial behavior, regardless how noble in appearance, is ultimately motivated by some form of self-benefit may seem cynical. But it is the dominant view in contemporary psychology. Moreover, it has long been the dominant view in Western thought (see, for example, Bentham, 1789; A. Freud, 1937; Freud, 1918, 1930; Hobbes, 1651; Machiavelli, 1513; Nietzsche, 1910; Rand, 1961; Skinner, 1978).

B. PROSOCIAL MOTIVATION AS EGOISTIC AND ALTRUISTIC:
AN ALTERNATIVE VIEW

But there has also been an alternative view in Western thought—that in some circumstances and to some degree humans are capable of acting from unselfish motives. This possibility was first discussed under the heading of "benevolence" (see Hume, 1740, 1751; Smith, 1759); more recently, it has been discussed as "altruism" (Comte, 1851; MacIntyre, 1967). This alternative view postulates the existence of a motivational system directed toward benefiting others, a system separate from and not reducible to motivation to benefit oneself.

Auguste Comte (1851), who first coined the term altruism, did not deny the existence of self-serving motives, even for helping; the impulse to seek self-benefit and self-gratification he called egoism. But Comte believed that some social behavior was an expression of an unselfish desire to "live for others" (1851, p. 556). This second type of prosocial motivation he called altruism. Building upon Comte's distinction, we may say that *prosocial motivation is egoistic when the ultimate goal is to increase one's own welfare; it is altruistic when the ultimate goal is to increase another's welfare.*

One popular rejoinder made by philosophers of his day to Comte's proposal of altruism went as follows: even if it were possible for a person to be motivated to increase another's welfare, such a person would be pleased by attaining this desired goal, so even this apparently altruistic motivation would actually be a product of egoism. This argument, based on the general principle of psychological hedonism, has been shown to be flawed by later philosophers, who have pointed out that it involves a confusion between two different forms of hedonism. The strong form of psychological hedonism asserts that attainment of personal pleasure is always the goal of human action; the weak form asserts only that goal attainment always brings pleasure. The latter form is not inconsistent with the possibility that the ultimate goal of some action is to benefit another rather than to benefit oneself, because the pleasure obtained can be a consequence of reaching the goal without being the goal itself. The strong form of psychological hedonism *is* inconsistent with the possibility of altruism, but this form of hedonism suffers from many counter examples and has few adherents among philosophers today. (See MacIntyre, 1967; Nagel, 1970, for further discussion of these philosophical arguments.)

To understand more clearly Comte's distinction between egoistic and altruistic motives, let us apply it to the example with which we began. Upon seeing the young auto accident victim, you rushed off and called an ambulance in order to relieve her distress. But why? If seeing her caused you distress, and you sought to relieve her distress in order to relieve your own distress, then your motivation was egoistic. True, you sought to make her feel better, but that was not your ultimate goal; it was only instrumental in allowing you to reach the ultimate goal of feeling better yourself. Similarly, if you helped in order to avoid feelings of guilt that you anticipated were you to "pass by on the other side," then your motivation was egoistic. If, on the other hand, you acted in order to relieve her distress as an end in itself, then your motivation was altruistic. True, by relieving her distress you probably relieved your own distress and avoided feeling guilty. Yet, if these outcomes were not ultimate goals but only consequences of your action, then your motivation was altruistic. Does such motivation actually exist?

II. Contemporary Psychological Discussions of Altruism

In spite of the dominance in Western thought of an exclusively egoistic view, the term altruism has reappeared in contemporary psychology. But what is now meant by altruism is usually something quite different from what Comte had in mind. Most contemporary psychologists who use the term have no intention of challenging the dominant view that all human behavior, including all prosocial behavior, is motivated by self-serving, egoistic desires. Quite the opposite, these psychologists intend to redefine altruism so that it fits within this dominant view. Accordingly, the views of these psychologists might most appropriately be called "pseudoaltruistic." They use the term altruism, but not to refer to a motivational state the ultimate goal of which is to increase another's welfare. Instead, they apply this term to one or another subtle form of self-benefit. So, by the definitions of egoistic and altruistic motivation proposed above, what these psychologists call altruism is not truly altruistic; it is a form of egoism.

A. PSEUDOALTRUISTIC VIEWS

Contemporary pseudoaltruistic views can be classified into three types.

1. Altruism as Prosocial Behavior, Not Motivation

First there are those who ignore the issue of motivation altogether, simply equating altruism with helping behavior, i.e., with benefiting another organism relative to oneself. This first pseudoaltruistic approach has been popular with developmental psychologists, especially those studying children from a social learning perspective (see Rushton, 1980, for a review), and with sociobiologists, who wish to apply the term altruism across a very broad phylogenetic spectrum—from the social insects (Hamilton, 1964, 1971) to man (Dawkins, 1976; Trivers, 1971; Wilson, 1975).

To illustrate this approach, consider the definition of altruism employed by sociobiologists Ridley and Dawkins (1981):

> In evolutionary theory, altruism means self-sacrifice performed for the benefit of others. In everyday speech the word altruism carries connotations of subjective intent. . . . We do not deny that animals have feelings and intentions, but we make more progress in understanding animal behavior if we concentrate on its observable aspects. If we use words like altruism at all, we define them by their effects and do not speculate about the animal's intentions. An altruistic act is one that has the *effect* of increasing the chance of survival (some would prefer to say "reproductive success") of another organism at the expense of the altruist's. . . . It follows that an indubitably unconscious entity such as a plant, or a gene, is in principle capable of displaying altruism. (pp. 19–20, italics in original)

I admire the clarity with which Ridley and Dawkins state their definition, but to use the term altruism in the manner they propose strikes me as roughly equivalent to defining psychokinesis to include changing the channels on a TV by employing a remote control switch. One could find much evidence for psychokinesis so defined; yet the more intriguing question of the existence of psychokinesis as ordinarily defined would remain. So too with the more intriguing question of whether self-sacrificial behavior is ever directed toward benefiting the other as an ultimate goal. To know that self-sacrificial behavior exists raises this motivational question; it does not answer it.

2. Altruism as Prosocial Behavior Seeking Internal Rewards

Pseudoaltruistic views of the second and third type address the issue of motivation for helping, but rather than treating altruistic motivation as an alternative to egoistic motivation, as Comte intended, these views treat it as a special form of egoistic motivation. The second view—by far the most common view among contemporary psychologists—redefines altruism to include seeking benefits for the self, so long as these benefits are internally rather than externally administered.

For example, Robert Cialdini and his associates (Cialdini, Baumann, & Kenrick, 1981; Cialdini, Darby, & Vincent, 1973; Cialdini & Kenrick, 1976) speak of an internalization process through which by adulthood "altruism . . . comes to act as self-reward" (Cialdini et al., 1981, p. 215). Daniel Bar-Tal and his associates (Bar-Tal, 1976; Bar-Tal, Sharabany, & Raviv, 1982) also focus on self-rewards for altruism—"feelings of self-satisfaction and . . . a rise in . . . self-esteem" (Bar-Tal et al., 1982, p. 387). For them, altruism is helping that is (1) self-chosen rather than chosen in compliance to external authority, and (2) self-reinforced rather than externally reinforced. Shalom Schwartz and his associates (Schwartz, 1977; Schwartz & Howard, 1982) view altruism as "motivated by *personal* (as opposed to social) norms, situation-specific behavioral expectations generated from one's own internalized values, backed by self-administered sanctions and rewards'' (Schwartz & Howard, 1982, p. 329, italics in original). Joan Grusec (1981) defines altruism as "the development of consideration for others which no longer depends on external surveillance'' (p. 65); instead, it depends on internalized values. Ervin Staub (1978, 1979) has a similar but more differentiated view:

> A prosocial act may be judged altruistic if it appears to have been intended to benefit others rather than to gain either material or social rewards. Altruistic prosocial acts are likely to be associated, however, with internal rewards (and the expectation of such rewards) and with empathic reinforcing experiences. (1978, p. 10)

It seems clear that none of these views describes what Comte meant by altruism, for in each case the ultimate goal is self-benefit in the form of self-reward. Benefiting the other is simply an instrumental goal on the way to reaching this egoistic ultimate goal. Therefore, the considerable empirical evidence that has been mustered to support these various views does not permit an affirmative answer to the question with which we began: Does anyone ever act with an ultimate goal of benefiting someone else? Rather than demonstrating altruism, this evidence simply documents some subtle forms of egoistic self-benefit.

3. Altruism as Prosocial Behavior to Reduce Aversive Arousal

The third pseudoaltruistic view assumes that altruism is helping motivated by a desire to reduce some internal state of aversive arousal or tension. Perhaps the best-known example of this view is the arousal-reduction model originally developed by Jane and Irving Piliavin (1973) and later revised by Jane Piliavin et al. (1981, 1982). Although its authors are careful to call this a model of bystander or emergency intervention rather than of altruism, it has often been adopted as an account of altruistic motivation by others (e.g., Karylowski, 1982). The heart of the Piliavin model is summarized in two propositions:

> Proposition II: In general, the arousal occasioned by observation of an emergency and attributed to the emergency becomes more unpleasant as it increases, and the bystander is therefore motivated to reduce it. Proposition III: The bystander will choose that response to an emergency that will most rapidly and most completely reduce the arousal, incurring in the process as few net costs (costs minus rewards) as possible. (Piliavin et al., 1982, p. 281, italics in original)

Of course, one way for the bystander to reduce his or her unpleasant arousal is to help, because helping removes the stimulus causing the arousal.

Variations on the theme of altruism as arousal reduction are provided by Harvey Hornstein (1976, 1978, 1982), Janusz Reykowski (1982), and Melvin

Lerner (1970). Appealing to a Lewinian view of motivation, Hornstein suggests that when certain others are in need—specifically, those whom one cognitively links to self as "us" and "we" rather than "them" and "they"—one experiences a state of promotive tension, in which one is "aroused by *another's* needs almost as if they were one's own" (Hornstein, 1982, p. 230, italics in original). Once so aroused, one is motivated to reduce this tension:

> In some circumstances human beings experience others as "we," not as "they." When this happens, bonds exist that permit one person's plight to become a source of tension for his or her fellows. Seeking relief, they reduce this tension by aiding a fellow we-grouper. . . . Self-interest is served and tension is reduced when one acts on the other's behalf. (Hornstein, 1978, p. 189).

Reykowski (1982) proposes a quite different source of prosocial motivation, but still one that involves reduction of a tension state: "The sheer discrepancy between information about the real or possible state of an object and standards of its normal or desirable state will evoke motivation" (p. 361). Specifically, if one perceives a discrepancy between the current and expected or ideal state of another's welfare, this will produce cognitive inconsistency and motivation to reduce the upsetting inconsistency. Reykowski calls the result "intrinsic prosocial motivation."

Lerner's (1970) just-world hypothesis led him to a view similar to, but more specific than, Reykowski's. Lerner suggested that most of us believe in a just world—a world in which people get what they deserve and deserve what they get—and that the existence of a victim of innocent suffering is inconsistent with this belief. In order to reduce the arousal produced by this inconsistency a person may help—or may derogate—the victim.

According to each of these arousal-reduction views of prosocial motivation, the potential helper's ultimate goal is to reduce some unpleasant arousal or tension. Increasing the other's welfare is simply one instrumental means of reaching this egoistic goal.

B. ALTRUISTIC VIEWS

Each of the foregoing pseudoaltruistic views involves a redefinition of the term altruism. But there are also several contemporary psychologists who have attempted to consider the issue of altruistic motivation, using the term altruism in a way that retains Comte's original intent. I shall call these views altruistic. Lest false hopes arise, however, it must be admitted at once that these contemporary altruistic views tend to share two problems. First, perhaps because of the lack of precision with which they are stated, these views tend to be unstable; they seem inevitably to get transformed into one or another of the pseudoaltruistic views just described. Second, again perhaps because of imprecise statement, the empirical evidence presented is unconvincing; it can easily be accounted for by one or more egoistic explanations. These problems may be illustrated by looking at several of the best known contemporary discussions of the existence of altruistic motivation—those by Martin Hoffman, Dennis Krebs, David Rosenhan, Jerzy Karylowski, Melvin Lerner, and Jane Piliavin.

1. Hoffman

Probably the best known altruistic view has been provided by Martin Hoffman (1975, 1976, 1981a,b). Hoffman proposes that empathy—defined as "an affective response appropriate to someone else's situation rather than one's own" (Hoffman, 1981b, p. 44)—is the basis for an altruistic motive that is independent of egoistic, self-serving motives. Hoffman considers empathy to evolve through a developmental sequence, beginning with the reactive cries of infants to the cries of other infants (Sagi & Hoffman, 1976; Simner, 1971). Ultimately, the individual develops a clear sense of other as distinct from self and "imagines how he or she would feel in the other's place" (Hoffman, 1981b, p. 47). If the other is in distress, this leads the individual to experience "empathic distress," which may be generalized not only beyond the other's immediate situation to his or her general plight (e.g., a feeling of sadness at seeing a happy child unaware that he has a terminal illness), but also to the plight of an entire group or class of people (e.g., the poor or oppressed).

Out of empathic distress emerges a second vicarious emotion: "sympathetic distress." It is sympathetic distress that Hoffman claims evokes altruistic motivation:

> Once people are aware of the other as distinct from the self, their own empathic distress, which is a parallel response—a more or less exact replication of the victim's presumed feeling of distress—may be transformed at least in part into a more reciprocal feeling of concern for the victim. That is, they continue to respond in a purely empathic, quasi-egoistic manner—to feel uncomfortable and highly distressed themselves—but they also experience a feeling of compassion, or what I call sympathetic distress for the victim, along with a conscious desire to help because they feel sorry for him or her and not just to relieve their own empathic distress. (1982, p. 290; see also 1981b, p. 51)

The motivation to help associated with empathic distress is egoistic; the helper's goal is to relieve his or her own distress:

> Empathic distress is unpleasant and helping the victim is usually the best way to get rid of the source. One can also accomplish this by directing one's attention elsewhere and avoiding the expressive and situational cues from the victim. Such a strategy may work with children but provides limited relief for mature observers who do not need these cues to be empathically aroused. (Hoffman, 1981b, p. 52)

Only the motivation associated with sympathetic distress is directed toward increasing the other's welfare as an ultimate goal.

Hoffman's view is elaborate and rich in heuristic potential. But it dramatically illustrates both problems typical of contemporary altruistic views. First, it has proved unstable, tending to become a pseudoaltruistic view. In his early writings on altruism, Hoffman (1975, 1976) made a sharp distinction between the vicarious emotions of empathic distress and sympathetic distress, as well as between their associated egoistic and altruistic motivation. Although these distinctions may still be found in his more recent writings, as the passages just quoted reveal, these distinctions have tended to recede into the background, and another theme has become dominant. The term empathic distress is now used "generically to refer to both empathic and sympathetic distress" (Hoffman, 1981b, p. 52; also 1982, p. 281), and the clear distinction between egoistic and altruistic motivation outlined above is blurred: "Empathy is uniquely well suited for bridging the gap between egoism and altruism, as it has the property of transforming another person's misfortune into one's own distress and thus has elements of both egoism and altruism" (p. 55).

On what grounds does Hoffman infer that this generic empathic distress evokes an altruistic motive?

> First, it is aroused by another's misfortune, not just one's own; second, a major goal of the ensuing action is to help the other, not just the self; and third, the potential for gratification in the actor is contingent on his doing something to reduce the other's distress. It is thus more appropriate to designate empathic distress as an altruistic motive—perhaps with a quasi-egoistic component—than to group it with such obviously self-serving motives as material gain, social approval, and competitive success. (1981b, p. 56)

But as we know from examining pseudoaltruistic views, the three characteristics Hoffman mentions here apply to a variety of subtle egoistic motives for helping. What began as an argument for an altruistic motive independent of egoistic motives has, over the years, become indistinguishable from an argument for a combination of two pseudoaltruistic motives—subtle self-rewards and reduction of one's own aversive arousal.

The second problem with Hoffman's argument is the empirical evidence that he cites as support for an independent altruistic motive. The evidence, which he claims must necessarily be circumstantial, is the following (Hoffman, 1981b, p. 42). (1) Most people across a wide range of ages and cultures try to help others in distress (see also Hoffman, 1982, pp. 291–293); (2) people are less likely to help when approval needs are aroused; and (3) helping can occur relatively quickly (e.g., in some bystander intervention studies the average reaction time is 5–10 seconds). Elsewhere, Hoffman (1981a, p. 131; also 1982, p. 293) refers to a fourth piece of evidence: (4) latency of helping decreases as the intensity of the victim's distress cues increases, and following helping there is a decrease in the helper's arousal.

The first, third, and fourth of these points cited by Hoffman are empirically correct, but they say nothing about the nature of the motivation to help; the motivation could as easily be egoistic as altruistic. The second point is only correct under some circumstances (see Cialdini *et al.,* 1981; Reis & Gruzen, 1976), and it is easily handled by an egoistic explanation that allows for internalized self-reward (see Bandura, 1977; Thomas & Batson, 1981; Thomas, Batson, & Coke, 1981). Hoffman also presents some biological evidence for the existence of altruistic motivation, but this evidence is equally unpersuasive. It is either purely hypothetical or easily amenable to egoistic interpretations (see Hoffman, 1981a). The same may be said for the circumstantial evidence that Hoffman mentions for the transformation of empathic distress into sympathetic distress (1982, p. 290).

How can Hoffman conclude that altruism exists based on this clearly equivocal empirical evidence? He reasons as follows: Empirical evidence for the view that "altruism can ultimately be explained in terms of egoistic, self-serving motives . . . has not been advanced," and as a result, "the burden of proof rests as much on an egoistic interpretation as on an interpretation that humans are by nature altruistic" (1981b, p. 41). Given these premises, Hoffman chooses to interpret the evidence as supporting altruism.

Unfortunately, both Hoffman's premises here seem false. First, there is ample evidence that increased potential for self-benefit can increase prosocial behavior (see Piliavin *et al.,* 1981; Rushton, 1980; Staub, 1978, for reviews). That egoistic motives can underlie prosocial behavior—as well as many other behaviors—cannot be denied. The issue in doubt is whether egoistic motives are the whole story, or only part. Second, given that egoistic motives exist and altruistic motives may or may not exist, parsimony clearly favors an exclusively egoistic view. If all we can do is muster evidence that is equally consistent with egoistic and altruistic explanations, then we have no good reason for claiming that altruistic motives exit.

2. *Krebs*

Like Hoffman, Dennis Krebs (1975) claims that empathic emotion leads to altruistic motivation. And like Hoffman's view, Krebs's view is unstable, leading him at times clearly to assert that empathy leads to altruistic as opposed to egoistic motivation, and at other times to suggest an arousal-reduction pseudo-altruistic view. Initially, Krebs makes the motivational distinction clear:

> Psychologists have manipulated various antecedents of helping behaviors and studied their effects, and they have measured a number of correlated prosocial events; however, they have done little to examine the extent to which the acts that they investigated were

oriented to the welfare of either the person who was helped or the helper. It is the extent of self-sacrifice, the expectation of gain, and the orientation to the needs of another that define acts as altruistic. People help people for a variety of reasons. Some of them may be altruistic; some of them may not.

The present study sought to cast some light on the phenomenon of altruism by investigating the idea that empathic reactions mediate altruistic responses. (1975, p. 1134)

Later on, however, this clear motivational distinction fades into a pseudoaltruistic view:

When the pains and pleasures of others become intrinsically tied to the affective state of observers, it can be in their best interest to maximize the favorableness of the hedonic balance of others in order to maximize the favorableness of their own hedonic state. (Krebs, 1975, pp. 1144–1145)

Krebs apparently feels that the latter view is all that can be meant by altruism, because one can never show that an act is not motivated by expectation of reward:

The main reason why classical debates about human capacity for altruism have flourished is because scholars have defined altruism as helping behavior that is not motivated by expectations of reward. As Krebs (1970) pointed out, the existence of altruistic behavior can never be proved when defined in this manner because it requires proving the null hypothesis (i.e., establishing the absence of expectation of reward). (1975, pp. 1134–1135)

I think Krebs has made a logical slip here. It is not necessary to establish the absence of expectation of reward, nor is it even necessary that an absence of expectation of reward exist, for an act not to be motivated by expectations of reward—so long as obtaining the reward is not the actor's goal. Krebs has failed to make the crucial distinction between the goals and the consequences of an action. Failure to make this distinction leads him to substitute for his initially altruistic view an arousal-reduction pseudoaltruistic view of the prosocial motivation associated with empathy.

Although Krebs's (1975) empirical evidence is more suggestive than that cited by Hoffman, it is equally inconclusive because it is equally amenable to egoistic explanations. Krebs found that subjects observing someone similar to themselves undergo positive and negative experiences were more likely than subjects observing someone dissimilar (or someone undergoing affectively neutral experiences) to (1) show physiological arousal, (2) report identifying with the other, (3) report feeling worse while waiting for the other to experience pain, and (4) subsequently help the other at some cost to self. Krebs claimed that because helping in this situation was personally costly it provided an index of altruistic motivation. But there is no reason to make this assumption, any more than there is reason to assume that helping was an index of egoistic motivation to—as Krebs himself suggested—maximize the favorableness of the helper's own hedonic state. Krebs demonstrated that empathy was associated with pro-social motivation, but he provided no clear evidence about the nature of that motivation. It could have been egoistic or altruistic.

3. Rosenhan

Unlike Hoffman and Krebs, David Rosenhan and his associates (Rosenhan, 1970, 1978; Rosenhan, Salovey, Karylowki, & Hargis, 1981b) do not focus only upon empathy or sympathy; they speak more generally of affect and emotion as sources of altruistic motivation:

> The ordinary laws of reinforcement seek to maximize rewards to the self. Technically speaking, they forbid altruism, which by definition is behavior directed toward the welfare of others at the expense of one's own welfare, even of one's life. . . . As we shall see, certain affects are the fulcra upon which the ordinary laws of reinforcement are violated. While experiencing those affects, people are led away from stances that maximize their own rewards and find instead that their attention, cognitions, and behaviors are directed toward the needs of others, often without regard for the quid pro quo. (Rosenhan *et al.*, 1981b, p. 234)

Like the views of Hoffman and Krebs, the view of Rosenhan *et al.* (1981b) proves unstable, and the empirical evidence equivocal. Rosenhan *et al.* quickly shift away from the stringent definition of altruism just quoted and instead use the term to apply to any prosocial behavior (1981b, pp. 235ff.). For empirical evidence, Rosenhan *et al.* rely primarily on two studies. In the first, Thompson, Cowan, and Rosenhan (1980) found that subjects who focused on the worry, anxiety, and pain of a friend dying of cancer subsequently spent more time trying to answer difficult multiple choice questions for a graduate student in Education than either control subjects or subjects who focused on their own pain and sorrow caused by the friend's death. In the second study, Rosenhan, Salovey, and Hargis (1981a) found that subjects who attended to their own joy at being given a trip to Hawaii subsequently spent more time answering multiple choice questions than control subjects, who in turn spent more time than subjects who attended to a close friend's joy at being given a trip to Hawaii.

At least in the Thompson *et al.* study, one might assume that high empathy or sympathy resulted when subjects were instructed to focus on the friend (although no measures of emotion other than sadness were reported) and that this vicarious emotion (1) sensitized subjects to feel empathy (sympathy) for the graduate student, (2) predisposed subjects to take the perspective of the graduate student and to feel empathy as a result, or (3) led subjects to misattribute some of their empathy for the friend to the graduate student. Although each of these interpretations goes well beyond the data, each would be quite compatible with the relationship between empathy (sympathy) and altruism proposed by Hoffman and Krebs.

But instead, Rosenhan *et al.* (1981b) suggest a pseudoaltruistic interpretation of the Thompson *et al.* and Rosenhan *et al.* findings: "It seems reasonable that altruism should occur only when there is a perceived imbalance of resources between self and other, and when that imbalance is weighted in favor of the self" (p. 244). Although Rosenhan *et al.* do not clearly specify why this imbalance should motivate helping, the underlying mechanism could easily be a personal need to conform to some internalized standard of equity (Hatfield, Piliavin, & Walster, 1978) or justice (Lerner, 1970). Once again, an altruistic view of prosocial motivation is transformed into a pseudoaltruistic view, and the empirical evidence proves as compatible with an egoistic interpretation as with an altruistic one.

4. Karylowski

Jerzy Karylowski (1982) proposes a distinction between doing good to feel good about oneself (e.g., by maintaining or heightening a positive self-image)—"endocentric altruism"—and doing good to make someone else feel good—"exocentric altruism." Endocentric altruism is clearly pseudoaltruistic, but exocentric altruism appears to be truly altruistic; the goal seems to be to increase the other's welfare: "Exocentric approaches assume that improvement of the partner's condition may possess inherent gratification value for the observer, regardless of whether it has been caused by him or not" (Karylowski, 1982, p. 399). Exocentric altruism is said to develop when attention is focused on the person in need rather than on the self.

On closer inspection, however, even Karylowski's exocentric altruism is indistinguishable from a pseudoaltruistic view. This becomes apparent when he begins enumerating contemporary views of prosocial motivation that he considers to reflect exocentric altruism. Included are the views of Hornstein, of Piliavin and Piliavin (including Piliavin, Dovidio, Gaertner, & Clark), of Lerner, of Reykowski, and of Hoffman (see Karylowski, 1982, pp. 399–403). It soon becomes clear that, although exocentric altruism is not motivated by a desire to gain rewards or to avoid punishments, however subtle, no attempt is made to differentiate between acting in order to reduce one's own aversive arousal caused by witnessing another's distress and acting in order to reduce the other's distress. But this distinction seems absolutely crucial in answering the question of the existence of altruism—the former is self-serving; the latter is not.

Karylowski's empirical evidence for the existence of exocentric altruism is also weak. Relying on self-reports of what subjects consider the most likely thoughts and feelings of a potential helper, Karylowski finds that more exocentric (as opposed to endocentric) choices are made by subjects who experienced those socialization practices thought to increase sensitivity to the needs of others. Egoistic interpretations of this finding are, of course, readily available. To mention only the most obvious, the finding may reflect no more than differential socialization for what are the "right" responses to another's need (i.e., the ones for which one can self-reward). In general, it seems unlikely that self-reports of thoughts, feelings, and reasons for doing good are going to move us any closer to an answer to the question of whether altruistic motivation exists. Such reports can tell us that people differ in systematic ways in their prosocial values, but they cannot tell us the nature of these people's prosocial motivation. Those who espouse exocentric values could easily be endocentrically motivated to act in accordance with them.

5. *Lerner*

In recent years Melvin Lerner (1982; Lerner & Meindl, 1981) has sought to go beyond his initial analysis of prosocial motivation in terms of a pseudoaltruistic desire to maintain one's belief in a just world. He has suggested that there are a variety of forms of justice, one of which—the justice of need—transcends self-concern for justice and is oriented instead to the welfare of the other. Lerner believes that the form of justice operative in a given situation depends on the perceived relationship among the participants in the encounter.

Most relevant for our present concern, the justice of need is evoked when we perceive an identity relationship, in which "we are psychologically indistinguishable from the other and we experience that which we perceive they are experiencing" (Lerner & Meindl, 1981, p. 224). Paralleling Hoffman's developmental view, Lerner claims that there is a prototype for such identity relationships in early childhood in "the persistent and powerful empathic experience of sharing the emotional state of others," which is especially likely to occur when those with whom one is closely associated (e.g., family) transmit affective cues (Lerner & Meindl, 1981, p. 224). With maturation, this prototype becomes elaborated to include goal-directed activities. Specifically, when those with whom we perceive an identity relation desire some resource, we may engage in "identity-based activities":

> The "identity" activities are those activities designed to allow another person to acquire a desired resource. Our only "acquisition" of the resource in question under these circumstances occurs vicariously, as we experience some form of that which the other, who having gained the resource, is experiencing. (Lerner & Meindl, 1981, p. 225)

Lerner's analysis here might seem to imply a model of altruistic motivation based on identity relations. He certainly leads one to expect such a model, both by his sweeping indictment of the egoistic "economic" assumptions underlying every "well recognized theory of prosocial or altruistic behavior" (Lerner,

1982, p. 251) and by his listing of the emergent activities in identity relations as "nurturant concern for the other's welfare" and "meeting other's needs" (Lerner & Meindl, 1981, p. 228).

But a closer look suggests that the implied model is at least as amenable to a pseudoaltruistic interpretation as an altruistic one. For, when we help in an identity relation, it seems that the goal sought is our own vicarious experience of rescue:

> If the empathic tie is dominant it would be natural for us to engage in acts which we or others might label as self-sacrificial or martyrdom. However, with that emotional bond we of course vicariously share in their fate. We experience their pain or rescue. (Lerner & Meindl, 1981, p. 227).

This statement suggests a view much like Hornstein's (1978, 1982) pseudoaltruistic view, in which a cognitive link of "we-ness" leads another's need to cause us to feel tension, which we are then motivated to reduce.

But perhaps the most appropriate interpretation of Lerner's view here is that it is neither egoistic nor altruistic. Both of these terms assume a distinction between self and other: at issue in each is whether one's ultimate goal is the self's welfare or the other's welfare. In contrast, Lerner's identity relation appears to assume a dissolution of the self–other distinction. Although it seems unlikely that such a dissolution ever fully occurs—except perhaps in some mystical states—if it does, then the resulting self–other identity cannot properly be spoken of as either egoistic or altruistic. The question of whether the ultimate goal is to increase one's own *or* the other's welfare cannot meaningfully be asked; these two welfares have become one.

6. Piliavin, Dovidio, Gaertner, and Clark

In their revision, expansion, and update of the earlier Piliavin and Piliavin (1973) aversive arousal-reduction model, Piliavin et al. (1981, 1982) differentiate two subcategories of costs attendant upon a bystander's knowledge that a person in need has received no help. (1) *Personal costs* associated with the bystander's failure to intervene include "self-blame for one's inaction, public censure, recriminations from the victim, and in some countries even prosecution as a criminal" (Piliavin et al., 1981, p. 85). (2) *Empathy costs* are "unrelated to bystanders' actions on behalf of the victim, but [depend] solely on their knowledge that the victim is continuing to suffer" (Piliavin et al., 1981, p. 85). Piliavin et al. imply that the prosocial motivation associated with empathy costs is more altruistic than the clearly egoistic prosocial motivation associated with aversive arousal reduction and anticipated personal costs: "To the extent that arousal is interpreted as alarm and concern for another person, rather than personal distress and upset, and the salience of empathic considerations associated with the victim's plight (e.g., the victim is suffering) exceed personal cost considerations, the motive for helping has a sympathetic rather than a selfish tone'' (1982, p. 286).

But a closer look at the Piliavin *et al.* discussion of empathy costs suggests that the associated motivation is probably pseudoaltruistic rather than altruistic. In describing the "sympathetic" motives induced by empathy costs, Piliavin *et al.* state that ". . . the needs of another can become undifferentiated from one's own, . . . can become coordinated with those of the bystander or become incorporated into the bystander's self-interest. . ." (1982, p. 286). Piliavin *et al.* note the similarity of their position here to Hornstein's promotive tension view. They add: " 'Empathy costs' involve internalizing the need or suffering of the victim and include continued unpleasant arousal related to the perceived distress of the victim" (1982, p. 288). "The more clear and more severe the emergency is, the more unpleasant and costly the continued suffering of the victim will be for the bystander" (Piliavin *et al.*, 1981, p. 99). "We-ness," similarity, and attraction are all assumed to increase empathy costs, which are related to a "disposition to take instrumental action for relief of one's own distress" (1981, p. 203).

This description of empathy costs and the associated sympathetic motives does indeed sound reminiscent of Hornstein's view. Unfortunately, like his view, this description does not exclude the possibility that the motivation to help associated with "empathy costs" is directed toward the egoistic goal of reducing these empathy costs rather than the altruistic goal of reducing the victim's distress.

There is an additional ambiguity in the Piliavin *et al.* (1981, 1982) discussion of empathy costs. Often, as in the passages just quoted, the emphasis seems to be on reduction of unpleasantness that the potential helper is currently feeling as a result of knowing that the victim is suffering. But in other passages (e.g., Piliavin *et al.*, 1981, p. 127), the emphasis seems to be on unpleasantness that the potential helper anticipates feeling in the future if he or she does not help. These different emphases imply two different egoistic motives—escape from present aversive arousal and avoidance of anticipated future aversive arousal. The former is akin to the motivation of a rat on a charged shock grid trying to escape the shock; the latter, to the motivation of a rat bar-pressing to escape before the shock is turned on. Learning is necessary for the latter motivation to occur; it is not for the former. These two motivational processes are psychologically distinct, but certainly not mutually exclusive. They may even occur simultaneously.

Although the ambiguities in their discussion leave me far from certain of their precise intent, the differentiation in prosocial motivation made by Piliavin *et al.* (1981, 1982) does not seem to be between egoistic and altruistic motives but between three different egoistic motives: (1) egoistic motivation to reduce one's feelings of disgust, anxiety, and upset caused by seeing someone suffer (direct aversive arousal reduction), (2) egoistic motivation to avoid shame, guilt, and recrimination for a failure to help (personal costs), and (3) pseudoaltruistic motivation to reduce one's own present or future empathic distress produced by witnessing the suffering victim (empathy costs). The self-benefit may be more subtle in the last case, but the motivation still seems egoistic.

In their 1981 discussion, Piliavin *et al.* introduced a somewhat different view of the prosocial motivation associated with empathy costs. They suggested that " 'empathy costs' involve internalizing the need or suffering of the victim and include a continued and perhaps increasing level of unpleasant arousal related to the perceived distress of the victim and associated feelings of inequity or unfairness" (1981, p. 85). This statement is less reminiscent of Hornstein's view than of Reykowski's (1982) view that another's suffering can violate one's standards and expectations and so evoke motivation to avoid unpleasant cognitive inconsistency. Like Reykowski's view, this unfairness view of empathy costs is easily amenable to a pseudoaltruistic interpretation: the knowledge that at least certain others are continuing to suffer is unpleasant because it violates the bystander's sense of justice, and he or she is therefore motivated to help in order to reduce this unpleasantness.

Whichever version of the Piliavin *et al.* empathy cost analysis one considers—the version that emphasizes present and future empathic distress or the version that emphasizes unfairness—the result seems the same. Although these authors imply that empathy costs introduce sympathetic motives that transcend selfishness, the specific motivational processes described seem easily amenable to a pseudoaltruistic (i.e., egoistic) interpretation.

7. Hoffman's Genetic View

Finally, although standard sociobiological positions are pseudoaltruistic, failing to consider the issue of motivation at all, a genetically based altruistic view is possible. All that is required is the assumption that there is not simply a genetic predisposition to act in ways that benefit others but also a predisposition to want at least some others to benefit. Perhaps the best developed model of this kind is Hoffman's (1981a) view that there is a genetic proclivity toward empathic emotion which, in turn, evokes altruistic motivation (see Smith, 1759; McDougall, 1908, for earlier statements of a similar view). Although intriguing, Hoffman's genetic view suffers from the same instability noted previously in Hoffman's other work; what he claims is inherited is actually a pseudoaltruistic predisposition to experience empathic distress and to act to reduce this distress. Moreover, as already noted, the empirical evidence cited by Hoffman (1981a) for a genetically based empathically mediated altruistic impulse is easily amenable to egoistic interpretations.

C. SUMMARY OF REVIEW OF CONTEMPORARY DISCUSSIONS
OF ALTRUISM

To summarize thus far, psychological theories of motivation have assumed that all human action, including all prosocial behavior, is directed toward the ultimate goal of increasing the actor's own welfare. Contemporary psychological discussions of altruism seem to involve either intentionally or unintentionally redefining the term so that the question of whether prosocial behavior is ever directed toward the ultimate goal of benefiting another is not clearly addressed. Perhaps as a result, the evidence cited in these discussions provides us with no good basis for claiming that prosocial motivation is ever truly altruistic.

Does this then mean that the contemporary discussions of altruism are of no value in our attempt to determine whether prosocial motivation is ever altruistic, and that we must start again from scratch? Not at all. The contemporary work makes two very important contributions. First, it reveals a number of subtle forms of egoistic prosocial motivation—and how easy it is to slip from discussing altruism to discussing instead one or another of these pseudoaltruistic alternatives. This revelation makes it clear that if we are fruitfully to pursue the question of altruism, then our first step must be to develop an explicit and detailed map of how an altruistic view not only relates to but also differs from various egoistic alternatives—especially from those subtle forms of egoism reflected in the pseudoaltruistic views. Such a map seems essential if we are to have any hope of generating from an altruistic view empirical predictions that differ from the predictions made by one or more of the egoistic views. And until such differential predictions can be made, the empirical evidence for altruistic motivation will necessarily remain unconvincing.

Second, the recent work offers a number of clues as to where one might look for altruistic motivation. Certainly the most frequently named source of altruistic motivation is the other-directed vicarious emotion called empathy or sympathy; it is mentioned in one way or another by Hoffman, Krebs, Karylowski, Lerner, and Piliavin *et al*. Although there are other possible sources of altruistic motivation—certain cognitions, emotions, moods, values, or personality characteristics—the suggestion that empathic emotion evokes altruistic motivation is the most common. This *empathy–altruism hypothesis* is the only possibility that I shall consider in the remainder of this chapter, because I too think empathic (sympathetic) emotion is a likely source of altruistic motivation. Moreover, because empathic emotion seems most likely to occur in situations in which another person is in need, I shall limit my discussion to prosocial motivation evoked by the perception of another in need. Situations in which one person may be motivated to do something nice for another who is not in need— e.g., giving a surprise gift or party—are certainly of interest (see Schoenrade, Batson, Brandt, & Loud, 1986), but I shall not consider them here.

In considering the possibility that empathy evokes altruistic motivation, I shall try to follow my own advice and first provide an explicit and detailed map that summarizes and systematizes the previous discussions of prosocial motivation, highlighting similarities and differences between empathically induced altruistic motivation and the major egoistic accounts of prosocial motivation. This map—which is in the form of a three-path model—will then be employed to generate explicit empirical predictions that differ depending on whether the prosocial motivation evoked by empathy is egoistic or altruistic. Indeed, a major virtue of the proposed model is that it yields empirically testable differential predictions depending on whether the prosocial motivation evoked by empathy follows the altruistic or one of the egoistic paths. These differential predictions permit empirical tests for the existence of empathically evoked altruism. Once the three-path model is outlined, existing research relevant to the predictions will be reviewed and future research proposed.

III. A Three-Path Model Comparing and Contrasting Egoistic and Empathically Induced Altruistic Motivation for Helping

A. EGOISTIC ACCOUNTS OF PROSOCIAL MOTIVATION: PATHS 1 AND 2

As was suggested by the preceding review of pseudoaltruistic views, one of two egoistic motives is usually invoked in psychological explanations of prosocial motivation. One of these motives involves social learning and reinforcement; the other involves arousal reduction. These two egoistic motives are summarized in Paths 1 and 2 of the flowchart in Fig. 1. The reinforcement model (Path 1) is further subdivided to differentiate (a) reward-seeking and (b) punishment-avoiding motives. Each path begins with perception of another person in need.

1. Perception of Another in Need

Perception of another in need involves recognition of a negative discrepancy between the other's current and potential states on one or more dimensions of well-being. Dimensions of well-being include the absence of physical pain, negative affect, anxiety, stress, and so on, as well as the presence of physical pleasure, positive affect, security, and so on.

Perception of need would seem to be a threshold function of three factors: (1) a perceptible discrepancy (real or apparent) between the other's current and

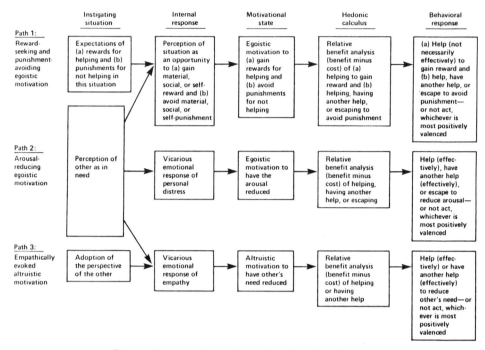

Fig. 1.   Flowchart of egoistic and altruistic paths to helping.

potential states on some dimension(s) of well-being, (2) sufficient salience of these states, so that each can be noticed and a comparison made (Clark & Word, 1972, 1974; Latané & Darley, 1970), and (3) the perceiver's attention being focused on the person in need, not on the self or some other aspect of the environment (Duval & Wicklund, 1972; Gibbons & Wicklund, 1982; Mathews & Canon, 1975; Weiner, 1976; Wicklund, 1975). It appears that all three of these conditions must simultaneously be satisfied before another's need can be perceived. Of course, satisfying these conditions does not guarantee a perception of need; they are necessary but not sufficient conditions. A variety of cognitive and situational factors, including pluralistic ignorance and social cueing, may lead to the minimization or even denial of the need (Latané & Darley, 1970).

Given that some need is perceived, it can vary in magnitude. The magnitude of the perceived need appears to be a function of three factors: (1) the number of dimensions of well-being on which discrepancies are perceived, (2) the size of each discrepancy, and (3) the potential helper's perception of the importance of each of these dimensions for the person in need (Schaps, 1972).

2. Expectation of Rewards and Punishments

Perception of another as in need is all that is required to instigate Path 2 motivation but, by itself, this perception is not sufficient to instigate Path 1 motivation. Before motivation to help can be elicited along Path 1, the potential helper must also have the expectation of receiving rewards for helping or punishments for not helping—or both—in the particular situation. These expectations are the product of the potential helper's learning history, including rewards and punishments he or she has previously received in similar situations, as well as rewards and punishments he or she has observed others receiving in similar situations. (See Bandura, 1977; Cialdini *et al.*, 1981; Eisenberg, 1982, for reviews of research on the socialization processes by which such expectations are learned.)

3. Internal Response

Perceiving the other's need, combined with expectations based on one's learning history, can lead to the anticipation of rewards for helping or punishments for not. The anticipated rewards and punishments may be obvious and explicit, such as being paid (Fischer, 1963), gaining social approval (Baumann, Cialdini, & Kenrick, 1981; Gelfand, Hartmann, Cromer, Smith, & Page, 1975; Kenrick, Baumann, & Cialdini, 1979; Moss & Page, 1972), or avoiding censure (Reis & Gruzen, 1976). They may also be more subtle, such as receiving esteem in exchange for helping (Hatfield, Piliavin, & Walster, 1978), complying with social norms (Berkowitz, 1972; Gouldner, 1960; Leeds, 1963; Staub, 1971), complying with internalized personal norms (Lerner, 1970; Schwartz, 1975, 1977; Zuckerman, 1975), seeing oneself as a good person (Bandura, 1977; Cialdini *et al.*, 1973; Cialdini & Kenrick, 1976; Weyant, 1978; Wilson, 1976), or avoiding guilt (Hoffman, 1976, 1982; Steele, 1975). This internal response of anticipating rewards and punishments is represented on Path 1 of Fig. 1.

Independent of the anticipated rewards and punishments on Path 1, seeing another in need may cause an individual to experience aversive vicarious emotions of personal distress (cf., Hoffman's empathic distress)—to feel upset, anxious, disturbed, and the like (Batson & Coke, 1981; Batson, O'Quin, Fultz, Vanderplas, & Isen, 1983; Hoffman, 1981a, 1981b; Piliavin & Piliavin, 1973; Staub & Baer, 1974). The magnitude of this personal distress appears to be a function of three factors: the magnitude of the perceived need, its salience, and its personal relevance to oneself (Piliavin & Piliavin, 1973; Staub & Baer, 1974). As Piliavin *et al.* (1981) have noted, the salience and personal relevance of another's need seem to increase as a result of perceived "we-ness," similarity, and attraction. This second internal response is represented on Path 2 of Fig. 1.

Reward and punishment anticipation (Path 1) and aversive feelings of distress (Path 2) are distinct internal responses to perceiving another in need, but
they are not mutually exclusive. In many helping situations—notably emergencies—each of these internal responses will be instigated, and in proportional
magnitudes. In other helping situations—such as making a routine annual contribution to a charity—a person may be very aware of the rewards for helping and
the punishments for not, yet feel little personal distress. In still other situations—
such as witnessing a gory accident—much distress may be aroused, and little or
no attention paid to the possible reward and punishment opportunities of the
situation.

4. Motivational State

Reward anticipation, punishment avoidance, and feelings of distress each
evoke their own form of egoistic motivation. On Path 1, perception of the
opportunity to get reward or avoid punishment evokes motivation to gain the
reward (Path 1a) or avoid the punishment (Path 1b). The magnitude of the
reward-seeking or punishment-avoiding motivation appears to be a function of
two factors: (1) the magnitude of the anticipated rewards and punishments, and
(2) the potential helper's current need state with regard to the anticipated rewards
and punishments. The potential helper's current needs might include, for example, a need for enhanced self-esteem (Steele, 1975), for relief from feeling bad
(Cialdini et al., 1973; Weyant, 1978), or for continuance of feeling good (Isen &
Levin, 1972).

On Path 2, experiencing personal distress leads to motivation to have this
distress reduced. The magnitude of this arousal-reduction motivation appears
simply to be a direct function of the magnitude of the distress experienced
(Gaertner & Dovidio, 1977; Hoffman, 1981a; Piliavin et al., 1981).

The egoistic motives on Path 1 and Path 2 are distinct but not mutually
exclusive; they may be experienced simultaneously. When they are, obtaining
their goals may be compatible or incompatible. Sometimes, actions that move
one toward gaining reward or avoiding punishment also reduce one's personal
distress—as when one saves a person trapped in a burning building by putting
out the fire. At other times, acting to gain reward or avoid punishment increases
distress—as when one helps by comforting a mangled accident victim. If perception of another in need simultaneously evokes Path 1 and Path 2 egoistic motivation, then to the extent that the goals of the motives are compatible, their
magnitudes should sum.

5. Hedonic Calculus

If the magnitude of one or more egoistic motives is above some minimal
threshold, then the individual will consider various behavioral means of reaching

the goals of these motivational states. Helping may be one means of reaching the goal(s), but often there are other means. Before acting, a "hedonic calculus" is performed. That is, the motivated individual conducts some form of relative-benefit analysis, weighing benefit against cost for each potential response.

The magnitude of the benefit in the hedonic calculus is a function of the magnitude of the motivational state, because the benefit is to reach the goal. The magnitude of the cost is the sum of the various costs perceived to be associated with the behavior. Perhaps the simplest way to think about these costs is in terms of additional egoistic motives. It is likely that the potential helper, in addition to experiencing one or more motives evoked by perception of the other in need, also simultaneously experiences motives to avoid pain or risk of pain, to save time, to keep his or her money, and so on (Piliavin, Piliavin, & Rodin, 1975). As a general principle, if more than one motive exists, and if a given behavior can reach the goal of one of these motives but not others, then failure to obtain the incompatible goals is the cost associated with this behavior. The magnitude of this cost will be a function of the magnitude of the motivational force to reach the unobtained goals.

On Path 1a, the desired rewards are likely to be associated with being helpful, so the motivation to obtain these rewards specifies the behavioral means: The motivated individual must try to help. Yet, many of the rewards may be obtained even if one's helping is not effective. We do not usually insist on knowing that our charity dollars are well spent before collecting our social and self-rewards for contributing. As people say, "It's the thought that counts." On the other hand, if someone else helps, even effectively, we will receive no reward—unless we can take credit for the other person's helping (e.g., "I talked her into contributing"), and so claim to have helped indirectly.

The behavioral options are quite different on Path 1b. If another person helps effectively we may escape possible punishments for not helping (e.g., social censure, guilt, shame), because the other's help removes the situation requiring our help. Alternatively, if we can psychologically escape from the need situation—by, for example, becoming involved in a distracting task—then we may successfully escape self-inflicted punishments such as guilt and shame. Thus, the hedonic calculus on Path 1a focuses on helping as the only behavioral means of obtaining the desired rewards, but on Path 1b there are three means of avoiding punishment: helping, another person helping, and escaping.

Escaping deserves some additional comment. In general, escape may be accomplished by eliminating any of the three conditions necessary for perceiving need. That is, we can (1) redefine the situation so that no perceptible discrepancy exists between the other's current and potential states of well-being, (2) reduce the salience of the other's need through increasing the physical or psychological distance from it, or (3) shift the focus of attention away from the person in need toward some other aspect of the environment. Note that in order to escape self-inflicted punishments of shame and guilt on Path 1b it may not be enough for us physically to escape the need situation, because we may take the situation and our action (or inaction) with us in memory. To reach the goal of avoiding punishment, we need to escape psychologically. Of course, the old adage, "Out of sight, out of mind," suggests that physical escape may often permit psychological escape as well, and there is some recent empirical evidence that supports this view (see Batson, Bolen, Cross, & Neuringer-Benefiel, 1986).

Because many of the rewards can be obtained and punishments avoided by simply trying to help, Path 1 egoistic motivation should produce a bandwagon effect. The person who arrives at the scene of an accident after the ambulance and busily begins "helping" can expect many of the same rewards and can avoid many of the same punishments as the person who was first on the scene and who used his new shirt to wrap the victim's bleeding arm. If the preferred behavior is the one that maximizes benefit relative to cost, then the safe, clean, low-cost helping of the late arriver looks more attractive. Recognizing this, societies often try to make dangerous, dirty, high-cost helping more attractive by labeling initial helpers "heroes," lavishing them with extra social and even material rewards.

The same three behavioral options that can be used to avoid punishment on Path 1b can reduce aversive arousal on Path 2. The cause of one's distress can be removed either by helping or by another person helping. Alternatively, contact with the cause of one's distress can be removed by escaping. But note that the potential helper is escaping something different here than on Path 1b. On Path 1b the escape is from anticipated punishment, especially self-punishment in the form of shame and guilt; on Path 2 the escape is from the stimulus causing one's distress. Given this difference, physical escape should be even more effective on Path 2 than Path 1b.

Unlike helping on Path 1, helping on Path 2 must be effective if the goal of arousal reduction is to be reached. The help must reduce the other's need, because that is the cause of one's distress. Moreover, having someone else help can be just as effective in reducing one's distress, and it is probably less costly than being the helper oneself. Therefore, the motivation to help aroused on Path 2 should produce quite the opposite of a bandwagon effect.

If no one else can help, Path 2 motivation should lead the potential helper to help or escape, whichever is the least costly means of reducing one's distress. Typically, escaping is less costly than helping, so when escape is possible, Path 2 motivation might be expected to lead to relatively little helping, except when a rapid rise in feelings of distress produces a poorly thought-out, impulsive response.[1]

---

[1]Although a careful weighing of the pros and cons of the behavioral alternatives may take some time, it seems likely that various heuristics exist, permitting a rough hedonic calculus to be per-

The hedonic calculus is often even more complicated than suggested thus far, because the distressed individual has almost certainly also been socialized to expect rewards for helping and punishments for not. As a result, he or she will likely experience Path 1a and 1b motivation at the same time as Path 2 motivation. Piliavin *et al.* (1981) highlight this point through attention to the simultaneous evocation of aversive arousal (Path 2), personal costs (Path 1a), and empathy costs—both present (Path 2) and anticipated (Paths 1b and 2). The goals of motivation on Paths 1a, 1b, and 2 can all be reached by helping, but escaping will bring no rewards. Thus, the anticipated loss of praise and esteem are part of the cost of escaping in a more comprehensive hedonic calculus that deals with Path 1 and Path 2 motives simultaneously.

6. Behavioral Response

The motivated individual will help, let someone else help, or escape, depending on which available response has the greatest perceived relative benefit to self. If no available response is perceived to have relative benefit, i.e., if the anticipated cost of each exceeds the benefit, then the individual will not respond. He or she will pursue some unrelated goal or will do nothing. If no need-related response occurs, then the force of the need-related egoistic motives should slowly dissipate.

---

formed, when necessary, in less than a second. If so, then, contrary to the suggestions of Hoffman (1975, 1981a) and Piliavin and Piliavin (1973) that rapid, "impulsive" helping bypasses the hedonic calculus altogether, we may assume that a relative-benefit analysis is performed even when helping occurs very rapidly. The analysis may be limited in the number of response options considered and in the consideration given to the benefits and costs of these options, but that should not lead us to conclude that no analysis was made.

To illustrate: Imagine that coming upon the young auto accident victim you experience a quick and sizeable increase in aversive arousal and, as a result, a quick and sizeable increase in motivation to reduce that arousal. The benefit of reducing the arousal—and of doing so before it gets any more intense—is likely to be the most prominent, perhaps the only, factor considered in the hedonic calculus. As a result, you may almost instantly rush to call for help, and may afterward report—as do many who rush into burning buildings or dive into dangerous waters—that you "didn't think" before you acted. In spite of this report, it seems likely that you, and they, did think. Otherwise, these "impulsive" responses would not be as adaptive as they are, allowing the helper to circumvent barriers to reach the goal.

It seems best to account for impulsive helping by assuming that the heuristic of the impulsive helper focuses upon the benefit of helping and fails to consider the cost (see Clark & Word, 1974). Other individuals confronted with the same situation might employ a heuristic that focuses on cost to the exclusion of benefit, leading them impulsively to respond, "No way!" Each of these impulsive responses requires some thought, although neither may be well thought-out. (For a view of impulsive helping similar to the one proposed here, see Piliavin *et al.*, 1981.)

7. Summary

Although these two egoistic paths have not previously been laid alongside one another in a single model, Paths 1 and 2 are primarily a summary and integration of the work of other researchers (most notably, Bar-Tal, 1976; Cialdini & Kenrick, 1976; Hoffman, 1981a,b; Latané & Darley, 1970; Piliavin et al., 1981; Schwartz, 1977). No doubt, one or more of these researchers would disagree with me on some of the details of my portrayal. Yet, I shall not focus on these disagreements because none is relevant to what follows, and I believe there would be general agreement among researchers studying prosocial motivation on the major themes and logic presented.

Much can be said in favor of using these two egoistic paths to account for the motivation for helping. Each path makes considerable intuitive sense; each is internally consistent; each is complex, yet permits relatively precise behavioral predictions; in combination, they include two classic psychological approaches to motivation—reinforcement and arousal reduction; and finally, there is much empirical research consistent with each (some key studies have already been cited; see Eisenberg, 1982; Dovidio, 1984; Krebs & Miller, 1985; Piliavin et al., 1981; Rushton & Sorrentino, 1981; Staub, 1978, 1979, for more extensive recent reviews).

But as already noted, contemporary psychologists such as Hoffman and Krebs have at times suggested that these egoistic accounts may not be adequate to provide a full explanation of why people help. The work of these psychologists suggests that the two egoistic paths may need to be supplemented by a third path, one based on the hypothesis that empathic emotion evokes altruistic motivation.

B. EMPATHICALLY EVOKED ALTRUISTIC MOTIVATION TO HELP: PATH 3

The hypothesis that empathy evokes altruistic motivation can be made explicit and, as a result, empirically testable by detailing the psychological process involved in this third path (Path 3 of Fig. 1), just as has been done for the two egoistic paths.

1. Perception of Another in Need

Like Paths 1 and 2, Path 3 begins with a perception of need. The existence and magnitude of the perceived need are assumed to be a function of the same factors specified for egoistic motivation. That is, existence of perceived need is a threshold function of (1) a perceptible discrepancy between the other's current and potential states on some dimension(s) of well-being, (2) sufficient salience of these states, and (3) the perceiver's attention being focused on the other. The magnitude of the perceived need is a function of (1) the number of dimensions of well-being on which discrepancies are perceived, (2) the size of each discrepancy, and (3) the perceived importance of each of these dimensions for the person in need. But on Path 3, perceiving the other's need is claimed to lead to a unique internal response—empathic emotion. Following Hoffman (1975, 1976), Krebs (1975), and Stotland (1969), it is proposed that this unique emotional response is a result of the perceiver adopting the perspective of the other.

2. Adopting the Perspective of the Other

Adopting the other's perspective involves more than simply focusing attention on the other. One may focus attention on another's need but maintain a relatively objective perspective, dispassionately observing that person's plight. In contrast, adopting the other's perspective involves imagining how that person is affected by his or her situation (Stotland, 1969). Recollection of one's own or others' reactions in similar situations—as well as imagining oneself in the other's situation—often provides information that facilitates adopting the other's perspective, but there are limits to this facilitation. One may get so wrapped up in reminiscences or in one's own possible reactions to the situation that one fails to consider the specific way the situation is affecting the other (Hygge, 1976; Karinol, 1982). It is consideration of the effect on the other that is the essence of perspective taking, and it is perspective taking—in combination with a perception of the other as in need—that I am suggesting leads to empathic emotion.

Adoption of the perspective of the other appears to be a threshold function of two factors: (1) the ability to take another's perspective (Hoffman, 1976, 1981b; Krebs & Russell, 1981), and (2) a perspective-taking set (Stotland, 1969). A perspective-taking set may be induced by prior experience in similar situations, by instructions, or by the existence of a feeling of attachment to the other. In the laboratory, perspective taking has often been induced by instructions (see Stotland, 1969; Coke, Batson, & McDavis, 1978; Toi & Batson, 1982). In the natural stream of behavior, perspective taking may also be the result of instructions, including self-instructions (e.g., "I should walk a mile in his moccasins"). More often, however, it is the result of prior similar experience or of attachment.

3. Attachment

Feelings of emotional attachment to certain other people seem quite important in our social relations; yet emotional attachment remains poorly understood. It is not possible even to articulate the defining features of attachment, only to provide some general clues and examples.

First, some general clues. When attachment exists—for example, a mother's attachment to her child—there is a general feeling of heartache and sadness at separation from that person and a feeling of warmth and joy at reuniting (Ainsworth, Blehar, Waters, & Wall, 1978; Bowlby, 1969). Cognitive processes such as perceived similarity and attractiveness can contribute to attachment, but its basic character seems to be emotional. Some attachments—such as the parent's attachment to the child and the child's to the parent—probably have a genetic base (see Batson, Darley, & Coke, 1978; Bowlby, 1969; Hoffman, 1981a). although this genetic base is clearly subject to broad cognitive generalization, as in cases of adoption (Batson, 1983). Like the related but more general concepts of attitude and sentiment, attachment involves a relatively enduring predisposition or orientation toward the other person.

The prototypic example of attachment is the parent's attachment to the child. But attachments can occur in a variety of interpersonal relationships—including other family relationships, friendships, love relationships, relationships with pets, and so on. Typically, attachments are based on personal contact. They may also be based on cognitive generalization from personal contact, as seems to be the case with similarity-based attachments. Attachments tend to be reciprocated, though they need not be. They may vary in strength. Attachments based on cognitive generalization are usually weaker than those based on personal contact. Extended intimate contact and dependency relations seem to produce particularly strong attachments. Other names for the phenomenon I am calling attachment might be "love," "caring," "feeling close," "we-feeling," or "bonding."[2]

4. Internal Response of Empathic Emotion

The arousal of empathic emotion appears to be affected by attachment in two ways. First, the stronger the attachment to the other, the greater the likelihood of adopting the other's perspective. And, as already discussed, adopting the other's perspective is assumed to be a necessary precondition for empathic emotion to be aroused. Second, the strength of attachment can affect the magnitude of empathic emotion. If the perceiver adopts the perspective of the other, then the magnitude of empathic emotion is predicted to be a function of two factors: (1) the magnitude of the perceived need, and (2) the strength of the

---

[2]As may be apparent, I am proposing a priority of emotional attachment over cognitive unit formation (Heider, 1958) in the experience of "we-feeling." This view stands in opposition to the view proposed by Hornstein in his discussion of promotive social relationships (1976, 1982). For Hornstein, cognitions take priority: "Dichotomizing the world into groups of 'we' and 'they' reflects a process of social categorization" (1982, p. 235); he places "a theoretical premium on cognitive factors" (1982, p. 244). I am placing the theoretical premium on emotional factors, suggesting that cognitive categorization (e.g., perceived similarity) has the power to produce we-feeling because it extends emotional attachments originally developed through personal contact.

attachment. Thus, the arrows of influence at the beginning of Path 3 represent two types of functions. Some represent threshold functions: perception of the other as in need and perspective taking are both necessary for empathy to occur at all. Others represent continuous functions: magnitude of the other's need and strength of the attachment (not included in Fig. 1) combine to determine the magnitude of the empathic emotion.

It has been suggested that there are at least two different types of vicarious emotion evoked by perceiving someone in need (Batson, Duncan, Ackerman, Buckley, & Birch, 1981; Batson et al., 1983; Hoffman, 1975, 1976). One, which I am calling *personal distress* (cf., Hoffman's empathic distress), has already been discussed. This vicarious emotion includes feeling anxious, upset, disturbed, distressed, perturbed, and the like and is assumed to evoke Path 2 egoistic motivation to have the distress reduced. The second vicarious emotion, which I am calling *empathy* (cf., Hoffman's sympathetic distress), includes feeling sympathetic, compassionate, warm, softhearted, tender, and the like.

Empathy, as I am using the term, does not mean feeling the same emotion one imagines the person in need is feeling, nor does it mean feeling the emotion one would if suffering the other's plight. Instead, it is a more other-oriented emotional response elicited by and congruent with the perceived welfare of someone else (see Batson & Coke, 1981, 1983). The specific label for this other-oriented congruent emotional response is, of course, not crucial. In recent years it has most often been called empathy, but it has also been called sympathy (Heider, 1958; Smith, 1759; Wispé, 1968, 1986), compassion (Hume, 1740), and "the tender emotion" (McDougall, 1908).

When perceiving someone in distress, empathy will be an unpleasant, aversive emotion. But it is suggested that empathy—unlike personal distress—does not evoke Path 2 egoistic motivation to have this aversive arousal reduced; instead, it evokes altruistic motivation directed toward the ultimate goal of reducing the other's need.

5. Altruistic Motivation

The proposal that empathic emotion can evoke motivation directed toward the ultimate goal of reducing the other's need has been called the *empathy–altruism hypothesis* (Batson & Coke, 1981; Batson et al., 1981). According to this hypothesis, the magnitude of altruistic motivation is assumed to be a direct function of the magnitude of empathic emotion. Of course, reducing the other's need is likely also to bring social and self-rewards (Path 1a), avoid social and self-punishments (Path 1b), and reduce the helper's own aversive arousal (Path 2). But it is proposed that feeling empathy for the person in need evokes motivation to help in which these benefits to self are not the goal of helping; they are simply consequences of helping.

Even though it is hypothesized that the motivation evoked by empathy is altruistic, not egoistic, it is recognized that the instigating conditions that arouse empathic emotion and, as a result, altruistic motivation are also likely to arouse Path 1 and Path 2 egoistic motives. These egoistic and altruistic motives are assumed to be distinct, but to the extent that the goals of these motives are compatible, their magnitudes should sum.

6. Hedonic Calculus

If the magnitude of the altruistic motivation or the summed egoistic and altruistic motivation is above some minimal threshold, then the individual will proceed to consider behavioral means of reaching the goal of this motivation. As on the egoistic paths, the altruistically motivated individual will perform a relative-benefit analysis before acting. To suggest a relative-benefit analysis for altrustic motivation may seem contradictory, because the goal of this analysis is clearly egoistic—to reach the desired altruistic goal while incurring minimal costs to self. Yet, the existence of this egoistic goal does not mean that the motivation to have the other's need reduced has now become egoistic; it only means that the impulse to act on this altruistic motivation is likely to evoke an egoistic motive as well. The existence of the latter motive need not negate or contaminate the former, although it certainly complicates the relationship between the altruistic motive and behavior.

The magnitude of the benefit in the relative-benefit analysis is, as on the egoistic paths, a function of the magnitude of the motivational force, because the benefit is to reach the goal or goals. The magnitude of the cost is the sum of the various costs associated with the behavior, including physical harm or risk, discomfort, exertion, mental strain, time, monetary expense, and so on.

The relative-benefit analysis on Path 3 should be restricted to consideration of helping or having someone else help; no consideration should be given to the cost of escaping, because escape is not a viable behavioral means of reaching the altruistic goal. Moreover, on Path 3 one's helping must be effective if the goal is to be reached. And having someone else help effectively should be as viable—but no more viable—a means of reaching the altruistic goal of having the other's need reduced as is being the helper oneself. There should be no bandwagon effect.[3]

---

[3]As with egoistic motivation, it seems likely that heuristics exist for conducting the relative-benefit analysis and that the sophistication of these heuristics varies widely. If the magnitude of the altruistic motivation increases very rapidly, then one may expect a rapid response based on a relatively crude heuristic. As on the egoistic paths, the potential helper may focus exclusively on the benefits of reaching the altruistic goal, failing to give weight to the associated cost. This would result in "impulsive" altruistic helping. Impulsiveness per se does not distinguish altruistic from egoistic motives in the present analysis; either type of motivation could lead to impulsive or to well thought-out responses.

7. Enacting a Behavior to Reach the Altruistic Goal

The altruistically motivated individual will help if (a) helping is possible, (b) the relative benefit of helping is perceived to be positive, and (c) the relative benefit of helping is perceived to be more positive than the relative benefit of having someone else help (assuming someone else is available to help). If the relative benefit is negative, i.e., the cost of helping exceeds the benefit, then the individual will not help. In this case, the force of the altruistic motivation should slowly dissipate. Alternatively, the individual could deny the person's need, break the attachment by derogating the person in need (Lerner, 1970), or change other factors leading to adoption of that person's perspective. These responses would not enable the individual to reach the altruistic goal, but they should eliminate the empathic emotion and, hence, the altruistic motivation.

IV. Making the Theoretical Assumptions Explicit: Three Hypotheses

It is possible to state the theoretical assumptions implicit in this discussion of the empathy–altruism relationship in terms of three empirical hypotheses. These hypotheses, if valid, justify the specification of Path 3 in Fig. 1 as distinct from Paths 1 and 2.

Hypothesis 1. Personal distress and empathy are distinct vicarious emotional responses to perceiving someone in need.

Hypothesis 2. Empathic emotion is evoked when the perceiver adopts the perspective of the person in need; the magnitude of this emotion is a function of the perceived magnitude of the need and the strength of the perceiver's attachment to the person in need.

Hypothesis 3. Empathic emotion evokes altruistic motivation to have the other person's need reduced; the magnitude of this motivation is proportional to the magnitude of the empathic emotion.

Hypothesis 3 is the one hypothesis most central to the argument. Hypothesis 1 is also central, because it states a necessary precondition for the motivation evoked by empathy to be qualitatively different from the motivation evoked by personal distress. Hypothesis 2 is less central. It must also be true if the specific model of altruistic motivation outlined in Path 3 is correct, but were it to prove false, a modified version of the model might be worth retaining. Were either Hypothesis 1 or 3 to prove false, however, the claim that empathic emotion evokes altruistic motivation should be rejected.

Empathic emotion is the only source of altruistic motivation specified by the model. I do not assume that feeling empathy is the only possible source of altruistic motivation, but if there are other sources—for example, one or another personality characteristic, including a disposition to feel empathy—these other sources lie outside the scope of the present model. (But see Batson *et al.*, 1986, for evidence that several "altruistic" personality characteristics, including a disposition to feel empathy, produce egoistic rather than altruistic prosocial motivation.)

In summary, then, the theoretical argument I am proposing for the existence of altruistic motivation is as follows. Empathy is a specific type of vicarious emotion produced by taking the perspective of a person perceived to be in need. It is distinct from personal distress. The magnitude of empathic emotion is a function of the magnitude of the perceived need and the strength of the perceiver's attachment to the person in need. Empathic emotion evokes altruistic motivation to have the other's need reduced. This motivation is called altruistic because the ultimate goal is to increase the other's welfare, not one's own.

In its general form this argument is not original with me; similar arguments have been made by Hoffman (1975, 1976), Krebs (1975) and, much earlier, by McDougall (1908). What is original with the present statement is (1) the precision of the argument, and (2) embedding the argument in a more general framework that includes egoistic prosocial motivation. These characteristics render the argument empirically testable in a way that earlier altruistic views are not.

V.   Empirical Evidence for Empathically Evoked Altruistic Motivation

To fully assess the empirical status of this argument, it would be necessary to review the evidence relevant to each of the three hypotheses. Because, however, Hypotheses 1 and 3 are most central, and because Hypothesis 2 is yet to be clearly tested (the evidence that does exist is generally supportive of it), I shall limit the present review to evidence relevant to Hypotheses 1 and 3. Clear evidence for these two hypotheses would be sufficient to call into question the widely held view of universal egoism; it would support instead the dualistic view that altruistic as well as egoistic motives exist.

A.   HYPOTHESIS 1. PERSONAL DISTRESS AND EMPATHY ARE
      DISTINCT VICARIOUS EMOTIONAL RESPONSES TO
      PERCEIVING SOMEONE IN NEED

There are three types of evidence relevant to this hypothesis. First, in a series of six studies, several colleagues and I factor analyzed individuals' self-reported emotional responses to encountering a person in need. Subjects in each study were asked to report on a 7-point scale (1 = not at all; 7 = extremely) how strongly they were feeling each emotion described in a list of emotion adjectives. The list included eight adjectives assumed to reflect the vicarious emotion of personal distress—alarmed, grieved, upset, worried, disturbed, perturbed, distressed, and troubled—and six adjectives assumed to reflect empathy—sympathetic, moved, compassionate, tender, warm, and softhearted. We reasoned that if distress and empathy are independent vicarious emotions, then subjects' ratings of the adjectives in these two sets should load on separate factors in a factor analysis. Alternatively, if these emotions combine to form a single vicarious emotion, as suggested by Piliavin and Piliavin's (1973) discussion of "empathic pain" and Hoffman's (1981a,b) recent discussions of generic "empathic distress," then responses to all 14 adjectives should load on a single factor. To provide a clear comparison of these alternatives, we used an orthogonal rotation, which ensures that each new factor is entirely unrelated to all previous factors.

The second type of evidence relevant to Hypothesis 1 comes from an experiment in which we tried to manipulate personal distress and empathy independently of one another (Batson *et al.*, 1981, Experiment 2). We reasoned that if distress and empathy are independent vicarious emotions, then it should be possible, using a misattribution technique, to manipulate subjects' perceptions of their experience of one of these emotions independently of the other.

The third type of evidence relevant to the claim that distress and empathy are qualitatively distinct vicarious emotions focuses upon the motivational difference claimed to result from the two emotions. If, as asserted in Hypothesis 3, empathy evokes altruistic motivation while distress evokes egoistic motivation, then empathy and distress must be functionally distinct.

1. Factor Analyses of Subjects' Vicarious Emotional Responses

Results from the factor analyses clearly support Hypothesis 1. Before looking at the factor analyses, however, let us consider the emotional responses themselves. Table I reports for each of six studies (1) subjects' mean response to each adjective, (2) the average response to the eight distress and to the six empathy adjectives, (3) the correlation between these averages, and (4) a *t*-test on the difference between the averages. As can be seen, the correlations between responses to the eight distress adjectives (averaged) and the six empathy adjectives (averaged) were positive in each study (all *p*'s < .001).

These correlations may seem to suggest that adjectives of both types reflect a single vicarious emotion. But although the correlations are certainly consistent with this possibility, they do not provide clear support for it because there are at least three other reasons to expect subjects' reports of these emotions to be positively correlated. First, since both distress and empathy are emotions, they

TABLE I

MEAN SELF-REPORTED EMOTIONAL RESPONSE TO ANOTHER IN NEED (6 STUDIES)

	Study[a]					
	1	2	3	4	5	6
Distress adjectives						
Alarmed	2.12	3.23	2.10	2.28	4.61	4.83
Grieved	2.00	4.20	3.57	3.28	3.90	4.43
Upset	2.18	3.10	2.59	2.64	4.03	4.47
Worried	2.58	2.73	2.40	2.56	4.74	4.70
Disturbed	2.48	3.77	2.86	3.14	4.52	4.70
Perturbed	1.97	1.60	1.60	1.96	3.23	3.94
Distressed	2.42	2.97	2.65	2.59	4.75	4.64
Troubled	2.48	2.50	2.51	2.69	4.92	4.78
Average	2.28	3.01	2.53	2.64	4.34	4.56
Empathy adjectives						
Sympathetic	—	5.27	5.14	5.04	5.03	5.23
Moved	4.24	4.07	4.10	3.92	4.03	4.47
Compassionate	4.09	3.63	3.40	3.81	4.67	4.70
Tender	—	3.30	3.11	3.37	3.79	4.24
Warm	3.36	2.40	2.79	2.81	4.13	4.32
Softhearted	4.21	3.53	3.19	3.68	4.20	4.55
Average	3.98	3.70	3.62	3.77	4.31	4.58
Correlation between distress and empathy averages						
$r =$	.59[b]	.75[b]	.59[b]	.66[b]	.44[b]	.59[b]
Test of difference between distress and empathy averages						
$t =$	8.59[b]	3.93[b]	7.29[b]	8.53[b]	.16	.14

[a]Studies are as follows: 1. Coke *et al.* (1978, Experiment 2), $N=33$, females only; 2. Batson *et al.* (1979), $N=30$, females only; 3. Coke (1980), $N=63$, females only; 4. Toi and Batson (1982), $N=78$, females only; 5. Fultz (1982), $N=61$, 26 males, 35 females; 6. Batson *et al.* (1983), $N=88$, 39 males, 49 females.

[b]$p < .001$.

should be similarly affected by individual differences in general emotionality or in readiness to report emotions. Second, since both distress and empathy are vicarious emotions evoked by perceiving a person in need, individual differences in perceptions of the magnitude of the need should have parallel effects on both. Third, in each of the six studies in this series, emotions were measured by self-reports on unidirectional adjective rating scales, with adjectives reflecting distress and empathy intermixed. Using this form of measurement, response-set biases could easily produce a positive correlation between reports of the two emotions.

Factor analysis can control for these potential confounds in the correlations, since factor analysis seeks systematic, independent patterns within as well as across individuals' responses. Turning then to the factor analyses, varimax-rotated principal-component analyses were performed for each of the six studies on subjects' responses to the 14 emotion adjectives. Results in each study revealed that a two-factor solution was more appropriate than a one-factor solution. The two-factor solution included all eigenvalues above 1.0 and only eigenvalues above 1.0 in five of the six studies, and all eigenvalues above 1.3 in the sixth (Batson, Cowles, & Coke, 1979). In addition, the two-factor solution included all factors accounting for at least 10% of the total variance in all six studies; the one-factor solution failed to meet this criterion in any study. Across the six studies, the variance accounted for by the two-factor solution ranged from 65% to 73% of the total.

To test the specific prediction that a two-factor solution fits the data better than a one-factor solution, goodness-of-fit tests were performed to compare the one- and two-factor solutions in each of the six studies. This was done by use of the goodness-of-fit criteria for maximum-likelihood principal component analyses (see Lawley & Maxwell, 1971). These comparisons revealed that the two-factor solution fit the data significantly better than the one-factor solution in all six studies (all p's < .001). Chi-squares for the differences in goodness of fit between the one- and two-factor solutions are presented in the first row of Table II.

Factor loadings for each of the 14 emotion adjectives are reported in the remaining rows of Table II. The loadings reveal a factor structure that is highly consistent across studies; in each, the eight distress adjectives tend to load on one factor and the six empathy adjectives to load on a second, orthogonal factor. The first factor, which I have called the Distress factor, received loadings greater than .60 from "alarmed," "upset," "disturbed," and "distressed" in all six studies, from "worried" and "perturbed" in five of the six, and from "grieved" and "troubled" in four of the six studies. The second factor, which I have called the Empathy factor, received loadings greater than .60 from "moved," "compassionate," "warm," and "softhearted" in all six studies and from "sympathetic" and "tender" in four of five studies (these last two adjectives were not used by Coke et al., 1978).

The robustness of the finding that distress and empathy are independent vicarious emotions is indicated by the consistency of the factor structure across studies employing quite different need situations. In the first study in this series (Coke et al., 1978, Experiment 2), the need was not especially great and it was relatively remote in time and place: a graduate student in the School of Education needed subjects for her M.A. research. In the next three studies, the victim's need was great, but it was still relatively remote in time and place: subjects learned that the victim was struggling to deal with the consequences of a tragic automobile accident. She had horrible scars on her face (Batson et al., 1979), on her legs (Coke, 1980), or was faced with having to give up her career aspirations

TABLE II

VARIMAX-ROTATED PRINCIPAL-COMPONENTS FACTOR STRUCTURE OF SELF-REPORTED EMOTIONAL RESPONSES TO ANOTHER IN NEED (6 STUDIES)

	Study[a]											
	1		2		3		4		5		6	

Difference in goodness of fit between one- and two-factor solutions (maximum likelihood factor analysis)

	1	2	3	4	5	6
$\chi^2 =$	48.12	41.40	121.84	106.79	115.35	219.38
$p <$	.001	.001	.001	.001	.001	.001

Factor loadings (least-squares component analysis)[c]

	D^b	E	D	E	D	E	D	E	D	E	D	E
Distress adjectives												
Alarmed	.75*	.01	.72*	.49	.63*	.15	.72*	.34	.77*	.11	.80*	.19
Grieved	.51	.49	.65*	.48	.55	.58	.70*	.33	.68*	.42	.72*	.30
Upset	.84*	.39	.82*	.32	.74*	.38	.80*	.38	.87*	.17	.89*	.28
Worried	.40	.60*	.87*	.18	.67*	.35	.72*	.34	.78*	.18	.81*	.39
Disturbed	.83*	.35	.82*	.38	.76*	.20	.76*	.38	.89*	.18	.90*	.24
Perturbed	.84*	.17	.59	-.11	.76*	-.18	.69*	-.13	.82*	-.02	.68*	.11
Distressed	.62*	.56	.65*	.48	.81*	.32	.67*	.48	.87*	.25	.86*	.28
Troubled	.88*	.23	.58	.54	.80*	.22	.75*	.33	.59	.39	.87*	.32
Empathy adjectives												
Sympathetic	—	—	.58	.53	.23	.74*	.29	.69*	.04	.84*	.20	.82*
Moved	.31	.75*	.37	.78*	.41	.78*	.42	.74*	.31	.67*	.40	.72*
Compassionate	.25	.80*	.09	.82*	.40	.73*	.24	.80*	.14	.86*	.17	.90*
Tender	—	—	.66*	.32	.18	.86*	.28	.78*	.31	.78*	.36	.74*
Warm	.05	.82*	.23	.71*	-.03	.80*	.19	.80*	.20	.68*	.15	.66*
Softhearted	.12	.85*	.14	.73*	.11	.80*	.17	.86*	.05	.83*	.29	.86*

[a] For identification of studies, see Table I.

[b] D = Distress factor (Factor 1); E = Empathy factor (Factor 2).

[c] Asterisk (*) denotes loading above .60.

(Toi & Batson, 1982). In each of these first four studies, subjects learned of the victim's need by listening to an audiotape of a (bogus) radio announcement. In the remaining two studies, the victim's need was great and was highly proximate in time and place: subjects watched over closed-circuit television (actually a videotape) while the victim, thought to be in a nearby room, unexpectedly reacted with increasing discomfort to a series of random electric shocks.

As revealed in Table I, in the first four studies there was a significant difference in the average amounts of distress and empathy that subjects reported; in the last two studies there was not. Yet the factor structure in all six studies clearly supports the hypothesized independence of the vicarious emotions of distress and empathy.[4]

Finally, the robustness of this two-factor structure is also supported by the findings of other researchers at another institution. Archer, Diaz-Loving, Gollwitzer, Davis, and Foushee (1981) and Davis (1983) have reported similar factor structures, with distress adjectives loading on one factor and empathy adjectives loading on another.[5]

The consistency of the two-factor structure across this range of need situations and range of relative magnitudes of distress and empathy seems to contradict the suggestion of Piliavin et al. (1981) that feelings of distress and empathy are actually components of a single vicarious emotion that is expressed as empathy in nonemergency situations and as distress in emergencies. It also seems to contradict the related suggestion of Piliavin et al. (1981, 1982) that distress and empathy are components of a single vicarious emotion that is expressed as

[4]Actually, the last two studies in Table I differed from the four earlier ones in two salient respects. First, as noted, subjects in the last two both saw and heard the victim, whom they thought was suffering in a nearby experimental room; in the four earlier studies, subjects heard a victim who was not physically present talk about a more remote problem. Second, the first four studies included only female subjects, while the last two included both males and females.

Apparently, it was the greater proximity and visibility of the victim's distress, not the sex difference, that accounted for the increased reporting of distress in the last two studies. For, when data for males and females in the last two studies were analyzed separately, there were no reliable differences between the amounts of distress and empathy reported by either sex in either study.

[5]Shelton and Rogers (1981) reported a study in which both distress and empathy adjectives loaded on a single factor. But that study differed from the studies discussed in this section in two important respects. First, the victims in the Shelton and Rogers study were an endangered species, whales, not other humans. Second, subjects in different conditions of the Shelton and Rogers study were given different information about the victims. Half the subjects saw a gory film clip in which whales were hunted, killed, and processed for market. The remaining subjects saw neutral scenes describing whales' natural habitats and behavior. In contrast, subjects in all conditions of the studies discussed in this section received the same information about the victim's needs. The information differences across conditions in the Shelton and Rogers study could easily account for distress and empathy responses loading on a single factor. Half of their subjects had little reason to experience either emotion; the other half had reason to experience both emotions (R. W. Rogers, personal communication, February, 1986).

empathy at low levels of intensity and distress at high levels. Contrary to these two suggestions, the factor analyses summarized in Table II reveal that people often report personal distress and empathy as independent emotions in both low- and high-impact situations and when reporting both relatively low and relatively high levels of distress and empathy.

This is not to say that the particular configuration of emotions experienced as distress and empathy, as well as the relationship between these configurations, will not differ for different need situations. As revealed in Table II, "grieved" and "worried" were sometimes more closely associated with the empathy than the distress factor, and in one study, both "sympathetic" and "tender" were more closely associated with the distress than the empathy factor. Moreover, in some need situations, e.g., when an innocent child or puppy is suffering, it seems likely that distress and empathy will be closely intertwined. In other need situations, e.g., when a peer is suffering, they may both be present but more clearly differentiated. The clearer differentiation in the latter case is expected due to an oscillation of focus of attention. We may more easily imagine the peer's plight befalling us, and so oscillate between focusing on the other's need and on our own need were we in the same situation. Focusing on the other's need should produce both distress and empathy; focusing on our own imagined need should produce only distress.

By itself, the factor analysis evidence cannot be considered conclusive. Some other discriminating features of the two sets of adjectives might be producing the two factors, for example, features such as relative social desirability or positivity of the empathy adjectives. Corroborating evidence using other research strategies is needed.

2. Independent Manipulation of Personal Distress and Empathy

Batson *et al.* (1981, Experiment 2) attempted to manipulate distress and empathy independently, using a placebo misattribution technique. They employed one of the research paradigms described previously. Female subjects watched over closed-circuit television while a young woman, Elaine, appeared to receive electric shocks. Elaine's reactions made it clear that she found the shocks quite uncomfortable. To manipulate subjects' emotional response to watching Elaine suffer, each subject had previously been given a drug capsule (actually a placebo) in the context of another study. Some were told that as a side effect the drug would create a feeling of "warmth and sensitivity, a feeling similar to that you might experience while reading a particularly touching novel"; others, that it would create a feeling of "uneasiness and discomfort, a feeling similar to that you might experience while reading a particularly distressing novel."

Batson *et al.* reasoned that if watching Elaine suffer elicited both feelings of personal distress and empathy, and if these feelings were independent vicarious emotions, then if subjects were induced to misattribute their feelings of warmth and sensitivity (empathic feelings) to the placebo, they would perceive their emotional reaction to Elaine's suffering to be predominantly personal distress. In contrast, if subjects were induced to misattribute their feelings of uneasiness and discomfort (distress feelings) to the placebo, they would perceive their emotional reaction to Elaine's suffering to be predominantly empathic.

Subjects' responses to two items on a postexperimental questionnaire were quite consistent with this reasoning. The first item asked subjects how much uneasiness they experienced as a result of observing Elaine; the second, how much warmth and sensitivity. Subjects who were told that the placebo would make them feel warm and sensitive reported experiencing a relative predominance of uneasiness as a result of watching Elaine; those told that the placebo would make them feel uneasy reported a relative predominance of warmth and sensitivity. This successful independent manipulation of perceived distress and empathy is entirely consistent with the suggestion that personal distress and empathy are independent vicarious emotions.

3. Summary

To summarize thus far, the results of the factor analyses and the misattribution study converge to provide clear and consistent support for Hypothesis 1. In doing so, these results suggest that the currently popular terms "empathic pain" and "empathic distress" (used generically) are inappropriate. Instead, as suggested by Hypothesis 1, personal distress and empathy appear to be two independent emotional responses to perceiving another in need. But as noted earlier, there is a third possible source of evidence for Hypothesis 1, evidence from studies designed to test Hypothesis 3. If distress and empathy evoke recognizably different types of motivation (Hypothesis 3), then they must be functionally distinct (Hypothesis 1). Let us turn, then, to evidence for Hypothesis 3.

B. HYPOTHESIS 3: EMPATHIC EMOTION EVOKES ALTRUISTIC
   MOTIVATION TO HAVE THE OTHER PERSON'S NEED
   REDUCED: THE MAGNITUDE OF THIS MOTIVATION IS
   PROPORTIONAL TO THE MAGNITUDE
   OF THE EMPATHIC EMOTION

Hypothesis 3, often called the empathy–altruism hypothesis, is the one most central to the proposed theory of altruistic motivation. It is also the one generally assumed to be most difficult to test. In order to test the claim that empathic emotion produces altruistic rather than egoistic motivation to help, we must have a method by which the egoistic motivation outlined in Paths 1 and 2 can be empirically distinguished from the altruistic motivation outlined in Path 3. For, if any evidence for this hypothesis can be explained as adequately by arguing that empathy leads to reward-seeking (Path 1a), punishment-avoiding (Path 1b), or arousal-reducing (Path 2) egoistic motivation, then parsimony argues against claiming that it leads to altruistic motivation.

The task of ruling out egoistic accounts of the motivation evoked by empathy is made more difficult by the fact that motives cannot be directly observed; they can only be inferred from behavior. And it seems that only rarely, if ever, can the nature of a motive or its magnitude be inferred from observation of a single behavior.

Still, I believe that it is possible to make meaningful inferences about motivation from behavioral observation. The key is to observe a *pattern* of behavior across systematically varied situations. The nature of a motive is defined by the ultimate·goal (as opposed to instrumental goals). Therefore, it should be possible to determine the nature of a motive by looking at the pattern of behavior when one systematically varies either (1) the direction to possible instrumental and ultimate goals, or (2) the cost associated with a given behavioral means of reaching one but not another possible goal. As the direction changes, the relationship of instrumental and ultimate goals changes, and the chosen behavior should always be directed toward the ultimate goal. Alternatively, as the cost associated with a behavior drops, the likelihood of the behavior being enacted should increase only if this behavior can lead to the ultimate goal.

Applying this logic, I have developed a taxonomy of variables for which it is possible to make different behavioral predictions depending on which of the four paths outlined in Fig. 1 (1a, 1b, 2, and 3) the motivation to help is following. This taxonomy, presented in Table III, takes advantage of the different behavioral options associated with each path (discussed in Section III above and summarized in Fig. 1) to generate different behavioral predictions. Although only one of the variables listed in Table III differentiates among all four possible paths, each differentiates between Path 3 and at least one of the egoistic paths. The taxonomy in Table III can be used to operationalize Hypothesis 3.

1. Evidence that the Prosocial Motivation Evoked by Empathy Follows Path 3 Rather Than Path 2

By far the most popular egoistic account of the prosocial effects of empathy is that it, like personal distress, produces arousal-reducing (Path 2) motivation (see Hoffman, 1981a; Hornstein, 1978; Krebs, 1975; Piliavin & Piliavin, 1973; Piliavin *et al.*, 1981, 1982). Therefore, to test the empathy–altruism hypothesis, Batson *et al.* (1981) sought to hold the potential rewards and punishments for helping (Path 1) constant, so that they could focus on whether the motivation to

TABLE III

VARIABLES THAT SHOULD DIFFERENTIATE BETWEEN EGOISTIC AND ALTRUISTIC
MOTIVATION TO HELP

Variable	Reward-seeking (Path 1a)	Punishment-avoiding (Path 1b)	Arousal-reducing (Path 2)	Altruistic motivation (Path 3)
1. *Acceptable helpers*: Whose help can attain the goal?	Only oneself	Oneself; others	Oneself; others	Oneself; others
2. *Necessity of one's help being effective*: Must one's help be effective to reach the goal?	Not necessary (if ineffectiveness justified)	Not necessary (if ineffectiveness justified)	Necessary	Necessary
3. *Viability of escape*: Can the goal be reached by escape without helping?	Escape not viable	Escape viable (from own shame, guilt)	Escape viable (from victim's distress)	Escape not viable
4. *Salient cognitions*: What cognitions are salient when deciding whether to help?	Anticipated rewards; costs of helping	Anticipated punishments; costs of helping	Aversive arousal; costs of helping	Victim's welfare; costs of helping
5. *Need for rewards of helping*: What is the effect of increased need for rewards of helping?	Increased motivation	No effect	No effect	No effect

help evoked by empathy followed Path 2 or Path 3, i.e., whether the ultimate goal was to increase one's own welfare by reducing the empathic emotion or to increase the welfare of the person in need by reducing that need.

As suggested by the taxonomy in Table III, one major difference between these two paths is that escape without helping is a viable behavioral means of reaching the goal on Path 2 but not on Path 3. If the motivation evoked by empathy follows Path 2, then either helping or escaping would permit one to reach the goal—reducing the aversive empathic arousal. As a result, assuming it is moderately costly to help, helping should occur more often when escape is difficult than when it is easy. But if the motivation evoked by empathy follows Path 3, then helping would permit one to reach the goal—reducing the other's need; escaping would not. As a result, helping should occur as often when escape is easy as when it is difficult. Thus, we have distinct empirical predictions for the effect of empathy on helping when escape is easy, depending on whether the prosocial motivation associated with empathy is following Path 2 or Path 3.

TABLE IV

PROPORTIONS OF LOW- AND HIGH-EMPATHY SUBJECTS WHO OFFERED HELP WHEN ESCAPE
WAS EASY OR DIFFICULT (7 STUDIES)

	Study[a]						
	1	2	3	4	5	6	7
Low empathy							
Easy escape	$.38_a^b$	$.00_a$	$.18_a$	$.33_a$	$.39_a$	$.40_a$	$.25_a$
	$(16)^b$	(15)	(11)	(12)	(23)	(10)	(8)
Difficult escape	—	—	$.64_b$	$.75_b$	$.81_b$	$.89_b$	$.89_b$
			(11)	(12)	(21)	(9)	(9)
High empathy							
Easy escape	$.94_b$	$.60_b$	$.91_b$	$.83_b$	$.71_b$	$.70_{ab}$	$.86_b$
	(17)	(15)	(11)	(12)	(17)	(10)	(7)
Difficult escape	—	—	$.82_b$	$.58_{ab}$	$.75_b$	$.63_{ab}$	$.63_{ab}$
			(11)	(12)	(20)	(8)	(8)

[a]Studies are as follows: 1. Coke *et al.* (1978, Experiment 2). Empathy condition determined by median split on empathic concern index. (A false-feedback manipulation of emotion produced parallel effects on helping in this study.) 2. Batson *et al.* (1979). Empathy condition determined by median split on empathy factor (orthogonal rotation). 3. Batson *et al.* (1981, Experiment 1). Empathy condition determined by similarity manipulation. 4. Batson *et al.* (1981, Experiment 2). Empathy condition determined by placebo misattribution manipulation. 5. Toi and Batson (1982). Empathy condition determined by median split on index of predominant emotional response (empathy index minus distress index). (A perspective-taking manipulation of empathy produced parallel effects on helping in this study.) 6. Batson *et al.* (1983, Experiment 1). Empathy condition determined by median split on index of predominant emotional response (empathy index minus distress index). 7. Batson *et al.* (1983, Experiment 2). Empathy condition determined by median split on index of predominant emotional response (empathy index minus distress index).

[b]Numbers in parentheses are the number of subjects in each cell. Cells within a given study not sharing the same subscript differ significantly, $p < .05$.

To date, there have been seven studies that have tested Hypothesis 3 by examining the effect of empathy on helping when escape is easy. The results of these studies are summarized in Table IV.

The first two studies in Table IV provide only a weak test of Hypothesis 3, because in these studies ease of escape was not manipulated; the need situation was always presented so that escape was easy. In the first study (Coke *et al.*, 1978, Experiment 2), participants learned indirectly of a graduate student's need for research participants by listening to a (bogus) taped radio broadcast; then they were given a written appeal for help. All that was necessary to escape continued exposure to the need situation was to lay the appeal aside and forget it. Yet, greater self-reported empathy was associated with more helping (see Column 1 of Table IV); moreover, greater self-reported personal distress was not. This was precisely the pattern of results that would be expected if the motivation evoked by increased empathy followed Path 3, while the motivation evoked by increased distress followed Path 2.

Results of the second study in Table IV (Batson *et al.*, 1979) provided additional evidence that greater self-reported empathy leads to helping when escape is easy, whereas greater personal distress does not. The procedure of this study was quite similar to the previous one, but a different need situation was employed. In this study, the taped radio broadcast presented the consequences of a rather gory automobile accident. There was evidence that this need situation evoked moderately high levels of both personal distress and empathy (see Column 2 of Table I). Escape without helping was made easy by the same technique used by Coke *et al.* Once again, consistent with Hypothesis 3, greater self-reported empathy was associated with increased helping, whereas greater self-reported personal distress was not.

In these first two studies, it was simply assumed that escape was easy enough that Path 2 egoistic motivation would not lead to any increase in helping, whereas Path 3 altruistic motivation would. A far stronger test of Hypothesis 3 would be provided by a design in which both the degree of empathic emotion and the ease of escape were varied. The last five studies in Table IV employed such a design. In each, ease of escape was manipulated by leading some participants to believe that if they did not help they would never again see the person in need; other participants were led to believe that if they did not help they would continue to see the suffering victim.

What pattern of helping would Hypothesis 3 predict in such a design? Presumably, if empathy is kept low, then personal distress will be the stronger vicarious emotion produced by witnessing the other's suffering. A predominance of distress should produce a predominance of Path 2 egoistic motivation. As a result, ease of escape should affect the rate of helping when empathy is low. In contrast, when empathy is high, empathy should be the stronger vicarious emotion, the result being a predominance of Path 3 altruistic motivation. So ease of escape should have no effect when empathy is high. Across the four cells of an empathy (low versus high) by escape (easy versus difficult) 2×2 design, we would expect a 1-versus-3 pattern of helping. The rate of helping should be relatively low in the low empathy–easy escape cell and high in the other three.

But what if, contrary to Hypothesis 3, empathy evokes Path 2 egoistic motivation, as suggested by a number of the pseudoaltruistic views considered earlier (e.g., Hoffman, Krebs, Karylowski, Piliavin *et al.*)? Then we would expect an escape manipulation to have the same effect on helping among high-empathy subjects as among low-empathy subjects; there should be a main effect for escape in each empathy condition. There might also be a main effect for empathy, high empathy leading to more helping than low, because the higher level of vicarious emotion should lead to stronger motivation to reduce that emotion. So, if empathy evokes Path 2 egoistic motivation to help, we would expect to observe one or two main effects; if, however, empathy evokes altruistic motivation as Hypothesis 3 predicts, we would expect the 1-versus-3 pattern.

Results of each of the last five studies in Table IV clearly conform to the 1-versus-3 pattern predicted by Hypothesis 3. In each study, the planned comparison testing this pattern accounted for all reliable between-cell variance. Moreover, individual between-cell comparisons in each study revealed that, as predicted, the low empathy–easy escape cell differed significantly, $p < .05$, from the low empathy–difficult escape cell (see subscripts in Table IV). The high empathy–easy escape and high empathy–difficult escape cells did not differ. These results clearly suggest that empathy does not evoke Path 2 egoistic motivation; instead, the results support the contention of Hypothesis 3 that empathy evokes altruistic motivation.

Another way to present the results of the last three studies summarized in Table IV is to examine the partial correlations with helping of self-reported distress (partialing self-reported empathy) and self-reported empathy (partialing self-reported distress) under conditions of easy and difficult escape. Partial correlations are needed to adjust for the previously noted positive correlation between measures of self-reported distress and empathy. Consistent with the 1-versus-3 pattern observed using median splits, the partial correlations between empathy and helping in the last three studies were consistently positive in the easy escape condition (ranging from .31 to .39) and near zero or even somewhat negative in the difficult escape condition (ranging from .03 to −.27). In contrast, the partial correlations between distress and helping were near zero or negative in the easy escape condition (ranging from −.08 to −.41) and near zero or positive in the difficult escape condition (.03 to .31). These partial correlation analyses are of course not independent of the median-split analyses reported in Table IV, but they do supplement those analyses by suggesting that the 1-versus-3 pattern is not simply an artifact of the median-split procedure.

The consistency of the 1-versus-3 pattern across the seven studies summarized in Table IV suggests that the pattern is fairly robust, because these studies differed in a number of ways. Low- and high-empathy conditions were created by four different techniques: subjects' self-reports of their vicarious emotion (Coke et al., 1978, Experiment 2; Batson et al., 1979; Toi & Batson, 1982; Batson et al., 1983, Studies 1 and 2), a perspective-taking instruction manipulation (Toi & Batson, 1982), a similarity manipulation (Batson et al., 1981, Experiment 1), and an emotion-specific misattribution manipulation (Batson et al., 1981, Experiment 2). Ease of escape was manipulated in two ways: subjects believed that they either would or would not continue to watch another introductory psychology student take electric shocks (Batson et al., 1981, Experiments 1 and 2; Batson et al., 1983, Studies 1 and 2), or subjects believed that they either would or would not see the needy person next week in their introductory psychology class (Toi & Batson, 1982). Finally, a variety of need situations was used in these studies—trying to keep one's family together, dealing with physical disfigurement, having to give up one's career aspirations, and reacting with increasing discomfort to a series of electric shocks. Across these different need situations and techniques for varying the levels of empathy and ease of escape, subjects' helping responses consistently conformed to the 1-versus-3 pattern predicted by Hypothesis 3.

Not only do these results provide support for Hypothesis 3, but they also provide further support for Hypothesis 1. If personal distress and empathy have different motivational consequences, as the evidence clearly suggests they do, then these two vicarious emotions must be distinct.

2. A Limit on the Generality of the Empathy– Altruism Relationship

This consistency of results notwithstanding, both the foregoing theoretical analysis and some empirical evidence suggest that there are limits on the conditions under which empathic emotion leads to altruistically motivated helping. Specifically, if the need situation is such that empathic emotion is evoked but then the potential helper's attention is directed away from the other's need and toward the self, the foregoing analysis predicts that altruistic motivation will disappear. Any remaining motivation to help should be egoistic.

Batson et al. (1983, Study 3) tested this prediction by informing subjects who were already empathically aroused that they would have to suffer quite a bit themselves if they wished to help the person in need. Subjects in a concurrent study (Batson et al., 1983, Study 2) were informed that the shocks the person in need was receiving, and that they would receive if they decided to help, were at a minimally uncomfortable level; subjects in Study 3, however, were informed that the shocks were at a relatively high level, being "clearly painful but of course not harmful." This information produced a dramatic effect on helping. Not only did the overall rate of helping decrease among subjects reporting a relative predominance of empathy (from 73% in Study 2 to 41% in Study 3), but the pattern also changed. Whereas in Study 2 there was a high rate of helping among high-empathy subjects regardless of whether escape was easy or difficult (see the last column in Table IV), in Study 3 the rate was significantly lower when escape was easy (14%) than when it was difficult (60%), $p < .05$. Presumably, this was because the high cost of helping in Study 3 directed empathic subjects' attention away from the victim and back upon themselves, replacing concern for the person in need with self-concern.

These results suggest that any altruistic motivation that blossoms from empathic emotion may be a fragile flower, easily crushed by overriding egoistic concerns. Not only did increasing the cost of helping in Study 3 reduce the overall level of helping, but it appeared to change the nature of the underlying motivation. No longer was the pattern of helping among high-empathy subjects the pattern that we would expect if their motivation were altruistic; it was the pattern that we would expect from Path 2 egoistic motivation.

3. New Egoistic Alternatives: The Empathy-Specific Punishment and Empathy-Specific Reward Hypotheses

The suggestion that the empathy–altruism relationship is fragile does not contradict the claim of Hypothesis 3 that empathic emotion evokes altruistic motivation. It only suggests that there are limiting conditions on the maintenance and expression of this motivation. There is, however, another and more serious question that must be raised about interpretation of the evidence supporting Hypothesis 3.

The pattern of helping reported in Table IV appears inconsistent with the claim that empathy evokes Path 2 egoistic motivation. But does it rule out the possibility that empathy evokes Path 1 egoistic motivation? It seems clear that no explanation that invokes some general reward for helping or general punishment for not helping can account for the different pattern of helping for low- and high-empathy individuals in the seven studies summarized in Table IV. Moreover, in each of the studies summarized in Table IV, an attempt was made to ensure that all anticipated rewards for helping and punishments for not helping were held constant across the different levels of empathy and ease of escape. To this end, a standardized procedure was used, and the experimenter was blind to the empathy manipulation. Thus far, I have assumed that this attempt was successful and, as a result, that the different pattern of helping under low and high empathy could not be the result of high-empathy subjects experiencing more Path 1 egoistic motivation. Yet this assumption may be wrong.

It is possible that feeling empathy may itself change the perceived reward structure of the situation, making helping more attractive and so increasing Path 1 egoistic motivation among high-empathy individuals. Consistent with this possibility, several researchers (R. B. Cialdini, personal communication, May, 1982; Dovidio, 1984; Piliavin et al., 1981) have suggested a Path 1 egoistic explanation for some or all of the results summarized in Table IV. They propose that feeling empathy may evoke an internalized social norm, a norm that dictates that one should help—or at least not abandon—others for whom one feels empathy. Having learned that violating this norm by not helping produces increased guilt and shame, the person feeling much empathy faces an anticipated punishment for failure to help that a person feeling little empathy does not.

This alternative explanation for the motivation to help evoked by empathy may be classed under the general heading of an *empathy-specific punishment hypothesis*. It claims that feeling empathy introduces a socialized sense of obligation to help above and beyond any obligation that may exist when empathy is absent. The thought that one might not live up to this obligation evokes additional punishment-avoiding (Path 1b) egoistic motivation.

Can this alternative explanation account for the results in Table IV? As is suggested by the taxonomy in Table III, although escape is not a viable behavioral means to obtain rewards for helping (Path 1a), it is a viable means to avoid punishment for not helping (Path 1b). So, if empathy evokes anticipation of empathy-specific punishments for not helping, then we would expect an effect of ease of escape among high-empathy individuals. The pattern of results in Table IV reveals no such effect. Thus, the results in Table IV may seem inconsistent with this empathy-specific punishment hypothesis.

Yet, this inconsistency may be more apparent than real. As noted in the taxonomy in Table III, there is an important distinction between what one is escaping on Path 1b and on Path 2. On Path 1b, one is escaping awareness that one failed to help when one should; on Path 2, one is escaping personal distress caused by exposure to another's suffering. It seems quite possible that the point at which escape becomes difficult is reached more quickly in the former case than in the latter: it may be easier to relieve one's distress by "passing by on the other side" than to escape the guilt and shame for doing so.

If there are different thresholds for these different types of escape, then individuals in the easy escape conditions in Table IV may have found avoidance of punishment for failing to live up to their empathy-specific obligations difficult to escape, even though they found their personal distress easy to escape. If so, then all of the high-empathy individuals would have been in a difficult escape condition with regard to empathy-specific punishment; only the low empathy– easy escape individuals would have been in an easy escape condition. The pattern of results predicted by the empathy-specific punishment hypothesis would then be precisely the 1-versus-3 pattern found in the studies summarized in Table IV.

As the preceding three paragraphs reveal, reconciliation of an empathy-specific punishment hypothesis with the existing data requires a rather fine-grained post hoc analysis. But if one is willing to accept this analysis, then the 1-versus-3 pattern found in Table IV is consistent with the possibility that empathy produces punishment-avoiding (Path 1b) egoistic motivation. Given this consistency, the evidence for Hypothesis 3 becomes equivocal, and parsimony favors the exclusively egoistic account.

A second egoistic explanation is also possible for the results summarized in Table IV—an *empathy-specific reward hypothesis*. This hypothesis suggests that the motivation to help evoked by empathy follows Path 1a. Perhaps individuals in our society are socialized to anticipate special rewards—such as a special sense of satisfaction or competence—when they help someone for whom they feel empathy (Meindl & Lerner, 1983). Or perhaps empathy produces a special need for the social and self-rewards associated with helping (Cialdini, Schaller, Houlihan, Arps, Fultz, & Beaman, 1987). This empathy-specific reward hypothesis may seem intuitively less plausible than an empathy-specific punishment hypothesis, but it can account for the results summarized in Table IV even more easily. As noted earlier, on Path 1a (as on Path 3) escape is not a viable means of reaching the goal, so if empathy evokes motivation to help in order to obtain empathy-specific rewards, then making escape relatively easy should not reduce the rate of helping of high-empathy subjects. No reduction is, of course, precisely what was found in the studies summarized in Table IV.

The emergence of these two new egoistic explanations may seem to support the contention that the egoism–altruism issue is not empirically resolvable. But, to the contrary, I would suggest that it is a sign of real progress and further underscores the usefulness of having an explicit and detailed map of the similarities and differences between an altruistic and various egoistic views. For, drawing upon the taxonomy in Table III of variables that should differentiate between egoistic and altruistic motivation to help, we can generate explicit empirical predictions to test these new egoistic explanations. To illustrate, let me briefly suggest some possible research strategies.

4. Research Strategies for Comparing the Empathy-Specific Punishment and Empathy–Altruism Hypotheses

The taxonomy in Table III suggests three variables that should produce different effects depending on whether the motivation evoked by empathy is punishment avoiding or altruistic. First, one's helping efforts need not be effective to reach the egoistic goal of avoiding punishment (if the ineffectiveness is justified), but one's efforts must be effective to reach the altruistic goal of increasing the victim's welfare. Second, escape (from one's own shame and guilt, not simply exposure to the victim's distress) is a viable route to the goal of punishment avoidance but not of increasing the victim's welfare. Third, if punishment avoidance is the goal, salient cognitions include the anticipated punishments; if increase in the victim's welfare is the goal, salient cognitions include this welfare.

These differences suggest several research possibilities. First, consider the effect of providing empathically aroused individuals with information about the likely effectiveness of their helping. If the motivation is following Path 1b, then knowing that one's help is not likely to be effective may have little effect on the rate of helping. If the motivation is following Path 3, however, such knowledge should lead to a reduction in helping.

Second, it might be possible to make the anticipated punishment arising from an empathy-specific punishment easier to escape by making individuals' helping decisions more anonymous or by making individuals aware that they can perform a highly engaging, distracting task if they decide not to help. Anonymity should reduce the threat of social censure and shame; a distracting task should reduce the threat of self-recrimination and guilt. Assuming that these techniques make the anticipated punishment easier to escape, then if the motivation is following Path 1b, these techniques should also reduce the rate of helping. But if the motivation is following Path 3, these techniques should not reduce the rate of helping.

Third, it might be possible to assess the relative predominance of punishment-related or victim-related cognitions by using information-processing measures, such as a Stroop technique (Stroop, 1938; Schadler & Thissen, 1981) or incidental learning (Hull & Levy, 1979; Smith, Ingram, & Brehm, 1983).

5. Research Strategies for Comparing the Empathy-Specific Reward and Empathy–Altruism Hypotheses

The taxonomy in Table III suggests four variables that should produce different effects depending on whether the motivation evoked by empathy is reward seeking (Path 1a) or altruistic (Path 3). First, only a person's own helping qualifies him or her for rewards, but either one's own or someone else's helping can achieve the altrustic goal of increasing the victim's welfare. Second, one's helping efforts need not be effective to reach the goal of attaining rewards (if the ineffectiveness is justified), but one's efforts (or someone else's) must be effective to increase the victim's welfare. Third, if getting rewards is the goal, salient cognitions should include anticipated rewards; if increasing the victim's welfare is the goal, salient cognitions should include this welfare. Fourth, increased need for the rewards associated with helping should increase helping if the goal is to obtain rewards; it should not affect the rate of helping if the goal is to increase the victim's welfare.

Research possibilities employing the second and third variables have already been mentioned in suggesting tests of the empathy-specific punishment hypothesis. The first variable, acceptability of other helpers, suggests measuring the mood of empathically aroused individuals after they learn that someone else has already relieved the victim's distress. If these subjects are seeking rewards for helping, their mood should not be enhanced; it might even grow worse. But if they are altruistically motivated, these subjects should feel better. The fourth variable, need for the rewards of helping, might be manipulated by extending the logic of Cialdini's negative-state relief model (Cialdini *et al.*, 1973). Empathically aroused individuals could be led to either anticipate or not anticipate a self-rewarding experience if they decide not to help. Anticipating such an experience should reduce helping if empathically aroused individuals are helping to gain self-rewards; it should have no effect if they are helping to benefit the other. Some research relevant to this last strategy has begun to appear—e.g., Cialdini *et al.* (1987), but results are not yet clear.

A caution is in order at this point. In any research exploring whether empathy evokes Path 1 as opposed to Path 3 motivation, we must be attentive to possible effects of manipulations on Path 2 motivation. So, were we to pursue one or more of the proposed research strategies, we would need to hold the behavioral consequences of Path 2 motivation constant by ensuring that escape without helping is always a less costly way of reducing one's own aversive arousal than is helping. Then any differences in helping across experimental conditions should not be due to Path 2 motivation.

In sum, research exploring the predicted behavioral differences resulting from Path 1 and Path 3 motivation should enable us to assess the viability of the empathy-specific punishment and empathy-specific reward hypotheses as alternatives to the empathy–altruism hypothesis. And the viability of these alternative hypotheses must be determined before we can claim that Hypothesis 3 has received clear and unequivocal empirical support.

At the same time, the emergence of the empathy-specific punishment and reward hypotheses as alternative egoistic accounts of the motivation to help evoked by empathy should not be allowed to overshadow the fact that, to date, attempts to test Hypothesis 3 have produced supporting evidence. The most popular egoistic account of the motivation to help evoked by empathy has long been in terms of arousal-reduction (Path 2). And in light of the evidence summarized in Table IV, it seems that this popular and long-standing egoistic account of the motivation to help evoked by empathy can and should be rejected. Still, until there is also clear empirical evidence that the motivation to help evoked by empathy is not an example of egoistic motivation to avoid punishment or gain rewards, the evidence for Hypothesis 3 must be considered only suggestive.

VI. Conclusion

Before the empathy–altruism hypothesis is accepted, more evidence is needed. Specifically, we need to determine whether the motivation to help evoked by empathy can be the product of empathy-specific punishment or reward. Fortunately, a conceptual framework for empirical exploration of these new alternative hypotheses is provided by (1) the explication in Fig. 1 of the egoistic and altruistic paths, and (2) the resulting taxonomy in Table III of variables that permit differential predictions for the different paths. So empirical tests of these new alternatives are possible. If the motivation evoked by empathy can be accounted for by one of these new egoistic alternatives, then parsimony favors an exclusively egoistic view. If it cannot, then the evidence for the empathy–altruism hypothesis would seem strong indeed, and the core of the proposed theoretical argument for altruistic motivation—Hypotheses 1 and 3—would have clear support. Hypothesis 2 could then be tested more carefully to determine whether the specific model of altruistic motivation outlined in Path 3 of Fig. 1 is correct.

As noted at the outset, the idea that some motivation for helping might be to some degree truly altruistic contradicts the exclusively egoistic assumptions that have dominated Western thought for the past four centuries. Because universal egoism is a widely held and basic belief both in and outside of psychology, it is only prudent to require that the evidence be clear before accepting the existence of altruism. If altruistic motivation exists, then we will have to make some fundamental changes in our conception of human motivation—and indeed, of human nature. As yet, the evidence is not sufficiently clear to justify such changes. But if the conceptual analysis and research outlined here have merit, then we may be on the threshold of an empirical answer to the question of why we care for one another. And the answer may require us to change our views—both about human motivation and human nature.

ACKNOWLEDGMENTS

Thanks to Donn Baumann, Jack Brehm, Bob Cialdini, Jay Coke, Nancy Eisenberg, Jim Fultz, Cheryl Flink, Alice Isen, Virginia Pych, and Pat Schoenrade for helpful comments on an earlier draft, and to Jim Fultz and Susan Embretson for valuable suggestions as statistical consultants. Preparation of this paper was funded in part by University of Kansas General Research Fund Grant 3472-XO-0038 and by NSF Grant BNS-8507110, C. Daniel Batson, Principal Investigator.

REFERENCES

Ainsworth, M. D. S., Blehar, M. C., Waters, E., & Wall, S. (1978). *Patterns of attachment: A psychological study of the strange situation.* Hillsdale, N.J.: Erlbaum.

Archer, R. L., Diaz-Loving, R., Gollwitzer, P. M., Davis, M. H., & Foushee, H. C. (1981). The role of dispositional empathy and social evaluation in the empathic mediation of helping. *Journal of Personality and Social Psychology, 40,* 786–796.

Aronfreed, J. (1970). The socialization of altruistic and sympathetic behavior: Some theoretical and experimental analyses. In J. Macaulay & L. Berkowitz (Ed.), *Altruism and helping behavior* (pp. 103–126). New York: Academic Press.

Bandura, A. (1977). *Social learning theory.* Englewood Cliffs, N.J.: Prentice-Hall.

Bar-Tal, D. (1976). *Prosocial behavior: Theory and research.* Washington, D.C.: Hemisphere.

Bar-Tal, D., Sharabany, R., & Raviv, A. (1982). Cognitive basis for the development of altruistic behavior. In V. J. Derlega & J. Grzelak (Eds.), *Cooperation and helping behavior: Theories and research* (pp. 377–396). New York: Academic Press.

Batson, C. D. (1983). Sociobiology and the role of religion in promoting prosocial behavior: An alternative view. *Journal of Personality and Social Psychology, 45,* 1380–1385.

Batson, C. D., & Coke, J. S. (1981). Empathy: A source of altruistic motivation for helping? In J. P. Rushton & R. M. Sorrentino (Eds.), *Altruism and helping behavior: Social, personality, and developmental perspectives* (pp. 167–187). Hillsdale, N.J.: Erlbaum.

Batson, C. D., & Coke, J. S. (1983). Empathic motivation of helping behavior. In J. T. Caccioppo & R. E. Petty (Eds.), *Social psychophysiology: A sourcebook* (pp. 417–433). New York: Guilford.

Batson, C. D., Bolen, M. H., Cross, J. A., & Neuringer-Benefiel, H. (1986). Where is the altruism in the altruistic personality? *Journal of Personality and Social Psychology, 50,* 212–220.

Batson, C. D., Cowles, C., & Coke, J. S. (1979). *Empathic mediation of the response to a lady in distress: Egoistic or altruistic?* Unpublished manuscript, University of Kansas.

Batson, C. D., Darley, J. M., & Coke, J. S. (1978). Altruism and human kindness: Internal and external determinants of helping behavior. In L. Pervin & M. Lewis (Eds.), *Perspectives in interactional psychology* (pp. 111–140). New York: Plenum.

Batson, C. D., Duncan, B., Ackerman, P., Buckley, T., & Birch, K. (1981). Is empathic emotion a source of altruistic motivation? *Journal of Personality and Social Psychology, 40,* 290–302.

Batson, C. D., O'Quin, K., Fultz, J., Vanderplas, M., & Isen, A. (1983). Self-reported distress and empathy and egoistic versus altruistic motivation for helping. *Journal of Personality and Social Psychology, 45,* 706–718.

Baumann, D. J., Cialdini, R. B., & Kenrick, D. T. (1981). Altruism as hedonism: Helping and self-gratification as equivalent responses. *Journal of Personality and Social Psychology, 40,* 1039–1046.

Bentham, J. (1879). *An introduction to the principles of morals and legislation.* Oxford: Clarendon (first published, 1789).

Berkowitz, L. (1972). Social norms, feelings, and other factors affecting helping and altruism. In L. Berkowitz (Ed.), *Advances in experimental social psychology* (Vol. 6, pp. 63–108). New York: Academic Press.

Bowlby, J. (1969). *Attachment and loss: Vol 1. Attachment.* New York: Basic Books.

Bryan, J. H., & Test, M. A. (1967). Models and helping. *Journal of Personality and Social Psychology, 6,* 400–407.

Campbell, D. T. (1975). On the conflicts between biological and social evolution and between psychology and moral tradition. *American Psychologist, 30,* 1103–1126.

Campbell, D. T. (1978). On the genetics of altruism and the counterhedonic components in human culture. In L. Wispé (Ed.), *Altruism, sympathy, and helping: Psychological and sociological principles* (pp. 39–57). New York: Academic Press.

Cialdini, R. B., Baumann, D. J., & Kenrick, D. T. (1981). Insights from sadness: A three-step model of the development of altruism as hedonism. *Developmental Review, 1,* 207–223.

Cialdini, R. B., Darby, B. L., & Vincent, J. E. (1973). Transgression and altruism: A case for hedonism. *Journal of Experimental Social Psychology, 9,* 502–516.

Cialdini, R. B., & Kenrick, D. T. (1976). Altruism as hedonism: A social development perspective on the relationship of negative mood state and helping. *Journal of Personality and Social Psychology, 34,* 907–914.

Cialdini, R. B., Kenrick, D. T., & Baumann, D. J. (1982). Effects of mood on prosocial behavior in children and adults. In N. Eisenberg (Ed.), *The development of prosocial behavior* (pp. 339–359). New York: Academic Press.

Cialdini, R. B., Schaller, M., Houlihan, D., Arps, K., Fultz, J., & Beaman, A. L. (1987). Empathy-based helping: Is it selflessly or selfishly motivated? *Journal of Personality and Social Psychology, 52,* 749–758.

Clark, R. D., & Word, L. E. (1972). Why don't bystanders help? Because of ambiguity? *Journal of Personality and Social Psychology, 24,* 392–401.

Clark, R. D., & Word, L. E. (1974). Where is the apathetic bystander? Situational characteristics of the emergency. *Journal of Personality and Social Psychology, 29,* 279–288.

Coke, J. S. (1980). Empathic mediation of helping: Egoistic or altruistic? (Doctoral dissertation, University of Kansas, 1979). *Dissertation Abstracts International, 41B,* 405. (University Microfilms No. 8014371)

Coke, J. S., Batson, C. D., & McDavis, K. (1978). Empathic mediation of helping: A two-stage model. *Journal of Personality and Social Psychology, 36,* 752–766.

Comte, I. A. (1875). *System of positive polity* (Vol. 1). London: Longmans, Green (first published, 1851).

Darley, J. M., & Latané, B. (1970). Norms and normative behavior: Field studies of social interdependence. In J. Macaulay & L. Berkowitz (Eds.), *Altruism and helping behavior* (pp. 83–101). New York: Academic Press.

Davis, M. H. (1983). The effects of dispositional empathy on emotional reactions and helping: A multidimensional approach. *Journal of Personality, 51,* 167–184.

Dawkins, R. (1976). *The selfish gene.* New York: Oxford University Press.

Derlega, V. J., & Grzelak, J. (Eds.) (1982). *Cooperation and helping behavior: Theories and research.* New York: Academic Press.

Dovidio, J. F. (1984). Helping behavior and altruism: An empirical and conceptual overview. In L. Berkowitz (Ed.), *Advances in experimental social psychology* (Vol. 17, pp. 361–427). New York: Academic Press.

Duval, S., & Wicklund, R. A. (1972). *A theory of objective self awareness.* New York: Academic Press.

Eisenberg, N. (Ed.). (1982). *The development of prosocial behavior.* New York: Academic Press.

Fischer, W. F. (1963). Sharing in preschool children as a function of amount and type of reinforcement. *Genetic Psychology Monographs, 68,* 215–245.

Freud, A. (1937). *The ego and the mechanisms of defense.* London: Hogarth.

Freud, S. (1918). From the history of an infantile neurosis. *Sammlung kleiner Schriften zur Neurosenlehre, 4,* 578–717. (Standard ed., Vol. 17, 1955).

Freud, S. (1930). *Civilization and its discontents.* London: Hogarth.

Fultz, J. N. (1982). *Influence of potential for self-reward on egoistically and altruistically motivated helping.* Unpublished M.A. thesis. University of Kansas.

Gaertner, S. L., & Dovidio, J. F. (1977). The subtlety of white racism, arousal, and helping behavior. *Journal of Personality and Social Psychology, 35,* 691–708.

Gelfand, D. M., Hartmann, D. P., Cromer, C. C., Smith, C. L., & Page, B. C. (1975). The effects of instructional prompts and praise on children's donation rates. *Child Development 46,* 980–983.

Gibbons, F. X., & Wicklund, R. A. (1982). Self-focused attention and helping behavior. *Journal of Personality and Social Psychology, 43,* 462–474.

Gouldner, A. W. (1960). The norm of reciprocity: A preliminary statement. *American Sociological Review, 25,* 161–179.

Grusec, J. E. (1981). Socialization processes in the development of altruism. In J. P. Rushton & R. M. Sorrentino (Eds.), *Altruism and helping behavior* (pp. 65–90). Hillsdale, N.J.: Erlbaum.

Hamilton, W. D. (1964). The genetic evolution of social behavior. *Journal of Theoretical Biology, 7,* 1–51.

Hamilton, W. D. (1971). Selection of selfish and altruistic behavior in some extreme models. In J. F. Eisenberg & W. S. Dillon (Eds.), *Man and beast: Comparative social behavior.* Washington, D.C.: Smithsonian Institution Press.

Hatfield, E., Piliavin, J. A., & Walster, G. W. (1978). Equity theory and helping relationships. In L. Wispé (Ed.), *Altruism, sympathy, and helping: Psychological and sociological principles* (pp. 115–139). New York: Academic Press.

Heider, F. (1958). *The psychology of interpersonal relations.* New York: Wiley.

Hobbes, T. (1651). *Leviathan; or the matter, forme, and power of a commonwealth, ecclesiasticall and civill.* London: A. Crooke.

Hoffman, M. L. (1975). Developmental synthesis of affect and cognition and its implications for altruistic motivation. *Developmental Psychology,* **11,** 607–622.

Hoffman, M. L. (1976). Empathy, role-taking, guilt, and development of altruistic motives. In T. Lickona (Ed.), *Moral development and behavior: Theory, research, and social issues* (pp. 124–143). New York: Holt, Rinehart.

Hoffman, M. L. (1977a). Empathy, its development and prosocial implications. In C. B. Keasey (Ed.), *Nebraska Symposium on Motivation* (Vol. 25, pp. 169–218). Lincoln: University of Nebraska Press.

Hoffman, M. L. (1977b). Moral internalization: Current theory and research. In L. Berkowitz (Ed.), *Advances in experimental social psychology* (Vol. 10, pp. 86–135). New York: Academic Press.

Hoffman, M. L. (1981a). Is altruism part of human nature? *Journal of Personality and Social Psychology,* **40,** 121–137.

Hoffman, M. L. (1981b). The development of empathy. In J. P. Rushton & R. M. Sorrentino (Eds.), *Altruism and helping behavior: Social, personality, and developmental perspectives* (pp. 41–63). Hillsdale, NJ.: Erlbaum.

Hoffman, M. L. (1982). Development of prosocial motivation: Empathy and guilt. In N. Eisenberg (Ed.), *The development of prosocial behavior* (pp. 281–313). New York: Academic Press.

Hornstein, H. A. (1976). *Cruelty and kindness: A new look at aggression and altruism.* Engelwood Cliffs, N.J.: Prentice-Hall.

Hornstein, H. A. (1978). Promotive tension and prosocial behavior: A Lewinian analysis. In L. Wispé (Ed.), *Altruism, sympathy, and helping: Psychological and sociological principles* (pp. 177–207). New York: Academic Press.

Hornstein, H. A. (1982). Promotive tension: Theory and research. In V. J. Derlega & J. Grzelak (Eds.), *Cooperation and helping behavior: Theories and research* (pp. 229–248). New York: Academic Press.

Hornstein, H. A., Fisch, E., & Holmes, M. (1968). Influence of a model's feeling about his behavior and his relevance as a comparison other on observer's helping behavior. *Journal of Personality and Social Psychology,* **10,** 222–226.

Hull, J. G. & Levy, A. S. (1979). The organizational functions of the self: An alternative to the Duval and Wicklund model of self-awareness. *Journal of Personality and Social Psychology,* **37,** 756–768.

Hume, D. (1896). *Treatise of human nature* (L. A. Selby-Bigge, Ed.). Oxford: Oxford University Press (first published, 1740).

Hume, D. (1902). *An inquiry concerning the principles of morals* (L. A. Selby-Bigge, Ed.). Oxford: Oxford University Press (first published, 1751).

Hygge, S. (1976). Information about the model's unconditioned stimulus and response in vicarious classical conditioning. *Journal of Personality and Social Psychology,* **33,** 764–771.

Isen, A. M., & Levin, P. F. (1972). Effect of feeling good on helping: Cookies and kindness. *Journal of Personality and Social Psychology,* **21,** 344–348.

Isen, A. M., Shalker, T. E., Clark, M., & Karp, L. (1978). Affect, accessibility of material in memory and behavior: A cognitive loop? *Journal of Personality and Social Psychology,* **36,** 1–12.

Karinol, R. (1982). Settings, scripts, and self-schemata: A cognitive analysis of the development of prosocial behavior. In N. Eisenberg (Ed.), *The development of prosocial behavior* (pp. 251–278). New York: Academic Press.

Karylowski, J. (1979). Self-focused attention, prosocial norms and prosocial behavior. *Polish Psychological Bulletin*, **10**, 57–66.

Karylowski, J. (1982). Two types of altruistic behavior: Doing good to feel good or to make the other feel good. In V. J. Derlega & J. Grzelak (Eds.), *Cooperation and helping behavior: Theories and research* (pp. 397–413). New York: Academic Press.

Kenrick, D. T., Baumann, D. J., & Cialdini, R. B. (1979). A step in the socialization of altruism as hedonism: Effects of negative mood on children's generosity under public and private conditions. *Journal of Personality and Social Psychology*, **37**, 747–755.

Krebs, D. L. (1970). Altruism—an examination of the concept and a review of the literature. *Psychological Bulletin*, **73**, 258–302.

Krebs, D. L. (1975). Empathy and altruism. *Journal of Personality and Social Psychology*, **32**, 1134–1146.

Krebs, D. L. (1978). A cognitive-developmental approach to altruism. In L. Wispé (Ed.), *Altruism, sympathy, and helping: Psychological and sociological principles* (pp. 141–164). New York: Academic Press.

Krebs, D. L. (1982). Altruism—a rational approach. In N. Eisenberg (Ed.), *The development of prosocial behavior* (pp. 53–76). New York: Academic Press.

Krebs, D. L., & Miller, D. T. (1985). Altruism and aggression. In G. Lindzey & E. Aronson (Eds.), *Handbook of social psychology: Vol. 2. Special fields and applications* (3rd ed., pp. 1–71). New York: Random House.

Krebs, D. L., & Russell, C. (1981). Role-taking and altruism: When you put yourself in the shoes of another, will they take you to their owner's aid? In J. P. Rushton & R. M. Sorrentino (Eds.), *Altruism and helping behavior: Social, personality, and developmental perspectives* (pp. 137–165). Hillsdale, N.J.: Erlbaum.

Kropotkin, P. (1902). *Mutual aid, a factor of evolution*. New York: McClure, Phillips.

Latané, B., & Darley, J. M. (1970). *The unresponsive bystander: Why doesn't he help?* New York: Appleton.

Lawley, D. N., & Maxwell, A. E. (1971). *Factor analysis as a statistical method* (2nd ed.). New York: American Elsevier.

Leeds, R. (1963). Altruism and the norm of giving. *Merrill-Palmer Quarterly*, **9**, 229–240.

Lerner, M. J. (1970). The desire for justice and reactions to victims. In J. Macaulay & L. Berkowitz (Eds.), *Altruism and helping behavior* (pp. 205–229). New York: Academic Press.

Lerner, M. J. (1982). The justice motive in human relations and the economic model of man: A radical analysis of facts and fictions. In V. J. Derlega & J. Grzelak (Eds.), *Cooperation and helping behavior: Theories and research* (pp. 249–278). New York: Academic Press.

Lerner, M. J., & Meindl, J. R. (1981). Justice and altruism. In J. P. Rushton & R. M. Sorrentino (Eds.), *Altruism and helping behavior: Social, personality, and developmental perspectives* (pp. 213–232). Hillsdale, N.J.: Erlbaum.

Macaulay, J., & Berkowitz, L. (1970). (Eds.), *Altruism and helping behavior: Social psychological studies of some antecedents and consequences*. New York: Academic Press.

Machiavelli, N. (1513). *The prince*.

MacIntyre, A. (1967). Egoism and altruism. In P. Edwards (Ed.), *The encyclopedia of philosophy* (Vol. 2, pp. 462–466). New York: Macmillan.

Mathews, K. E., & Canon, L. K. (1975). Environmental noise level as a determinant of helping behavior. *Journal of Personality and Social Psychology*, **32**, 571–577.

McDougall, W. (1908). *Introduction to social psychology*. London: Methuen.

Meindl, J. R., & Lerner, M. J. (1983). The heroic motive: Some experimental demonstrations. *Journal of Experimental Social Psychology*, **19**, 1–20.

Midlarsky, E. (1968). Aiding responses: An analysis and review. *Merrill-Palmer Quarterly*, **14**, 229–260.

Midlarsky, E., & Midlarsky, M. (1973). Some determinants of aiding under experimentally induced stress. *Journal of Personality*, **41**, 305–327.

Mill, J. S. (1863). *Utilitarianism*. London: Parker, Son, & Bourn.

Moss, M. K., & Page, R. A. (1972). Reinforcement and helping behavior. *Journal of Applied Psychology*, **2**, 360–371.

Nagel, T. (1970). *The possibility of altruism*. Princeton, N.J.: Princeton University Press.

Nietzsche, F. (1910). *The complete works of Friedrich Nietzsche* (Oscar Levy, Ed.). London: T. N. Foulis.

Piliavin, I. M., Piliavin, J. A., & Rodin, J. (1975). Costs, diffusion and the stigmatized victim. *Journal of Personality and Social Psychology*, **32**, 429–438.

Piliavin, J. A., Dovidio, J. F., Gaertner, S. L., & Clark, R. D., III (1981). *Emergency intervention*. New York: Academic Press.

Piliavin, J. A., Dovidio, J. F., Gaertner, S. L., & Clark, R. D. III (1982). Responsive bystanders: The process of intervention. In V. J. Derlega & J. Grzelak (Eds.), *Cooperation and helping behavior: Theories and research* (pp. 279–304). New York: Academic Press.

Piliavin, J. A., & Piliavin, I. M. (1973). *The Good Samaritan: Why does he help?* Unpublished manuscript, University of Wisconsin.

Rand, A. (1961). *The virtue of selfishness: A new concept of egoism*. New York: New American Library.

Reis, H. T., & Gruzen, J. (1976). On mediating equity, equality, and self-interest: The role of self-presentation in social exchange. *Journal of Experimental Social Psychology*, **12**, 487–503.

Reykowski, J. (1982). Motivation of prosocial behavior. In V. J. Derlega & J. Grzelak (Eds.), *Cooperation and helping behavior: Theories and research* (pp. 352–375). New York: Academic Press.

Ridley, M., & Dawkins, R. (1981). The natural selection of altruism. In J. P. Rushton & R. M. Sorrentino (Eds.), *Altruism and helping behavior: Social, Personality, and Developmental Perspectives* (pp. 19–39). Hillsdale, N.J.: Erlbaum.

Rosenhan, D. L. (1970). The natural socialization of altruistic autonomy. In J. Macaulay & L. Berkowitz (Eds.), *Altruism and helping behavior* (pp. 251–268). New York: Academic Press.

Rosenhan, D. L. (1978). Toward resolving the altruism paradox: Affect, self-reinforcement, and cognition. In L. Wispé (Ed.), *Altruism, sympathy, and helping: Psychological and sociological principles* (pp. 101–113). New York: Academic Press.

Rosenhan, D. L., Salovey, P., & Hargis, K. (1981a). The joys of helping: Focus of attention mediates the impact of positive affect on altruism. *Journal of Personality and Social Psychology*, **40**, 899–905.

Rosenhan, D. L., Salovey, P., Karylowski, J., & Hargis, K. (1981b). Emotion and altruism. In J. P. Rushton & R. M. Sorrentino (Eds.), *Altruism and helping behavior: Social, personality, and developmental perspectives* (pp. 233–248). Hillsdale, N.J.: Erlbaum.

Rushton, J. P. (1980). *Altruism, socialization, and society*. Englewood Cliffs, N.J.: Prentice-Hall.

Rushton, J. P., & Sorrentino, R. M. (1981). (Eds.), *Altruism and helping behavior: Social, personality, and developmental perspectives*. Hillsdale, N.J.: Erlbaum.

Sagi, A., & Hoffman, M. L. (1976). Empathic distress in newborns. *Developmental Psychology*, **12**, 175–176.

Schadler, M., & Thissen, D. M. (1981). The development of automatic word recognition and reading skill. *Memory and Cognition*, **9**, 132–141.

Schaps, E. (1972). Cost, dependency, and helping. *Journal of Personality and Social Psychology*, **21**, 74–78.

Schoenrade, P. A., Batson, C. D., Brandt, J. R., & Loud, R. E. (1986). Attachment, accountability, and motivation to benefit another not in distress. *Journal of Personality and Social Psychology,* **51,** 557–563.

Schwartz, S. H. (1975). The justice of need and the activation of humanitarian norms. *Journal of Social Issues,* **31,** 111–136.

Schwartz, S. H. (1977). Normative influences on altruism. In L. Berkowitz (Ed.), *Advances in experimental social psychology* (Vol. 10, pp. 221–279). New York: Academic Press.

Schwartz, S. H., & Howard, J. (1982). Helping and cooperation: A self-based motivational model. In V. J. Derlega & J. Grzelak (Eds.), *Cooperation and helping behavior: Theories and research* (pp. 327–353). New York: Academic Press.

Shelton, M. L., & Rogers, R. W. (1981). Fear-arousing and empathy-arousing appeals to help: The pathos of persuasion. *Journal of Applied Social Psychology,* **11,** 366–378.

Simner, M. L. (1971). Newborn's response to the cry of another infant. *Developmental Psychology,* **5,** 136–150.

Skinner, B. F. (1978). The ethics of helping people. In L. Wispé (Ed.), *Altruism, sympathy, and helping: Psychological and sociological principles* (pp. 249–262). New York: Academic Press.

Smith, A. (1759). *The theory of moral sentiments.* London: A. Miller.

Smith, T. W., Ingram, R. E., & Brehm, J. J. (1983). Social anxiety, anxious self-preoccupation, and recall of self-relevant information. *Journal of Personality and Social Psychology,* **44,** 1276–1283.

Spencer, H. (1872). *The principles of psychology* (Vol. 2, 2nd ed.). London: Williams & Norgate.

Staub, E. (1971). Helping a person in distress: The influence of implicit and explicit "rules" of conduct on children and adults. *Journal of Personality and Social Psychology,* **17,** 137–145.

Staub, E. (1978). *Positive social behavior and morality: Social and personal influences* (Vol. 1). New York: Academic Press.

Saub, E. (1979). *Positive social behavior and morality: Socialization and development* (Vol. 2). New York: Academic Press.

Staub, E., & Baer, R. S., Jr. (1974). Stimulus characteristics of a sufferer and difficulty of escape as determinants of helping. *Journal of Personality and Social Psychology,* **30,** 279–285.

Steele, C. M. (1975). Name-calling and compliance. *Journal of Personality and Social Psychology,* **31,** 361–369.

Stotland, E. (1969). Exploratory studies of empathy. In L. Berkowitz (Ed.), *Advances in experimental social psychology* (Vol. 4, pp. 271–313). New York: Academic Press.

Stroop, J. R. (1938). Factors affecting speed in serial verbal reactions. *Psychological Monographs,* **50,** 38–48.

Thomas, G. C., & Batson, C. D. (1981). Effect of helping under normative pressure on self-perceived altruism. *Social Psychology Quarterly,* **44,** 127–131.

Thomas, G. C., Batson, C. D., & Coke, J. S. (1981). Do Good Samaritans discourage helpfulness?: Self-perceived altruism after exposure to highly helpful others. *Journal of Personality and Social Psychology,* **40,** 194–200.

Thompson, W. C., Cowan, C. L., & Rosenhan, D. L. (1980). Focus of attention mediates the impact of negative affect on altruism. *Journal of Personality and Social Psychology,* **38,** 291–300.

Toi, M., & Batson, C. D. (1982). More evidence that empathy is a source of altruistic motivation. *Journal of Personality and Social Psychology,* **43,** 281–292.

Trivers, R. L. (1971). The evolution of reciprocal altruism. *The Quarterly Review of Biology,* **46,** 35–57.

Wagner, C., & Wheeler, L. (1969). Model, need and cost effects in helping behavior. *Journal of Personality and Social Psychology,* **12,** 111–116.

Wallach, M. A., & Wallach, L. (1983). *Psychology's sanction for selfishness: The error of egoism in theory and therapy.* San Francisco: Freeman.

Weiner, F. H. (1976). Altruism, ambiance, and action: The effect of rural and urban rearing on helping behavior. *Journal of Personality and Social Psychology, 34,* 112–124.

Weyant, J. M. (1978). Effects of mood states, costs, and benefits on helping. *Journal of Personality and Social Psychology, 36,* 1169–1176.

Wicklund, R. A. (1975). Objective self awareness. In L. Berkowitz (Ed.), *Advances in experimental social psychology* (Vol. 8, pp. 233–275). New York: Academic Press.

Wilson, E. O. (1975). *Sociobiology: The new synthesis.* Cambridge, MA: Harvard University Press.

Wilson, J. P. (1976). Motivation, modeling and altruism: A person X situation analysis. *Journal of Personality and Social Psychology, 34,* 1078–1086.

Wispé, L. G. (1968). Sympathy and empathy. In D. L. Sills (Ed.), *International encyclopedia of the social sciences* (Vol. 15, pp. 441–447). New York: Free Press.

Wispé, L. G. (1972). (Ed.), Positive forms of social behavior. *Journal of Social Issues, 28* (whole issue).

Wispé, L. G. (1978). (Ed.), *Altruism, sympathy, and helping: Psychological and sociological principles.* New York: Academic Press.

Wispé, L. G. (1986). The distinction between sympathy and empathy: To call forth a concept a word is needed. *Journal of Personality and Social Psychology, 50,* 314–321.

Zuckerman, M. (1975). Belief in a just world and altruistic behavior. *Journal of Personality and Social Psychology, 31,* 972–976.

DIMENSIONS OF GROUP PROCESS: AMOUNT AND STRUCTURE OF VOCAL INTERACTION

James M. Dabbs, Jr. and R. Barry Ruback

DEPARTMENT OF PSYCHOLOGY
GEORGIA STATE UNIVERSITY
ATLANTA, GEORGIA 30303

I. Introduction

The process of group interaction is seldom studied in social psychology. There has been much writing about groups, their performance, and the forces that drive them, but how groups actually transform input into outcome is largely unknown. We know that leadership, conformity, cohesion, polarization, establishing norms, generating ideas, solving problems, getting acquainted, and the like are important, but we do not know how these things manifest themselves in the moment-to-moment life of a group.

It is generally assumed that an understanding of groups requires attention to process, that set of verbal and nonverbal activities whereby members solve problems, influence one another, and change themselves over the life of a group. Process bears upon such questions as why some groups do better than others, how groups with similar inputs can produce different outcomes, and how groups with different inputs can produce similar outcomes. But the nature of group process is as elusive as it is important, and calls for its study have been repeated for decades (Dashiell, 1935; Kelly & Thibaut, 1954; McGrath & Kravitz, 1982).

The overriding problem is lack of agreement on the meaning of "process." Different theoretical models of groups emphasize different elements, but on the whole they simply bypass the question. Research has tended toward a black-box approach; certain inputs (e.g., group size or leadership) produce certain outcomes (e.g., performance on a task or cohesiveness) by means of a largely unspecified intervening system.

It is this lack of precise definition that concerns us most. We do not know

123

ADVANCES IN EXPERIMENTAL
SOCIAL PSYCHOLOGY, VOL. 20

what variables are important nor how they should be measured. As Hackman and Morris (1975) noted, many interaction coding systems yield only summary frequency scores. While frequency scores help us understand some aspects of group interaction, they alone are inadequate. Hackman and Morris' example of the game of chess illustrates the shortcomings of frequency measures; to understand chess one must understand not frequency but *sequences* of moves. This distinction between frequency and sequence suggests we might benefit from more consideration of the basic dimensions along which group process can vary. At the same time, we need to develop better techniques to deal with the complexity of group interaction (Hackman & Morris, 1975).

Research on group process is relatively rare in contemporary social psychology for several reasons, among them "the practical difficulties and costs of such studies, the apparent theoretical sterility of many earlier efforts, and the attractiveness of individual-level paradigms for studying related processes" (McGrath & Kravitz, 1982, p. 210). In this paper we offer a methodological approach that we believe at least overcomes the first obstacle. Our belief is that if process research becomes easier to do than it is now, more of it will be done, and this increased research will, in turn, lead to more sophisticated theoretical integrations than what we present here. Our major goal, then, is to discuss a reasonably simple and straightforward method of investigating group process that can provide detailed time-based data.

It is important to realize that there are many ways of approaching the study of group process. Some of these are on the fringes of or outside the area of traditional social psychology. For example, Gottman (1979) has studied the process of conversation in distressed and nondistressed couples; Ellis and Fisher (1975) have performed Markovian analyses of the sequencing of arguments; and Weick (1974) has explored the process of mastering a performance in a jazz group. Computer simulations have been used to understand social influence process (Tanford & Penrod, 1984) and jury decision making (Penrod & Hastie, 1980).

As in many research enterprises, there is really no "right" way to approach the problem. Campbell's (1969) notion of fish scales—independent but overlapping and jointly defining a whole entity—and McGrath, Martin, and Kulka's (1982) caution that single studies and approaches are inherently flawed should lead us to welcome divergent approaches. We need to consider all possibilities in trying to advance theorizing and research on group process.

While process encompasses many things—working, thinking, feeling, building up interpersonal relationships, and just "being together"—we have chosen to focus upon talk, especially the paralinguistic features of talk. We believe that talk constitutes an ideal variable for research on group processes, because it is present in a large number of interactions and can be examined at a number of levels, from simple to complex. Several researchers have coded process as sound or silence in a stream of behavior (e.g., Chapple, 1949; Kasl & Mahl, 1956; Verzeano & Finesinger, 1949). Conrad and Conrad (1956) focused on the use of personal pronouns in group discussions. More sophisticated coding schemes, like that of Bales, are also primarily concerned with talking in groups. We have found a distinction between *amount* and *structure* of talk to be particularly useful. We will try to demonstrate the usefulness of this distinction both in the traditional Bales research and in more recent research on paralinguistic features of vocalizations. Then we will present some of our own work on talk and suggest how our general approach might be used to study other factors involved in group process.

II. Amount and Structure of Vocal Exchange

A. THE BALES SYSTEMS

Most of the research on talk in group interaction dates from the early 1950s and was conducted by Bales and his colleagues (e.g., Bales, 1950a,b, 1953; Bales & Slater, 1955; Bales & Strodtbeck, 1951; Borgatta & Bales, 1953), although there have been other content-oriented systems (e.g., Bion, 1961; Freedman, Leary, Ossorio, & Coffey, 1951; Stock & Thelen, 1958). The initial research by Bales used the Interaction Process Analysis (IPA), a 12-category observational coding system. Six of the categories reflected socioemotional activity (e.g., showing solidarity, agreement, or tension) and six reflected task activity (e.g., giving a suggestion or asking for an opinion). Trained observers noted who made each statement, to whom it was directed, and which of the 12 categories best described its content.

More recently, Bales (Bales & Cohen, 1979) has moved from IPA to SYMLOG (the Systematic Multiple Level Observation of Groups). Under the SYMLOG Interaction Scoring system, five or six observers describe all behavior and verbal content during a group interaction in terms of three dimensions: dominant vs. submissive, friendly vs. unfriendly, and instrumentally controlled vs. emotionally expressive. The same dimensions can be used by observers or group members to rate a group retrospectively using adjective rating scales. SYMLOG is more flexible but also more complex than IPA. Because it is still relatively new and untried outside of the research of Bales and his colleagues, it is too early to assess its usefulness (McGrath, 1984).

While Bales did not use these terms, it is apparent from a reading of his work that he investigated both the *amount* of communication from different members and the *structure* of members' vocal interaction over time. With regard to amount, Bales and his colleagues found consistent regularities. One such regularity is that some group members talk much more than others. The distribution of participation in groups resembles a J-curve, with a few members accounting for most of the talking, regardless of the size of the group. Attempts to represent this downward-tending curve mathematically by a decreasing exponential function have been somewhat, but not totally, successful (e.g., Horvath, 1965; Stephan & Mishler, 1952; Tsai, 1977). Bales and his colleagues also found that those individuals who initiate the most communication in a group also tend to receive the most communication; the number of communications initiated by a member is highly correlated with the number of communications received.

With regard to structure, Bales and his colleagues found a pattern in which those who initiate more communication tend to direct more communication to the group as a whole, while those who initiate less communication tend to direct more comments to specific individuals within the group. Analysis of the content revealed that individuals who communicate most tend to give out more information and opinion than they receive, while those who communicate least tend to give out more agreement, disagreement, and requests for information than they receive. Based on these results, Bales and colleagues concluded that the group member who initiates the most communication acts as the central focus of the communications network in the group, receiving questions from other group members and communicating information and opinions to the group as a whole as well as to other specific individuals.

Bales also suggested that communication is structured over time by attempts of the group to maintain an equilibrium between task and socioemotional activity. If the group works only on the task, interpersonal strains develop, which must be addressed by socioemotional activity. If the group pays too much attention to socioemotional activity, strain develops because nothing is getting done. McGrath interpreted Bales' notion as being a process that is primarily directed toward solving the task but is "punctuated by social-emotional activities that reinforce, guide, and regulate the flow of essentially task-oriented behavior" (1984, p. 151). Bales also suggested that group process develops through the phases of getting information, evaluating the information, and deciding on a course of action. As this sequence unfolds, the group seeks an equilibrium between task and socioemotional activity. Over time, there is an increase in tension, evidenced by increased negative reactions, which in turn lead to an increase in positive reactions as the group attempts to deal with this tension, so that by the end of the session there is the highest level of positive and negative reactions.

The Bales research has produced what McGrath has called "the most consistent and robust findings in the field" (1984, p. 145). Nevertheless, this research has been conducted almost exclusively at the Harvard Interaction Laboratory. There are several reasons why the Bales approach has not been more widely used. First, the Bales coding systems (1970; Bales & Cohen, 1979) are labor intensive, requiring several highly trained individuals for the coding of ongoing group interactions. Interactions must be coded live rather than from audiotapes or written transcripts, because the relative impoverishment of these data sources might lead to error (McGrath, 1984). Even if group interactions were videotaped, multiple audio channels would be needed to localize voices to particular speakers, and multiple cameras would be needed to observe the nonverbal detail sometimes necessary to interpret the meaning of a communication.

Second, although the method is useful for investigating the relatively simple questions of amount of activity and the source and target of communication acts, the Bales coding systems have been less useful for investigating more complex questions. In part, this may be due to the fact that, like any coding system, they impose a limiting structure that may not always accurately capture the essence of group interaction. Thus, for example, with both IPA and SYMLOG an act can be instrumental or expressive, but not both. Moreover, Bales' methods of data collection make it difficult to observe rapidly moving phenomena, such as the vocalizations and turn takings in a group of individuals. In the more than 30 years since Bales first presented his work, there have been advances in technology that allow for the rapid collection and analysis of data from group interaction. Methodological and statistical advances may now make it possible to address more intricate questions.

A third reason why Bales's research has not led directly to much work on the part of others is that he focuses almost completely on the meaning of his category systems to the exclusion of other information. Concerning his IPA system, he said:

> It has been my experience that it is not until one translates the numbers in the cells of the matrix back into the *categories and category sequences* they represent that one finds himself able to penetrate their social psychological meaning (Bales, 1970, p. 89, emphasis in original).

By focusing only on the content of interaction, Bales may have missed important information in the paralinguistic and nonverbal features of group interaction.

B. CONTENT-FREE SYSTEMS

Beyond the meaning of words in conversation, there is a simpler matter of the sound of speech. Here we would consider group process in terms of the patterning of utterances—onset, offset, delays, interruptions, and sequencing of communication acts—rather than the content they express. Sound and silence make up the substrate of vocal exchange, a substrate that contains a great deal of information and allows comparisons across content domains. We are proposing a content-free analysis of group discussion, which we would intend not to supplant but to supplement work in the tradition of Bales and other researchers who focus upon content. Indeed, our own research has relied on subjects' ratings of their fellow group members and the group itself and on judges' ratings of the group to supplement our content-free data.

One of the strong traditions in social psychology is an emphasis on the content of interpersonal interactions. Although we agree that meaning is important, we also believe that content has often been emphasized to the detriment of other factors that can provide information about the nature of an interaction. Measures of content are generally used without question as to whether they provide the best measure of process, and it is worth considering why we might rely on them less heavily.

There are at least four reasons why vocal content should not be the only dependent variable in studies of group process. First, studying content may involve coding the intent of the actor, and, given the biases and limitations inherent in observers, errors are inevitable. Second, content can be an unreliable dependent variable because individuals sometimes attempt to deceive others (Zuckerman, DePaulo, & Rosenthal, 1981). Although group members and independent observers might look to content in trying to detect deception (Kraut, 1978), sometimes content is less important than characteristics of the voice (O'Sullivan, Ekman, Friesen, & Scherer, 1985). Third, a group activity or conversation may be only a ritual with little significant content. That is, the form of the interaction is more important than the content of what is said. For example, the reading and approval of the minutes from the last business meeting of an organization is often a pro forma action. Similarly, the groupthink discussions of the Bay of Pigs invasion described by Janis (1972) were essentially superfluous because the decision to invade Cuba had already been made by President Kennedy. Fourth, there may be some interactions where content is virtually impossible to code. In this category would fall studies of sounds made by interacting animals, preverbal children, and adults speaking in languages with which the researcher is unfamiliar (e.g., see Ruback & Dabbs, 1987).

Sometimes content is obviously important (as in weighty intellectual discussions), and at other times it probably matters little (as in the brief moments of greeting arriving members). But on–off patterns of vocalization always underlie vocal content, and we believe these patterns can provide useful information about group process. In this belief we follow the tradition of Jaffe and Feldstein (1970), who analyzed in great detail the patterns of sound and silence in monologues and dialogues. We will later show how the Jaffe and Feldstein approach can be extended to the study of groups.

The question immediately arises as to whether content-free measures can reveal important or interesting findings. Content-free measures ignore what is traditionally thought of as "meaning." They constitute a radical departure from the mainstream of social psychology. However, research summarized by Cappella (1981), Feldstein and Welkowitz (1987), Lustig (1980), Matarazzo and

Wiens (1972), and Siegman and Feldstein (1979) has shown such measures can be useful. Content-free measures have been related to stress, personality differences, the relationship between partners, and the winning and losing of arguments, and they could prove useful in contributing to an understanding of group process.

For example, Meltzer, Morris, and Hayes (1971) found that amplitude differences between partners and changes in amplitude accounted for 62% of the variance in who would "win" when there were moments of simultaneous speech. Martindale (1971) found that among students playing the role of defense or prosecuting attorneys, turns were longer (and persuasion attempts more successful) for students arguing in their own dormitory rooms. Hayes and Meltzer (1972) found that a speaker's total amount of talking by itself was a sufficient basis for making interpersonal judgments. Alberti (1974) found the present tense used more frequently in conversations where there was more frequent turn taking or a more rapid pace of vocal exchange among members. Feldstein, Alberti, BenDebba, and Welkowitz (1974) found that subjects scoring low on the 16PF factor I—participants described as tough minded, unsentimental, self-reliant, and practical—initiated less simultaneous speech than those scoring high on this factor. Dabbs, Evans, Hopper, and Purvis (1980) found, contrary to expectation, that low self monitors changed their vocal parameters to match their partners more than high self monitors did. Ruback and Hopper (1986) found that prison inmates who paused longer between vocalizations were judged by parole board interviewers to be less honest than were inmates who had shorter pauses; inmates with shorter interviews also proved more likely to have their subsequent paroles revoked. In sum, content-free measures based upon the amount and timing of sound and silence have proved useful in the past. They might also be used to indicate whether group conversation moves quickly or slowly, speakers are talkative or laconic, listeners are responsive or dull, and the overall interaction is smooth or clumsy.

In this chapter we wish to extend the Bales work on the amount and structure of communication to the content-free domain studied so effectively by Jaffe and Feldstein. We will describe a conceptual model that speaks directly to questions related to the dimensions of amount and structure and will discuss data from three studies that are suggestive of the importance of these two dimensions to an understanding of group process. We will also present an automated data collection system that requires no human observers.

C. AMOUNT AND STRUCTURE OF CONTENT-FREE MEASURES

Our approach is to define process in terms of talking (Shaw, 1964), including both the amount of talking and the patterns of talking among group members. We are aware that process can involve much more than talk, an issue to which we will return in the concluding section of the chapter. But first we will consider the amount and structure of content-free measures and how they both can be affected by factors about the task facing the group, the overall group, and the individual members.

1. Amount of Talk

Amount of vocal activity ranges from silence to everyone speaking at once. Although much of the research on brainstorming has contrasted nominal groups (where there is no interaction among members) with real groups, group interaction can range from none at all (in nominal groups) to various levels (in various real groups). Thus, for example, a real group in which there is little talking would be somewhat like a nominal group. Group interaction, as indexed by amount of talking, is a continuous variable, and it might be more fruitful to map performance onto this continuous variable than onto the dichotomy of "real" versus nominal groups.

The amount of communication in a group depends upon aspects of the task, the group, and the individual members. Task factors include the nature of the task and the type of communication network. For example, we have found more talking in social groups (Dabbs & Ruback, 1984) than in problem-solving groups (Dabbs, Ruback, & Evans, in press) and brainstorming groups (Ruback, Dabbs, & Hopper, 1984). Research would also suggest more communication in decentralized networks than in centralized networks (e.g., Cohen, Bennis, & Wolkon, 1961). Moreover, there is evidence suggesting that when the issue is more relevant, there will be longer communications, fewer interruptions, and fewer pauses (Schachter, 1951). The amount of communication might also be related to the difficulty of the goal (Locke, 1968; Locke, Shaw, Sasri, & Latham, 1981) and the amount of time the group has to work on the task (Kelly & McGrath, 1985).

One of the most important group factors is attractiveness of the group, which we expect to contribute to high levels of communication. Because attractive groups are high in cohesiveness (the members like each other and are attracted to the group), the groups are likely to be highly motivated (Bass, Pryer, Gaier, & Flint, 1958) and to have stronger pressures to communicate (Festinger, 1950). We might also expect such groups to produce a situation of relatively low communication anxiety. Groups that are cohesive, attractive, highly motivated, and have a norm of encouraging members to talk should evidence higher levels of communication than groups that have the opposite characteristics. However, Back's (1951) research has indicated that different ways of creating cohesiveness do not always have identical effects on communication. There may be times when highly cohesive groups stifle discussion due to overzealous members who punish attitudinal deviates or to members who deliberately withhold comments they know to be contrary to majority sentiment (Janis, 1972). In addition, in groups that have a norm of little communication, increased cohesion might further reduce their amount of talking.

One of the most important of the factors about members concerns individual differences in their talkativeness. Groups containing talkative members (whom Bales called "high initiators") should have higher amounts of communication than groups containing members who are low initiators. This difference in the talkativeness of members has been observed in research on groups (e.g., Bales, 1953) and on speech communication anxiety (e.g., McCroskey, 1984). Our own research (Dabbs & Ruback, 1984) has found that all-female groups have higher levels of communication than all-male groups. Interestingly, we have not found that measures of affiliation, introversion–extraversion, and verbal ability relate to amount of talking (Ruback & Dabbs, 1986; Ruback et al., 1984). How much any particular individual talks is positively related to his or her own characteristic amount of talking in a group ("basic initiating rate") and negatively related to the "basic interaction rates" of the other group members (Borgatta & Bales, 1953). Thus, removing the high interactors from the group will cause an increase in the communication rate of the remaining group members (Stephan & Mishler, 1952). An individual's rate of communication will also increase if the leader encourages equal participation (Bovard, 1951). McGrath (1984) suggests five other factors that relate to an individual's amount of talking in a group: (1) position in the group's communication network (central vs. peripheral), (2) prominence of his or her seating position (e.g., head vs. side of a table), (3) status in the group, (4) motivation to perform the task, and (5) value to the group (e.g., expert or deviate from modal opinion). Finally, Festinger (1950) has suggested that communicators who are in an emotional state are more likely to talk than individuals who are not happy or angry.

In terms of outcome, we generally expect members to be more attracted to groups with higher levels of communication. Such groups should do well on tasks requiring high levels of communication (e.g., social conversations) but to do less well on tasks that require creative thought, because talking may interfere with the production of ideas (Ruback et al., 1984). If this model is correct, we would expect that by manipulating the amount of conversation in a group we could affect both the amount of liking for the group and the group's performance on the task.

2. Structure of Talk

Some discussion of the meaning of "structure" is called for here, although we are generally of the view that definitions should remain loose in the exploratory stages of an enterprise. In describing Bales' work, we used structure to refer to patterns of member interaction and changes over time. Structure to us carries meanings of order, predictability, form, regularity, clarity, design. Things without structure are disorderly, unpredictable, amorphous, fuzzy, random. Structure describes the way in which a thing is distributed across time, space, or other dimensions. Readers familiar with information theory will recognize that more structure in a data set implies less information or uncertainty. There is probably no single definition of "structure" that will be completely acceptable to everyone. In this chapter we refer to the structure of vocal activity in a number of different ways. Further research will be needed to decide which are the most useful.

Manifestations of structure in group vocal behavior can be quite varied. Turn taking can alternate regularly among members, or turns from each individual can cluster together, with clusters separated by periods of relative inactivity. Individual members can mimic or copy one another, showing greater similarity in their vocal parameters than would be expected by chance alone, or they can diverge in contrast to one another. The sequential patterning of talk can be random, or it can be orderly and predictable. If one examines turn taking, information statistics (Attneave, 1959) can index the overall predictability in who follows whom. Sequential chains involving particular pairs or sets of group members can be examined to provide more detail (Parker, 1984).

Our notions of group structure bear some similarity to the work on communication networks. In both instances communication is seen as occurring in a variety of patterns, ranging from essentially random (e.g., when anyone can communicate with anyone else) to highly structured (e.g., when a group member can speak to only one or two others). Since the initial studies by Bavelas (1948) and Leavitt (1951), it has been found that group members prefer decentralized to centralized networks, regardless of the type of task the group is performing. In contrast, the effectiveness of groups in problem solving depends on group structure and the complexity of the task involved (Shaw, 1964). With simple problems (e.g., symbol-identification tasks), centralized groups make fewer errors and solve the problems faster. With complex problems (e.g., discussion problems), decentralized groups make fewer errors and solve the problems faster. It should be noted that in these studies structure and amount of communication are confounded, with decentralized networks generally sending more messages. However, it does appear that for easy tasks more communication is counterproductive, whereas for difficult tasks more communication is likely to be related to better performance.

As with amount of communication, we expect the communication structure to be affected by factors about the task, the group, and the individual members. In terms of the task, differences are likely to appear as a function of the cognitive effort required. For example, some intellective tasks require a group to pursue an idea, and structure would be demanded by the material. Other tasks, like getting acquainted, should have more spontaneity or randomness. With regard to factors about the group, we expect structure to be more marked in established groups than in groups with no prior history, because established groups are more likely to have developed roles and norms concerning when it is appropriate for different members to talk. We would also expect more structured conversational patterns in groups with a clear hierarchy than in those that are more egalitarian and in groups with a rigid, unchanging structure than in those where leadership and degree of individual involvement are likely to change in different situations. We expect more contribution to structure (1) by members who are especially responsive to others, speaking more in reply (cf. Davis & Perkowitz, 1979; Weiss, Lombardo, Warren, & Kelley, 1971) and thereby helping to keep the others going, and (2) by pairs of members who like one another and contribute recurring brief dyadic exchanges to the overall group discussion. In groups that are more highly structured, it is easier to predict who will follow whom, and there should be more chains of conversations between two individuals (e.g., A-B-A-B, indicating that individuals A and B are talking with one another).

In terms of how structure is likely to affect outcome, our predictions are based to a large extent on the results of studies of communication networks. Overall, we expect group members to enjoy being in groups with little structure. These groups are characterized by more uncertainty about who will speak next, and participation should appear to members (and to observers) to be more spontaneous and fun. With regard to task performance, we expect groups with high structure to do well on simple tasks, and groups with little structure to do well on complex tasks.

III. The Grouptalk Model

We have been discussing vocal measures and the kind of information that might be extracted from the moment-by-moment analysis of content-free speech. Let us consider in more detail exactly what kind of data might be involved in such an analysis.

A simple means of data collection and analysis comes from the work by Jaffe and Feldstein (1970), and earlier Chapple (1949), whose approaches deal with the temporal organization of sound and silence. Jaffe and Feldstein collected data using the Automatic Vocal Transaction Analyzer (AVTA), a system that includes a cancellation network to eliminate the spillover of one person's voice into another person's microphone. AVTA determines the on–off state of each person's voice at each moment and transforms these data into psychologically meaningful scores.

When we listen to conversation we hear not sound and silence but a pattern of alternation among speakers. The basic parameter in the Jaffe and Feldstein scheme is the individual *turn,* which is made up of a speaker's *vocalizations* and *pauses.* Silence that ends a turn is a *switching pause,* and it is always followed by the beginning of the other speaker's turn. When one person is speaking in his or her turn and the other joins in, the speech on the part of the second person is called simultaneous speech; *interruptive simultaneous speech* leads to a change of turn, and *noninterruptive simultaneous speech* does not.

The situation becomes more complicated when more than two people are conversing. In a dyad one partner's turn begins when that partner speaks alone and ends the instant the other partner speaks alone. But in groups larger than dyads a speaker's turn may end with several others speaking at once, in which case there is no obvious way to decide who should be assigned the turn. No new turn taker has emerged (no one else is speaking alone), but it hardly seems appropriate to continue crediting the turn to the original speaker, who by now is silent. Thus, in contrast to Jaffe and Feldstein, who argue that their model can be adapted without change from dyads to groups, the "Grouptalk" model (Dabbs, Ruback, & Evans, 1987), proposes the notion of *group turn* to cover this contingency.

A group turn begins when an individual turn taker has fallen silent and two or more other persons are speaking. The other persons may have jointly interrupted the original turn-taker, or they may simultaneously have begun to speak following a silence. The group turn ends the instant an individual again speaks alone. Analogously to individual turns, group turns may contain *group vocalizations* and *group pauses* and end with *group switching pauses.* During a group turn the set of people who are speaking together may vary, but there will be no one speaking alone. In our research we have found that group turns occupy between 0.04 and 10.88% of the total discussion time. Although accounting for a relatively small percentage of group conversation time, we believe that group turns are important because, in addition to adding conceptual completeness, they describe what we have observed to be a very real and variable phenomenon in groups.

The Grouptalk model includes the six Jaffe and Feldstein codes and the four group turn codes (all ten italicized in the above three paragraphs). This model is graphically displayed in Fig. 1, which also summarizes the probability of occurrence of various states and transitions, computed from the data from three studies described below. In the left portion of the figure are individual turn states, and in the right portion are group turn states. The solid circles define a set of mutually exclusive and exhaustive states, and the numbers and arrows show the probability of each state's occurrence and the probability of all possible transitions among the states.

The most common state is a vocalization (which may or may not be accompanied by simultaneous speech emitted by someone other than the turn taker). Pauses can follow a vocalization, and pauses are always followed by another

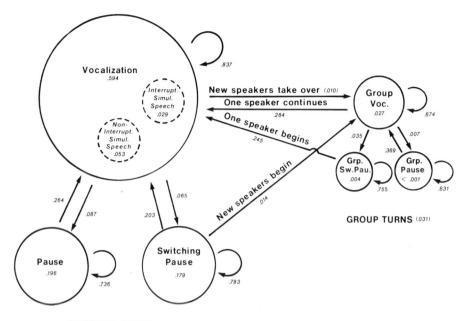

Fig. 1.   Diagram of conversational states in the Grouptalk model. Solid circles constitute a set of mutually exclusive and exhaustive states. Dashed circles are additional events that may occur during the vocalizing state. Numbers inside circles are simple probabilities of the occurrence of each state or event. Numbers beside arrows are transitional probabilities of each state occurring at the next point in time. The data are summarized from 60 five-person group conversations, lasting an average of 15–20 minutes each, in which the conversational state was coded ever quarter-second.

vocalization by the same speaker. Switching pauses lead to a vocalization by a new speaker or, more rarely, to a group vocalization, in which several new speakers begin at once. A group turn can emerge out of the silence of a switching pause and be followed by the silence of a group switching pause, but more typically group turns emerge from the vocalization of an individual speaker as two or more others take over, and they are transformed again into the vocalization of an individual speaker when all but that one fall silent. Group pauses are possible, if all the speakers vocalizing together fall silent at once, and then two or more speakers begin together. Group pauses are infrequent, however, because usually only one person will begin again after several have fallen silent together.

We differ from Jaffe and Feldstein in that we would define an individual turn as ending when an individual turn taker has fallen silent and two or more others are speaking together. Jaffe and Feldstein would have an individual turn continue directly through the activity of other simultaneous speakers to the point where a new individual turn begins. For some purposes (e.g., comparability with the research of Jaffe and Feldstein) it might be desirable to disregard group turns, coding all occasions of multiple speaking as part of the preceding individual turn. Some of our computer programs will recode data in this fashion, making it possible to regard conversation wholly in terms of a pattern of alternation among individual turns. In general, however, we feel that the group turn is a unique emergent property of group conversation and should not be defined out of existence.

IV. Data Collection and Management

Data collection is more complicated with a group than with a dyad. The system must recognize a person speaking alone and also recognize several persons speaking at once. Each subject's voice will be heard on all subjects' microphones, and the crosstalk cancellation network used in Jaffe and Feldstein's AVTA cannot be readily expanded to include more than two microphones. The system we use was developed by Dabbs and Swiedler (1983), following the general approach of an earlier system developed by Brown (1979).

The system consists of both electronic hardware and computer software. Each subject in a group wears a small lavaliere microphone. An electronic device amplifies each microphone signal and continuously compares it to a standard "trigger" level, which corresponds to the level of a very soft voice. The trigger level generally remains the same from group to group. Signals above the trigger level are amplified to 5 volts and monitored through a parallel port into an Apple II computer. These signals reveal which microphones are active at a given moment, but more information is needed to determine whether a sound on a given microphone comes from the person wearing the microphone or from someone else.

The relative intensity of microphone signals provides this information. The equipment is calibrated ahead of time such that the amplification is identical on all channels. Each speaker's voice will then be louder, and thus be above the trigger level longer, on his or her microphone than on any other microphone. The computer checks each microphone line about eight times per millisecond to see whether or not a signal is present. Every 10 milliseconds, the computer summarizes its findings and designates the microphone that has been above the trigger level most often as belonging to the true speaker. The computer cancels isolated spikes of noise and fills in brief (less than 300 milliseconds) pauses within and between the speaker's words.

This same procedure allows the computer to recognize several subjects speaking at once. When people speak together, their voices are not perfectly synchronized. In the continuous mix of syllables, accents, and pauses, even the softest-spoken speaker will have moments of being loudest. In picking the most active microphone every 10 milliseconds, the computer monitoring simultaneous speech will find rapid alternation in which of several microphones is most active. The same procedure that filled brief gaps in the speech of a single person will now fill gaps caused by the computer's alternation among the microphones of the several simultaneous speakers. The computer in effect "looks over" its current array and designates all these microphones as belonging to active speakers. Every quarter-second the computer saves one 8-bit byte, each bit representing the on–off state of one person's voice in a group of up to eight members.

Computer systems become rapidly outdated, and we are under no illusion that our system should be used by all investigators interested in this kind of data. Other approaches could be more elaborate, recording levels of loudness in addition to the simple on–off state of each person's voice. A. W. Siegman and S. Feldstein (personal communication) are currently working with such a "loudness AVTA" in a project on vocal patterns and coronary heart disease. High-speed machines, such as (in 1986) the Apple Macintosh, Commodore Amiga, or Atari ST, could be programmed to construct and display a sociogram of a conversing group, recording how much each person talks and displaying a diagram showing the turn transitions from each person to each other person. A printout of a sociogram could be provided to a group during a session, to give them feedback on group process. The possibilities are virtually unlimited, and we present our system primarily as an example of what can be done with relatively simple equipment.

The data are stored on a computer disk and later transferred to a mainframe computer. The raw data of on–off vocal states sampled every quarter-second for one group of five persons talking a half-hour constitutes 36,000 data points. When many such groups are run in an experiment, the amount of data can be overwhelming, and we have followed some of the guidelines suggested by Bakeman and Dabbs (1976). The importance of careful data management cannot be overemphasized. Psychologists sometimes collect data without thinking through how they will analyze it. When data are as voluminous as that described here, a cavalier approach to data management can lead to disaster.

We use a program called GRPTFD (Dabbs *et al.*, 1987) to expand the raw on–off voice data into the Grouptalk codes and store these codes in Bakeman's (1975) Time Frame Data format. With the data in Time Frame Data format we can compute total time, number, and mean duration for each vocal code for each group and each group member. We can examine the conditional probabilities of events (e.g., the probability of each group member's interrupting each other member), similarities among subjects (e.g., in mean pause length), or the distribution of times between turns. We can generate transitional matrices showing who follows whom in the flow of conversational turn taking, or transform the data into a time series showing how many group members (from zero to *n*) are speaking at each moment. Reanalysis is relatively easy because of the time-based format in which the data are stored.

The Grouptalk model can describe the behavior of both individuals and groups. For each individual we have total time, number, and mean duration of turns, vocalizations, pauses, switching pauses, and two kinds of simultaneous speech. For each group we have total time, number, and mean duration of group turns, group vocalizations, group pauses, and group switching pauses, as well as mean scores summarizing the vocal codes of all individuals within the group. Group scores can also be derived from the way behavior is patterned among subjects and over time. Group members can be similar or dissimilar to one another in their vocal codes. Turns can be distributed evenly or clustered together. A transitional matrix showing who follows whom in turn taking can be generated, and chains of turn taking can be extracted from the data. We can examine the clustering of turns, and we can use Fourier analysis to characterize a group as having slow-moving or fast-moving cycles of speech and silence; cycle length in dyads has been interpreted as a measure of the "cognitive load" of a conversation (Dabbs, 1983a,b).

V. Initial Studies

The approach outlined here has not yet been established in the literature, and we are obliged to show that it works. We have so far completed three studies, involving a total of 60 five-person groups. The first study (Dabbs *et al.*, 1987) involved 20 mixed-sex groups that worked on the desert survival problem (Lafferty & Pond, 1974) for 10–30 minutes each. Subjects played the role of being stranded in the desert after a plane crash. Before discussing the problem they individually ranked 15 items (e.g., knife, compass, water) in terms of importance for survival. They then discussed the problem to reach consensus on the ranking of each item. Vocal data were recorded using the microcomputer system described above. After the discussion, subjects completed questionnaires on which they rated their peers and the group as a whole.

The vocal and questionnaire data were analyzed at both individual and group levels. At the individual level, results showed talking related to ratings of leadership and, less strongly, to ratings of liking. When amount of talking was controlled for, leadership was found to be related positively to vocalizing in one's own turn and negatively to emitting simultaneous speech in others' turns. At the group level, subjects rated their groups as having more spirit when there was more vocalization, more simultaneous speech, more time spent in group turns, and more equal distribution of talking time among subjects.

The second study (Ruback *et al.*, 1984) involved 20 mixed-sex groups that worked for 20 minutes each brainstorming how to increase the number of tourists visiting the United States. During the brainstorming session, two judges watching on a video monitor recorded the originator of each new idea and (using extra switches in the data acquisition system) the time of the occurrence of the idea. Again, speech was recorded automatically, and subjects completed questionnaires at the end of the session.

At the individual level, high levels of talking were related to peer ratings of leadership and, less strongly, to liking. When amount of talking was controlled for, ratings of leadership were still positively related to amount of time vocalizing in one's own turns. Leaders spent more time in latencies before their turns and in switching pauses at the end of their turns. At the group level, liking was related positively to vocalizations and negatively to switching pauses. A conditional probability analysis indicated ideas were especially likely following a switching pause; in other words, silence between speakers, rather than talk, tended to precede the emergence of ideas.

The third study (Dabbs & Ruback, 1984) involved 20 same-sex five-member groups engaged in social conversation. Subjects were asked to get to know one another for 20 minutes. At the individual level, high levels of talking were again positively related to rated leadership and, again less strongly, to rated liking. When talking was held constant, leadership was again positively related to vocalizing in one's own turn and negatively related to simultaneous speech. A contrast between male and female groups showed female groups spent significantly more time in vocalizations and less time in switching pauses, and females liked their groups more and rated their groups as having more spirit.

Two common findings emerge from the three studies. First, as has been widely reported before (e.g., Bass, 1981; Stein & Heller, 1979), individuals who talk more are rated higher on leadership. But even when talking is held constant, leaders vocalize more in their own turns and emit less simultaneous speech in the turns of others. Second, groups are liked more when members vocalize more and, in two of the three studies, when there is more simultaneous speech. Our findings lead to the conclusion that simultaneous speech may be good at the group level (where it is associated with more group spirit) but not at the individual level (where it is associated with lower ratings of leadership).

The brainstorming study also provided a clue as to how ideas are produced. Ideas did not emerge following high levels of vocalization or simultaneous speech, as might have been predicted from work by advocates of brainstorming (Osborn, 1957), but rather following periods of silence between speakers. It is possible that the widely cited finding that brainstorming is less effective with groups than with individuals arises because simultaneous speech in groups is distracting and/or arousing and interferes with the complex task of generating novel ideas.

Data from these three studies, originally gathered to deal with questions of leadership, peer ratings, and group satisfaction, could be pooled to cast some light upon the nature of group process. The vocal data had been treated identically in the three groups, but some work was needed to make peer ratings and group ratings comparable across the studies. Five peer rating items were common to the three studies (attention, leadership, contribution, liking, meet again). On each of these items Kenney's SOREMO program (Kenny, Lord, & Garg, 1983) was used to correct for individual differences in rater bias in a round-robin design, and the resulting scores were combined into a single mean rating characterizing each subject.

We also needed a single overall rating to characterize each group. Five items on which members had rated their groups were common to the three studies (liking, group spirit, work again, task performance, group enthusiasm). Two outside judges watched videotape recordings of each session that had been made with a camera in the ceiling directly above the group. The judges viewed six 20-second segments distributed approximately equally across each session. Segments were viewed at twice normal speed, to save time and keep the verbal content unintelligible. After viewing all six segments each judge rated group enthusiasm on a 9-point scale. Interjudge reliability was $r = .80$, $df = 58$, $p < .001$. In order to weight equally the impressions of group members and outside judges, we standardized judges' mean ratings of each group, standardized members' mean ratings of each group, and combined judge and member standardized ratings into an overall mean rating of group attractiveness. The material below deals with analyses of vocal and verbal data from the three combined studies.

VI. Amount of Vocal Activity

A. TALK, TURNS, INTERRUPTIONS

We found both individuals and groups evaluated more favorably when they talked more. The pooled within-group correlation between percentage of time a person talked and mean peer ratings given that person was $r = .73$. At the group level, among the 60 groups, the correlation between percentage of time there was talking in the group and overall rating of the group was $r = .85$. Talking is apparently very desirable, at least in short-lived groups like those we studied.

The significance of talk is shown in more detail in Table I, which summarizes results for five vocal codes. There were striking differences between findings for individuals and for groups. Individuals who paused more were rated more favorably, while groups that paused more were rated less favorably. This difference is likely related to how one perceives differently sound and silence

TABLE I

RELATIONSHIP OF VOCAL CODES TO EVALUATION OF INDIVIDUALS
AND GROUPS

Vocal code	Correlation with peers' ratings of individuals[a]	Correlation with ratings of groups
Vocalization	.73[b]	.82[b]
Pause	.67[b]	−.72[b]
Switching pause	.62[b]	−.70[b]
Noninterruptive simultaneous speech	.03	.73[b]
Interruptive simultaneous speech	.42[b]	.68[b]

[a]Pooled within-group r.
[b]$p < .001$.

from individuals or from groups. The concept of turn is important here, as it was for Jaffe and Feldstein (1970). In attending to an individual, one hears not just sound and silence but turns, which include vocalizations, pauses, and switching pauses. Vocalizing and pausing both increase the length of a turn and thus the amount of time dominated by the turn taker. In attending to a group, on the other hand, one may hear overall vocal activity rather than the turns of individual members. Activity seems to be desirable, while pausing does not contribute to and can actually interfere with group discussion.

It is less clear why noninterruptive simultaneous speech operates differently for individuals and groups. The findings were that both interruptive and noninterruptive simultaneous speech added to the positive evaluation of a group, but only interruptive simultaneous speech added to the positive evaluation of an individual. Again, the notion of turn may be useful. Both kinds of simultaneous speech add to overall group activity. But at the individual level, interruptive simultaneous speech is special in that it triggers the beginning of a new turn, while noninterruptive simultaneous speech is completely "out of turn," leaving the original turn state unchanged. Individuals are viewed more favorably when they emit more interruptive simultaneous speech, leading to more turns for themselves. Thus, it may be that the winners of these "battles" for turns are rated more positively.

Another way to talk about noninterruptive and interruptive simultaneous speech operating differently at individual and group levels is to say that at the group level both kinds of simultaneous speech show involvement with the discussion. In contrast, at the individual level noninterruptive simultaneous speech shows an interest in the conversation of another person, whereas interruptive simultaneous speech shows an interest in one's own ideas. Thus, at the individual level only interruptive simultaneous speech would be recognized as contributing to one's ranking as a leader.

B. COMPARISON TO PRIOR RESEARCH

Our findings concerning amount of talking are consistent with prior research for both groups and individuals. At the group level, studies of communication networks generally show that people are more satisfied with groups in which more messages are sent (Leavitt, 1951; Shaw, 1964), just as we found groups with higher levels of talking were liked more. At the individual level, there is much prior research indicating, as we found, that individuals are rated higher in leadership if they talk more (e.g., Bass, 1981; Stein & Heller, 1979).

But some of our findings are different; we found that pauses and interruptive simultaneous speech contribute to rated leadership, whereas noninterruptive simultaneous speech does not. Essentially, we have articulated vocal parameters more finely, breaking down overall talk into the utterances and pauses that compose the turns of individual group members in the Grouptalk model. Our conceptualization is not basically new, except for the notion of "group turn"; instead it follows directly from the turn-taking model of dyadic conversation in Jaffe and Feldstein's *Rhythms of Dialogue*. What is new is a data acquisition and management scheme that allows us to disentangle and summarize in a coherent fashion the overlapping streams of utterances from many group members at once.

VII. Structure of Vocal Activity

Going beyond amount of vocal activity and how it is partitioned among different vocal codes, there are questions of how vocal activity is structured among group members and over time.

A. VOCAL SIMILARITY

One kind of structure is vocal similarity among group members. Such similarity could have several origins. It could be the result of selection, either planned or fortuitous, in which like members are brought together into the group. It could reflect environmental or process forces that produce similar effects on all group members. Or it could reflect a tendency for members to mimic, copy, or imitate one another. We are concerned here less with the origins of vocal similarity than with documenting its existence and its effects.

1. Congruence

Feldstein and Welkowitz (1987), in reviewing the vocal behavior of dyads, defined "congruence" as a tendency for subjects within dyads to be more similar to one another than would be expected by chance, and they used the intraclass correlation coefficient as an index of congruence. Congruence in loudness of speech is quite general (Natale, 1975), perhaps reflecting a natural tendency for persons to talk louder to maintain intelligibility in a noisier environment. Similarity of accents and speech styles is also common (see Giles & Powesland, 1975, pp. 70–81). Feldstein and Welkowitz report that among content-free parameters of speech it has most often been the mean lengths of switching pauses, and to some extent of pauses, that show congruence. Congruence in lengths of vocalization is less common. Perhaps this is because the length of a vocalization is constrained by the need to select appropriate words to express particular thoughts, while pauses, having no content, can easily be varied in length to match the pauses of a partner.

We examined congruence among subjects in each of the 60 groups, using Kenny's LEVEL program (Kenny & Stigler, 1983) to compute intraclass r's on all the vocal parameters. We partialed out mean differences among the three studies that might otherwise have inflated the intraclass r's. While most of the analyses in this chapter were based upon the percentage of time a vocal code occurred, the present analyses used percentage of time for some vocal codes and mean length for others. Mean length is a more satisfactory measure when the sum of the percentages would approach the total session time, because as total session time is approached the scores take on an ipsative quality, making it impossible for all group members to be equally high or low in their scores. When this happens the intraclass r must equal $-1/(n-1)$, which for our groups is $-.25$. Thus, we used mean duration (as Feldstein and Welkowitz did) in analyzing vocalizations, pauses, and switching pauses. For noninterruptive and interruptive simultaneous speech, which are generally brief and do not account for much of the session time, we used percentage scores in the analysis.

The intraclass r's are shown in the left column of Table II. The intraclass r's were significant for all five vocal codes. The intraclass r was somewhat higher for vocalizations and lower for pauses and switching pauses than generally reported by Feldstein and Welkowitz. Feldstein and Welkowitz did not report any findings on congruence in simultaneous speech. Apparently the tendency toward vocal congruence is more pervasive in groups than it has been found to be in dyads.

TABLE II

VOCAL SIMILARITY AMONG MEMBERS AND ITS RELATIONSHIP TO OVERALL EVALUATION
OF THE GROUP

	Intraclass r showing vocal similarity within group[a]	Partial r between group similarity scores and ratings of groups[b]
Vocalization (M)	.17***[c]	.27*
Pause (M)	.18***	.42**
Switching pause (M)	.32***	.14
Noninterruptive simultaneous speech (%)	.53***	.01
Interruptive simultaneous speech (%)	.55***	.13

[a]Partial intraclass r, with difference among three experiments removed.

[b]Similarity is the algebraic negative of the group standard deviation on each vocal code. Partial r controls for mean vocal activity and for differences among the three studies.

[c]* indicates $p < .05$; ** indicates $p < .01$; *** indicates $p < .001$.

Going beyond the existence of vocal congruence, we looked to see how similarity was related to the attractiveness of a group. The extensive social psychological literature on similarity and attraction might be brought to bear upon vocal patterns if we could derive a suitable index of vocal similarity to describe each group. Marcus, Welkowitz, Feldstein, and Jaffe (1970) defined congruence for a dyad as the absolute difference between partners on the mean length of a vocal code. We extended this approach and defined congruence for a group as the negative of the standard deviation among members on a vocal code, with lower standard deviations defining higher congruence.

We wished to compute the correlation between this standard deviation measure of congruence and the attractiveness rating of a group. In examining the data, however, it became apparent that standard deviations and means were correlated within groups, with higher standard deviations when mean vocal activity was higher. Correlations between mean and standard deviation are not unusual; differences are often "cheaper" toward the higher end of a scale. We corrected for any spurious effect this confounding of mean and standard deviation might have produced by partialing out of the relationship between the standard deviation scores and the rating of the group the mean percentage of time a vocal code occurred. We also partialed out of this relationship mean differences among the three studies. The results are shown in the right column of Table II.

Congruence within groups appeared generally desirable. Congruence in mean length of vocalization and of pause was significantly related to group attractiveness. While congruence in mean length of switching pause was not significantly related to attractiveness, a separate analysis showed similarity in percentage of time in switching pauses was so related ($r = .42$, again controlling for mean percentage of switching pause and for study differences). More activity is desirable, as described earlier, but groups are also more attractive when members are more similar in their vocal parameters.

2. Equality in Amount of Talk

Congruence refers to similarity among group members in the occurrence or mean duration of specific vocal codes. Another kind of similarity is equality among members in their overall amounts of vocal activity. Here we will discuss equality in information theory terms. It is not essential to use such terms, but we believe they provide a vocabulary that adds to our understanding of group process.

Information theory gained some popularity among psychologists in the 1950s and early 1960s (cf. Miller, 1956). Attneave (1959) has a readable presentation of the topic, and Davis (1963) and Gottmann and Bakeman (1979) present applications to social behavior. Information is equivalent to the uncertainty in a set of symbols. The less certain one is about which symbol will appear next, the more information there is in the set. If there is only one symbol in the set, there is no uncertainty, and information is zero. If there are several equiprobable symbols, there is maximum uncertainty, and information is at its maximum value. Thus, equal amounts of vocal behavior from different group members would produce the greatest uncertainty; one listening to such a group would be "uncertain" about who would speak at any given moment.

The standard measure of information is H, a summary of the average amount of information in a set. H is expressed in bits, or binary units. When symbols in the set are equiprobable, $H = \log c$, where log is to the base 2 and c is the number of symbols. The value of H would be 0 with one symbol, 1 with two symbols, 2 with four symbols, 3 with eight symbols, and so on. When symbols are not equally likely to occur, each symbol is weighted by the probability of its occurrence in the classic Shannon and Weaver (1949) formulation,

$$H = \Sigma\, p_i\, \log(1/p_i),$$

which is equivalent to

$$H = -\Sigma\, p_i\, \log(p_i).$$

The turns of five speakers in a group may be regarded as five symbols in a set. H can be computed based upon the percentage of time occupied by each speaker's turns. H would take on its minimum value of zero if only one member in the group ever spoke, and it would take on its maximum value, $H = \log 5 = 2.32$, if all five members had turns equally.

We computed H for each group based upon the percentage of time each subject held the turn in the group. The mean value of H across the 60 groups was 2.16, which is quite high. Thus, across all the groups there was a great deal of what might be called uncertainty or unpredictability in who would speak at an average given moment.

Further, H proved to be related to other measures. Among the 60 groups there was a correlation of $r = .23$ ($df = 55$, $p < .05$) between H and the overall attractiveness of a group, with amount of talk and differences among the three studies partialed out. Subjects showed a significant (albeit modest) tendency to prefer groups where there was more uncertainty about who would speak. Note that subjects may not have perceived this state of affairs as uncertainty. They might instead have perceived the group as an egalitarian one, in which all members participate equally.

H was also significant in another and unexpected way. Using Kenny's SOREMO program (Kenney et al., 1983), we partitioned peer rating variance into components attributable to raters, ratees, and the relationship between rater and ratee. (Relationship is an interaction effect; in our data it includes both error and idiosyncratic preferences of specific raters for specific ratees.) With amount of talk and mean differences among the three studies partialed out, there was less ratee variance in groups where H was higher ($r = -.43$, $df = 55$, $p < .001$). Apparently when participation is equal, subjects have little basis for differentiating among their partners, and as a result their ratings are due more to error and to idiosyncratic preferences. This was indicated by a positive correlation between H and the relationship component of peer rating variance ($r = .35$, $df = 55$, $p < .01$), again with amount of talk and differences among the studies partialed out. It was not the case that subjects simply displayed more bias in their ratings. The correlation between H and rater variance (a measure of bias) was only $r = .17$ (not significant). Regardless of the exact explanation of these correlations, they suggest that differential amounts of talk may provide much of the basis for objective peer ratings.

B. SEQUENTIAL INTERRELATIONSHIPS

Similarity among group members is a kind of structure, but a structure based upon summary scores rather than moment-by-moment relationships. There are other more dynamic kinds of structure, involving patterns of alternation among group members in their vocal behavior. Analysis of this kind of patterning or sequencing is not common in social psychology, and there have been suggestions that the field might benefit from such work (e.g., Steiner, 1986). In this section, we examine the predictability in who follows whom and see how this predictability is related to other measures.

1. The Turn-Taking Matrix

Bales (1953) described a turn-taking matrix that summarized the conversational history of a group in terms of how often each member spoke to each other member. A similar transitional matrix can be generated from our grouptalk data, showing the likelihood that each speaker will follow each other speaker. This transitional matrix is akin to the preference matrix of sociometry, where an entry in cell *ij* shows whether the person in the *i*th row chooses the person in the *j*th column. A speaker in a group conversation does not exactly choose who will speak next, but there is often some tie between the two people in a sequence. The raw data in our matrices comprise frequencies of all observed transitions; the frequency of A following B, C following D, and so forth. To control for different amounts of talking, we usually convert these frequencies to conditional probabilities, describing the likelihood that, "given the person in this row speaks, the person in that column will speak next." With conditional probabilities, rows always sum to 1.0, indicating the certainty that someone will always follow. In generating this transitional matrix we chose to ignore the group turn state so as to be more comparable with the data from Jaffe and Feldstein. We recoded each group turn so that it was absorbed into the preceding speaker's turn. Conversation was thus treated as moving continuously from the turn of one speaker to the turn of another.

The turn transition matrix can take either of two forms, depending upon whether the quarter-second time frames that make up turns or whole turns are the units of analysis. When the units are time frames, each transition can be either to a moment in a new turn or to a continuing moment in the old turn. When the units are turns, each transition will be to a new person's turn; it is not possible to have two consecutive turns from the same person. When turns are the unit of analysis, there will be empty cells in the diagonal of the first order (i.e., *t* to *t* + 1) transitional matrix. These empty cells constitute "structural" zeros, necessarily there because a person's turn cannot be followed immediately by another turn from that same person. Structural zeros are different from "observed" zeros, where transitions would have been possible but did not occur. This restriction of structural zeros exists only in the turn-to-turn matrix, not in the time frame-to-time frame matrix.

Table III shows how these two approaches can be used to summarize a group conversation. The table summarizes one group of five subjects in the brainstorming study. The matrix on the left is based upon 176 individual turn transitions in a session that lasted almost 20 minutes, and the matrix on the right is based upon 4781 quarter-second time frame transitions in the same session. In both cases cell entries show the conditional probability that, given a turn or a time frame belonging to the subject in row *i*, the next turn or the next time frame

TABLE III

TRANSITIONAL MATRICES SHOWING TURN TAKING AMONG FIVE SUBJECTS
IN A BRAINSTORMING GROUP[a]

		Speaker at turn $t + 1$				
		A	B	C	D	E
Speaker at turn t	A	—	.43	.25	.21	.11
	B	.20	—	.17	.35	.28
	C	.38	.48	—	.05	.10
	D	.11	.57	.09	—	.23
	E	.13	.58	.06	.23	—

		Speaker at time $t + 1$				
		A	B	C	D	E
Speaker at time t	A	.95	.02	.01	.01	.00
	B	.01	.97	.00	.01	.01
	C	.02	.03	.93	.00	.01
	D	.00	.02	.00	.97	.00
	E	.04	.02	.00	.01	.97

[a]The upper matrix is a summary of 176 turns, and transitions are from turn to turn. The lower matrix is a summary of 4781 quarter-second time frame units, and transitions are from time frame to time frame. Cell entries are conditional probabilities. Entry in cell ij represents the conditional probability that the speaker in row i at time t will be followed by the speaker in column j at lag $t + 1$.

will belong to the subject from column j. Diagonal entries on the left are empty, because the same subject cannot immediately follow himself or herself with a new turn. Diagonal entries on the right are high, because with moments as brief as a quarter-second it is very likely that the next moment will be a continuation of the same speaker's turn. Diagonal entries in each of the matrices would be quite different in other than first-order transitional matrices (i.e., matrices summarizing the state of affairs at varying lags into the future). Subjects can always have another turn again after a lag in which someone else has had a turn, and the likelihood that the same turn will continue unchanged decreases as the lag in quarter-second time frames increases.

2. Overall Predictability of Turn Taking

We wish to know whether there is predictability in the turn-taking matrix. If we find an overall predictability, we can go on to search for the specific sequences of turns, coalition formations, and other group processes that might account for the predictability. Overall predictability can be expressed in terms of a contingency between rows and columns in the turn-taking matrix. If there is contingency, rows and columns are not independent of one another; knowing who the speaker is at time t will tell us something about who the speaker will be at time $t + 1$.

A chi square test for quasi-independence appears to us the best way to analyze the turn-by-turn matrices, where structural zeros in the diagonal make true independence impossible. We used Bakeman's ELAG program (1983) to tabulate the observed turn-taking matrix for each of the 60 groups in the three studies. We then used an iterative procedure described by Castellan (1979) to generate expected values for each cell, with diagonal cells set equal to zero and cell entries otherwise computed so as to be proportional to row and column totals. Chi squares were then computed to test the difference between observed and expected values in the matrix for each group. Degrees of freedom for each chi square test were [(rows—1) (columns—1)]—(number of structural zeros) = 11, requiring that chi square be greater than 19.68 to be significant at the $p < .05$ level. Sixteen of the sixty chi squares were significant at the $p < .05$ level. The individual chi squares and degrees of freedom can also be summed to produce an overall chi square of 981.02 with 660 degrees of freedom. Estimating significance for this large number of degrees of freedom using the procedure given by Dixon and Massey (1969), the overall chi square is significant at the $p < .001$ level. There is contingency in turn taking; knowing who has the turn at turn t helps tell us who will have the turn at turn $t + 1$.

We examined predictability in the time frame-to-time frame matrices using a similar procedure, but here there were no structural zeros to complicate matters. We used Bakeman's JNT4 program (1979b) to tabulate the observed frame-to-frame turn-taking matrix for each of the 60 groups, then computed chi square tests for each group. Without the structural zeros, degrees of freedom for each chi square test were (rows—1) (columns—1) = 16, requiring that chi square be greater than 26.30 to be significant at the $p < .05$ level. All of the 60 chi squares were significant at this level, indicating greater predictibility from time frame to time frame than from turn to turn. The chi square values ranged from 1,705.40 to 20,354.82, which are high enough to arouse suspicion. Examination of the matrices revealed that by far the largest entries were in the diagonal cells. It appears that while transition among frames is predictable, the predictability is largely trivial, arising from the fact that the average turn lasts for several time frames. One can thus predict with assurance that the average next frame will be a continuation of the same speaker's turn.

3. Turn Taking among Pairs of Members

Analysis of the t to $t + 1$ turn-taking matrix indicates some overall degree of predictability or order. We need now identify more specifically the patterns that contribute to this order. In so doing, we move from a test of overall significance to more detailed findings.

One way of examining turn taking more closely would be to look for recurring sequences or chains of turns. Such chains have been examined in studies of family conversation by Haley (1964) and more recently by Parker (1984), both of whom found more structure in disturbed than in normal families. For example, in disturbed triads Haley found father–mother–child rather than the more direct father–child chains, and Parker found chains linking mother–father and mother–child, but not father–child. Bakeman's ESEQ program (1979a) is well suited for this kind of analysis. ESEQ will count specified chains and compute z scores to indicate the degree to which these chains occur more or less frequently than expected by chance. Unfortunately, with our homogeneous and short-lived ad hoc groups of subjects there is little reason to employ such a detailed analysis of chains, because there is little basis for specifying what chains we expect to appear. With hierarchical groups, or groups that have existed for a longer period of time, or groups in which clear leadership has emerged, it would be interesting to examine in detail the various possible sequential patterns of chains.

A second way of examining the turn-taking matrix in more detail would be to see how often overall group activity becomes centered in particular subgroups. For example, subjects in a given pair may tend to interact with one another to the exclusion of other group members. Kenny's SOREMO program (Kenney et al., 1983) provides a way of computing, for each subject A and each other subject B, the average correlation of A's talking after B with B's talking after A. SOREMO is designed for use with peer ratings but can be applied to any data in matrix form, such as the conditional probability scores shown in the left matrix in Table III.

One of SOREMO's outputs is the reciprocity correlation, the correlation between cell ij and cell ji, computed across all the cross-diagonal pairs of cells in a matrix. These are the cells that could show reciprocity of talking, and the example in Table III shows some of this kind of reciprocity between subjects A and C. The highest conditional probability in C's column is for turns following subject A (.25), and the highest conditional probability in A's column is for turns following subject C (.38). Insofar as such pairings tend to appear in all of the groups, the reciprocity correlation will be significant. We should note here that C following A and A following C does not necessarily imply the existence of A-C-A-C chains of turns. Instead, A may follow C a number of times and then C follow A a number of times, without direct alternation back and forth between the two. But regardless of whether reciprocity reflects sequential pairs or longer sequential chains, it indicates a link between two persons.

The SOREMO reciprocity correlation pooled across all 60 groups was $r = .42$, $df = 540$, $p < .001$, indicating a significant tendency for such cross-diagonal pairing. When the three studies were analyzed separately, reciprocity correlations in the problem-solving, brainstorming, and get-acquainted groups were .27, .40, and .62, respectively ($df = 180$, $p < .001$ for each). The reciprocity correlations for the problem-solving and brainstorming groups were not significantly different from each other, but both were significantly different from the reciprocity correlation for the get-acquainted groups, z's = 4.22 and 2.84, respectively ($p < .01$). Perhaps the get-acquainted groups, being least restrained by task demands, allowed most freedom for subjects to respond to others who had responded to them.

We also computed the SOREMO reciprocity correlation separately for each group, and the resulting r for each group was taken as an index of subgroup pair formation within the group. We then compared this r with the chi square representing contingency from t to $t + 1$ in the turn-to-turn transitional matrix. The correlation between r and chi square values, computed across the 60 groups and partialing out differences between the three studies, was $r = .40$ ($df = 56$, $p < .001$). It appears that the overall chi square for the turn-taking matrix at least in part reflected a tendency toward subgroup pairing within a group.

4. Turn Taking at Various Lags

In addition to looking for systematic patterns of turn taking in the t to $t + 1$ matrix, one can look for patterns at greater lags: $t + 2$, $t + 3$, $t + 4$, etc. Here we find useful the information statistic T. Where H referred to uncertainty in a set of states, T refers to predictability in pairs of states. H applies when one wants to know the state that exists at some instant and is ignorant of both past and future. T applies when one knows one state of a two-state sequence and wants to predict the other state. T, representing transmitted or shared information, is the degree to which knowledge of the state at time t reduces our uncertainty about the state at time $t + 1$. T can be computed for any lag, quantifying the extent to which the present state predicts the future at that lag.

In the case of a transitional matrix, H refers to the marginals and T refers to the whole matrix. T is analogous to chi square, describing the contingency between rows and columns. It has advantages over chi square in being expressed in the common metric of bits and in not being inflated by the number of cases that enter into the computations. The lowest value T can have is zero, when knowledge of the row state (the speaker at time t) reduces none of our uncertainty about the ensuing column state (the speaker at time $t + 1$). This could happen if A, B, C, D, and E followed one another randomly in all the 25 possible pairings in a 5 $\times$ 5 matrix; that is, knowing the speaker at a given moment would provide no clue as to who would speak next. The highest value T can have is the value of H for columns, which happens when the row state predicts perfectly the ensuing column state. For example, if A, B, C, D, and E have turns equally, H for

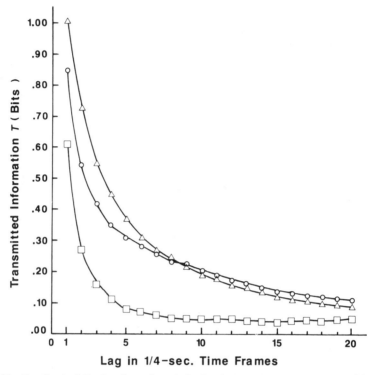

Fig. 2.   Graph of T values for each study for lags in quarter-second time frames. ☐——☐, problem solving; △——△, brainstorming; ○——○, getting acquainted.

columns will be equal to log 5 = 2.32, and there will be maximum uncertainty about who will speak at a given moment. But if B always follows A, C follows B, D follows C, E follows D, and A follows E, knowing the speaker at a given moment will predict perfectly who will speak next; all the uncertainty about the ensuing state will be reduced, and the value of T will be 2.32.

We examined T in the turn-taking matrix at various lags, to see how predictability might decline as we moved further into the future. Using Bakeman's JNT4 program, we tabulated the time frame-to-time frame transitional matrix for each group at lags of 1, 2, . . . 20 seconds. T was computed for each group at each of the resulting 20 one-second lags. The results are summarized for the three studies in Fig. 2.

A note is in order concerning problems of computing T for turn-by-turn rather than frame-by-frame transitional matrices. Structural zeros in the diagonal cells of the turn-by-turn matrix, arising because subjects cannot follow themselves immediately, impose a degree of order, or predictability, upon the transitional matrix. Computing T with these zeros included thus inflates the sequential contingency among speakers. This problem is discussed at length by Steier, Stanton, and Todd (1982). It can be handled with some difficulty by using an iterative procedure to generate a pseudo matrix for each group, with diagonal cells set equal to zero and cell entries otherwise computed so as to be proportional to row and column totals. T computed from this pseudo matrix represents the theoretical minimum value that can be obtained when subjects do not follow themselves, and T computed from the observed matrix can be interpreted in terms of the degree to which it exceeds this theoretical minimum. But the problem becomes increasingly difficult as the number of lags increases, and we chose not to pursue this turn-by-turn analysis.

Figure 2 shows, for all studies, an initial high level of transmitted information declining toward asymptote over a period of 20 seconds. Initial predictability exists because the average turn lasts several seconds and is therefore likely to continue unchanged (i.e., the "transition" is likely to be back to itself) from one moment to the next. This predictability declines rapidly over a period of a few seconds. It would be important to know what variables affect the overall predictability of turn taking. In this regard the differences between the three studies shown in Fig. 2 are provocative but difficult to interpret. Analysis of variance based upon the mean T for each group (averaged across all 20 lags) showed significant differences among the studies, $F(2, 57) = 11.16$, $p < .001$, with desert survival problem-solving groups especially low in predictability.

5. Is Turn Taking a Markov Process?

Jaffe and Feldstein (1970) concluded that transitions between states of sound and silence in dialogues approximate a first-order Markov model. Such a model may apply to the larger groups we studied. We do not view mathematical modeling as being of central importance to our work here, but we are pursuing it for several reasons. It may show that questions of group process can be addressed fruitfully by investigators who come from the mathematical modeling tradition of psychology. It may strengthen our argument that understanding of conversation can be advanced independent of analyses of content. And it may add a new language, and therefore to some extent a new way of thinking, to the study of group processes.

In the Grouptalk model, considering only the turns of individuals, conversation in a five-person group moves always within a set of five mutually exclusive and exhaustive states, the turn states of persons A, B, C, D, and E. The state of the conversation at time $t + 1$ depends to a large extent upon its state at time t. Predictability declines dramatically as time increases. This situation is suggestive of the operation of a first-order Markov process, a stochastic process in which knowledge of the state at time t is sufficient to predict the state at time $t + 1$. Such a process has very limited "memory"; one need only know what has happened at a single given time, not also what happened at earlier times, to predict what will happen next. People obviously remember much of what they have been talking about, and their memory affects what they will say next. But with simple matters of sound and silence and of who speaks now and who speaks next, knowledge of the current state alone may be enough to allow one to predict the next state.

To the extent that a phenomenon approximates a first-order Markov model, one can predict future conditional probabilities at successive time lags (t to $t + 2$, $t + 3, \ldots ,t + n$) by raising to successive powers the first-order transitional matrix (the t to $t + 1$ matrix). The adequacy of a first-order Markov model is usually assessed by squaring the first-order transitional matrix and seeing how closely the resulting predicted conditional probabilities at time $t + 2$ correspond to the observed conditional probabilities at time $t + 2$. We did this with each of the 60 groups in the present data. We squared each transitional matrix to obtain predicted conditional probability values, used Bakeman's JNT4 and ELAG programs to tabulate observed conditional probability values from the raw data at lag $t + 2$, and used chi square tests to assess the goodness of fit between predicted and observed conditional probability values.

We did this with whole speaking turns and with quarter-second time frames as the unit of analysis. In the frame-by-frame analysis, the chi square goodness-of-fit tests were nonsignificant for 56 of the 60 groups. The median chi square value was 4.24, and a value of 26.30 is required for significance at the .05 level with the $df = 16$ of a 5×5 matrix. These general failures of the chi square tests indicate that the first-order Markov model is probably an adequate fit; we cannot reject the hypothesis that the frame-to-frame transitions in turn taking follow such a model.

In the turn-by-turn analysis the situation was different. Here the chi square tests were significant for 50 out of the 60 groups, with a median value of 37.24. The turn-to-turn transitions, unlike the frame-to-frame transitions, do not fit the predictions of a first-order Markov model very well. Something more than knowledge of the current state is needed to predict the next state. We suspect this may be in part due to the fact, as indicated below, that turns from the same speaker tend to be "clustered" together, rather than distributed randomly over the course of a session.

C. DISTRIBUTION AND CLUSTERING OF TURNS

The analysis of turn-taking sequences revealed some structure, although perhaps less than we would have found in natural groups outside the laboratory. Another kind of structure involves the way in which turns are clustered over time. In listening to the group conversations, it seemed to us that activity would sometimes increase into a flurry of turn taking and at other times decrease and be replaced by long pauses and switching pauses. Perusal of the turn-taking matrices also revealed some unevenness in the flow of turns. Subjects seemed especially likely to follow themselves after one or two others had interjected turns. A subject would speak, another would speak, and the original subject would speak again. This might reflect a tendency for subjects to speak in clusters of turns, or "megaturns," holding the floor more or less continuously for a period of time while others offered brief comments, questions, or back-channel utterances (Dabbs, 1983a,b).

In examining this phenomenon, it may be appropriate first to determine how the whole set of turns in a group discussion is distributed over time. Jaffe and Feldstein (1970) found that vocalizations and pause lengths in monologues and dialogues were distributed exponentially, and subsequent analyses of their data revealed that turn lengths were also exponential (S. Feldstein, personal communication), with shortest turns most frequent. For each group we tabulated the time, in seconds, from the beginning of each turn to the beginning of the next turn. Turns of the five group members constitute a set of five mutually exclusive and exhaustive states; in Markovian language the time between changes of turn states would be called "wait time." We produced frequency distributions of the wait times for each group and used Kolmogorov–Smirnov tests in Phillips' (1972) Goodness-of-Fit program to see whether each distribution departed significantly from a theoretical exponential distribution of the same data. The tests were not statistically significant for any of the 60 groups, indicating that turn lengths probably are exponentially distributed for groups, as Jaffe and Feldstein found them to be for dyads.

It remained to be seen how the turns of individuals were distributed and whether they might be clustered together more than would be expected by chance. It is not immediately apparent what theoretical model best describes the distribution of turns, but we began by exploring the Poisson distribution. The Poisson distribution is used in queuing theory and in quality control applications to describe errors and equipment failures. Poisson distributions result from multiplicative combinations of random effects, where an event does not appear unless several determining factors occur at once. In our data, we considered that a new turn does not appear for a given subject unless the subject has finished speaking, someone else has spoken, and the original subject again has something to say and can get the floor to say it. Because of the essentially random quality of many determining factors, turns will not appear on a perfectly even schedule. Even when the rate of turn taking is constant over longer periods of time, local fluctuations will necessarily produce some clustering. A few longer-than-average turns will require that others be shorter than average, and a few placed closely together will require that others be farther apart, and the result will be some unevenness in the distribution, or some clustering. We were interested in knowing whether clustering in our data was in excess of this expected amount.

We assessed the clustering for each of the 300 subjects by tabulating the time, in seconds, from the beginning of one turn to the beginning of that subject's next turn. There is no standard designation in the literature for this time period, during which the turn states of several other subjects might have intervened, but here we will call it "cycle time." We produced frequency distributions of cycle times for each subject. These frequency distributions had the appearance of being Poisson, but their positive skew was extreme. The expected values of mean and variance are equal for a Poisson distribution, but for most of our subjects the mean was far smaller than the variance. We used Kolmogorov–Smirnov tests in Phillips' (1972) Goodness-of-Fit program to see whether each distribution departed significantly from a theoretical Poisson distribution of the same data. The tests were statistically significant at the .05 level for 299 of the 300 subjects, indicating far more clustering than would be predicted on the basis of a Poisson distribution.

The Poisson distribution thus provides a poor model of how an individual's turns are distributed, perhaps because it underestimates the frequency of short turns and therefore the amount of clustering. However, the Poisson distribution may provide a useful benchmark against which to quantify individual differences in turn clustering. We used the Kolmogorov–Smirnov D as an index of the extent to which clustering of turns exceeded that predicted by the Poisson model for each individual, and we correlated D for each subject with the peer ratings given that subject. Subjects whose turns were less clustered, or more evenly distributed over time, were rated more highly by their peers. The pooled within-group correlation between peer ratings and clustering was $r = -.60$ ($df = 239$, $p < .001$).

Because the Poisson distribution did not provide an adequate model for the distribution of individual cycle times, we used the Goodness-of-Fit program to see whether these times might be exponentially distributed. It appeared that they were; Kolmogorov–Smirnov tests failed to reject the hypothesis that the distributions were exponential in 287 of the 300 cases. Perhaps this is to be expected, because the cycle between two turns for a subject lasts through the intervening turns of other subjects, which themselves presumably come from exponential distributions. The analogy we drew between turns and the equipment failures the Poisson distribution describes so well may have been misleading for the following reason. Equipment failures have no sequential dependency, and there can be an indefinite wait between two of them, while turns must follow other turns with little delay or the conversation will end.

In trying to describe the distribution of turns and turn clustering, we are left with a less than satisfying situation. Turns are distributed exponentially, for groups and for individuals. But there are differences among individuals, and these differences are related to how much a set of turns is clustered or distributed evenly over time. We need to characterize both the overall phenomenon of turn distribution and individual differences in this distribution. An adequate analysis of the clustering of turns in conversations may depend upon better statistical techniques, some of which are being developed for applications in epidemiology and health (cf. Schweder, 1984; Tango, 1984) and elsewhere in social psychology (cf. Bond, Jones, & Weintraub, 1985).

Finally, looking at an overall contrast between the two halves of each session, we examined the extent to which each subject's turns occurred more toward the beginning of a group discussion. Each subject was assigned a score representing the percentage of his or her total turns emitted during the first half of the session. This score also proved to be negatively correlated with peer ratings (pooled within-group $r = -.30$, $p < .001$). Low-rated members, in addition to not participating much, participate less as time goes on.

D. COMPARISON TO PRIOR RESEARCH

In contrast to our results concerning amount of vocal activity, which are consistent with a large body of research, our results concerning structure generally add more to our knowledge of groups. We have examined two general kinds of structure: vocal similarity and sequential relationships among group members. Some of our findings are consistent with prior research. Vocal similarity, or congruence, among group members exists and is associated with liking for the group, as described by Feldstein and Welkowitz for dyads and as would be expected from a large body of literature in social psychology on similarity and attraction. Our finding that leaders tend to participate equally throughout the session whereas nonleaders tend to participate less over time is consistent with results of a study by Collins (cited in Collins & Guetzkow, 1964, p. 175), who found that while a status hierarchy is being formed individuals tend to communicate relatively more to low-status persons, while after the hierarchy is formed high-status individuals tend to communicate among themselves.

Other findings are more novel, such as that greater uncertainty in who will speak is associated with attractiveness of the group; that the reciprocity correlation, indicating more vocalization among subset pairs of group members, is higher in purely social groups; that the moment-to-moment transitions among turn states approximate a first-order Markov model; that the predictability of turn taking extends further into the future with some kinds of groups than with others; and that the turns of individual members are clustered rather than distributed evenly over time. To a large extent these positive findings arise from our avoidance of static summary measures. Conversation is a continuously changing sequential process, and vocal measures recorded on a time base can be analyzed to reveal complex interrelationships among group members that change over time.

VIII.   Conclusion

We have argued that at least part of the process of group interaction can be described in terms of content-free measures and that these measures can be considered in terms of two dimensions, amount and structure. In this final section, we deal with three issues. First, we examine the question of whether amount and structure are really independent dimensions. Second, we consider what these dimensions tell us about traditional measures of the outcome of group interaction. Finally, we explore the question of whether these dimensions can be useful for understanding other measures of group process.

A.   INDEPENDENCE OF AMOUNT
AND STRUCTURE DIMENSIONS

Thus far, we have assumed that amount and structure are independent dimensions. However, it is certainly reasonable to ask whether the two are really orthogonal. For example, one might expect increased talking by many speakers to interfere with orderly patterns of turn taking, because potential speakers will not inhibit their talk and "wait their turn," and the episodes of "dyadic turns" will be interrupted by other group members. But one could equally well argue that a conversation could have both a high level of vocal activity and a high level of order in the sequential patterning among members.

Ultimately the question of the independence of these dimensions is an empirical one. Our observation of small groups both inside and outside the laboratory suggests that the activity level and orderliness of conversations are to a large extent unrelated to one another. In addition, in partial answer to the question of independence, we correlated the amount of talking (the percentage of time someone was talking) in each of the 60 groups with measures of structure examined in this chapter. These correlations, controlling for differences among the three studies and presented in the order the measures were discussed above, were as follows: with member congruence in mean length of vocalization, pause, and switching pause, $r = .35$, $-.37$, and $-.32$, respectively; with member equality in amount of talk (H), $r = -.03$; with chi square for predictability from t to $t + 1$ in the frame-to-frame turn-taking matrix, $r = .33$; with chi square for predictability from t to $t + 1$ in the turn-to-turn matrix, $r = .05$; with the SOREMO "relationship" coefficient in cross-diagonal pairing in talking part-

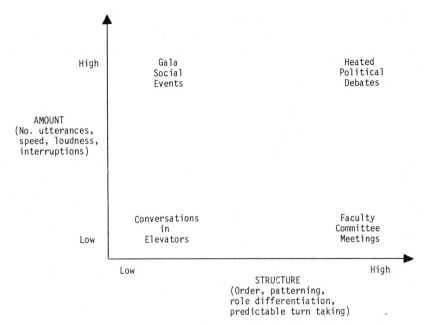

Fig. 3.   Typical groups at different levels of vocal activity and structure.

ners, $r = .12$; and with turn clustering (D) at the group level, $r = .10$. These generally low correlations indicate considerable independence between amount and structure, as we have operationalized the terms.

Given that amount and structure are relatively independent, a next question might be how they jointly predict group process. Our belief is that a conversation can have a high or low level of vocal activity and a high or low level of order in the patterning among members. The situation as we see it is summarized in Fig. 3. Moving up from bottom to top, we find group members talking louder and faster, pausing less, and interrupting each other more. Moving from left to right, we find more of several kinds of "order," with more congruence or matching, longer turns, and more predictable sequences of turn taking among the group members. Intuitively, the abscissa (order) and ordinate (amount) seem to us to correspond to task and social dimensions of group activity. Obviously, however, this conjecture calls for further research. In the figure, we have speculated about the kinds of groups that might fit in the four combinations of amount and order.

In drawing the figure we have emphasized the arousal of positive affects as we move up the ordinate. It is also possible that negative affects—anger, hostility, argument—would be associated with more vocal activity, which would change the labels of groups we have placed in the four cells. A program of research oriented around this figure would have to deal both with treatment conditions that move group process to different points of this surface and with outcomes that result from having group process positioned at different points. There also remains an unresolved question of whether our dimensions, particularly structure, are sufficiently unidimensional to be treated as the dimensions of a two-coordinate system.

B.   RELATION TO OUTCOME

Assuming that the vocal measures we have discussed in this chapter are reflective of underlying group process, it is reasonable to ask whether these same measures have any relationship to what are usually considered to be measures of the outcome of group process. Our research (Dabbs and Ruback, 1984; Dabbs *et al.*, 1987; Ruback *et al.*, 1984) showed that at both the individual and the group level, measures of amount are related to liking. At the individual level, individuals who talked more were rated higher in leadership. Even when amount of talking was controlled for, these leaders still showed variations in the amount of silence that surrounded their vocalizations. These leaders had a higher percentage of time in latencies before they started talking and in switching pauses after their vocalizations, and their mean latencies and switching pauses were longer than those of nonleaders. At the group level, groups were liked more if there was more talking and liked less if there was more time spent in switching pauses. In terms of structure, liking for the group was positively related to congruence and to uncertainty about who will speak next. The fact that some kinds of structure (congruence) seem to add to group attractiveness while others (certainty in speaking order) seem to detract suggests that it is premature to pick any one statistic as a measure of structure.

The only measure of group productivity we used in the three studies was the number of ideas in the brainstorming study (Ruback *et al.*, 1984). There we found that ideas tended to follow periods of switching pauses rather than vocalizations or pauses. In sum, our research suggests that amount and structure of vocal interaction do relate to measures of outcome. But it is also clear that the groups we investigated were all composed of five previously unacquainted college students. The question of how our process measures might relate to outcomes in established groups needs to be investigated further.

C.   APPLICATION TO OTHER DOMAINS OF PROCESS

Given that amount and structure capture the nature of vocal interaction in groups and that they are related to measures of group output, the next question is whether amount and structure can be used to describe other areas of group process (i.e., thinking, feeling, working). It is with this in mind that we propose the model shown in Table IV.

Table IV is an elaboration of a model proposed by Hackman and Morris (1975), based upon an earlier model by McGrath (1964), that specifies a number of input, process, and outcome variables. Our focus is upon process, the first three areas of which we have listed as working, thinking, and feeling. These three reflect the familiar tripartite division of human nature, ranging from the heart, head, and gut of Plato to the behavior, cognition, and affect of contemporary social psychology. Other writers might use other terms. For example, McGrath (1984) describes process in terms of communication, action, attraction, and influence. We think the particular terms are less important than that a range of terms be used that is sufficiently broad to capture what goes on in group process.

The main point we wish to make about this model is that variables in each one of these areas can be measured in terms of amount and structure. For example, for working, amount could be measured by effort expended and structure measured by the degree of integration of member contributions. For thinking, amount could be measured by number of ideas produced and structure measured by the similarity among members in number or quality of ideas produced. For feeling, amount could be measured by the number of nonverbal displays and structure measured by the patterns of these behaviors over time.

Our analyses were conducted on time-patterned frequency data. In like fashion, similar scores could be obtained for measures of the other types of group process. These scores could be summed to produce total amount of group activity, and structure could be analyzed using the same statistics we used here to investigate the patterning of talk among group members.

D. FUTURE DIRECTIONS

The methods we have outlined here can be used to investigate a number of theoretically important questions. In the introduction, we hypothesized a number of relationships among (1) factors about the task, the group, and the individual members, (2) the amount and structure of activity during the group interaction, and (3) the group's performance and group members' liking for the group. Although some of these hypothesized relationships have empirical support, many, particularly those involving the structure of group interaction, have not been tested. It seems to us that testing these hypotheses, even if they are relatively atheoretical, would establish a stronger knowledge base for later theoretical developments.

Although we believe the methods and statistical procedures we have discussed here are useful in their own right, we also believe that they would be best

TABLE IV

ELABORATED MODEL OF GROUP INTERACTION

Input	Process	Outcome
Individuals	*Working*	*Individuals*
Personality: Sex, age, talkativeness, ethnic origin, experience, confidence	Expending physical energy, assigning tasks, forming work subgroups, coordinating performances, using resources, working toward goals	Evaluations of one another Attraction to the group Mood, fatigue, boredom, excitement, achievement
Ability: Ideas, specific knowledge, cognitive skills, social skills		
Motivation: High or low, task or social	Measures:	*Group*
Expectations: Of status, of roles	Amount: Effort and time expended	Cohesiveness, esprit Reaction to success or failure Final role structure, hierarchy
	Structure:	Leadership
Group	Member similarity of contribution	Summary of communication patterns
History, prior experience	Member interaction	
Esprit	Complexity of production process	*Production*
Attractiveness, cohesiveness, conformity pressures	Development of role structure	Achievement of goals
Homogeneity of membership		Amount and complexity of work accomplished
Role structure		Quality of work accomplished
Leadership, assigned or not, directive or democratic	*Thinking*	Number and complexity of ideas produced
Expectation of success	Using ideas, remembering, creating, evaluating, supporting, opposing	Quality of ideas produced
Clarity of goals	Measures:	
	Amount:	
Situation	Number of ideas processed	
Task: Type, complexity, interest, familiarity, difficulty	Quality of processing (thoroughness, efficiency, tenacity)	
Reward structure, time pressures	Use of all members' inputs	
Autonomy, authority, legitimacy	Structure:	
Others' expectations: Supportive, critical, demanding	Member similarity of contribution	
Environmental factors: Shape of table, noise, temperature, time of day	Complexity of member interaction	
	Coalition formation and change, polarization, groupthink	
	Feeling	
	Sharing, encouraging, emot-	

TABLE IV *(Continued)*

Input	Process	Outcome
	Feeling (cont.)	

Feeling (cont.)
ing, cajoling, empathizing,
criticizing, attacking
Measures:
Amount:
  Affective statements,
    laughter, shouts
  Nonverbal displays
    (smiles, movements,
    expressions, tones of
    voice)
Structure:
  Member similarity of
    affect
  Nonverbal or affective
    interaction among
    members
  Affective coalitions
  Affective changes over
    time

Talking
Speaking, pausing, interrupt-
ing, taking turns
Measures:
Amount:
  Number, percentage,
    mean duration of indi-
    vidual and group vocal
    codes
  Rate, loudness, inflection
Structure:
  Member similarity in vo-
    cal behavior (vocal
    codes, loudness, rate,
    inflection, accent,
    dialect)
  Patterns of turn taking
  Temporal clustering of
    vocalizations
  Episodic and cyclical
    changes in
    vocalization

used in conjunction with other, more traditional procedures. For example, consider Steiner's (1972) notion of process loss, the interference with group performance that arises from lack of coordination, low motivation, and other factors. In trying to understand exactly what is entailed in process loss, researchers would certainly have to consider the content of group members' statements as well as the content-free variables we have discussed. Similarly, distinctions between stages in ongoing groups, such as Tuckman's (1965) forming, storming, norming, and performing or McGrath's (1984) generate, choose, negotiate, and execute, might be tested by using both content and content-free measures to determine whether the underlying processes are the same for all types of tasks.

Moreover, it would be worthwhile to use the techniques we have described here to examine the socialization process in small groups (Moreland & Levine, 1982). Moreland and Levine posit changes over time at both the individual and group level as new members become socialized into an existing group, changes that might appear in the content and in the amount and structure of group conversations. It seems to us that theories like group socialization, which deal with variables at both the individual and group level, would be particularly amenable to the procedures outlined here.

In addition, we would like to see applications to areas of group activity beyond talk. Ruback et al. (1984) used a moment-by-moment sequential analysis of the production of ideas in brainstorming, finding that ideas emerged following times of increased switching pauses. Group processes might be traced through a fabric of words, gaze, facial expressions, gestures, bodily postures, affect, arrival and departure of members, problem assignments, and problem solutions. Work groups, especially in the mundane world outside the laboratory, are often involved in processes that employ no vocalizations at all. Sophisticated equipment would not be needed for much of this work; Parker (1984) produced an enlightening study of turn taking among family members using paper and pencil recording. All that is really needed is careful attention to detail and acceptance of the notion that group process involves changes over time.

E. SUMMARY

We have attempted to bring together the work of Hackman and Morris, Bales, and Jaffe and Feldstein into a model that is both manageable and intricate enough to capture subtle details of ongoing group process. The measures we have used have been content free, and clearly they alone cannot do justice to group phenomena. But the approach of dividing process variables into amount and structure and of recording variables on a time base that will allow complex sequential analyses has proved useful with the vocal data. Moreover, this approach can be extended to other domains of group interaction. We hope this work will encourage others to look more closely at the form and function of group process.

ACKNOWLEDGMENTS

We would like to thank David Kenny and Joseph McGrath for their helpful comments on earlier versions of this chapter.

REFERENCES

Alberti, L. (1974). *Some lexical correlates of speaker switching frequency in conversation.* Paper read at Eighteenth International Congress of Applied Psychology, Montreal.

Attneave, F. (1959). *Applications of information theory to psychology.* New York: Holt.

Back, K. (1951). Influence through social communication. *Journal of Abnormal and Social Psychology,* **46,** 9–24.

Bakeman, R. (1975). Data analyzing procedures (Tech. Rep. 2). Atlanta: Georgia State University, Infancy Laboratory.

Bakeman, R. (1979a). *Analyzing event sequence data: Computer programs ELAG and ESEQ.* Unpublished paper, Georgia State University.

Bakeman, R. (1979b). *Analyzing sequential data: Computer programs JNT1, JNT3, and JNT4.* Unpublished paper, Georgia State University.

Bakeman, R, (1983). Computing lag sequential statistics: The ELAG program. *Behavior Research Methods and Instrumentation,* **15,** 530–535.

Bakeman, R., & Dabbs, J. M., Jr. (1976). Social interaction observed: Some approaches to the analysis of behavior streams. *Personality and Social Psychology Bulletin,* **2,** 335–345.

Bales, R. F. (1950a). A set of categories for the analysis of small group interaction. *American Sociological Review,* **15,** 257–263.

Bales, R. F. (1950b). *Interaction process analysis: A method for the study of small groups.* Cambridge, MA: Addison-Wesley.

Bales, R. F. (1953). The equilibrium problem in small groups. In T. Parsons, R. F. Bales, & E. A. Shils (Eds.), *Working papers in the theory of action.* Glencoe, IL: Free Press.

Bales, R. F. (1970). *Personality and interpersonal behavior.* New York: Holt.

Bales, R. F., & Cohen, S. P. (1979). *SYMLOG: A system for the multiple level observation of groups.* New York: Free Press.

Bales, R. F., & Slater, P. E. (1955). Role differentiation. In T. Parsons, R. F. Bales *et al.* (Eds.), *The family, socialization, and interaction process.* Glencoe, IL: Free Press.

Bales, R. F., & Strodtbeck, F. L. (1951). Phases in group problem solving. *Journal of Abnormal and Social Psychology,* **46,** 485–495.

Bass, B. M. (1981). *Stogdill's handbook of leadership.* New York: Free Press.

Bass, B. M., Pryer, M. W., Gaier, E. L., & Flint, A. W. (1958). Interacting effects of control, motivation, group practice, and problem difficulty on attempted leadership. *Journal of Abnormal and Social Psychology,* **56,** 352–358.

Bavelas, A. (1948). A mathematical model for group structure. *Applied Anthropology,* **7,** 16–30.

Bion, W. R. (1961). *Experiences in groups: And other papers.* New York: Basic Books.

Bond, C. F., Jr., Jones, R. L., & Weintraub, D. L. (1985). On the unconstrained recall of acquaintances: A sampling-traversal model. *Journal of Personality and Social Psychology,* **49,** 327–337.

Borgatta, E. F., & Bales, R. F. (1953). Interaction of individuals in reconstituted groups. *Sociometry*, **16**, 302–320.

Bovard, E. W., Jr. (1951). Group structure and perception. *Journal of Abnormal and Social Psychology*, **46**, 398–405.

Brown, B. L. (1979). Effects of speech rate on personality attributions and competency evaluations. In H. Giles, W. P. Robinson, & P. M. Smith (Eds.), *Language: Social psychological perspectives*. Oxford: Pergamon.

Campbell, D. T. (1969). Ethnocentrism of disciplines and the fish-scale model of omniscience. In M. Sherif & C. W. Sherif (Eds.), *Interdisciplinary relationships in the social sciences*. Chicago: Aldine.

Cappella, J. N. (1981). Mutual influence in expressive behavior: Adult-adult and infant-adult dyadic interaction. *Psychological Bulletin*, **89**, 101–132.

Castellan, N. J. (1979). The analysis of behavior sequences. In R. B. Cairns (Ed.), *The analysis of social interactions*. Hillsdale, N.J.: Erlbaum.

Chapple, E. D. (1949). The interaction chronograph: Its evolution and present application. *Personnel*, **25**, 295–307.

Cohen, A. M., Bennis, W. G., & Wolkon, G. H. (1961). The effects of continued practice on the behaviors of problem-solving groups. *Sociometry*, **24**, 416–431.

Collins, B. E., & Guetzkow, H. (1964). *A social psychology of group processes for decision-making*. New York: Wiley.

Conrad, D. C., & Conrad, R. (1956). The use of personal pronouns as categories for studying small group interaction. *Journal of Abnormal and Social Psychology*, **52**, 277–279.

Dabbs, J. M., Jr. (1983a). Fourier analysis and the rhythm of conversation. Atlanta: Georgia State University. (ERIC Document Reproduction Service No. ED 222 959).

Dabbs, J. M., Jr. (1983b). Measuring the cognitive load of a conversation: Speech rhythm and speech-gaze patterns. *Psychological Documents*, **13**, 3 (Ms. 2532).

Dabbs, J. M., Jr., Evans, M. S., Hopper, C. H., & Purvis, J. A. (1980). Self-monitors in conversation: What do they monitor? *Journal of Personality and Social Psychology*, **39**, 278–284.

Dabbs, J. M., Jr., & Ruback, R. B. (1984). Vocal patterns in male and female groups. *Personality and Social Psychology Bulletin*, **10**, 518–525.

Dabbs, J. M., Jr., Ruback, R. B., & Evans, M. S. (1987). Grouptalk: Patterns of sound and silence in group conversation. In A. W. Siegman & S. Feldstein (Eds.), *Nonverbal behavior and communication* (2nd ed., pp. 501–520). Hillsdale, NJ: Erlbaum.

Dabbs, J. M., Jr., & Swiedler, T. C. (1983). Group AVTA: A microcomputer system for group voice chronography. *Behavior Research Methods and Instrumentation*, **15**, 79–84.

Dashiell, J. F. (1935). Experimental studies of the influence of social situations on the behavior of individual human adults. In C. Murchison (Ed.), *Handbook of social psychology*. Worcester, MA: Clark University Press.

Davis, D., & Perkowitz, W. T. (1979). Consequences of responsiveness in dyadic interaction: Effects of probability of response and proportion of content-related responses on interpersonal attraction. *Journal of Personality and Social Psychology*, **37**, 534–550.

Davis, J. H. (1963). The preliminary analysis of emergent social structure in groups. *Psychometrika*, **28**, 189–198.

Dixon, W. J., & Massey, F. J., Jr. (1969). *Introduction to statistical analysis* (3rd ed.). New York: McGraw-Hill.

Ellis, D. G., & Fisher, A. (1975). Phases of conflict in small group development: A Markov analysis. *Human Communication Research*, **1**, 195–212.

Feldstein, S., Alberti, L., BenDebba, M., & Welkowitz, J. (1974). *Personality and simultaneous speech*. Paper presented at annual meeting of the American Psychological Association, New Orleans.

Feldstein, S., & Welkowitz, J. (1987). A chronography of conversation: In defense of an objective approach. In A. W. Siegman & S. Feldstein (Eds.), *Nonverbal behavior and communication* (2nd ed., pp. 435–499). Hillsdale, NJ: Erlbaum.

Festinger, L. (1950). Informal social communication. *Psychological Review, 57,* 271–282.

Festinger, L., & Thibaut, J. (1951). Interpersonal communication in small groups. *Journal of Abnormal and Social Psychology, 46,* 92–99.

Freedman, M. B., Leary, T. F., Ossorio, A. B., & Coffey, H. S. (1951). The interpersonal dimension of personality. *Journal of Personality, 20,* 143–161.

Giles, H., & Powesland, P. F. (1975). *Speech style and social evaluation.* New York: Academic Press.

Gottman, J. M. (1979). *Marital interaction: Experimental investigations.* New York: Academic Press.

Gottman, J. M., & Bakeman, R. (1979). The sequential analysis of observational data. In M. E. Lamb, S. J. Suomi, & G. R. Stephenson (Eds.), *Social interaction analysis: Methodological issues.* Madison: University of Wisconsin.

Hackman, J. R., & Morris, C. G. (1975). Group tasks, group interaction process, and group performance effectiveness: A review and proposed integration. In L. Berkowitz (Ed.), *Advances in experimental social psychology* (Vol. 8, pp. 45–99). New York: Academic Press.

Haley, J. (1964). Research on family patterns: An instrument measurement. *Family Process, 3,* 41–65.

Hayes, D., & Meltzer, L. (1972). Interpersonal judgments based upon talkativeness: Fact or artifact. *Sociometry, 35,* 538–561.

Horvath, W. J. (1965). A mathematical model of participation in small group discussion. *Behavioral Science, 10,* 164–166.

Jaffe, J., & Feldstein, S. (1970). *Rhythms of dialogue.* New York: Academic Press.

Janis, I. L. (1972). *Victims of groupthink.* Boston: Houghton Mifflin.

Kasl, S. V., & Mahl, G. F. (1956). A simple device for obtaining certain verbal activity measures during interviews. *Journal of Abnormal and Social Psychology, 53,* 388–390.

Kelley, H. H., & Thibaut, J. W. (1954). Experimental studies of group problem solving and process. In G. Lindzey (Ed.), *Handbook of social psychology* (Vol. 2). Cambridge, MA: Addison-Wesley.

Kelly, J. R., & McGrath, J. E. (1985). Effects of time limits and task types on task performance and interaction of four-person groups. *Journal of Personality and Social Psychology, 49,* 395–407.

Kenny, D. A., Lord, R. G., & Garg, S. (1983). *A social relations analysis of peer ratings.* Unpublished manuscript, University of Connecticut.

Kenny, D. A., & Stigler, J. W. (1983). LEVEL: A FORTRAN IV program for correctional analysis of group-individual data structures. *Behavior Research Methods and Instrumentation, 15,* 606.

Kraut, R. E. (1978). Verbal and nonverbal cues in the perception of lying. *Journal of Personality and Social Psychology, 36,* 380–391.

Lafferty, J. C., & Pond, A. (1974). *The desert survival situation.* Plymouth, MI: Human Synergistics.

Leavitt, H. J. (1951). Some effects of certain communication patterns on group performance. *Journal of Abnormal and Social Psychology, 46,* 38–50.

Locke, E. A. (1968). Toward a theory of task motivation and incentives. *Organizational Behavior and Human Performance, 3,* 157–189.

Locke, E. A., Shaw, K. N., Sasri, L. M., & Latham, G. P. (1981). Goal setting and task performance: 1969–1980. *Psychological Bulletin, 90,* 125–152.

Lustig, M. W. (1980). Computer analysis of talk—silence patterns in triads. *Communication Quarterly, 28,* 3–12.

Marcus, E. S., Welkowitz, J., Feldstein, S., & Jaffe, J. (1970). *Psychological differentiation and the congruence of temporal speech patterns*. Paper presented at the meeting of the Eastern Psychological Association, April, Atlantic City.

Martindale, D. A. (1971). *Effects of environmental context in negotiating situations: Territorial dominance in dyadic interactions*. Unpublished doctoral dissertation, City University of New York.

Matarazzo, J. D., & Wiens, A. N. (1972). *The interview: Research on its anatomy and structure*. Chicago: Aldine-Atherton.

McCroskey, J. C. (1984). The communication apprehension perspective. In J. A. Daly & J. C. McCroskey (Eds.), *Avoiding communication: Shyness, reticence, and communication apprehension* (pp. 13–38). Beverly Hills, CA: Sage.

McGrath, J. E. (1964). *Social psychology: A brief introduction*. New York: Holt.

McGrath, J. E. (1984). *Groups: Interaction and performance*. Englewood Cliffs, NJ: Prentice-Hall.

McGrath, J. E., & Kravitz, D. A. (1982). Group research. In M. R. Rosenzweig & L. W. Porter (Eds.), *Annual review of psychology* (Vol. 33). Palo Alto, CA: Annual Reviews.

McGrath, J. E., Martin J., & Kulka, R. A. (1982). Some quasi-rules for making judgment calls in research. In J. E. McGrath, J. Martin, & R. A. Kulka (Eds.), *Judgment calls in research*. Beverly Hills, CA: Sage.

Meltzer, L., Morris, W., & Hayes, D. (1971). Interruption outcomes and vocal amplitude: Explorations in social psychophysics. *Journal of Personality and Social Psychology, 18*, 392–402.

Miller, G. A. (1956). The magical number seven, plus or minus two: Some limits on our capacity for processing information. *Psychological Review, 63*, 81–97.

Moreland, R. L., & Levine, J. M. (1982). Socialization in small groups: Temporal changes in individual-group relations. In L. Berkowitz (Ed.). *Advances in experimental social psychology* (Vol. 15, pp. 137–197). New York: Academic Press.

Natale, M. (1975). Convergence of mean vocal intensity in dyadic communication as a function of social desirability. *Journal of Personality and Social Psychology, 32*, 790–804.

Osborn, A. F. (1957). *Applied imagination* (rev. ed.). New York: Scribner.

O'Sullivan, M., Ekman, P., Friesen, W., & Scherer, K. (1985). What you say and how you say it: The contribution of speech content and voice quality to judgments of others. *Journal of Personality and Social Psychology, 48*, 54–62.

Parker, K. C. H. (1984). *Speaking sequence based models of group interaction: Relational dominance and involvement in groups and families*. Unpublished doctoral dissertation. University of Western Ontario (Waterloo, Ontario).

Penrod, S., & Hastie, R. (1980). A computer simulation of jury decision making. *Psychological Review, 87*, 133–159.

Phillips, D. T. (1972). *Applied goodness of fit testing*. Norcross, GA: American Institute of Industrial Engineers.

Ruback, R. B., & Dabbs, J. M., Jr. (1986). Talkativeness and verbal aptitude: Perception and reality. *Bulletin of the Psychonomic Society, 24*, 423–426.

Ruback, R. B., & Dabbs, J. M., Jr. (1987). *Group vocal patterns and leadership in India: The effects of type of task, language, and sex of subjects*. Unpublished manuscript, Georgia State University, Atlanta, Georgia.

Ruback, R. B., Dabbs, J. M., Jr., & Hopper, C. H. (1984). The process of brainstorming: An analysis with individual and group vocal parameters. *Journal of Personality and Social Psychology, 47*, 558–567.

Ruback, R. B., & Hopper, C. H. (1986). Decision making by parole interviewers: The effect of case and interview factors. *Law and Human Behavior, 10*, 203–214.

Schachter, S. (1951). Deviation, rejection, and communication. *Journal of Abnormal and Social Psychology, 46*, 190–207.

Schweder, T. (1984). Investigating group-specific clustering in univariate spatial data with many small groups. *Biometrics, 40*, 767–776.

Shannon, C. E., & Weaver, W. (1949). *The mathematical theory of communication.* Urbana, IL: University of Illinois Press.

Shaw, M. E. (1964). Communication networks. In L. Berkowitz (Ed.), *Advances in experimental social psychology* (Vol. 1, pp. 111–147). New York: Academic Press.

Siegman, A. W., & Feldstein, S. (1979). *Of speech and time: Temporal speech patterns in interpersonal contexts.* Hillsdale, NJ: Erlbaum.

Steier, F., Stanton, M. D., & Todd, T. C. (1982). Patterns of turn-taking and alliance formation in family communication. *Journal of Communication, 32,* 148–160.

Stein, R. T., & Heller, T. (1979). An empirical analysis of the correlations between leadership status and participation rates reported in the literature. *Journal of Personality and Social Psychology, 37,* 1993–2002.

Steiner, I. D. (1972). *Group process and productivity.* New York: Academic Press.

Steiner, I. D. (1986). Paradigms and groups. In L. Berkowitz (Ed.), *Advances in experimental social psychology* (Vol. 19, pp. 251–289). Orlando, Fl.: Academic Press.

Stephan, F. F., & Mishler, E. G. (1952). The distribution of participation in small groups: An exponential approximation. *American Sociological Review, 17,* 598–608.

Stock, D., & Thelen, H. A. (1958). *Emotional dynamics and group culture: Experimental studies of individual and group behavior.* New York: New York University Press.

Tanford, S., & Penrod, S. (1984). Social influence model: A formal integration of research on majority and minority influence processes. *Psychological Bulletin, 95,* 189–225.

Tango, T. (1984). The detection of disease clustering in time. *Biometrics, 40,* 15–26.

Tsai, Y. (1977). Hierarchical structure of participation in natural groups. *Behavioral Science, 22,* 38–40.

Tuckman, B. W. (1965). Developmental sequence in small groups. *Psychological Bulletin, 63,* 384–399.

Verzeano, M., & Finesinger, J. E. (1949). An automatic analyzer for the study of speech in interaction and in free association. *Science, 110,* 45–46.

Weick, K. E. (1974). Middle range theories of social systems. *Behavioral Science, 19,* 357–367.

Weiss, R. F., Lombardo, J. P., Warren, D. R., & Kelley, K. A. (1971). Reinforcing effects of speaking in reply. *Journal of Personality and Social Psychology, 20,* 186–199.

Zuckerman, M., DePaulo, B. M., & Rosenthal, R. (1981). Verbal and nonverbal communication of deception. In L. Berkowitz (Ed.), *Advances in experimental social psychology* (Vol. 14, pp. 1–59). New York: Academic Press.

THE DYNAMICS OF OPINION FORMATION

Harold B. Gerard and Ruben Orive

DEPARTMENT OF PSYCHOLOGY
UNIVERSITY OF CALIFORNIA, LOS ANGELES
LOS ANGELES, CALIFORNIA 90024

I. Introduction

This paper casts informational social comparison within a framework of opinion formation in which an opinion is conceived of as a preparatory set for action by the person (P) toward an object or issue (X).[1] When P anticipates transaction with X, an opinion-forming imperative is induced in P to reduce ambivalence he or she may have toward X. There are two major strategies P may use to reduce ambivalence: reduce the opinion-forming imperative and/or generate supportive information. Subsumed under the latter strategy are several avenues classified into two broad categories of information generation, nonsocial and social. The nonsocial type is a subset of avenues that leads to the generation of information directly relating to specific features of X (e.g., pro and con arguments, positive and negative features) whereas the social category of avenues, e.g., social comparison, refers to indirect information relating to X generated via referral to others. The ubiquitous process of social projection, the tendency for P to assume that others (O's) share his or her opinion, is the basis for such informational social comparison.

The three-tiered theory proposed here is a blend of revisions of Festinger's (1950, 1954, 1957) theories of social comparison and cognitive dissonance with a heavy reliance on Lewin's (1931, 1935, 1938) and Hull's (1932, 1938) concep-

---

[1]We use the term opinion to refer to an evaluative belief held by P about X that has both cognitive content and affective quality. Opinion, as we use it here, is thus synonymous with the concept "attitude." Excluded from our definition of opinion are non-evaluative "opinions" that are based on the interpretation of facts, such as a medical or legal opinion.

ADVANCES IN EXPERIMENTAL
SOCIAL PSYCHOLOGY, VOL. 20

tions of conflict and F. H. Allport's (1924) theory of social projection. Some experimental studies testing derivations from the theory will be presented. They fall into two areas: the general dynamics of opinion formation and the specific utilization of information from others in the service of forming opinions.

II. Theoretical Background

Studies of opinion change, though viewed in different contexts and from different perspectives, have in recent years converged on a common focal point—opinion polarization. For example, in the ''group polarization'' context originally referred to as the ''risky shift'' phenomenon, an individual's opinion will become more extreme after he or she has been informed of the group's opinion or of the prevailing (popular) opinion (Lamm & Myers, 1978). Some of this work suggests that consensus information alone may be sufficient to produce these opinion shifts (Cotton & Baron, 1980), whereas other investigators argue that *thinking* about the group members' opinions so as to generate more supportive arguments is necessary for polarization to occur (Burnstein & Vinokur, 1975). And, in a line of work related to the latter position, Tesser (1978) has shown that an individual's attitude toward an object will polarize when he or she is instructed merely to think about the object in an ''alone'' situation.

As Cialdini, Petty, and Cacioppo (1981) point out, the ''cognitive responses'' approach to persuasion contends that self-generated thoughts or arguments about a persuasive message mediate, and hence determine, the amount of opinion polarization that occurs both in groups (Burnstein & Sentis, 1981) and individually. Thus, that approach focuses on the cognitive processes and structures (e.g., encoding processes, integrative schemas, recall availability, etc.) that presumably mediate these shifts. This view, however, fails to consider the conditions that motivate the individual either to process the message or to generate the bolstering information which it assumes is necessary for the polarizing effect to occur. This is understandable given that cognitive responses theory is a direct descendant of the more general learning approach to persuasion originated by Hovland and his colleagues (Hovland, Janis, & Kelley, 1953), which views the person as a passive recipient of a message. Like the learning approach, the ''cognitive responses'' approach, even with its more active processing bent, has also failed to consider the functions that opinions serve for the person, i.e., his or her motivation to form, hold and modify them (see Katz, 1960). In a recent analysis of the problem, Petty and Cacioppo (1981), who themselves take a ''cognitive responses'' perspective, argue that it is indeed necessary to delineate the conditions that motivate the person to process messages. The present approach, which stems from a tradition in which the person is seen as actively structuring his or her inner and outer worlds, is directly concerned not only with the conditions that motivate the person to generate information, but also with the nature of the underlying processes that provide such cognitive bolstering. Specifically, the motivation for information generation is determined by the person's level of opinion preparedness relative to the imperative for action which he or she faces or expects to face. The less prepared the person is to act on an opinion, the more inclined he or she will be to generate supportive information, reduce the action imperative, or some combination of the two. In this view, the motivation to process information depends directly on the person's need for information.

A key development in the study of opinion formation was Festinger's (1954) theory of social comparison processes. Festinger assumes that P has a built-in need to evaluate his or her opinions. When P is uncertain of an opinion, he or she may utilize two means for increasing certainty—checking the opinion against physical reality or checking it against social reality, that is, against the opinions of others. Although there are ambiguities and some downright puzzles in the theory, there is no denying its bold-stroke brilliance (reviewed in Suls & Miller, 1977). With the exception of the literature on the selection of a comparison O, however, and despite its citation prominence, relatively little work was stimulated directly by the theory itself. In contrast, the theory of cognitive dissonance (Festinger, 1957), which was published 3 years later, opened a veritable sluice-gate of research activity.

The lack of actual research impact of the 1954 paper was only partly due to the then-developing cognitive *Zeitgeist* in social psychology which eventually engulfed much of the field, but also to problems in the theory that gave it a dead-end character. As we see it, there are three main problems with it: (1) the lack of specification of the individual dynamics underlying opinion formation, which was somewhat better elaborated in cognitive dissonance theory, (2) confusion between informational and normative processes (Festinger claimed he was only interested in how P utilizes information from others as benchmarks, but, as we shall see, he inadvertently introduced normative pressures as well), and (3) related to this, the peculiar status of the "cohesiveness" variable which assumed center stage in the research.

In the distinction drawn by Deutsch and Gerard (1955) between informational and normative pressure, informational pressure, which prompts P to utilize opinion-relevant information from a suitable comparison O, results from P's desire to be correct. Normative pressure, on the other hand, stems from P's desire to maintain or improve his or her status in O's eyes. Although Festinger maintained that social comparison theory focuses on informational comparison, the experiments designed to test the theory typically placed subjects in face-to-face contact where they were aware that their opinions differed from others and that the others, in turn, might react negatively to them because of such apparent opinion opposition. It is therefore highly likely that normative pressures did develop in those experiments. In both the earlier (Festinger, 1950) and later versions (Festinger, 1954) of the theory, cohesiveness played a central role in the tendency for group members to utilize the opinions of others in the group as comparison referents. Cohesiveness as a group-level concept was defined vaguely as the sum total of all the attractions of the members for the group. Clearly, to the extent that a given member is attracted to the group, he or she will be concerned with maintaining membership in the group; the greater that concern, the less likely would that member be to take or maintain a deviant opinion since a deviant opinion might be seen as challenging or threatening to the other group members. Thus, status concerns are undoubtedly implicated in a cohesive group, and in the face of opinion discrepancies normative pressures will arise to reduce those discrepancies. Thus, not only was there confusion at the conceptual level, but in the individual experiments both informational *and* normative influence were probably at work.

To carry the argument further, if social comparison theory is indeed concerned strictly with social influence occurring as a result of informational comparison, P's concern with selecting a suitable comparison O would be based on his or her judgment as to the reliability of O's opinion, which would, in turn, presumably be based on P's judgment as to O's qualifications to form and hold veridical opinions about X. O's attractiveness to P on bases other than such qualifications would presumably not enter into P's choice of O as a comparison referent. Given these considerations, it would follow that group cohesiveness as a factor should be immaterial to informational comparison.

Comparison theory was couched mostly in group-level concepts. The desire on the part of each group member to increase his or her own opinion certainty generates "pressures toward uniformity" which then take over and mediate the vicissitudes of the comparison-influence process. The research studies, as they were formulated and designed, tested relationships between manifestations of pressures toward uniformity, such as communication and opinion change, and group characteristics, such as cohesiveness and homogeneity of the group composition without reference to the underlying dynamics of individual opinion formation. The research hypotheses were cut off, as it were, from the real source of opinion comparison—individual cognitive dynamics. Lacking a firm basis for formulating penetrating questions, the theory all but died on the vine. The present theory treats social comparison processes as one manifestation of the dynamics of opinion formation and incorporates dissonance-like processes as central to opinion dynamics. We shall first discuss this central process, opinion dynamics.

A. THE ACTION IMPERATIVE

In Chapter 6 of Jones and Gerard (1967), cognitive dissonance is cast within a framework of action with a pragmatic, functionalist basis. In that framework, dissonance is viewed as a negative state induced by cognitions having incompatible behavioral implications. For example, after a decision the negative features of the chosen alternative and the positive features of the rejected one(s) induce action tendencies in P (approach toward the rejected and avoidance of the chosen alternative) that are incompatible with maintaining an unequivocal behavioral orientation (UBO) toward transaction with the chosen alternative. These incompatible action tendencies prevent effective, nonconflicted transaction. If such transaction is to occur, incompatible action tendencies must be reduced or eliminated. Viewed in this light, dissonance reduction is an attempt to reduce or eliminate incompatible action tendencies in the service of maingaining UBO. The present theory builds upon the UBO concept by arguing that the imperative induced by an impending transaction with X requires that P develop a well-formed opinion toward X which then enables him or her to maintain UBO. In line with this argument, Jones and Regan (1974) found that social comparison information, which could serve to reduce conflict, was more useful pre- than postdecisionally. We are thus arguing that in order for P to maintain UBO toward X, the underlying opinion must be relatively unequivocal.

B. OPINION FORMATION

We assume, as Kurt Lewin (1935) does implicitly in his life-space notion, that P holds opinions only about objects and events that have some potential direct or indirect hedonic consequences for him or her, and, as such, opinions are preparatory sets to transact with or avoid such objects or events. Prepared opinions allow us to act toward objects and issues effectively and expediently. Transaction can be successful only when P maintains UBO toward X; whole-hearted, not half-hearted, transaction is likely to be effective. P will therefore attempt to reduce his or her ambivalence toward X since ambivalence prevents UBO maintenance. Further, the reduction of ambivalence will tend to polarize P's opinion toward X. Consequently, a well-formed opinion toward X tends, although not invariably, to be more polarized than a less well-formed one. A great deal of research dating back 60 years (e.g., Allport & Hartman, 1925; Suchman, 1950) has clearly demonstrated the robustness of the relationship between opinion confidence and extremity.

Since our focus in this chapter is on P's concern with the subjective validity of his or her opinions and not with how he or she is perceived by O, we do not consider conditions under which P will prefer weak rather than firm opinions. For example, in the face of an anticipated confrontation with O, P may prefer to remain tentative rather than be committed to an opinion since he or she can then easily change the opinion in order to avoid possible rejection and censure

(Cialdini, Levy, Herman, Kozlowski, and Petty, 1976). This, of course, involves normative processes.

C. CONFLICT AND TRANSACTION

In his penetrating analysis of conflict and conflict resolution, Lewin (1931, 1935, 1938) saw P's behavior at any moment as coming to terms with competing "force-fields" induced by the configuration of valences and barriers in P's life-space. Lewin argues that the strength of the force-field for both positively and negatively valent activity regions increases the closer P comes to that region, the gradient of a negative force-field increasing more sharply than that of a positive one. Thus, in an approach–avoidance conflict, as transaction with X becomes more imminent, its positive features, which induce approach, loom larger and its negative features, which induce avoidance, loom larger still (see Fig. 1).

In his analysis of approach–avoidance conflict,[2] Lewin distinguishes between the situation in which a positive and a negative valence are both embodied in the same object or activity from one in which P is prevented from transacting with a positive object by a negative force-field extrinsic to the positively valent object itself. These two types of approach–avoidance conflict call for different resolutions. The latter situation is illustrated by Lewin's example of the little boy at the beach who wants to fetch a rubber swan out of the water.The child's approach to the swan is inhibited by his fear of the water. As a result of the two opposing force-field gradients induced by the child's desire for the swan and his fear of the water, the child, after initially vacillating back and forth, will finally position himself at a point near the water's edge facing the swan where the gradients are exactly balanced. This "equilibrium point," which is depicted in Fig. 1, occurs where the two gradients are of equal and opposite strength. If, in the vicinity of the goal, the child backs away from the equilibrium point (i.e., moves to the left on the abscissa in Fig. 1), his position on the positive gradient will be higher than his position on the negative gradient, thus inducing approach. If he moves forward of the equilibrium point (i.e., moves to the right on the abscissa), his avoidance tendency will be greater than his approach tendency, which will move him back toward the equilibium point. This subtype of ap-

---

[2]Lewin (1935) distinguished three types of conflict: (1) approach–approach, in which P must choose between two positively valent activities, (2) avoidance–avoidance, in which P must choose between two negatively valent activities, and (3) approach–avoidance, in which P must choose to engage or not engage in an activity that has both positive and negative valence. There is also the double approach–avoidance conflict in which P is faced with a choice between two transactions, each of which embodies both positive and negative valence. In our discussion we will consider primarily the approach–avoidance case. Although each of the other cases has its own peculiarities, the general principles of opinion formation apply equally to all four cases.

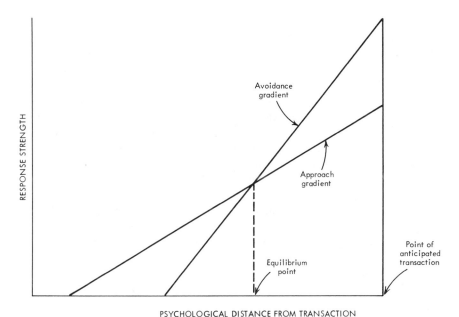

PSYCHOLOGICAL DISTANCE FROM TRANSACTION

Fig. 1. The approach–avoidance gradient structure.

proach–avoidance conflict is characterized by the existence of an extrinsic barrier or threat that prevents transaction with a desired object. The opposite case can also occur, in which a person is offered an extrinsic reward for engaging in negatively valent behavior, as in the forced compliance paradigm utilized in dissonance theory research (e.g., Festinger & Carlsmith, 1959). The gradient structure underlying forced compliance is essentially the same as in the threat case.

The other major subtype of approach–avoidance conflict in which anticipated transaction with the object itself is seen as having both positive and negative hedonic consequences is illustrated by Lewin's example of the child who wants to climb a tree but is afraid of falling out of it. A similar conflict would exist for a person who wants to eat a rich, gooey dessert but is deterred by the number of calories it contains.

In the case where one of the valences is extrinsic to the activity region, as in the rubber swan example, the problem can be solved in two stages. The child can resolve his conflict by cajoling an adult into fetching the swan for him. By circumventing the source of the negative force-field, as in the so-called *Umweg* (detour) solution, the child temporarily turns away from the desired goal in order to get around a barrier that blocks his or her direct access to it. In the case where the object itself embodies both positive and negative valence, a two-stage solution is not possible; P must cope with the negative consequences inherent in X if he or she chooses to transact with it. The forced compliance paradigm notwithstanding, many instances of opinion formation are of the second subtype in which P attempts to come to terms with the inherent negative consequences of potential transaction with X.

If the approach gradient is everywhere above the avoidance gradient, P will have little difficulty consummating the transaction, whereas if the avoidance gradient is higher at every point, P will move away from X. It is only when the gradients intersect that P has a true approach–avoidance conflict. If P is at such an equilibrium point, he or she can resolve the conflict by raising the approach gradient or by lowering the avoidance gradient or both. Raising the approach gradient is accomplished by increasing the positive valence associated with transaction, that is, by anticipating an increase in the positive consequences of transaction. Such an increase can occur by adding anticipated positive consequences or by increasing the weight of already anticipated positive consequences. Similarly, the avoidance gradient can be lowered by denying or eliminating negative consequences or by lowering their weights.

Thus, if P is to resolve the conflict, he or she must do the cognitive work necessary to shift the gradients. Successful conflict resolution occurs when, through these gradient shifts, the equilibrium point is eliminated entirely, enabling P to transact with X. By virtue of the typical difference in slope of the two gradients, it is more efficient for P to lower the avoidance gradient than to raise the approach gradient since the amount by which the equilibrium point shifts by moving the gradients is directly proportional to the relative slopes of the two gradients. Evidence from a study by Rabbie, Brehm, and Cohen (1959), which utilized the so-called "forced compliance" paradigm, suggests that when P is in an approach–avoidance conflict, the mere decision to transact with X (without actual transaction) engages gradient shifts of the kind we have been discussing. In that experiment, the subject was asked to write an essay supporting a point of view that was opposed to his or her actual opinion. The results indicate that the mere decision to write the essay (without actually writing it) was sufficient to produce attitude change in the direction of the to-be-advocated opinion.

A seminal contribution to conflict theory was Hull's (1938) *Psychological Review* paper which formalized, in S-R terms, Lewin's earlier and vaguer force-field conception of goal gradients. Hull acknowledges Lewin's "admirable perspicacity" in realizing that avoidance gradients typically begin later and are steeper than those of approach, and, further, if the gradients cross, there will be an equilibrium point where the force-fields are exactly balanced. If a rat is shocked in a goal box where on previous learning trials it received food, the rat will, on subsequent trials, run toward the goal box, stop some distance away from it, move back then forward and back again, hovering at the equilibrium point, as in the example of the boy and the rubber swan.

Except for barely a handful of inconclusive studies with humans, much of the work on the goal gradient approach to conflict has been done with rats under Neal Miller's aegis (see Miller 1944, 1959, for summaries of that work). Heilizer (1977a,b), in his critical reviews of Miller's postulate system, which is a formalization of Lewin's original goal gradient framework, concludes that the postulate system has empirical support.

All five deductions from Miller's postulate system regarding approach–avoidance conflict have received empirical support in animal studies in which hunger and fear produced approach and avoidance responses, respectively. These deductions are (1) the subject should approach part way to the food and then stop (the stopping point is the point at which the approach and avoidance responses are equal); (2) increasing the strength of hunger should cause subjects to approach nearer the goal (the approach gradient has been raised); (3) increasing the number of reinforced training trials should cause the subject to approach nearer the goal (approach gradient raised); (4) increasing the strength of fear should cause the subject to stop further from the goal (avoidance gradient raised); and (5) increasing the number of reinforced avoidance trials should cause the subject to stop further from the goal (avoidance gradient raised).

As Miller (1959) so perceptively points out, the approach gradient is typically and primarily based on internal cues stemming from a drive state such as hunger or sex which remains relatively constant in the period just prior to anticipated transaction with the object (e.g., food or a member of the opposite sex). As the organism enters the immediate vicinity of the object, external cues provided by incoming sensory information and attendant anticipated consumatory responses raise the gradient. Data from harness-pull studies with rats suggest that the approach gradient typically does have a rather shallow positive slope. An avoidance tendency, on the other hand, is primarily under the control of external negatively toned cues. Transaction with the object portends an unpleasant experience. Typically, avoidance attendant upon the anticipation of an upcoming painful experience shows a sharp increase in the immediate vicinity of the potential source of the pain. Human studies of neophyte parachutists (Epstein & Fenz, 1962) provide evidence of a sharply inclined avoidance gradient as the time for the jump nears. As Miller (1959) suggests, however, the greater steepness of avoidance as compared with approach gradients is typical but probably not invariant. There may be situations in which an organism under a very strong drive state may show a steep approach gradient in the vicinity of the goal. Definitive studies that might define boundary conditions for steep versus shallow approach gradients are lacking. Given the current evidence, it is reasonable to follow Lewin, Hull, and Miller in assuming that typically avoidance gradients are steeper than approach gradients.

Since we conceive of the approach gradient in the opinion formation context as being the sum total of all P's anticipated positive consequences attendant on transaction and the avoidance gradient as being based on all anticipated negative consequences, the gradients may be raised or lowered, as we have indicated above, by either adding or deleting anticipated consequences (relevant cognitions) or by changing their weights. If P is to resolve an approach–avoidance conflict, P must attempt through cognitive work to conjure up cognitions that would shift the gradients accordingly. The situational forces, as specified in the gradient structure, determine the amount and direction of cognitive modification necessary for ambivalence reduction. Thus, for successful transaction to occur, P must engage in the cognitive maneuvers necessary to reduce ambivalence so that a relatively unconflicted transaction can occur.

D. THE "REQUIREDNESS" LEVEL (RL)
   AND OPINION PREPAREDNESS (OP)

The amount of ambivalence that has to be reduced will depend upon P's judgment as to what level of opinion preparedness will be required for him or her to maintain UBO toward X. This requirement is what we referred to earlier as the action imperative. To the extent that P's opinion preparedness is below this level of requiredness, he or she will experience uncertainty and will attempt to reduce this uncertainty. The requiredness-level concept, which generates the opinion-forming pressure, is the cornerstone of the present theory.

Three factors determine the RL: the importance of the anticipated action, its immediacy, and an individual difference variable, "tolerance for ambivalence." The "importance of the anticipated action" factor embodies the likelihood and amount of anticipated positive and/or negative hedonic consequences occurring as a result of P's transacting with X. Because we hold opinions only about objects or events having some personal hedonic relevance, and since anticipated consequences appear greater the closer P is to transaction, immediacy reduces to importance. That is, more immediate transactions are more important than less immediate ones. The RL for a given transaction will differ among individuals in accordance with their individual level of tolerance for ambivalence, a relatively stable personality trait. In order to illustrate how this trait operates, we use the following hypothetical example.

Imagine that genetic engineers have cloned two individuals, identical in every respect except for one personality trait—tolerance for ambivalence—with one individual being high and the other low in that trait. Imagine also that they go to the local ice cream parlor for an ice cream cone, a treat they indulge in only rarely because they are on a special diet. Upon arriving at the parlor, our clones must choose between two equally desired ice cream flavors: marble fudge or sticky-chewy-chocolate. After taking a number (they get a "14" and the last number called was "5"), they continue with their conversation. In this scenario, our theory predicts that as the numbers called get closer to 14, the clone who is

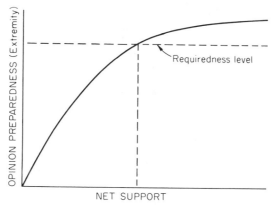

Fig. 2.   Opinion dynamics: preparedness and net support.

low in tolerance for ambivalence will be the one to break off the conversation in order to decide which ice cream flavor to get. It is not that for him the transaction is objectively more immediate or important than it is for the high-tolerance clone, but that he perceives it to be so. Although for both individuals the degree of ambivalence in choice of flavors is the same, the low-tolerance clone perceives a greater action imperative and feels pressure to decide sooner (i.e., at a lower number being called) because his RL is comparatively higher. This higher RL will in turn produce an OP–RL discrepancy sooner for the low-tolerance clone and, as will be discussed shortly, induces uncertainty that can be reduced only by preparing for transaction.

The key relationship involved in the dynamics of opinion formation is depicted in Fig. 2. Opinion content or cognitive "net support," represented on the abscissa, is the resultant or net amount of supportive information the person has about X. Underlying this content continuum is the cognitive structure of the opinion including various beliefs about X, the values P judges are implicated in potential transaction with X, as well as the perceived extrinsic social support P may have for the beliefs and values he or she may hold about X. For some opinions this underlying calculus may be very complex, taking into account the anticipated rewards versus costs of transaction as well as the rewards and costs of not transacting. Opinion preparedness or extremity is shown on the ordinate. As can be seen, the positive function relating preparedness to cognitive content is decelerating; each marginal increment of net support produces a smaller increase in preparedness than did the previous increment. Thus far our model of opinion dynamics has a good deal in common with other conceptions such as the Fishbein and Ajzen (1975) framework. Fishbein and Ajzen include in their formulation, as we do in ours, how transaction with the attitude object will implicate certain of the values P holds (the attitude) as well as the amount of extrinsic social support (norms) he or she believes exists for the transaction.

A general working formula for the underlying cognitive net support base for P's opinion can be represented by the following:

$$\text{Net support} = \Sigma(\text{supportive cognition} \times \text{weight}) - \Sigma(\text{nonsupportive cognition} \times \text{weight}),$$

where weights are measured by the perceived importance of each cognition. Note that this formulation is related to Festinger's (1957) formula for magnitude of dissonance and also to one used by Cotton and Baron (1980), which was in turn modified from another employed by Burnstein and Vinokur (1975). The latter formulas have been used in the "thought-listing" procedure for assessing cognitive responses to persuasive appeals (see Cacioppo, Harkins, & Petty, 1981, for other methods).

Viewed in the light of our discussion thus far, the arousal of cognitive dissonance is not so much a postdecisional phenomenon as Festinger (1964) argues (although it is that too, since a decision typically moves P closer to transaction), but rather a function of the importance and immediacy of anticipated transaction and tolerance for ambivalence. For example, if P must choose between two positively valued alternatives, the initial information search serves to spread the alternatives apart in value sufficiently for P to transact with one of them. If each is unequivocally positive, the thought of giving one of them up is experienced by P as a negative consequence, the negativity of which increases the closer P is to committing him- or herself to the other alternative. This anticipated loss acts as a nonsupportive cognition. The process alternates in generating supportive and nonsupportive cognitions for each alternative as P contemplates choosing each in turn. If each alternative has both positive and negative features, the net support structure will be characterized by considerable complexity, shifting back and forth from one net support configuration to the other as P contemplates choosing one and then the other alternative.

In order for P to subsequently act with equanimity toward the chosen alternative, his or her opinion preparedness must continue to increase until it reaches the RL. To the extent that P is below that level, he or she will experience uncertainty. Postdecisionally, P will continue to spread the alternatives apart until his or her opinion preparedness reaches the RL.

In a recent experiment White and Gerard (1981) found clear, unmistakeable evidence that the act of deciding in itself does not result in cognitive accommodation, but it is, rather, the anticipated immediacy of transaction with the chosen alternative that does so. Subjects in the experiment chose between performing one of two tasks (working on a jigsaw puzzle or a taste discrimination task), anticipating no postdecision delay, a 10-minute delay, or a 30-minute delay in transaction with the chosen task. On a composite liking measure administered immediately after the choice (see Table I), subjects in the "no delay" condition spread the choice alternatives apart in value more than did those who anticipated a 10-minute delay. Subjects who anticipated a 30-minute delay in transaction

TABLE I

THE EFFECT OF IMMEDIACY OF TRANSACTION ON THE EVALUATION
OF THE CHOSEN AND REJECTED TASK ALTERNATIVES

Task alternative	Immediacy of transaction		
	Immediate	10 minutes	30 minutes
Chosen	77.40[a]	72.05	65.30
Rejected	45.46	51.37	46.69
Difference	31.95	20.68	18.61

[a]Mean composite scale score; a higher score indicates a more positive
evaluation of the task.

showed the least spreading apart. The results are consistent with the hypothesis
that the more immediate the transaction, the higher will be the RL, and the higher
the RL, the more will P attempt to increase OP through cognitive bolstering.
Thus, the act of deciding in and of itself did not induce cognitive bolstering,
since subjects in all three conditions had made a decision; it was instead the
relative nearness in time to transaction that produced the observed differential in
the so-called "dissonance effect." Note also that the amount of spread is due
almost entirely to the relative evaluation of the chosen task.

In an experiment utilizing a double approach–avoidance conflict, Gerard
and White (1983) also found strong evidence that postchoice uncertainty reduction consists of reducing ambivalent feelings toward the chosen alternative,
which is in line with the results of the previous study. Initially the subject ranked
20 paintings and was then asked to choose between a pair consisting of the third
and thirteenth ranked paintings, and a pair consisting of the sixth and sixteenth
ranked paintings. Thus, the alternative pairs consisted of one high- and one low-
ranked painting.

Consistent with our theoretical framework, the postdecisional reevaluation
data, which are presented in Table II, suggest that the subject's efforts were
focused primarily on the negative feature of the chosen alternative, i.e., the

TABLE II

RANK CHANGE[a] OF THE PAINTINGS FROM BEFORE
TO AFTER THE CHOICE

	Chosen	Rejected
Liked painting	.02	−.52
Disliked painting	2.48	.03

[a]A positive change reflects greater liking and a
negative score indicates less liking.

disliked chosen painting. As indicated in the table, the disliked chosen painting increased in liking, whereas the liked chosen painting and both rejected paintings showed virtually no change.[3] Thus, when faced with imminent transaction, it is adaptive for P to reduce ambivalence by focusing on the chosen alternative rather than continuing to consider forgone options. P's "problem" consists of coming to terms with the negative features of the chosen alternative. By virtue of the affective gradients involved, its negative features will typically loom especially large as P contemplates immediate transaction. In response to this action imperative, P's efforts will be focused on reducing ambivalence primarily by lowering the negativity of the negative features of the chosen alternative. This ambivalence-reduction strategy will move P to the right on the net support continuum (see Fig. 2), thereby tending to raise opinion preparedness up toward the RL.

E. OPINION DYNAMICS: ACCOMMODATION
    TO DISCREPANCY

Figure 3 represents the full model as a process which depends on P's comparison of his or her current opinion prepareness (OP) with his or her RL. When the OP level is at or above RL, P is sufficiently prepared—action can be predicated on his or her opinion. However, when OP is below RL, subjective uncertainty, which is directly proportional to the discrepancy between OP and RL, motivates P to decrease the OP–RL gap so as to induce UBO toward X. Accommodation to this discrepancy can be achieved via two basic strategies available to P: increasing preparedness through information generation, lowering the RL itself, or some combination of the two. These two strategies have divergent implications for opinion formation. Lowering the RL involves utilizing one or both of the two factors upon which opinion importance is based, the immediacy and the importance of the transaction. Hence, P may attempt to minimize the hedonic relevance (importance) of the transaction and/or delay transacting with X, if that is possible. In contrast to lowering the RL, information generation necessitates sorting out aspects of the issue, generating a consensus base, and so on. It is widely assumed by others (e.g., Cialdini et al., 1981; Collins & Raven, 1969), as it is here, that accommodation to a cognitive discrepancy involves the principle of least effort. Assuming this, we can predict that lowering the RL is

[3]One might argue that the lack of an increase in liking for the liked chosen painting was due to a "ceiling effect" since its initial rank was nearer the top than was the disliked chosen painting. The key comparison, however, should be with the liked rejected painting, which had exactly as much room to move down in rank as had the disliked chosen painting to move up. Dissonance theory would therefore have predicted equal movement in opposite directions since a movement upward of the disliked chosen painting or a movement downward by the same amount of the liked rejected alternative would presumably have an equal dissonance-reducing effect.

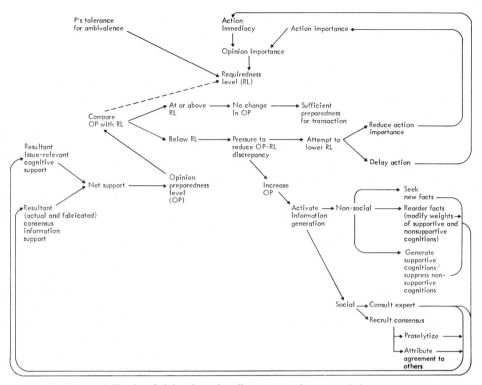

Fig. 3.   Opinion dynamics: discrepancy and accommodation.

typically the strategy of first choice if it is an available option—some action deadlines, however, cannot be delayed. One consequence of the RL-lowering strategy is that the opinion itself will have lower intensity. RL lowering will thus result in an opinion that is more moderate and more susceptible to change than if the opinion had been bolstered via information generation.[4]

It would therefore follow that when the strategy of lowering RL is taken, P becomes more vulnerable to being influenced by counterattitudinal communication. For example, Petty, Cacioppo, and Goldman (1981) found that issues having high importance as compared to those having low importance required stronger arguments for persuasion to occur. Furthermore, subjects confronting a

[4]Suchman's (1950) work on the relationship between attitude intensity and attitude extremity clearly shows that the two variables take on a U-shaped function so that a more extreme attitude is held with greater intensity. Kelley and Lamb's (1957) study of influence on taste judgments showed that a more extreme judgment is more resistant to influence from others. We can thus expect that a more moderate or less intensely held opinion that results from RL lowering will be more susceptible to change than one which is more extreme.

low-importance issue were susceptible to persuasion by a highly credible source, but not by one of low credibility, when weak arguments were presented by both. This suggests that the influence of "expertise" provided by the highly credible source had its effect, despite the weak arguments, because RL was low. The initial opinion was thus less firm, rendering the subject less prepared and more persuadable. The credible source appears to have provided indirect support for the new opinion position even though the underlying cognitions about X may not have been altered directly (see Fig. 3).

If uncertainty induces information generation and is accompanied by relatively little RL lowering, the opinion will tend to polarize because the supportive cognitions will increase relative to nonsupportive ones in the service of reducing the initial OP–RL discrepancy. This explanation provides the theroretical foundation for Petty and Cacioppo's (1981) contention that thought is required for durable opinion change and is supported by data from a study by Cialdini *et al.* (1976). In that study enduring opinion polarization emerged only when the opinion issue was clearly important and action could not be delayed. In line with the present model, net support increased and the subject's opinion polarized, remaining so even after anticipated transaction was eliminated. The opinion remained extreme because the subject's OP had already increased above RL. On the other hand, when the issue was unimportant, the subject's opinion did not polarize since, in terms of the present conception, RL remained low. In the experiment, the subject was to subsequently confront someone who disagreed with him or her on the issue. The situation thus embodied two imperatives, one having to do with the issue and the other with the confrontation. With low issue importance, the imperative induced by the anticipated confrontation was relatively more salient than the imperative due to the importance of the issue itself. Cialdini *et al.* (1976) interpret moderation effects under low importance as having been due to relatively higher self-presentational (normative) concerns. In our model this difference in opinion extremity is attributed to an attention difference between one kind of imperative (the issue) and another (the confrontation).

As indicated in Fig. 3, information generated to increase net support can be of two types, social and nonsocial, corresponding to the two bases for net support: consensus information that provides indirect support for the "correctness" of an opinion and direct issue-relevant information that pertains to features or contents of the opinion object or issue itself. Within each of these two broad paths there are a number of available avenues of information generation that may be open to P in his or her attempts to reduce any existing ambivalence. Avenues categorized under the nonsocial pathway are attempts by P to directly modify or add cognitions about various aspects of the object or issue. These avenues may be used singly or in various combinations. When the means to do so are available, P may attempt to augment his or her cognitive structure about X by seeking new supportive facts, by modifying the weights of supportive or nonsupportive cognitions, or by generating new supportive cognitions and suppressing old nonsupportive ones. On the other hand, avenues categorized under the social pathway are indirect in that P refers to others for information. P may consult an expert, refer to a peer or group of peers who share P's perspective about X, or fabricate a consensus (more about that later). Note that an expert, though primarily a social source, also serves a nonsocial function in that he or she may also provide facts about the issue.

In keeping with the principle of least effort, P will prefer using those avenues that raise OP with minimum effort. The overall effect of utilizing either the social or the nonsocial pathway or both would be to increase net support and thus reduce the RL–OP gap. Once the gap is closed, P has, by definition, established UBO by virtue of having met the situational requirements for opinion-based action. It is, however, the situation itself that circumscribes which combination of avenues of the two general strategies are available for P to utilize. We can expect P not to use those avenues which have been foreclosed by circumstances. For example, when transaction with X has high hedonic consequences for P, is immediate, and cannot be delayed, the only possible way in which the RL-lowering strategy can be used by P is for P to delude him- or herself into believing that the transaction is not really important. This denial is a refusal to acknowledge the hedonic consequences of the transaction. When hedonic consequences are truly high and are perceived to be so, it is doubtful that this potentially risky approach would be used, unless, of course, P is unable to generate information.

F. THE ROLE OF COMMITMENT

Two basic features of commitment to a decision are identified in the dissonance literature: the irrevocability of the decision and the costs that would be incurred if that decision were to be undone (Gerard, 1968). In our model, that decision occurs when P begins his or her attempt to reduce the approach–avoidance conflict by increasing net support. In that attempt, P can exert varying amounts of cognitive effort, depending on the means that are available. Some means of resolving the conflict require more effort than others. For example, passively receiving information about the degree of consensual support for an opinion requires little cognitive effort. On the other hand, generating supportive cognitions, suppressing nonsupportive ones, or altering their weights requires considerably more effort.

Implicated in effortful cognitive work are the two features of commitment—costs and irrevocability. When P engages in effortful information generation in support of a given opinion, whether that generation avenue is social (e.g., proselytizing) or nonsocial (e.g., self-generating arguments), P will expend energy and invest time which, once exerted, cannot be recouped. As P modifies the cognitive structures underlying X, structures underlying other potentially important opinions that are structurally interconnected with X will also be altered (see Jones & Gerard, 1967, Chapter 5, for a discussion of the infrastructure of an opinion). P must "walk the line," so to speak, in altering the cognitive substratum and simultaneously maintaining the integrity of that substratum so as not to reduce his or her preparedness toward other important X's that may arise. Additionally, in order to undo or revoke the opinion, additional costs would have to be incurred. Commitment thus involves the costs of P's having prepared his or her opinion as well as the anticipated costs of undoing or changing that opinion. The amount of those anticipated costs is what contributes to its irrevocability. An actual cost incurred by effortful resolution is the foreclosing of the denial avenue of the RL-lowering strategy. P gives up that avenue of accommodation because in resolving the conflict P, in effect, acknowledges the potential hedonic consequences of transaction with X. It would be difficult for P to subsequently deny the consequences he or she has already clearly acknowledged. Thus, the net effect of more effortful cognitive work is to increase P's commitment to the opinion position he or she has taken.

III.   Consensus and Informational Social Comparison

As indicated above, a major source of net support is the consensus P perceives he or she has for an opinion. For example, in groups P's opinion will tend to polarize by simply knowing what the prevailing opinion is (Cotton & Baron, 1980). But even in the absence of this information, there is a tendency for P to fabricate such a consensus. The basis for such support is *social projection*, which is a pervasive tendency for P to attribute identical judgments and opinions to others, even in their absence. When others are present, the tendency is realized if and only if they are first perceived by P as sharing his or her vantage point toward X. We use the term "cooriented other" to refer to an O who is judged by P to be similar in relevant background with respect to X.[5] The power of the Asch (1956) line judgment paradigm derives from the tendency for the subject to assume that the others, who are cooriented with respect to the task, see the lines

[5]Jones and Gerard (1967) use this term in a more restricted sense to refer to value background similarity. Here we have broadened the use of the term to include any common characteristic that may provide the basis for holding an opinion toward some X. In his recasting of Heider's P–O–X paradigm, Newcomb (1953) used the term coorientation to refer to the simultaneous holding by P of attitudes toward both O and X.

the way he or she does. Disagreement with the others on the critical trials represents an unexpected and distressing disconfirmed projection to which the subject attempts to accommodate. In the subject's past history such projections onto others of judgments of distance or length were almost invariably confirmed.

This tendency for P to project his or her opinion onto others is at the heart of informational social comparison. Although projection occurs irrespective of whether or not P is below his or her RL, it may also provide an avenue of increasing opinion preparedness by adding consensus information as supportive cognitions when P is below his or her RL. Increasing OP via social projection is accomplished by a process that typically occurs rapidly and below the level of P's awareness: (1) Initially, P reacts to X with some level of extremity; (2) if a potential comparison O is available, P will estimate the degree of relevant background similarity of O, i.e., O's coorientation; (3) if, and only if, P judges that O shares a similar vantage point will P project his or her opinion onto O; (4) this attributed opinion, which appears to P as emanating from O, acts back reciprocally on P as a confirmation of P's opinion (as indicated above, consensus fabrication occurs whether or not P is below his or her RL); and (5) when P is below his or her RL, the self-generated consensus provides information that bolsters P's opinion, tending to make it more extreme, thus providing P with increased opinion preparedness.

Although his description of the process was incomplete, F. H. Allport (1924) was the first to describe fabricated consensus through social projection in the service of intensifying opinions. He identified three steps, projection, reciprocal consensus, and increased opinion intensity, but he failed to note the necessary condition for projection to occur and the sufficient condition for the intensifying effect to occur. The necessary condition for projecting onto a specific O is that O be perceived by P as cooriented (step 2 above); the sufficient condition for the intensifying effect is that P be below his or her RL (step 5). Since Allport's original formulation, others have discussed the attributive aspect of social projection (e.g., Murstein & Pryer, 1959; Holmes, 1968), but none have noted the potential reciprocal opinion-enhancing effect that may occur as result of projection. The opinion-enhancing effect of projection, we contend, is mediated by a fabricated consensus that often manifests as an overestimation of actual consensus (e.g., Calvin, Hanley, Hoffman, & Clifford, 1959; Ross, Greene, & House, 1977).

Let us follow the latter point a bit further. Since the 1940's psychologists have been aware of the tendency for P to overestimate the extent to which others agree with his or her opinions (e.g., Travers, 1941; Wallen, 1943). Ross *et al.* (1977) have recently called this phenomenon the "false consensus effect." Yet, in a sense, "false consensus" is a misnomer because the extent of consensus that is perceived may not always be false. In a study that has been cited all too infrequently, Stone and Kamiya (1957) examined estimated and actual agreement for opinions on novel issues in groups of high school students. They found that for most opinion issues the degree of consensus was typically overestimated, but in certain cases where actual group consensus for a given opinion was very high (e.g., 90% actual agreement), the degree of consensus was underestimated (subjects perceived 80% agreement in the group). In most cases consensus was overestimated, in some cases it was underestimated, and in still other cases it was accurately estimated. As Stone and Kamiya note, the striking finding is that, regardless of the proportion of the group that actually agreed on a given issue, subjects always perceived that they were in the majority. Even subjects whose opinion was shared by only 10% of the group estimated that 55% to 60% of the group held a similar opinion. In effect, subjects in this study, as in other studies, were generating their own consensus (a majority) on those issues. Given that the effect has greater implications for the self-bolstering of opinion support and less to do with how accurate P is in estimating the actual degree of consensus, a more appropriate term for the phenomenon would be "self-generated consensus" rather than "false consensus." We contend that projection is the mechanism underlying a fabricated consensus and is the process that produces an intensified opinion (see Orive, 1984, for a discussion of the elementary nature and possible evolutionary origins of social projection).

Armed with the projection notion, we can now take a new perspective on the early social comparison studies and consider social comparison as an avenue of information generation in the service of increasing cognitive net support.

Figure 4 presents a schematic of opinion dynamics in the social comparison context showing the consequences of either a confirmed or a disconfirmed projection. On the far left of the figure, three eventualities of projection onto a similar (cooriented) O are shown. If O does in fact agree with P's opinion, the projection is confirmed; if O disagrees, the projection is disconfirmed. Also indicated is the eventuality of no information about O's opinion. The two opinion-preparedness referents, P's initial level and the requiredness level (RL), are shown. Also depicted are a variety of recourses, including RL lowering, that may be available to P for attempting to reestablish his or her initial level of opinion preparedness in the face of disconfirmation. Among these are the three avenues examined in the early research on social comparison: P changing his or her opinion to agree with O; P attempting to change O's opinion to agree with him or her; and P rendering O noncomparable (e.g., Festinger and Thibaut, 1951; Festinger, Gerard, Hymovitch, Kelley & Raven, 1952).

The consequences of utilizing one or another avenue are indicated in the figure. For example, if P is successful in changing O's opinion, P's disconfirmed projection is transformed into a confirmed one, thus completing a feedback loop. As indicated, the other avenues, when utilized, may complete other feedback loops. It should be noted that the avenues in Fig. 4 that are not included in Fig. 3

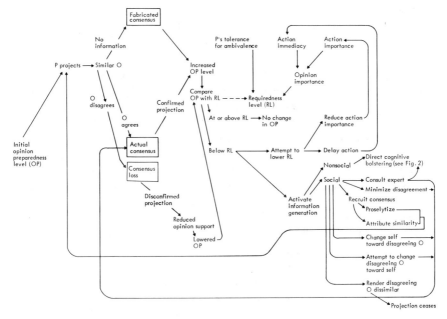

Fig. 4. Opinion dynamics and social comparison.

are all social because P is accommodating to the disconfirmed projection which was the result of an explicit social comparison. Otherwise, the process is identical to that depicted in Fig. 3.

A. DISAGREEMENT AS A DISCONFIRMED PROJECTION

In the early experiments on social comparison, in which group cohesiveness and homogeneity of group composition were manipulated, the subject was confronted with an array of opinions in the group that were either the other's actual opinions (e.g., Festinger & Thibaut, 1951) or were presented as false feedback (e.g., Festinger et al., 1952). It is likely that under high cohesiveness or high homogeneity the subject judged the others to be cooriented with respect to the judgment at hand. Therefore, under those conditions, agreement with others was tantamount to a confirmed projection, whereas disagreement represented a disconfirmation. A confirmed projection would tend to bolster the subject's opinion if he or she were below his or her RL, whereas a disconfirmed projection would tend to lower his or her opinion preparedness. If OP fell below the subject's RL, mechanisms of information generation and/or RL lowering would be engaged in order to restore an acceptable relative level of OP. Certain manifestations of information search were the dependent variables studied in the various experiments.

More recently, Orive (1981) created a social comparison paradigm that captured the essence of a number of the earlier studies. The likelihood that social projection would occur was varied by inducing two levels of background similarity (high versus low). These were cross-cut by three treatments of comparison information: agreement with another, disagreement, and a baseline condition of no comparison information. In line with the model, only in the similar-disagree condition would the subject's projection be disconfirmed. A variety of dependent measures were taken including the subject's reactions to the comparison other and to the issue, as well as his or her desire to exchange information with the other. Thus, several of the accommodation avenues indicated in Fig. 4 were examined. Also, the subject's emotional response to the comparison information was measured by questionnaire and by skin resistance changes.

The procedure used in the experiment was as follows. Four subjects, reporting to the laboratory for a study of "opinion and impression formation," initially answered a survey-type questionnaire that was used to establish high or low background similarity. After responding to the questionnaire, which contained items relevant to the issue about which he or she was to later form an opinion, the subject "exchanged" questionnaires with only one of the others. In actuality, the questionnaire the subject received was prepared in such a way as to have the other appear either similar or dissimilar in background. They all then read a variation of the "Johnny Rocco" case (Schachter, 1951; Raven, 1959), which was modified to make it more ambiguous than the original regarding Johnny's culpability for the severe battering of an old woman. Each subject was subsequently provided with the opinion of "the other subject," about whom he or she already had background information, to help him further in forming an impression of the other.

As predicted, the results showed a negatively toned emotional reaction only in the cell in which projection was disconfirmed, the similar-disagree condition. Only in this condition was disagreement negatively arousing. There were also decreases in opinion confidence, opinion importance (lowered RL), and readiness to act on the opinion (lowered opinion preparedness). In addition, the similar other who disagreed was both derogated and rendered less similar. Evidence also emerged that comparison with the dissimilar other was initially avoided. The fact that subjects did not indicate a desire to influence the other or expose themselves to influence by the other when disconfirmation occurred suggests that RL lowering and/or nonsocial accommodation to a disconfirmed projection may be preferred over social information generation, a finding that provides supporting evidence for the least-effort principle of accommodation. These data also show that a combination of accommodation strategies can be used. Additionally, as we would predict, the dissimilar-disagree and the similar-agree conditions produced no significant emotional impact and no cognitive accommodation in comparison with their respective controls.

On the other hand, unexpected agreement with a dissimilar other came as a pleasant surprise to the subject. It produced a positively toned emotional response that increased both opinion confidence and readiness to take opinion-relevant action. These findings are reminiscent of the "triangulation" effect reported by Goethals (1972). In land surveying and sea navigation, triangulation is a trigonometric operation whereby the position or location of an object can be determined when the direction of the object is measured from two fixed points known to be a certain distance apart. Analogously, when a dissimilar other whose perspective divergence is known to P agrees with P, P's judgment of X is corroborated. But this triangulation interpretation also raises an interesting issue regarding the limits of support provided by consensus information. The relationship between degree of coorientation between P and O and the utility for P of agreement with O about X will take the form of a "Wundt curve" (cf. Berlyne, 1971), which resembles an inverted U or one-half of a butterfly curve (McClelland, Atkinson, Clark, & Lowell, 1953). Curves of this general shape have been obtained when subjects judge the pleasantness or unpleasantness of a variety of stimuli, such as those involving taste and temperature. As the stimulus diverges from that which the subject expects, pleasantness increases, peaks, and then decreases. At the extreme end, the stimulus is judged negatively (Berlyne, 1971). Thus, if O is similar to P, finding him- or herself in agreement with O will come as no surprise to P. The preparedness-enhancing utility for P of such information and P's affective response to it will be low. If, however, O has a slightly different perspective, agreement with him or her has potentially greater utility since O, in effect, triangulates X for P; P's affective response will therefore be correspondingly more positive. As perspective difference increases, there will be some point of optimum difference that provides for P the maximum information utility and increased confidence about X. As perspective difference increases beyond that point, however, P will render O less and less comparable, such that knowledge that O agrees with him or her will have less and less information utility. As indicated by the shape of the "Wundt curve," at the extreme end of perspective difference, agreement with a highly dissimilar O will produce in P a decrease in confidence about X. It is worthwhile noting that a dissimilar other in this extreme region becomes a "negative referent" (Collins & Raven, 1969) who, in circumstances where P is initially uncertain about X, can be utilized by P to provide triangulating information about X. Although there is some suggestive evidence for the information utility provided by the dissimilar O

(Fazio, 1979), the affective and utilitarian effects of agreement with the full range of perspective-divergent others has never been satisfactorily demonstrated.

There is probably considerable complexity underlying P's judgment of his or her opinion-relevant background similarity to O. An important clue to this complexity and its effect on social comparison is provided in a study by Goethals and Nelson (1973). Building on the distinction between belief and value comparison made by Jones and Gerard (1967), they found that agreement with a dissimilar O bolsters confidence in a belief (a nonvalue-laden opinion) but not in a value-laden opinion. We see this finding not as evidence for the lack of triangulation provided by agreement with a dissimilar O regarding value-laden opinions, but as possibly suggesting that the Wundt curve relating information utility of agreement to the similarity of a comparison O rises and falls more sharply to the extent that an opinion is value laden. That is, in the case of such opinions, an agreeing O can provide useful (opinion bolstering) information only if O is within a narrow range of opinion-relevant background similarity. It will still be the case that within that range, the less similar O is to P the more useful will agreement with O be in bolstering P's opinion up to a point. Since the Goethals and Nelson study manipulated dissimilarity over rather grossly defined levels, it may not have been possible to detect triangulation for their value-laden opinions. Counterposing the Goethals and Nelson interpretation of their data with our interpretation of them presents a challenge to experimental ingenuity since it will involve careful parametric manipulation of several levels of background similarity and somehow equating degree of similarity for value-laden and nonvalue-laden opinions. In the absence of evidence such an experiment might provide, we prefer our interpretation on the grounds of parsimony since it assumes that the process of social comparison for all opinions, value laden or not, is essentially the same. What Goethals and Nelson take to be different processes in opinion comparison may merely be an artifact of a difference in the range of an O's acceptable background similarity for the comparison of value-laden as compared with nonvalue-laden opinions.

In the case where O disagrees with P, the more similar O is to P, the greater will be the negative effect on P's opinion preparedness. Disagreement with O will be given more weight the more similar O is to P, lowering net support proportionately. Again, the same relationships should hold for both value-laden and nonvalue-laden opinions.

B. OPINION IMPORTANCE

In an early social comparison experiment, Gerard (1953) manipulated opinion importance by informing or not informing subjects in a group that immediately after the session they were, as a group, going to have to debate the issue with some well-informed people "who will very likely disagree with you." Seen within our present framework, the debate instruction presumably had the effect of raising each subject's RL. There was clear evidence of greater information generation, as indicated by more intense influence and opinion change (see Fig. 4), when the subjects anticipated confrontation than when they did not. Several other experiments that were recently completed tested more directly this and other aspects of the theory as it applies to informational social comparison. We will briefly describe those studies.

1. Coorientation, Immediacy of Transaction, and Opinion Polarization

Gerard and Wagner (1984) attempted to create a situation in which evidence of the effects of social projection and immediacy (to vary RL) could be examined. Subjects, who were UCLA undergraduates, were run in same-sex groups of four and were cautioned not to communicate with each other in any way. The procedure was similar to the one used by Orive (1981). Subjects were fed back a "value profile" of the group tailored to give each subject the impression that the three others shared his value perspective or did not. In a third condition no value profile feedback was given. We can assume that in the "no similarity information" treatment the subjects attributed some degree of similarity to the others since they were fellow students drawn from the introductory psychology subject pool. In order of perceived similarity, therefore, the "similar" treatment would induce the greatest attributed similarity, the "dissimilar" treatment the least, with the "no similarity information" treatment falling somewhere in between. Data from the manipulation check administered after the experiment reflected this ordering of the treatments.

In order to vary RL, subjects were told (as in the Gerard, 1953, study) that they were each going to debate someone *not in their present group* on the opinion issue (the "Johnny Rocco" case) immediately after the present session, next week, or possibly not at all "due to scheduling difficulties." Following these instructions, the subjects indicated their opinions on a 7-point scale as to whether Johnny should receive harsh or lenient treatment for his crime. They were also asked to estimate on a 9-point scale the average opinion of the other three subjects (a measure of projection).

The results indicated that both action imminence and similarity influenced projection, as measured by the extent to which the subject believed that the others agreed with his or her own opinion about what should be done with the delinquent boy. The anticipation of an immediate debate evoked more projection in the "similar" than in the "no information" and "dissimilar" conditions. When subjects were told that the debate was not likely, they projected less than when they expected it to take place. Opinion extremity scores were derived by

TABLE III

THE EFFECT OF DIFFERENTIAL GROUP SIMILARITY AND IMMEDIACY
OF THE DEBATE ON OPINION EXTREMITY

Immediacy of the debate	Group similarity		
	High similarity	No information	Low similarity
Immediate	2.30[a]	1.87	1.50
Next week	2.25	1.70	1.50
Probably not at all	1.50	1.40	1.50

[a]Cell means are based on extremity scores ranging from 1 to 4; a higher
score indicates greater extremity.

folding the 7-point scale at "4", which was the neutral point, yielding a 4-point
extremity scale for which the degree of harshness or leniency of the recommen-
dation was not distinguished. These data, which are presented in Table III, show
main effects of similarity and imminence. Under the two conditions in which the
subjects expected to express their opinions, "immediate" and "next week,"
increased similarity produced increased opinion extremity, whereas when the
debate was not likely to take place there was no effect of similarity on opinion
extremity. The data provide support for the theoretically derived effects of immediacy (which is one of the factors determining the height of the RL) and coorientation on opinion polarization. These results dovetail nicely with the White and
Gerard (1981) decision experiment described above, which showed a similar
effect of immediacy on opinion extremity (cf. Table I).

TABLE IV

IMMEDIACY OF MEASUREMENT, GROUP VERSUS
ALONE, AND OPINION POLARIZATION

	Measurement delay	
	Immediate	Delayed
Similar group	2.50[a]	3.44
Dissimilar group	2.00	2.13
Alone	2.50	2.25

[a]Mean extremity scores. The range of the scale is
0 to 5.

2. Measurement Delay, Coorientation, and Opinion Extremity

The work of Tesser and his colleagues on opinion polarization typically utilized a context in which several subjects, who were asked to individually form an opinion, were run simultaneously. The subjects were also cautioned to consider their opinions carefully since they were going to be asked questions later. The combination of both circumstances provided a situation that was ripe for the occurrence of social projection and opinion polarization. Cautioning the subjects about later questions increased opinion importance, thus creating a situation with a high RL. The presence of similar others made social projection-comparison a likely avenue for increasing opinion preparedness (extremity). As compared with those subjects whose opinions were measured immediately, those for whom measurement was delayed 90 seconds (the typical delay used by Tesser and his colleagues) had more extreme opinions, an effect we would have predicted from the present theory since a delay provides a greater opportunity for projection to occur. Tesser (1978) explains the effects by arguing that measurement delay allows the subject to pare away information inconsistent with whatever "schema" the subject initially applied to the information he had been given.

In order to separate out the effects of measurement delay on schema consistency development from the possibility for social projection-comparison, Gerard and Wagner (1984) utilized a format similar to the one used in the previous experiment in which four subjects were run under either a high or a low coorientation treatment. They were asked to form opinions on two issues, import quotas on Japanese cars and federal defense spending, which they would have to defend later. Opinion measurement was immediate for one issue and delayed 90 seconds for the other (the measurement delay used by Tesser), counterbalanced across conditions for issue order and measurement delay order. Also run was an "alone" baseline condition. The data, which are presented in Table IV, reflect the relative degree of polarization for the immediate and delayed measurement issues. As in the previous experiment, the 11-point scale was "folded" at the "6" midpoint to yield a 6-point degree-of-extremity scale. The data are clear: polarization as a result of measurement delay occurred only under the "similar others" condition. As shown in the table, the "alone" and "dissimilar others" treatment showed virtually no effect of delayed measurement on polarization. Tesser's explanation predicts greater extremity for delayed measurement across all three treatments. It is likely, therefore, that Tesser's polarization effects were due, at least in part, to the opportunity for social projection provided subjects by virtue of the presence of similar others and the high RL induced by the anticipated quiz (questions the subject expected the experimenter to ask). Since social projection probably occurs rapidly once the person has formed an opinion we would have expected some polarization in the similar-others immediate condition relative to the other two immediate conditions. That this did not occur can possibly be attributed to the fact that the two opinion issues were probably quite complex for the subjects so that it took time for them to form an opinion in the first place. In future studies, varying the delay period as well as issue complexity might be used to further elucidate this problem.

C. COMMITMENT AND OPINION FIRMNESS

As was mentioned earlier, the effect of commitment to an opinion position tends to eliminate denial of action importance as an accommodation strategy and thus limits the possibility of RL lowering. As we argued earlier, commitment increases when P engages in effortful information generation. That is, resolution of conflict without having to work it through, as is the case with effortless consensus generation (such as being told what the prevailing opinion is and in self-generating a consensus through projection), may not produce as firm an opinion because commitment does not increase even though opinion preparedness does.

Some evidence for this was reported by Orive (1984), who found that opinion polarization based on projection-induced fabricated consensus appears to be rather fragile. The study used the projection notion to explain opinion fluctuation (polarization and moderation) in the "deindividuation" context (cf. Diener, 1980; Zimbardo, 1969). In the study subjects were assembled in groups ranging from five to seven and, presumably on the basis of responses to a questionnaire previously taken, were told they shared a similar background, a dissimilar background, or were given no background information. Thus, the condition presumed to induce social projection, being in a "similar" group, was created and compared with conditions less likely to induce it, being in a "dissimilar" group or being in a "no background information" group. Subjects subsequently read an article on a current world crisis and gave their opinions on several statements about the crises. For half of the subjects, a second factor was introduced to disrupt ongoing projection in the group. This was accomplished by inducing public self-awareness (self-consciousness) through a procedure in which a camera was focused on the subject while he or she was forming the opinions. In another experiment reported in the same article, this procedure was found to induce self-awareness and to moderate opinions. As was found in our previous studies, only those who formed their opinions in the similar group showed greater opinion polarization (see Table V). And, interestingly enough, only those in the similar group, who would presumably be projecting (self-generating a consensus), *moderated* their opinions on the issues they were judging when self-awareness was induced. Those in the "dissimilar" and "no information"

TABLE V

GROUP BACKGROUND, INDUCED SELF-AWARENESS,
AND OPINION EXTREMITY

| | Group background | | |
Self-awareness	Similar	Dissimilar	No information
Low	10.78[a]	9.22	9.16
Heightened	7.12	8.59	9.30

[a]A higher score indicates greater extremity; the scale range is 0 to 18.
(Adapted from Orive, copyright 1984, by the American Psychological Association).

groups were not affected by heightened self-awareness presumably because they did not have the benefit of a "fabricated" consensus as did those in the "similar" group. Although projection tends to polarize opinions, it does not necessarily solidify them. In contrast to effortless consensus generation, however, we can expect effortful information generation to increase commitment and to produce a firmer opinion, one that is more resistant to change.

IV. Conclusion

The three-tiered conception presented here, in which informational social comparison is based on a substructure of individual opinion dynamics overlaid on goal gradient processes, offers a deeper understanding of some of the older literature and enables us to derive additional implications, some which have already been tested and others which are in the process of being tested. The theory serves to bridge the gap between the earlier theory and research on social comparison processes, which had an inadequate foundation, and the later work on decision making and postdecisional accommodation, both seen from the perspective of the person's attempt to prepare him- or herself for action. The approach represents a unified conception of information search and processing in the service of increasing opinion preparedness.

ACKNOWLEDGMENTS

Authorship order in no way reflects relative contribution to the work; it was truly a collaborative effort. The preparation of this article was supported in part by NSF Grant BNS 84-12866.

REFERENCES

Allport, F. H. (1924). *Social psychology.* Cambridge, MA: Riverside Press.
Allport, F. H., & Hartman, D. A. (1925). The measurement and motivation of atypical opinion in a certain group. *The American Political Review,* **19,** 735–763.
Asch, S. E. (1956). Studies of independence and conformity: A minority of one against a unanimous majority. *Psychological Monographs,* **70** (9, Whole No. 416), 416.
Berlyne, D. E. (1971). *Aesthetics and psychobiology.* New York: Appleton.
Burnstein, E., & Sentis, K. (1981). Attitude polarization in groups. In R. E. Petty, T. M. Ostrom, & T. C. Brock (Eds.), *Cognitive responses in persuasion.* Hillsdale, NJ: Erlbaum.
Burnstein, E., & Vinokur, A. (1975). What a person thinks upon learning he has chosen differently from others: Nice evidence for the persuasive-arguments explanation of choice shifts. *Journal of Experimental Social Psychology,* **11,** 412–426.
Cacioppo, J. T., Harkins, S. G., & Petty, R. E. (1981). The nature of attitudes and cognitive responses and their relationships to behavior. In R. Petty, T. Ostrom, & T. Brock (Eds.), *Cognitive responses in persuasion.* Hillsdale, NJ: Erlbaum.
Calvin, A., Hanley, C., Hoffman, F., & Clifford L. (1959). An experimental investigation of the "pull" effect. *Journal of Social Psychology,* **49,** 275–283.
Cialdini, R. B., Levy, A., Herman, C. P., Kozlowski, L., & Petty, R. E. (1976). Elastic shifts of opinion: Determinants of direction and durability. *Journal of Personality and Social Psychology,* **34,** 663–672.
Cialdini, R. B., Petty, R. E., & Cacioppo, J. T. (1981). Attitude and attitude change. In M. R. Rosenzweig & L. W. Porter (Eds.), *Annual review of psychology* (Vol. 32). Palo Alto, CA: Annual Reviews.
Collins, B. E., & Raven, B. H. (1969). Group structure: Attraction, coalition, communication, and power. In G. Lindzey & E. Aronson (Eds.), *The handbook of social psychology* (Vol. 4). Reading, MA: Addison-Wesley.
Cotton, J. L., & Baron, R. S. (1980). Anonymity, persuasive arguments, and choice shifts. *Social Psychology Quarterly,* **43,** 391–404.
Deutsch, M., & Gerard, H. B. (1955). A study of normative and informational influence upon individual judgment. *Journal of Abnormal and Social Psychology,* **51,** 629–636.
Diener, E. (1980). Deindividuation: The absence of self-awareness and self-regulation in group members. In P. B. Paulus (Ed.), *The psychology of group influence.* Hillsdale, NJ: Erlbaum.
Epstein, S., & Fenz, W. D. (1962). Theory and experiment on the measurement of approach-avoidance conflict. *Journal of Abnormal and Social Psychology,* **64,** 97–112.
Fazio, R. H. (1979). Motives for social comparison: The construction-validation distinction. *Journal of Personality and Social Psychology,* **37,** 1683–1698.
Festinger, L. (1950). Informal social communication. *Psychological Review,* **57,** 271–282.
Festinger, L. (1954). A theory of social comparison processes. *Human Relations,* **7,** 117–140.
Festinger, L. (1957). *A theory of cognitive dissonance.* Evanston, IL: Row Peterson.
Festinger, L. (1964). *Conflict, decision, and dissonance.* Stanford, CA: Stanford University Press.
Festinger, L., & Carlsmith, J. M. (1959). Cognitive consequences of forced compliance. *Journal of Abnormal and Social Psychology,* **58,** 203–210.
Festinger, L., Gerard, H. B., Hymovitch, B., Kelley, H. H., & Raven, B. H. (1952). The influence process in the presence of extreme deviates. *Human Relations,* **5,** 327–346.
Festinger, L., & Thibaut, J. W. (1951). Interpersonal communication in small groups. *Journal of Abnormal and Social Psychology,* **46,** 92–99.
Fishbein, M., & Ajzen, I. (1975). *Belief, attitude, intention and behavior: An introduction to theory and research.* Reading, MA: Addison-Wesley.

Gerard, H. B. (1953). The effect of different dimensions of disagreement on the communication process in small groups. *Human Relations, 6*, 249–271.

Gerard, H. B. (1968). Basic features of commitment. In R. P. Abelson, E. Aronson, W. J. McGuire, T. M. Newcomb, M. J. Rosenberg, & P. H. Tannenbaum (Eds.), *Theories of cognitive consistency: A source book* (pp. 456–463). Chicago, IL: Rand McNally.

Gerard, H. B., & Wagner, W. (1984). *Opinion importance, coorientation and social comparison.* Unpublished manuscript.

Gerard, H. B., & White, G. L. (1983). Post-decisional reevaluation of choice alternatives. *Personality and Social Psychology Bulletin, 9*, 365–369.

Goethals, G. R. (1972). Consensus and modality in the attribution process: The role of similarity and information. *Journal of Personality and Social Psychology, 21*, 84–94.

Goethals, G. R., & Nelson, R. E. (1973). Similarity in the influence process: The belief-value distinction. *Journal of Personality and Social Psychology, 25*, 117–122.

Heilizer, F. (1977a). A review of theory and research on the assumptions of Miller's response competition (conflict) models: Response gradients. *The Journal of General Psychology, 97*, 17–71.

Heilizer, F. (1977b). A review of theory and research on Miller's response competition (conflict) models. *The Journal of General Psychology, 97*, 227–280.

Holmes, D. S. (1968). Dimensions of projection. *Psychological Bulletin, 69*, 248–268.

Hovland, C. I., Janis, I. L., & Kelley, H. H. (1953). *Communication and persuasion.* New Haven, CT: Yale University Press.

Hull, C. L. (1932). The goal gradient hypothesis and maze learning. *Psychological Review, 39*, 25–43.

Hull, C. L. (1938). The goal gradient hypothesis applied to some "field force" problems in the behavior of young children. *Psychological Review, 45*, 271–299.

Jones, E. E., & Gerard, H. B. (1967). *Foundations of social psychology.* New York: Wiley.

Jones, S. C., & Regan, D. T. (1974). Ability evaluation through social comparison. *Journal of Experimental Social Psychology, 10*, 133–146.

Katz, D. (1960). The functional approach to the study of attitudes. *Public Opinion Quarterly, 24*, 163–204.

Kelley, H. H., & Lamb, T. W. (1957). Certainty of judgment and resistance to social influence. *Journal of Abnormal and Social Psychology, 55*, 137–139.

Lamm, H., & Myers, D. G. (1978). Group-induced polarization of attitudes and behavior. In L. Berkowitz (Ed.), *Advances in experimental social psychology* (Vol. 11). New York: Academic Press.

Lewin, K. (1931). Environmental forces in child behavior and development. In C. Murchison (Ed.), *A handbook of child psychology.* Worchester, MA: Clark University Press.

Lewin, K., (1935). *The dynamic theory of personality.* New York: McGraw-Hill.

Lewin, K. (1938). The conceptual representation and measurement of psychological forces. *Contributions to Psychological Theory, 1* (4).

McClelland, D. C., Atkinson, J. W., Clark, R. A., & Lowell, E. L. (1953). *The achievement motive.* New York: Appleton.

Miller, N. E. (1944). Experimental studies of conflict. In J. M. Hunt (Ed.), *Personality and the behavioral disorders* (Vol. 1). New York: Ronald.

Miller, N. E. (1959). Liberalization of basic S-R concepts: Extensions to conflict behavior, motivation, and social learning. In S. Koch (Ed.), *Psychology: A study of a science* (Vol. 3). New York: McGraw-Hill.

Murstein, B. I., & Pryer, R. S. (1959). The concept of projection: A review, *Psychological Bulletin, 56*, 353–374.

Newcomb, T. M. (1953). An approach to the study of communicative acts. *Psychological Review,* **60,** 393–404.

Orive, R. (1981). Emotional and cognitive reactions to confirmation and disconfirmation of interpersonal expectations. *Dissertation Abstracts International,* **41B,** 3237 (University Microfilms No. 81-02, 864).

Orive, R. (1984). Group similarity, public self-awareness, and opinion extremity: A social projection explanation of deindividuation effects. *Journal of Personality and Social Psychology,* **47,** 727–737.

Petty, R. E., & Cacioppo, J. T. (1981). *Attitudes and persuasion: Classic and contemporary approaches.* Dubuque, IA: Wm. C. Brown.

Petty, R. E., Cacioppo, J. T., & Goldman, R. (1981). Personal involvement as a determinant of argument-based persuasion. *Journal of Personality and Social Psychology,* **41,** 847–855.

Rabbie, J. M., Brehm, J. W., & Cohen, A. R. (1959). Verbalization and reaction to cognitive dissonance. *Journal of Personality,* **27,** 407–417.

Raven, B. H. (1959). Social influence on opinions and the communication of related content. *Journal of Abnormal and Social Psychology,* **58,** 119–128.

Ross, L., Greene, D., & House, P. (1977). The "false consensus effect": An egocentric bias in social perception and attribution processes. *Journal of Experimental Social Psychology,* **13,** 279–301.

Schachter, S. (1951). Deviation, reject⁻ and communication. *Journal of Abnormal and Social Psychology,* **46,** 190–207.

Stone, P., & Kamiya, J. (1957). Judgments of consensus during group discussion. *Journal of Abnormal and Social Psychology,* **55,** 171–175.

Suchman, E. A. (1950). The intensity component in attitude and opinion research. In S. A. Stouffer, L. Guttman, E. A. Suchman, P. F. Lazarfeld, S. A. Star, & J. A. Clausen. *Measurement and prediction* (Vol. IV of *The American Soldier*). New York: Wiley.

Suls, J. M., & Miller, R. L. (1977). *Social comparison processes.* Washington, D.C.: Hemisphere.

Tesser, A. (1978). Self-generated attitude change. In L. Berkowitz (Ed.), *Advances in experimental social psychology* (Vol. 11). New York: Academic Press.

Travers, R. M. W. (1941). A study in judging the opinions of groups. *Archives of Psychology,* **266.**

Wallen, R. (1943). Individuals' estimates of group opinion. *Journal of Social Psychology,* **17,** 269–274.

White, G. L., & Gerard, H. B. (1981). Postdecision evaluation of choice alternatives as a function of valence of alternatives, choice, and expected delay of choice consequences. *Journal of Research in Personality,* **15,** 371–382.

Zimbardo, P. G. (1969). The human choice: Individuation, reason, and order versus deindividuation, impulse and chaos. In W. J. Arnold & O. Levine (Eds.), *Nebraska symposium on motivation* (Vol. 17). Lincoln: University of Nebraska Press.

POSITIVE AFFECT, COGNITIVE PROCESSES, AND SOCIAL BEHAVIOR

Alice M. Isen

DEPARTMENT OF PSYCHOLOGY
UNIVERSITY OF MARYLAND—
BALTIMORE COUNTY
CATONSVILLE, MARYLAND 21228

I. Introduction

Consider the following situation. You are sitting in your office, and you answer your telephone to hear a very respected and admired colleague tell you that your new paper that you sent him recently for comments is really impressive—an elegant piece of work and a genuine contribution to knowledge. This makes you feel very happy. The conversation then goes normally and, after a few minutes, you and your caller hang up. Do you think that this conversation will influence your subsequent interactions with other people? Will it influence the way you go about solving problems?

Next, consider the following event. You are walking down the street on your way to work on a nice, sunny day, and suddenly you notice a $5.00 bill lying on the ground. You look around to see if the person who dropped it is nearby, but there is no one else in sight. So, you pick up the $5.00 and put it in your wallet. You feel good. You think of the little "extra" you will buy with your found money. You become more aware of what a nice day it is, and as you think of the work day ahead, you focus on the interesting things you have planned to do. Now let me ask again, do you think that *this* event, even though it is nonsocial and unreflective of your own ability, will influence your subsequent interactions with people and the way you go about solving problems?

Recent research suggests that, in fact, affect states induced by such mild, everyday positive events as those described above can have a substantial influence on both social behavior and thought processes. Persons in whom positive

ADVANCES IN EXPERIMENTAL
SOCIAL PSYCHOLOGY, VOL. 20

affect has been induced, compared with those in control conditions, have been found to be more sociable, cooperative, and helpful to others. In addition, a growing body of literature is demonstrating that such mild affect also has a marked influence on cognitive processes and that the relationship between affect and social behavior may be mediated by thoughts and cognitive processes that accompany or result from affect. This chapter will examine some of the literature demonstrating an impact of affect on social behavior and then will consider the influence of affect on cognition in an attempt to further our understanding of how cognitive processes may mediate the effect of feelings on social behavior. Among the topics that will be considered are recent work suggesting an influence of positive affect on flexibility in cognitive organization (that is, in the perceived relatedness of ideas) and the implications of this effect for social interaction.

One goal of this research has been to expand our understanding of social behavior and the factors, such as affect, that influence interaction among people. Another has been to extend our knowledge of affect, both as one of these determinants of social behavior and in its own right. And a third has been to increase our understanding of cognitive processes, especially as they play a role in social interaction.

The assumptions underlying this approach have been threefold: first, that a good way to understand affect is to gain insight into its effects on cognitive and behavioral processes; second, that a key to understanding social behavior is understanding the cognitive processes that underlie interpretations and choices and thus can play a role in social interaction. This latter is the basic assumption of the approach known as "cognitive social psychology." What the current program of research has hoped to add to this field is some appreciation of the ways in which affect influences cognitive processes and, thus, social behavior.

The third assumption guiding this program of work has been that models of cognition must include affect and must do so in a realistic way that accounts for the wide range of effects that feelings have been found to have. Recent reserach suggests that the long-held view of affect as merely "disorganizing" (e.g., Young, 1943, 1961; but see Arnold, 1970; Easterbrook, 1959; and Leeper, 1948, 1970, for earlier discussions of this issue) or as an "interrupt" in an otherwise goal-directed program of behavior (Simon, 1967) must be supplemented in order to provide a more complete picture of affect's influence on cognition and behavior.

Most recently, cognitive and social psychologists have investigated ways in which affective factors may participate in cognitive processes (not just interrupt them) and have begun to include affect as a factor in more comprehensive models of cognition. For example, Bower (1981) has proposed that affect may be considered a node in a network and spreading-activation model of cognition (e.g., Anderson & Bower, 1973). A review of the research literature on the influence of affect on cognition suggests that this associationist model may not account well for some of the effects that have been observed (Isen, 1984), but the goal of including affect in comprehensive models of cognition remains, and alternative models may be forthcoming.

Recent data showing an impact of positive affect on problem solving, together with the suggestion that affect may influence cognitive organization and promote creativity, also imply that an alternative or addition to the spreading-activation model as a way to understand affect's influence on cognition might be useful. These findings lead us to consider some points raised by a contextualist or constructivist approach (e.g., Bransford, 1979; Jenkins, 1974; Neisser, 1967), to supplement the more associationist models. Thus, the work to be discussed in this chapter may have implications for some aspects of cognitive theory, as well as for the understanding of affect and the ways in which affect may influence social behavior.

The research to be described has focused primarily on feelings rather than intense emotion, because feelings are probably our most frequent affective experiences. Intense emotions occur relatively rarely, whereas feelings are our daily companions. By ''feelings'' I mean generalized affective experiences that do not demand or seem to focus immediate attention on themselves. They are usually, but not necessarily, relatively low level. Examples would include the kinds of things one feels as one goes about the activities of the day—listens to music, finds money on the street, gets wet in a cold rain, receives a compliment, loses money in a snack machine, finishes a task and is satisfied with the product, or receives a useful free sample. Because feelings do not usually interrupt ongoing behavior and capture attention, it is possible to examine their effects on other thoughts and behavior.

Although I have included above examples of situations that might generate negative feelings as well as some likely to generate positive ones, it is not clear that these two kinds of states would be equally easy to induce, equally unlikely to focus attention on themselves or their source, or equally likely to produce cognitive and behavioral effects. In fact, research suggests that positive and negative affective states may differ in ease of induction (e.g., Isen, Johnson, Mertz, & Robinson, 1985) and may have quite different kinds of effects on cognition and behavior. Supposedly comparable positive and negative affect have sometimes been found to produce effects that are similar, but sometimes they have produced effects that are opposite, and sometimes their results appear unrelated (see Isen, 1984, and Isen, 1985, for discussion of this issue). Thus, the finding that positive affect produces a certain effect does not necessarily imply that negative affect will give rise to its opposite, as is often assumed. These results suggest that positive and negative responses may be independent rather than bipolar. Much more research on the relationship between negative and positive affect is needed.

However, for the present, because whatever is discovered about the effects of one type of affect apparently will not always help us to predict the effects of the other, it is necessary to investigate each type of affect specifically. The research to be described in this chapter has focused primarily on positive affect.

II.   The Influence of Positive Affect
on Social Behavior

A.   POSITIVE AFFECT AND HELPFULNESS

A large body of research indicates that positive affect can influence social behavior—in particular, sociability, cooperativeness in negotiation, and kindness. Many studies have shown, for example, that people exposed to conditions designed to induce happy feelings are more likely than those in comparable control groups to help others (e.g., Aderman, 1972; Aderman & Berkowitz, 1970; Batson, Coke, Chard, Smith, & Taliaferro, 1979; Cunningham, 1979; Fried & Berkowitz, 1979; Isen, 1970; Isen, Horn, & Rosenhan, 1973; Isen & Levin, 1972; Isen, Clark, & Schwartz, 1976; Levin & Isen, 1975; Moore, Underwood & Rosenhan, 1973; Weyant, 1978). This appears to be true for both children and adults and seems to apply in many situations.

In the research, affect has been induced in a large variety of ways, ranging from receiving a free sample or getting one's dime back in the coin return of a public telephone to success on a task or to thinking about positive or negative events that had occurred in the past. Moreover, many different measures of helping, generosity, and kindness have been used to demonstrate the effect.

For example, in one series of studies, it was found that persons who had found a dime in the coin return of a public telephone in a shopping mall were more likely than control subjects to help a stranger pick up papers that she dropped. Similarly, students who unexpectedly received cookies while studying in a college library (in individual carrels) were more likely than controls to volunteer to help someone, but less likely to volunteer to annoy someone, when later approached by an unknown third party with a request to volunteer (Isen & Levin, 1972). Moreover, persons participating in a laboratory study who, on a random basis, received information that they had succeeded on a test of perceptual-motor skills were later more generous in donating to charity than either controls or persons notified of failure on the test. In a follow-up study, similarly treated persons were found to be more helpful to a stranger who needed help in carrying books and papers and who dropped one of the books (Isen, 1970). The general conclusion that can be drawn from this work is that positive affect is associated with an increase in the tendency to help others.

1. A Qualification to This Effect: Behavior Is Determined by More Than One Factor

As might be expected, however, there are circumstances under which the generalization that positive affect promotes helping will not hold. For example, one study has demonstrated that a person who is feeling good may actually be less willing to help than someone in a neutral state, if she or he has reason to believe that engaging in the helping task will be depressing (Isen & Simmonds, 1978). In that study, subjects who had found a dime in the coin return of a public telephone were more likely than control subjects to help someone by reading and evaluating statements that they were told would put them in a good mood, but positive-affect subjects were *less* likely than the control group to help by reading statements that they were told would put them in a *bad* mood. A similar finding involving willingness to help a liked cause, but refusal to aid a disliked cause, suggests that people who feel good may be more likely to behave as they please: they were more likely than persons in a control condition to help a cause that they favored, but less likely than controls to help a cause that they did not like (Forest, Clark, Mills, & Isen, 1979).

Results of these studies suggest that positive affect may have more than one influence and that the behavior that results from positive feelings may depend on the interaction among these influences. Positive affect may tend to promote helping in general, but it may also give rise to concern about protecting one's own good feelings. Additionally, it may engender a sense of personal freedom or independence. Under some circumstances, either of these alternative tendencies may override the increased likelihood of behavior such as helping.

2. The Motivation Underlying the Link Between Positive Affect and Helping

These findings should not be taken to suggest that a person who is feeling happy will engage only in behavior that will *improve* his/her feeling state; nor that when an elated person helps, it is *in order to* maintain his or her positive state; nor, even if this goal is sometimes present, that it is the *only* reason that helping occurs among persons who are feeling happy. There has been some confusion in the literature regarding these points recently (e.g., Manucia, Bauman, & Cialdini, 1984; Shaffer & Graziano, 1983), and thus they merit some attention.

There are both logical and empirical reasons not to draw any of these conclusions from the finding reported by Isen and Simmonds (1978) and Forest *et al.* (1979). First, logically, the finding that happy people are more sensitive to, or more avoidant of, negative affect is not grounds for saying that happy persons should be more drawn to activities that *boost* mood. Such a conclusion would be appropriate only if avoidance of negative affect required the seeking of positive affect. But these are not inextricably linked logically. Empirically, too, there is evidence that positive-affect subjects will do things other than seeking positive affect, and they will help others in situations that do not ostensibly benefit themselves (e.g., Batson et al., 1979; Isen, 1970; Isen & Levin, 1972; Levin & Isen, 1975). While there is some evidence that altruism may be rewarding to the person performing the helpful act (e.g., Weiss, Buchanan, Alstatt, & Lombardo, 1971), this fact does not necessarily mean that self-reward is the motive behind every instance of helpful behavior. Moreover, Manucia et al. (1984) reported results suggesting that the goal of improving one's own feeling state might not be the only determinant of behavior (see below). It should be noted that this finding is in no way incompatible with those presented by Isen and Simmonds (1978). The latter point out that, in a situation where the positive-affect state is threatened, persons who are feeling happy may tend to be especially avoidant of negative affect, and this tendency may even extend to a helping situation and may override the tendency to help. This does not necessarily imply, however, as some authors seem to have inferred, that positive affect should promote only behavior that improves or maintains a positive state and should be of little impact where affect is not at stake.

The finding that positive affect results in avoidance of tasks that are expected to destroy the positive feelings is even farther, logically, from the conclusion that helping that does occur under conditions of positive affect occurs *because* the helping will improve or maintain the positive state. It says nothing necessary about the motive for helping among positive-affect subjects when they *do* help. It says only that whatever that motive is, it can be superseded by other motives, such as desire to maintain the good feeling state (Isen & Simmonds, 1978) or desire to avoid benefiting a disliked cause (Forest et al., 1979).

Moreover, the hierarchy of motives that might be inferred from such findings may be specific to the particular situations involved. That is, in contrast to the findings under discussion (e.g., Isen & Simmonds, 1978), the motive to help another might outweigh one's desire to maintain one's own pleasant feelings if the other's need were very great or somehow more "important." Studies showing that people in whom positive affect has been induced will not always help more than controls simply direct our attention to additional motives that may be operating or factors in situations that may be influential. The question of what the motives or mechanisms for increased helping *are* among persons in positive-affect states remains an interesting one for investigation.

Several authors have set as their goal understanding the motivation underlying helpful acts. Batson and his colleagues (e.g., Batson, Duncan, Ackerman, Buckley, & Birch, 1981; Batson, O'Quin, Fultz, Vanderplas, & Isen, 1983; Toi & Batson, 1982), for example, have conducted a program of research designed to investigate the role of empathy in helping and to distinguish between altruistic versus egoistic motivation for helping. Manucia et al., (1984) have sought to address the issue of the motivation underlying helpful acts, specifically raising the question of whether persons who are feeling happy, and those who are feeling sad, help *in order to* maintain their positive, or improve their negative, affective states.

Manucia *et al.* (1984) attempted to reveal motivations related to mood change by getting subjects to believe, differentially, that their affective states were either labile or fixed for a period of time (as a result of a drug they had ingested). Results indicated that people in whom positive affect had been induced helped equally as much regardless of whether they believed that their feeling states were fixed or labile, whereas persons in whom sadness had been induced were more likely to help in a situation in which they believed their emotions were open to change (i.e., improvement) than one in which they were fixed. The authors concluded from these results that people who are sad help in order to improve their affect states, but that mood maintenance is not a motive for helping among people in whom a positive state has been induced. These conclusions may be too sweeping.

One troubling aspect of the results of this study is that, although the two positive-affect groups helped equally, *neither* helped more than the control group. This means that *no* influence of positive affect on helping was actually observed, so that it is not possible to say that elated people helped more than controls regardless of whether their affect state was thought to be fixed or labile. It is only possible to say that lability appeared not to be a factor, but it is not clear why positive affect of either kind (fixed or labile) failed to promote helping.

This consideration suggests a need for caution in interpreting the findings of this study; however, with appropriate caution, the results of the study do provide some support for the suggestion that when people who are happy help, it need not be in order to maintain their own positive feelings. It is not possible to conclude from this study that desire to maintain or improve one's own positive affective state can *never* be the motivation underlying helping (or not helping) among persons in whom positive affect has been induced or that positive affect maintenance is irrelevant in helping situations (the fact that helping continued to occur under conditions where loss of affect was not possible does not mean that the goal of affect protection might not govern behavior in a situation in which the affect state *were* threatened). But they may indicate that such a goal is not the *only* possible motive for helping. There may be other factors that can promote helping when one is happy; and, in fact, several lines of research, including the recent work on the influence of positive affect on cognitive processes, have resulted from exploration of the question of just what such factors might be.

B. POSITIVE AFFECT AND BENEVOLENCE TO SELF

Returning to our consideration of the impact of positive feelings on social behavior, people who feel good have been found to be more kind to themselves as well as to others: they tend to reward themselves more than control subjects do (Mischel, Coates, & Raskoff, 1968) and to display a greater preference for positive than negative self-relevant information (Mischel, Ebbesen, & Zeiss, 1973, 1976). There is reason not to interpret this relative self-indulgence as impulsiveness or loss of self-control. For example, several studies found that children who had succeeded, unlike those who had failed, did not display impaired ability to resist temptation (Frey, 1975) or to delay gratification (Schwartz & Pollack, 1977; Seeman & Schwartz, 1974). Thus, all of these results might be interpreted as the products of decisions to behave in ways that are kind to oneself as well as to others.

C. POSITIVE AFFECT AND COOPERATIVENESS

Positive affect has been found to be associated with increased sociability and cooperativeness, as reflected in behavior such as willingness to initiate conversations with others (Batson et al., 1979; Isen, 1970) and expression of liking for people (Gouaux, 1971; Griffitt, 1970; Veitch & Griffitt, 1976). People in whom positive affect has been induced show less aggressiveness than others (e.g., Baron, 1984; Baron & Ball, 1974), and they may be more receptive to persuasive communication under some circumstances (Galizio & Hendrick, 1972, Janis, Kaye, & Kirschner, 1965). They have been found to take a cooperative, problem-solving orientation in negotiation, rather than a competitive one, and to obtain more optimal outcomes than persons in comparable neutral-affect control conditions in an integrative bargaining task (Carnevale & Isen, 1986).

An integrative bargaining task or problem situation is one in which the negotiators have different payoff possibilities for each of several issues and must make tradeoffs in order to reach optimal agreement. Reaching agreement in such a task involves seeing a large number of alternatives and thinking flexibly about how they might be combined. Integrative solutions are different from "compromise," in which concessions are made to a midpoint on a single, obvious dimension. A well-known illustration of this difference describes two persons who are arguing over which one will have an orange that is in their joint possession. They cut it in half and share it equally (compromise), only to discover that one drinks the juice from his half and discards the rind, while the other cuts the rind from his half to use in making a cake and throws the juice away. If they had negotiated integratively, they would have discovered their real needs and each obtained more of what he was seeking. Integrative solutions are also contrasted with "yielding," in which one party lowers his/her aspirations. Like compromise, this negotiation strategy can be seen as inferior to an integrative one, because it results in lower overall joint benefit than is possible to achieve in the situation. (For greater detail, see, for example, Pruitt, 1983.)

In one study, persons in whom positive affect had been induced by means of a small free gift (a tablet of paper) and humor (cartoons), and who then bargained face-to-face with another person on an integrative bargaining task, were significantly more likely than comparable control subjects, who bargained face-to-face but in whom positive affect had not been induced, to reach agreement, to reach the optimal agreement (i.e., achieve the highest possible joint and individual outcomes), and to have positive evaluations of the situation and of the other participant (Carnevale & Isen, 1986). In addition, there was a near-significant tendency among positive-affect subjects to have greater understanding of the other player's payoff matrix (priority preferences among three items about which negotiation was centered).

Both this latter finding and the better joint outcome of the negotiation for persons who bargained in a positive state suggest a better understanding of the overall situation among those persons. The task is not one in which simple liking for the other person and yielding, based on this liking or on desire to avoid conflict, would result in the optimal, or even an acceptable, outcome for either party. Thus, positive affect has been found to facilitate face-to-face negotiation and to promote the understanding of a complex interpersonal situation. In fact, improved understanding of the situation may even mediate the positive social outcomes that occurred (successful negotiation, liking for the other party, and enjoyment of the activity). This potential relationship between improved cognitive processes and improved social interaction is a topic to which we shall return later.

D. POSITIVE AFFECT AND RISK PREFERENCE

There is some evidence that positive affect can influence behavior and decision making in situations of risk or uncertainty, both social and nonsocial (e.g., Isen, Means, Patrick, & Nowicki, 1982). In situations in which the chance or amount of possible loss is inconsequential, there appears to be a tendency for positive affect to be associated with a greater inclination to take a risk; but, in contrast, where potential for loss is great or salient, subjects who are feeling good tend to be more conservative than those in a neutral condition (Arkes, Herren, & Isen, 1987; Isen & Geva, 1987; Isen & Patrick, 1983).

Several studies now indicate this tendency toward cautiousness in situations in which meaningful loss is possible, and a greater concern about such loss, among persons in whom positive affect has been induced. In one study, in which subjects were given the opportunity to gamble with chips representing fractions of their credit for participating in the experiment and in which the only bet open to them was a high-risk one (17% chance of winning), those in whom positive affect had been induced (by receipt of a coupon for a free hamburger) bet less than control subjects (Isen & Patrick, 1983). Similarly, in another study, in which the dependent measure was acceptable probability level for placing a predetermined bet of 1, 5, or 10 chips (again, representing fractions of participation credit), subjects in whom positive affect had been induced (by receipt of a small bag of candy), relative to controls, required a higher probability of winning before they were willing to bet 5 or 10 chips (but not for 1 chip). They also expressed a higher percentage of thoughts about losing than control subjects, in a thought-listing task (Isen & Geva, 1987). These two studies suggest that, relative to people in control conditions, positive-affect subjects are more concerned about possible loss and more cautious in gambling where the potential for loss is high.

Most recently, another study has indicated that positive affect influences the perceived negative utility of losses, making them loom larger (seem worse) than they normally might. This study used a procedure devised by Davidson, Suppes, and Siegel (1956) to estimate perceived utility while holding probability constant. The results indicated that potential losses held greater negative utilities for subjects who had received a small gift than for those in a control condition (Isen, Nygren, & Ashby, 1985).

Changes in subjective *probability* have been hypothesized to influence the risk preferences of persons in affective states (e.g., Isen *et al.*, 1982; Isen & Patrick, 1983), and Johnson & Tversky (1983) demonstrated such an effect (showing that positive affect reduced people's subjective probabilities of negative events occurring). However, these more recent results show that, independent of any effect that positive feelings may have on the subjective probability of negative events occurring, positive affect influences the perceived utility of such events, making them seem more aversive.

This finding is compatible with those showing increased cautiousness among possitive-affect subjects, and it suggests that the effect may be mediated by an impact on perceived utility, independent of any influence of affect on subjective probability of an event's occurrence. Moreover, because this study shows heightened negative utilities specifically for losses among positive-affect subjects, it goes one step further in suggesting a mechanism behind the increased preference for safety observed: it indicates that for people who are feeling happy avoidance of loss and affect maintenance may be a factor in decisions involving risk and potential loss. In this same study, it should be noted, the comparable effect of positive feelings on subjective utility of *gains* was much less than that involving losses. Generally, there were no significant differences between the affect groups, when considering gains, although the comparison for the largest potential gain was of borderline significance ($p = .08$). In other words, relative to the control group, persons in whom positive affect had been induced indicated that a given loss would seem more aversive to them; however, any given *gain* (except the very largest) did not seem more valuable or desirable. This suggests that the impact of positive affect on perceived utilities of losses may need to be considered independent of any impact on perceived utilities of gains.

It might be noted that these findings regarding risk taking are compatible with the hypothesis, discussed earlier (Section II,A), that a positive affective state is accompanied by an inclination to maintain that state (a tendency toward affect protection). In these studies, subjects in whom mild positive affect had been induced showed increased sensitivity to loss and behaved so as to avoid its occurrence. The data may also hold some support for the hypothesis of positive affect promoting an inclination to exercise one's freedom to behave as one wishes (in the finding that positive-affect subjects are more likely to take a chance where potential harm is low), but this is less clear.

In summary of this section, then, the evidence indicates that positive affect is associated with increased sociability, cooperativeness, and benevolence to both self and others, decreased aggressiveness, the presence of a problem-solving orientation in negotiation, and cautiousness in threatening situations. Studies investigating the influence of feelings on social behavior have also tried to explore the processes that might underlie such effects—the means by which feeling good oneself might lead one to be more generous and helpful to others, for example (e.g., Berkowitz, 1972; Isen, 1970; Isen & Levin, 1972). Initially, interpretations such as increase in frustration tolerance (Berkowitz, 1972) or increase in perceived resources (Isen, 1970) were proposed. But subsequently the level of analysis changed, and authors became concerned with the process by which feeling good might lead to increased frustration tolerance or sense of surplus. This led some authors to propose cognitive processes which might mediate such effects. Thus, interest in the processes by which happiness leads to helping produced studies of the influence of affect on decision making, memory, thinking, and problem solving. We will consider this work next.

III. The Influence of Positive Affect on Cognition

A. POSITIVE AFFECT AND MEMORY

Thus, a large body of literature now indicates that mild positive affect can have a marked influence on social behavior, and attention has begun to focus on the cognitive processes that may mediate such effects. Several studies suggest that happiness can influence cognitive processes of memory and judgment, and it has been proposed that these effects may mediate the influence of happiness on social behavior.

1. Effect at Time of Retrieval

One of the earliest findings in this area was that an affective state at time of attempted recall could influence memory. In particular, it was found that positive affect facilitated the recall of positive material that had been learned earlier in the study (Isen, 1975; Isen, Shalker, Clark, & Karp, 1978). People who had succeeded on a task, in comparison with those who had failed, showed better recall for positive trait adjectives such as "kind" and "friendly" than for other words (negative traits, neutral traits, or neutral nontrait words). Persons in the negative affect condition (failure) did not show parallel superiority for negative material, and there was no state-dependent learning effect (superior recall for material learned and recalled in the same state).

In order to understand the meaning of these results, it is helpful to consider the concepts of "accessibility" (Tulving & Pearlstone, 1966) and "priming" (Brown, 1979; Neely, 1976, 1977). Tulving and Pearlstone (1966) introduced the idea that memory depends not only on whether material was initially learned and is *available* in memory storage, but also upon the conditions present at time of attempted recall, which affect its relative *accessibility*. These authors demonstrated that the presence, at time of attempted recall, of a cue to the material, such as the name of the category to which the item belonged, facilitated the recall of the material. So, for example, subjects were found to be able to recall more words (for example, "elm," "spruce") from a learned list of words of different categories when the name of one of the categories (for example, "trees") was presented at time of attempted recall. Material of the category was said to be more accessible when the category was "primed" in this way. Several studies have now shown that people respond more quickly and easily to words that are related to material to which they have recently responded, including category names, category members, and other related words or social concepts (e.g., Higgins & King, 1981; Jacobson, 1973; Loftus, 1973; Loftus & Loftus, 1974; Meyer & Schvaneveldt, 1971; Posner & Snyder, 1975; Srull & Wyer, 1979; Warren, 1977).

Thus, in order to understand the impact of positive affect on memory described above, it was proposed that positive affect could serve as a retrieval cue for positive material in memory, rendering such material more accessible. It was also assumed that such a retrieval bias might also influence other cognitive processes (such as judgment, evaluation, expectations, and decision making) and behavior that follows from those processes, as well (Isen, 1975; Isen *et al.*, 1978). There is now considerable evidence that this is the case, and it seems that positive affective state can function like category name or other organizing unit as a cue to prime related cognitive material. Several additional studies, using various means of affect induction, have confirmed that positive affect can influence memory, both speeding up the recall of positive material (Teasdale & Fogarty, 1979) and rendering the recall of positive material more likely (e.g., Laird, Wagener, Halal, & Szegda, 1982; Nasby & Yando, 1982; Teasdale & Russell, 1983). Positive material seems to be more accessible to people who are feeling good.

In addition, it has been shown that induced mild positive affect can influence people's judgments. For example, in a study conducted in a shopping mall, people who had been given a small free sample note pad or nail clipper expressed more positive evaluations of their major consumer products on an apparently unrelated consumer opinion survey than did a control group that had not been given the free sample (Isen, 1975; Isen *et al.*, 1978).

This effect of happiness on judgment has been interpreted as resulting from the influence of positive feelings on memory noted above. In accord with Tversky and Kahneman's (1974) suggestion that judgments tend to be influenced by the material that is accessible in memory when the judgment is being made, it has been hypothesized that the greater accessibility of positive material that has been observed among persons who are feeling happy has an impact upon their judgments (e.g., Isen, 1975; Isen *et al.*, 1978).

2. Effect at Time of Encoding

A few studies have reported an encoding effect of positive feelings—that is, that affect at time of learning may influence the material that is learned. (This effect has been called "mood-congruent learning" by Bower and his colleagues.) These studies have found that people who are happy at time of learning later show better recall of positive material in the list of items or paragraph being learned than of other material, relative to controls. For example, Bower, Gilligan, and Montiero (1981) found that people in whom positive affect had been induced (by means of hypnosis) at the time of learning of the material (but not at time of recall) recalled more facts about persons described as happy (more facts compatible with a positive state). Nasby and Yando (1982), using fifth-grade children as subjects and nonhypnotic mood inductions, found that a positive encoding mood resulted later in better recall of positive trait adjectives than other words, relative to controls. Thus, people who are happy may find it easier to learn material that is compatible with their positive state, and this ease is reflected in their recall of the material later, even if they are not made happy at the time of recall. This finding, like the retrieval effect (though not observed as frequently as the latter), suggests that positive material somehow receives preferential treatment in memory when one is happy.

3. State-Dependent Learning

A third type of effect occasionally reported in the affect-memory literature is the state-dependent-learning effect. This refers to the facilitation of recall by the matching of feeling *states* (not the match between a feeling state and the content of the material to be recalled) at time of learning and recall—the tendency for material, regardless of its affective tone, learned in a specific state to be recalled better when one is again in that same state than at another time.

A state-dependent effect of positive feelings has been reported by a few authors (e.g., Bartlett, Burleson, & Santrock, 1982; Bartlett & Santrock, 1979; Bower, Montiero, & Gilligan, 1978), but it has more frequently not been found and has been considered unreliable, or at least weak and of limited application, by most researchers in the area from the first (e.g., Isen *et al.*, 1978; Laird *et al.*, 1982; Nasby & Yando, 1982; see Eich & Birnbaum, 1982; Isen, 1984; and Isen *et al.*, 1978, for discussion of this issue).[1] On the other hand, Bower and his colleagues had argued that state-dependent learning based on affect was a robust phenomenon and might even be the only basis on which effects thought to be retrieval effects of feelings occurred (Bower *et al.*, 1981). But more recently, Bower and Mayer (1985), like other researchers, have reported repeated failure to obtain the state-dependent-learning effect based on affective state and have suggested that the effect is not reliable.

This conclusion does not apply, more generally, to effects of feelings on memory: affective state (at least positive affect) does appear able to influence memory, but on the basis of the matching of the affective state and the tone (meaning) of the material, rather than on the basis of the matching of the affective states at learning and retrieval (the state-dependent effect). It is possible that state-dependent-learning effects of affect may occur under circumstances where meaning-based learning is unlikely (e.g., where material is meaningless, where affect is especially focal or salient, and/or where thinking, interpretation, and meaning-based learning are especially difficult for any reason).

4. *Asymmetry between Happiness and Sadness*

It should be noted that, for each of these three types of effects, it cannot be assumed that what holds true about happiness is also true for other affective states, particularly the assumed opposite of happiness, sadness. Although some investigators do report symmetrical effects of happiness and sadness (e.g., Bower, 1981; Bower *et al.*, 1981; Bower *et al.*, 1978; Laird *et al.*, 1982), most of the studies that report effects of happiness on memory, whether reporting encoding, retrieval, or state-dependent-learning effects, fail to find comparable effects for sadness. They suggest, instead, that sadness does not facilitate the recall of negative material or does so to a lesser extent than does comparable positive affect (e.g., Bartlett, Burleson, & Santrock, 1982; Bartlett & Santrock, 1979; Isen *et al.*, 1978; Nasby & Yando, 1982; Natale & Hantas, 1982; Riskind, 1983; Teasdale & Fogarty, 1979; Teasdale, Taylor, & Fogarty, 1980; see Isen, 1984, for fuller discussion of this issue).

---

[1]It should be noted that this refers to a state-dependent-learning effect based on normal, relatively mild, feeling state, not to state-dependent-learning effects more generally. State-dependent learning effects based on intense, dominating states such as alcoholic intoxication have been consistently reported by other investigators, for example, Weingartner and his colleagues (e.g., Weingartner & Faillace, 1971).

Two types of ideas for understanding this asymmetry between happiness and sadness have been proposed, one motivational and one structural.

  a. A Motivational Interpretation. The motivational interpretation suggests that the reason that happiness is a better cue than sadness is that people are naturally motivated to maintain a positive state, but are motivated to change an unhappy state. Thus, under normal circumstances, people use their positive affective states as cues and think about and enjoy the positive material that comes to mind as a result of that cueing process. In contrast, it might be expected that people would not use their sadness as a cue and, if any automatic effect occurred, would attempt to stop the process of thinking about negative material that might be cued by sadness.

Even some of the studies that report symmetrical effects of happiness and sadness are compatible with this interpretation, because they used hypnosis as the means of affect induction and instructed subjects under hypnosis to maintain their induced affect states throughout the session. This, then, might account not only for the symmetrical effects of positive and negative affect observed in those studies, but also for the encoding effects which were also observed under those conditions. (Instructions at the outset of the session to maintain one's affective state throughout the session might promote encoding effects, because such instructions might cause subjects to focus on affect-compatible material during the learning phase of the experiment more than they otherwise might.) The same observation may also be relevant to studies that induced affect via the Velten technique or requests to imagine or remember an affective state/event, since these techniques require of subjects that they make a specific effort to bring on the affective state and mentally concentrate on it.

  b. A Structural Interpretation. It is also possible to propose a structural interpretation of the asymmetry between happiness and sadness in effects on memory. That is, the cognitive structures or sets of material associated with positive and negative affect may differ in important ways that produce the observed asymmetry in recall-cue effectiveness. For example, it is possible that positive material is more extensive and at the same time better integrated, so that positive affect is able to cue a wide range of thoughts. In contrast, material related to sadness may be structured more specifically and kept in relative isolation from other thoughts, so that sadness can cue only a small range of thoughts that are very specifically related to sadness (not to all negative experiences) or even to the particular cause of the sadness being experienced.[2]

It seems plausible that such a structural difference may exist and contribute

---

[2]According to associative network theory, this might imply that, although sadness may cue a more limited range of material (i.e., only material that matches it precisely), it may be an especially effective cue for that bit of material. This would lead to the prediction that, although sadness may not provide access to as much material as positive affect, it may be a very effective cue for the small circle of material to which it is related.

to the observed asymmetry, in addition to any motivational effect that may play a role, because the asymmetry has been observed in memory, not just in behavior. While motivational factors can, of course, affect the results of memory experiments, it seems likely that a smaller range of material is accessed by a negative state than a positive one.

It is also possible that both kinds of processes (cognitive and motivational) may be in evidence in the observed asymmetry. In fact, habitual use of the motivational strategies described above might be one factor contributing to the creation of the asymmetrical cognitive structures for positive and negative affect that have been proposed. Exploration of the specifics of the cognitive structures associated with various affective states—the cognitive representations of affects—seems an exciting possibility for empirical research. In fact, we will have occasion to think about these matters again later in this chapter, when we discuss the work that has been done so far on the influence of positive affect on cognitive organization.

5. The Role of Meaning in the Effect of Feelings on Memory

In light of our earlier discussion of the impact of affect on memory, it appears that affect's influence on memory is usually mediated by meaning, rather than only mechanistically on the basis of peripheral cues present at time of learning and recall. As we have seen, the research literature shows that positive material is more readily recalled when one is happy than at another time, and that this effect is not usually based on a simple state-dependent-learning effect. This suggests that positive affect may serve as a retrieval cue for material meaningfully related to positive feelings, and thus, given the encoding-specificity principle, it suggests that positive affect may be the basis of a cognitive category that is actively used to organize material. The literature suggests that positive affect does not simply act automatically as a physical context cue, which a state-dependent-learning effect would imply, cueing anything that happened to be present at the time of the feelings. As noted above, it is rare (though not impossible) to observe affect-based state-dependent learning effects, which would involve the phenomenon of nonaffective material cued on the basis of affect as a physical cue, not a meaningful cue. Rather, positive affect appears more often to influence memory through an impact on meaning, cueing material that is meaningfully related to positive affect or "in" the positive affect category.

This brings to mind the question of what "positive material" is—that is, what precisely is included in the category that is cued by positive feelings. While this seems a reasonable question, and in general the answer would be something like "material with a pleasant meaning," more accurately the answer has to be "whatever the person has stored as related to that category." This may seem unsatisfying, but it is the same answer that would be given in response to a similar question about the contents of any category—for example, "Trees" or "Furniture" or "Fruits": the particular contents depend on the exemplars of the category a person knows and, to some extent, the experiences a person has had with them. There are certain commonalities that one can expect of people in our culture, but the specific content of categories depends on individuals' categorization schemes. Moreover, recent work is beginning to suggest that categorization can also be influenced by aspects of the categorization situation (e.g., Isen & Daubman, 1984; Murphy & Medin, 1985; Roth & Shoben, 1983; Smith & Medin, 1981). Thus, the contents of categories may vary from time to time or situation to situation, as well as person to person, as people construe the category in the situation. The same is likely true for the affect category.

Thus, the important points center not on precisely what the contents of the positive-affect category are, but rather on the fact that positive affect constitutes a category in the cognitive system and functions as a cognitive category, based on meaning; and, further, that affective *state* can cue and provide access to this meaning category. Exploration of the nature of affective categories and of the ways in which they are structured, accessed, used, and related to other material are exciting topics for continued research.

a. Encoding Specificity and State-Dependent Learning. These points, that positive affect can serve as the basis of a category or as an organizing principle in the cognitive system and that feeling state can cue material encoded as relevant to that category, depend on the distinction between state-dependent-learning effects (simple context effects) and meaning-based effects, and they relate to the encoding-specificity principle. Because the encoding-specificity principle was originally established using studies similar to state-dependent learning experiments and because it emphasizes the compatibility between learning and retrieval cues, the point that retrieval effects of affect are mediated by meaning, and not simply via physical context cues, and yet are compatible with the encoding-specificity principle, merits some discussion.

The encoding-specificity principle (e.g., Thomson & Tulving, 1970; Tulving, 1979; Tulving & Osler, 1968; Tulving & Thomson, 1973) maintains that a retrieval cue can be effective in recall only if the learned material was encoded as somehow associated with or relevant to that cue. Thus, it allows for state-dependent learning (if a learner happens to use a learning strategy that involves aspects of his/her physical state or of the physical context, and those aspects of the physical context are presented as cues at the time of retrieval), but it is more broad than the latter and also allows for meaning-based learning. In fact, since people are usually more likely to use meaning than physical context as a basis for learning (Tulving & Thompson, 1973), the encoding-specificity principle would suggest that meaning-based learning would be the general rule, with state-dependent learning (a special case of encoding specificity) less frequent.

Originally, this principle was established by studies demonstrating that a cue (e.g., a word paired with a target word in a list of words to be learned) present during learning (encoding) was later a more effective retrieval cue than one that had not been present at encoding (even, in some cases, in comparison with a word otherwise highly associated with the target word). This seems reminiscent of state-dependent learning, because it demonstrates improved recall where there is, in some sense, a match between "conditions" present at time of encoding and at time of retrieval. (In encoding-specificity studies, the matching condition is the presence of the same word among those presented; in state-dependent-learning studies, it is the presence of the same physical or affective state.)

In making this connection and equating the presence of a word with the presence of a state, one is viewing the words and the feeling states in terms of their physical properties, rather than their meanings, and equating them with physical context cues such as the color of the walls or temperature of the air. This associationist stance would hold that the encoding-specificity effect obtained in the studies described above occurs, not because of a subject's memorization strategy, but only because of a relatively automatic association between the words that were presented at the same time. In contrast, however, Tulving and his associates emphasized the importance of the learner's memorization strategy, which most often utilizes the meanings of words (e.g., Tulving & Thomson, 1973; Tulving, 1979).

The important point to be made here is that encoding specificity and state-dependent learning actually represent different principles, with very different potential implications—one focusing on the importance of learning strategy (which most often involves meaning) for memory, the other focusing on automatic association—even though the techniques used to establish the encoding-specificity principle appear similar to those used in state-dependent-learning studies.

   b.   *Differences between Encoding Specificity and State-Dependent Learning.*   On closer inspection, it is clear that encoding specificity and state-dependent learning are conceptually distinct, even despite this similarity in the way they have been investigated. The principle of encoding specificity maintains that the effectiveness of a cue at time of recall depends on whether it relates to the way in which the given stimulus was encoded. This is distinct, logically, from saying, as the state-dependent-learning position does, that every cue present at encoding should later be an effective retrieval cue. A retrieval cue cannot be effective if it does not relate to the way material was stored, but it need not have been physically present itself in order to serve an effective cue later; moreover, every cue present at time of learning does not automatically become an effective retrieval cue.

Encoding specificity and state-dependent learning also have different theoretical implications. The former concept, compatible with a contextualist approach, acknowledges that subjects' strategies, and the meaning of the material to the subjects in the context of these strategies, can play a role in learning (e.g., Tulving, 1979). In contrast, state-dependent learning, more an associationist view than a contextualist one, ignores the role of interpretation, meaning, and the subjects' goals and strategies in learning. Applied to the encoding-specificity paradigm, it treats the other words in the to-be-learned list only as a part of the physical context, important only because they were present rather than because they were *used* by subjects in learning the material. Applied to affect, likewise, the idea of affect-based state-dependent learning assumes that the affective state is only part of the physical context. Encoding specificity, in contrast, applied to the retrieval effects of positive affect, suggests a meaning basis, rather than a simple context basis, for the success of affect as a cue for positive material in memory. This implies further that, since positive affect can be an effective retrieval cue for positively toned material, positive material is a meaningful cognitive category, used by people in encoding information. Thus, the implications of a state-dependent-learning view regarding the processes of encoding and retrieval are quite different from those of the encoding-specificity principle, even though state-dependent learning appears only slightly different from encoding specificity, and especially, from the studies used to establish the latter.

Encoding specificity makes a flexible statement as to which cues present at encoding will be associated with the target cue and will therefore become effective retrieval cues. For example, Tulving (1979) voices agreement with Morris, Bransford, and Franks (1977) in saying that the most appropriate or valuable encoding strategy (and therefore, presumably, the cues that will best promote recall) will depend on the task demands or on the particular goals and purposes of the learner. No one strategy or basis for recall will always be superior to another. Encoding specificity maintains only that it is the compatibility of these learning cues with those presented at time of retrieval that determines ease of recall and that in order for a cue to be effective at retrieval, it must have played a role in the encoding of the material.

Thus, the most effective retrieval cue will not be just any cue that happened to be present also at encoding, but rather the one that corresponds to the strategy that was used in learning. Success in recall will depend upon a match between encoding strategy and cues provided at time of recall. The match that must be made to enable successful recall, however, according to the encoding-specificity principle, is a match between strategies, encodings, or meanings, and cues to those, rather than simply a match between any two cues that happen to be present at each occasion. The encoding-specificity principle, unlike the assumptions underlying the state-dependent-learning predictions, allows for the meaning and emphasis provided by the learner (e.g., Tulving, 1979) and the way in which a stimulus was experienced by a learner (e.g., Jenkins, 1974) to influence coding and memory. Thus, results that have been obtained showing that positive material is more easily recalled when one is in a positive affective state would suggest not only that positive affect can be the basis of a cognitive category or dimension (can serve as a way of organizing thoughts), but that it is one that tends to be actively *used* by subjects.

    c. Levels of Processing.   i.   Possible Effect of Degree of Elaboration of Material Learned.   The foregoing discussion raises the topic of levels of processing. For one thing, the failures to obtain affect-based state-dependent-learning effects, together with the prevalence of retrieval effects based on the meaning of the words, suggest that meaning-based retrieval cues may usually be more effective than the mere stimulus properties of the material to be learned. Such a possibility corresponds to what the cognitive literature refers to as the "levels of processing" distinction (e.g., Craik & Lockhart, 1972; Craik & Tulving, 1975; Fisher & Craik, 1977). It has been suggested that, all else equal, material encoded more deeply (e.g., according to its semantic meaning) will be recalled better than material encoded more shallowly (e.g., according to its stimulus properties). The precise meaning of the terms used in the levels-of-processing framework is not established, but researchers have considered the crucial factor in depth of processing to be something like "spread" or degree of elaboration, or number of encoding (and therefore potential retrieval) devices or cues with which the item is learned. This suggests that material learned according to its meaning or other "deep" level of processing may be more memorable because it is more elaborated.

    On the other hand, Tulving (1979) has pointed out that, given the encoding specificity principle, only the compatibility between encoding and retrieval cues determines the success of recall. Thus, no particular way of encoding can be said to be inherently better than any other. Its "goodness" will depend on the retrieval cues available later, at time of attempted recall. Likewise, Fisher and Craik (1977) found that retention levels were dependent not only on type of encoding but also on type of retrieval used. However, they also found evidence compatible with the interpretation that "deeper" processing led to superior recall. It may be that deeper encoding, more elaborated encoding, itself acts to increase potential compatibility between encoding and retrieval cues if it increases the number of ways in which material is encoded and therefore the number of potential retrieval cues that might be effective when later encountered.

    ii.   Positive Affect and Elaboration.   This issue may be important in understanding the impact of positive affect on recall, because positive affect, like deep encoding or encoding in terms of meaning, may involve extensive elaboration (that is, a wide range of associated thoughts). There is evidence that positive affect gives rise to an enlarged cognitive context. For example, persons in whom a positive affect *state* has been induced have been found to give more unusual word associations, and a greater diversity of first associates, to neutral stimulus words than do persons in control conditions (e.g., Isen, Johnson, Mertz, &

Robinson, 1985). This broader cognitive context may lead to, or itself reflect, cognitive elaboration. Likewise, positive *material* has been shown to have an advantage over other material on many cognitive measures, from recall to speed and diversity of word associations (e.g., Isen, Johnson, Mertz, & Robinson, 1985; Matlin & Stang, 1979). This situation is sometimes attributed to the negative affective pole instead of the positive, and thus to assumed irrational "defensive" processes; however, it may result from the greater elaboration of positive material, the fact that positive material has a diverse lot of associates (Isen, Johnson, Mertz, & Robinson, 1985).

6. Cognitive Theoretical Implications of the Affect-Memory Finding

It is sometimes assumed that the suggestion that affect may constitute a category in memory, and that feelings can serve as retrieval cues for material in memory, implies the network and spreading-activation view of the structure of memory, as described by Anderson and Bower (1973) and as related to affect by Bower (1981). This is not necessarily the case. These findings are equally compatible with a constructivist position as described by, for example, Jenkins (1974): they say nothing about the underlying structure of memory and cognition nor anything about whether this structure is static or changing.

Indeed, recently it has been noted that some of the data showing an effect of feelings on memory and judgment appear to raise some problems for the associative network account: feelings have not always produced the effects that might have been predicted by that theory (e.g., Isen, 1984; Johnson & Tversky, 1983). Some of these problems have been reviewed elsewhere recently (Isen, 1984) and will only be briefly mentioned here. They include (1) the failure of state-dependent-learning effects based upon induced feelings, (2) cue overload, (3) the ability of positive affect to serve as a retrieval cue for positive material learned during an experimental session, (4) the absence of gradients in the effects of feelings on judgment and memory, and (5) the asymmetry between positive and negative affect in effects on memory and other cognitive processes.

The Failure of State-Dependent-Learning Effects of Feelings. The easiest way for affect to be incorporated into associative network theory would be as a simple context cue. (Here the word "context" is not being used as the contextualists use it, to refer to the complex, cognitive aspects of context that influence meaning and interpretation, but rather as a simple stimulus element present in the situation.) However, if affect were only that simple kind of context cue (stimulus element), then state-dependent-learning effects based on feelings should be the rule. All words present during an affective state should show superior retrievability when the person were again in that affective state (Bower, 1981). But, as we have seen, state-dependent effects of feelings are not commonly observed and appear to occur only in a limited range of situations. In contrast, retrieval effects of positive affect have been observed rather consistently. Thus, it does not appear that affect serves only as a simple stimulus element. The failure of the state-dependent-learning paradigm to produce consistent effects with affect (together with the fact that retrieval effects of positive feelings are commonly obtained) suggests that the associative network model may not tell the whole story. This is because these data suggest that affective material (and perhaps other material as well) may not typically be encoded according to the stimulus context present at the time of learning, but rather according to meaning or feeling or some other "deeper" level of processing. This suggests that cueing and recall usually involve not the automatic activation of a relatively permanent "node" in memory, together with all of its associated material, but rather the active utilization of meaning or interpretation to organize a concept for storage and retrieval. Sometimes this process will involve the person's purposes and goals as well as stored knowledge. Thus, it has been suggested that schema or contextualist theories of memory may shed additional light on the way in which affect influences cognition (Isen, 1984).

Cue Overload.   According to associative network theory, the more items that are associated with a given simple context cue, the less effective that cue should be in prompting any single one of those stimuli. This has been termed "cue overload" (e.g., Watkins, 1979) or the "fan effect" (Anderson & Bower, 1973), and research has confirmed that something like this does occur, under some circumstances. For this reason a common cue, such as the neutral color of your living room walls, or mildly happy affective state, which is associated with thousands of events and associated memories, should not be very effective as a retrieval cue for any given memory. Thus, if affect functions as this kind of simple cue, then mild, everyday affect should not serve as a particularly good cue for specific material because it is associated with many things. In contrast, however, positive affect *has* been found to be a very effective cue, and it has been found to function more by means of meaning than via stimulus elements.

Retrieval Effects.   As suggested, the ability of positive affect to serve as a retrieval cue, on the basis of meaning, for positive material learned during an experimental session is also problematic for associative network and spreading activation theory (Bower *et al.*, 1981). As described above, the simplest way to incorporate affect into network theory would be via state-dependent-learning effects based on affect. This would limit affect's impact to that of a simple context cue. In contrast, the existing data suggest that positive affect organizes broad ranges of stimuli, by means of meaning, and is an effective retrieval cue.

Gradients.   A theory proposing spreading activation within a network would predict something like a generalization gradient in the effect of feelings on judgment and memory. That is, there should be a decline in the effects, as the particular stimulus to be judged is more and more different from the affect-inducing stimulus or the network node. Recent studies by Johnson and Tversky (1983) reported failure to observe such gradients.

These authors examined the impact of affect on subjects' judgments of the likelihood of certain tragedies occurring, and they found no gradient based on similarity of the judged event to the topic that had been used to induce affect. Induction of negative affect by exposure to the description of a tragedy had the same degree of effect on the estimated probabilities of several different types of negative occurrences, regardless of their degree of relatedness to the tragedy that was used to induce the negative affect. Moreover, positive affect was associated with a perception of reduced risk of these events occurring, also regardless of the degree of similarity between the affect-inducing stimulus and the type of event. The authors interpreted their results as evidence against a network and "spreading activation" interpretation of cognition's underlying structure (or at least of the organization and impact of affective material).

Asymmetry between Happiness and Sadness. As originally formulated, the associative network model of cognition did not contain ready provision for findings such as this asymmetry. A recent reformulation of the model (Anderson, 1983) can accommodate these findings somewhat more easily, because it has introduced the idea that "nodes" can differ in strength (ability to spread activation). However, this represents a rather major change in the theory. It opens the possibility, for example, that if affect is to be considered a "node" in the network, as suggested by Bower (1981), nonetheless it may not be like other nodes. Thus, conceptualization of affect as a "node" in the cognitive network is not as informative as it may have seemed when the idea was introduced, because the parameters associated with this node remain to be determined. The addition of these ideas to the network-and-spreading-activation model increases its flexibility and allows it to account for the data such as the asymmetry between negative and positive affect. At the same time, however, it tends to decrease the ability of the model to make precise predictions. In so doing, it decreases the distinctiveness and utility of the model.

This trade-off is essentially the dilemma faced by the two types of models that have been mentioned. The network model makes precise predictions but increasingly is finding itself unable to account easily for data. In response to this lack, its proponents have increased its flexibility by introducing effects of processing variables and differences among nodes, but as they have done so they have given up the precision that was the hallmark of the model. In contrast, schema or contextualist models make no assumptions about organization and are flexible enough to be compatible with many findings that are problematic for the network model. However, schema models typically have not offered the precise predictions possible with the network formulation. The goal, then, is to develop a model that is flexible enough to account for all of the data, yet precise enough to generate specific predictions.

We have spent some time considering cognitive processes, such as the role of meaning in memory, the role of elaboration in thinking, and the possible effects of feelings on such processes, and relating all of this to cognitive theory, because understanding these relationships may help us to understand affect and affect's influence on thought and behavior. In particular, relating affect to what is known about these matters may help us to anticipate the range of processes and activities that are influenced by affect. For example, it is now becoming clear that affect can influence not only memory but also problem solving and decision making, and it is possible that these are influenced through an effect on the even more fundamental processes such as elaboration and cognitive organization that relate to the issues raised here. We turn now to consideration of some of these other effects of feelings on cognition.

B. THE INFLUENCE OF POSITIVE AFFECT ON PROBLEM SOLVING

Recent studies have begun to examine ways in which affect may influence problem solving, both social and nonsocial. This work has grown out of the realization that affect's influence on memory implies an impact of affect on interpretation, elaboration of context, and related processes that can influence the way situations are approached and construed.

Some of this work on problem solving has suggested that affect may influence not only the *content* of material that becomes accessible and comes to mind, but also the *strategies* chosen in approaching and structuring problems. These strategies, in still another way, may influence the process and structure of cognition and the decisions and behaviors that result from these. Some of this work has indicated that people in whom positive feelings have been induced may tend to simplify, or integrate components of, decision situations. In one series of studies (Isen *et al.*, 1982), for example, subjects in whom good feelings had been induced either by giving them a small gift or by placing them in especially comfortable surroundings, complete with refreshments, were found to be more likely to use an intuitive solution and a heuristic in solving two different types of problems (a physics timer-tape problem used to study time–rate–distance relationships, and a relative frequency judgment).

1. Use of Intuition

In the physics problem, subjects were asked to reason about objects traveling at different rates of speed. They were shown several tapes and were asked to choose the one that would be made by an object traveling in a way described (e.g., speeding up, slowing down) if, attached to that object, there were a tape that passed through a device that marked the tape at a steady rate (called a timing device). Since the timing device marks the tape steadily, a tape passing through more quickly (i.e., attached to a speedier object) will bear markings that are farther apart than those of a more slowly moving tape.

However, for many people, this fact is counterintuitive. For some reason, it seems to many people that faster-moving objects should produce tapes with markings closer together. Perhaps this is because we think that intensity of speed should be paralleled by intensity of markings. It also seems possible that the error may result from failure to think about the problem carefully. Use of an intuitive strategy or overlearned relationship and failure to check on whether that intuition or relationship can be applied to the task at hand may be the crucial components of this error.

Whatever the reason, a large minority (about 40%) of college students tested tend to make this error in judgment, and it has been found that people in whom positive affect has been induced are significantly more likely than control subjects to give this intuitive answer to the problem (72%). Whether this is because an intuitive answer is more likely to occur to them, because this particular intuitive answer is more likely to come to mind, because an algorithmic answer is less likely to occur to them (the problem is actually a time–rate–distance problem, for which all college students have long since been taught a solution formula), or because they are less likely to think about the problem carefully (to see whether the intuitive answer actually applies) remains to be investigated. That is, since we do not know what portion of the 60% of control subjects who give the correct answer think of this incorrect intuition first but then check and reject it (as opposed to those who have the correct answer intuitively in that group), we cannot tell whether the difference between affect and control groups lies in differential inclination to rely on intuition without checking or in differences in the intuitions generated. A third possibility is that control subjects have no intuition about the problem but tend more to use the time–rate–distance formula to solve the problem.

2. Use of Heuristics

The other process investigated was use of heuristics. Use of heuristics in problem solving has been discussed recently by Tversky and Kahneman (e.g., 1974) and others (e.g., Sherman & Corty, 1984). The term refers to use of a "rule of thumb" (a simple, inexact, but practical rule) in problem solving, and it is usually contrasted with a strategy that involves application of an algorithm or complex, systematic rule or formula. Thus, it may be thought of as a simplifying strategy, because persons using heuristics are using simple, global, rather easily applied rules, instead of complex, tedious, or effortful strategies in solving the problem.

One problem-solving heuristic, or simple rule, that has been discussed, for example, is the "availability" heuristic (Tversky & Kahneman, 1973). It has been applied to situations in which frequency estimates are requested. Subjects using this heuristic to solve a frequency problem are thought to base their answers on the relative ease of recall of material in memory rather than on some more tedious method of estimating frequency or rather than holding frequency actually in memory. Thus, it has been shown that most people will estimate that there are more names of, for example, female celebrities than of male celebrities in a long list if the female names are of more famous persons (for example, where the list is composed of 39 names, 20 of males of moderate fame—e.g., Cal Ripkin, Jr.—and 19 of females of greater fame—e.g., Elizabeth Taylor). The same is true, naturally, for names of males if they are the more famous. Thus, people will say that the actually less numerous set (19, as opposed to 20 of the other gender) was more numerous. It is assumed that the reason that people say there were more female (male) names when in fact there were fewer is that they recall the more famous ones more easily and base their judgment on this accessibility or availability. Thus, they are said to be using the availability heuristic to solve this problem.

Use of this heuristic in this situation has been found to extend to about 80% of persons tested (Tversky & Kahneman, 1974). In one study in which the stimulus sets were adapted to consist of three more-famous and six less-famous names, most people no longer made this error; however, under these circumstances it was possible to see that persons in whom positive affect had been induced were more likely than members of a control group still to use the fame of the names as a guide to their numerosity in the list (Isen *et al.,* 1982). Thus, it has been suggested that persons who are feeling good may be more likely to use a heuristic in problem solving.

It is sometimes assumed that use of such heuristics impairs performance; and indeed, in these studies, it gave rise to the incorrect answer. It should be noted, however, that subjects in these studies were not told to memorize the names or to keep track of the number of each, and therefore it is likely that the task came as a surprise to them. Thus, there may have been no way for them to have solved the problem other than via the heuristic, once the task was put to them. In that case, it may be that the use of the heuristic did not impair performance but rather provided the only means even to attempt solution to the problem. If this is so, then use of heuristics, in itself, may not signal sloppy thinking but rather an attempt to cope with a problem for which one does not have the answer.

Nonetheless, it is true that in the adapted situation (where the list contained three names of more-famous persons and six of less-famous ones) positive-affect subjects differed significantly from controls in their tendency to give the incorrect answer (presumably based on use of the heuristic, which was misleading in this case). This suggests that positive affect may promote a tendency to use heuristics per se, or it may result in a greater need to use heuristics because of not knowing the correct answer. This could occur if positive affect promoted other cognitive activities or led subjects to think about other things, so that when asked the surprise question regarding frequency these subjects more than controls needed to use the heuristic—had nothing but the heuristic on which to base their answer. Thus, the increased use of the heuristic observed among positive-affect subjects may indicate that they, more than controls, did not know the answer. The reason for this state of affairs—perhaps attention to other things, perhaps lessened cognitive capacity, perhaps a different way of organizing the material— remains to be investigated.

We do not know whether positive affect would lead to use of heuristics in other circumstances, where the task was not a surprise. Moreover, it should also be noted that we have not studied the impact of positive affect on use of other heuristics discussed in the literature, such as "representativeness" (e.g., Tversky & Kahneman, 1974). Thus, it would be of interest to see whether positive affect promotes use of heuristics more generally or is specific to avail- ability in the kind of situation described.

3. Efficiency

In these problems, simplifying the situation and using a heuristic or an intuitive answer led to incorrect answers and therefore a subject's performance was impaired by the presence of positive affect. In other situations, however, it may be that being able to find a heuristic to use on an otherwise unsolvable task might improve performance. Studies designed to investigate this and related questions such as the impact of affect on incidental learning more generally might be useful. However, there are some studies showing that persons who are made to feel happy can sometimes perform better or more efficiently than control subjects, and I will describe some of those next.

For example, in a complex decision-making task involving choice of a car for purchase from among six alternatives differing along each of nine dimen- sions, subjects in whom positive affect had been induced were more efficient in reaching a decision than were control subjects (Isen & Means, 1983). Even though the cars chosen by the two groups did not differ on average, the experi- mental subjects reached a decision in 11 minutes, as contrasted with the control group's mean of 19 minutes, and they engaged in significantly less rechecking of information already considered and were more likely to eliminate unimportant dimensions from the material to be considered. (The dimensions eliminated by positive-affect subjects were those rated by *control* subjects as least important, in a questionnaire following the task.)

Persons in whom positive affect had been induced were also more likely than those in the control group to use a strategy similar to the one identified by

Tversky (1972) as Elimination By Aspects (EBA). This strategy involves the use of broad categories to deal with large amounts of data at once and quickly narrow the field of alternatives. For example, if a person choosing a record album eliminates from consideration all of those by a given composer, he/she may be said to be using EBA. In our situation, this was reflected by a subject ruling out cars on the basis of their standing on a single dimension such as purchase price or fuel economy (rather than some more complex strategy involving weightings of dimensions, combining of dimensions, and comparisons among alternatives).

The findings of the car-choice study, obtained after a different type of affect induction (success on a task of perceptual-motor skill), is entirely compatible with those of the studies that found increased use of heuristics in problem solving as a function of positive affect (induced by the presence of refreshments at the experimental session or by receipt of a small gift), even though the two types of studies revealed different effects on performance. Together they suggest that people who are feeling happy tend to simplify at least some types of decision or problem-solving situations; sometimes this tendency may impair performance and sometimes it may facilitate it, depending on the task and the circumstances (see Isen *et al.*, 1982, for a fuller discussion of this issue). It should also be noted, however, that the car-choice situation was one that involved a large amount of information to be managed and that subjects who did not simplify the problem became bogged down in it. Thus, this tendency that we observed of positive-affect subjects to simplify may apply only to complex, otherwise un-manageable, situations.

4. The Role of Feedback

Another aspect of the task that should be discussed is whether the task contains within it feedback regarding the correct answer. In all of the studies described here, in which positive affect was seen to promote task simplification and sometimes errors on this account, the task provided no feedback to subjects regarding whether their answers were correct. Many problems, in contrast, do provide immediate feedback as to whether a correct solution has been obtained. For example, studies involving creative problem-solving tasks (to be described next), which do provide immediate feedback about performance, indicate improved performance by persons in whom positive affect has been induced. It seems likely that task feedback makes a difference and that under conditions in which people know whether the answers they gave were right or wrong the strategies employed by persons who are feeling happy will not impair their performance. This is because there is reason to believe that they will show greater cognitive flexibility and will respond to feedback by trying something else.

5. Flexibility and Enhanced Creativity

One set of studies that tends to confirm this suggestion examined the influence of positive affect on performance of tasks requiring creative or innovative solutions. Two tasks which have been employed to investigate this relationship are the candle task used by Karl Duncker (1945) and a subset of items on the Mednicks' (1964) Remote Associates Test. In the candle task, the subject is presented with the common objects of a box of tacks, a candle, and a book of matches, and he/she is asked to attach the candle to the wall (a cork board) in such a way that it will burn without dripping wax on the table or floor beneath. The problem can be solved if the box is emptied of tacks, tacked to the wall, and used as a platform (candle holder) for the upright candle.

The Remote Associates Test is a measure of creativity designed by the Mednicks (Mednick, Mednick, & Mednick, 1964) in accord with S. Mednick's (1962) theory of creativity, which is based on the associative memory structure thought to be related to creative thinking. In it, each item consists of three words followed by a blank space. The subject's task is to provide in the blank space a word that relates to each of the three words in the item. An example of a Remote Associates Test item of moderate difficulty is

MOWER   ATOMIC   FOREIGN   _____.[3]

Several studies have found that positive affect, induced in either of two ways (gift of candy or comedy film) leads to improved performance on these tasks, which are generally thought to involve creative or innovative thinking (Isen, Daubman, & Nowicki, 1987). At the same time, conditions designed to induce negative affect (5 minutes viewing the film "Night and Fog," a documentary of Nazi death camps) and affectless arousal (2 minutes of exercise) did not produce the same effect, suggesting that the effect of happiness should not be attributed to mere arousal. (For fuller discussion of the arousal issue, see Isen, 1984; Isen, Daubman & Nowicki, 1987; Martindale, 1981; Zajonc, 1965.)

This improved performance as a function of positive affect suggests that the impairment in performance just previously discussed should not be assumed to be attributable to lessened cognitive capacity as a result of positive affect. Rather, it is likely that positive affect influences strategy and organization. It is also likely that the nature of the task to be solved—its complexity and its importance—may interact with these organizational changes to influence task performance.

Thus, in summary, we have observed several effects of positive feelings on

[3]The answer to this item appears on p. 247.

cognitive processes. First, we have identified an effect on memory—the processing of positive material is facilitated—and we have considered the nature of one cognitive factor that may play a role in this effect, a change in relative accessibility of positive material as a function of positive affect. (We have paid less attention to the influence of affect on learning or encoding, but this could also be examined.) In addition, we have seen an effect of positive feelings on problem solving and have considered the role of two possible strategies or characteristics of the problem-solving approach in the effect—simplification of the material to be dealt with and flexibility in thinking about material. The influence of affect on cognitive flexibility will come up again and be examined in more detail in the next section, which addresses the influence of affect on the way in which concepts are organized or related to one another.

C. POSITIVE AFFECT AND COGNITIVE ORGANIZATION

Now, we turn to the idea that positive affect results in a change in cognitive organization or perceived relatedness of cognitive material. This change may play a role in the kind of processing observed in the studies described above (more efficient, creative and flexible, but sometimes allowed to depend on an inappropriate cue or peripheral relationship). The hypothesis offered here is that positive affect results in a broader or more integrated organization of cognitive material, wherein more diverse ideas are seen as potentially related or similar or bearing upon one another. Moreover, more movement or interchange among categories, material, and approaches may be possible, resulting in more flexible thinking.

The precise mechanism underlying the proposed effect of positive feelings on cognitive organization is not clear, but it may be related to greater differentiation and integration of cognitive material. Such a two-part process has been identified before, for example, in the cognitive style literature, where it has been related to an individual difference stylistic termed Integrative Complexity (e.g., Harvey, Hunt, & Schroder, 1961). While integrative complexity is not exactly the same as the process proposed here, it is interesting to note that the ability to differentiate has been theorized to promote some of the kinds of flexible processing that we have observed to result from positive affect. The increased differentiation may involve recognizing more features or dimensions of objects or more aspects of ideas; but this may also enable greater integration and, when necessary, simplified processing, because the larger number of dimensions generated may allow for more bases for integration or combination. Thus, although this integration may be done on the basis of the more complex or elaborated (differentiated) schemata, it may result in what appears to be a simple schema or approach to the problem at hand.

Such a change in cognitive organization—in the way in which material is structured and related to other material—as an effect of positive affect would be compatible with the data on use of heuristics and simplification strategies, described above, and would help us to understand older data also indicating that positive material is organized more simply or globally than other material. For example, Goldstein and Blackman (1978) summarize evidence indicating that positive stimuli, whether they are liked housemates, liked political figures, liked students (by teachers), liked teachers (by students), socially close role stimuli, or even positively evaluated books, were rated as less complex using the Rep Test (Kelly, 1955). In addition, it would be compatible with several recent findings which will be discussed next.

1. Empirical Evidence

Four types of evidence support the possibility of an influence of positive feelings on cognitive organization. They include studies of categorization, word association, organization of memory, and creative problem solving.

a. Categorization. The studies of categorization were based on the idea that if positive affect influences categorization of material such that more material is grouped together, seen as related, and so forth, then people in a positive-affect condition might be more likely (1) to group more items together in a sorting task, and (2) to rate less prototypic exemplars more as members of the category in a categorization task. That is, those items that tend in general not to be seen as clear examples of a category might be more frequently classed as members of the category by persons who are feeling happy.

These results have been obtained in five studies, using two types of categorization tasks (rating and sorting), two types of materials (words and colors), and three types of positive-affect manipulation (refreshments, receipt of a small gift, and 5 minutes of a comedy film). In three studies, a rating task similar to that used by Rosch (e.g., 1975) in her seminal work on prototypes in categorization was used. In this task, subjects are given several exemplars of a category, varying in typicality for the category, and are asked to rate, on a scale from 1 to 10, the degree to which each exemplar seems a member of the category. For example, "shirt" would be a prototypic exemplar of the category "clothing" and presumably would be rated "10" by most subjects in this task. In contrast, "cane" is less typical as an article of clothing and therefore in general tends to receive a lower rating as an exemplar of the category "clothing."

In the three studies using this technique to examine the impact of positive affect on categorization, people in whom positive affect had been induced rated fringe exemplars of categories (for example, "purse" and "cane" as members of the category "clothing") higher than did subjects in control conditions. In addition, in two other studies, under a one-trial free sorting task, people in positive-affect conditions sorted stimuli into fewer groupings. This indicates that, relative to persons in control conditions, for positive-affect subjects more items were seen as "going together" (e.g., Isen & Daubman, 1984).

Together, these five studies suggest that persons in whom positive affect has been induced tend to see things as more related and to categorize them accordingly. The nature of the stimuli to which this effect extends remains to be investigated. The studies cited here used, for the most part, neutral material; thus the effect does not appear to be limited to positive material, as some might expect. Nonetheless, there may be some limit to the nature of the stimuli for which this process would be effective. Indeed, it has already been found that the generalization does not apply to some stimuli (Isen & Daubman, 1984).

Here it is of interest to note that the integrative process that is being proposed might predict more differentiation, rather than more clustering together, under circumstances where the subjects were asked how many different groupings they *could* identify. This is because the idea under discussion proposes that the person who is feeling happy may recognize more features or aspects of ideas or items and thus may be able to group the items together, often on the basis of an otherwise unrecognized relationship or dimension, when asked to identify the ones that "go together" or when asked how good an exemplar of a concept an item is. However, if asked to differentiate among categories, persons who are happy would be expected to be able to find more bases for differentiation, just as they have for similarity when asked about similarity.

In fact, recent studies on a related task (the task being to sort material as many times as necessary in order to include all of the ways in which the items might be grouped) offer support for this prediction. Results indicate that persons in whom positive affect had been induced sorted stimuli, this time aspects of their perceived selves, in more *different* ways than did persons in control conditions. That is, not on a single sort, but over repeated sortings, when asked to categorize the elements in as many ways as they saw, they produced more different groupings of self-components than did control subjects, indicative of more different perceived underlying dimensions and possibly more integration of the components (Isen & Daubman, 1986).

At first this situation, where positive-affect subjects group stimuli into larger units (Isen & Daubman, 1984) but also can be found to make more differentiation among stimuli (group the stimuli into more different groupings) when the task focuses on differentiation (Isen & Daubman, 1986), might seem confusing or contradictory. However, it is actually quite compatible both with theoretical accounts of the process of cognitive differentiation and integration and with empirical results in this and other areas showing that the way in which the items are presented, and the similarity or categorization questions that are asked, have a predictable, understandable effect on subjects' responses (e.g., Tversky & Gati, 1978).

  b. Word Association. Studies examining the unusualness of word association also support the view that positive affect can influence cognitive organization as proposed—that is, can lead to greater differentiation and integration. The suggestion that affect results in concepts having more components or implications and seeming more inclusive and in material seeming more interrelated than normally has at least two implications for a person's associations to a given concept. For one thing, a person in a positive state might be expected to have a broader range of associates to a given word. Second, if the pool of associates is broader among people who are feeling good, word associations might therefore be more unusual under those conditions.

Three studies using four different affect inductions (receiving refreshments, associating to positive trait adjectives before giving associates to the target words, viewing a few minutes of a comedy film, and receiving a small free gift) support this hypothesis. In these studies, it was found that persons in the positive-affect conditions gave significantly more unusual first associates to *neutral* words taken from the Palermo and Jenkins (1964) norms than did subjects in control conditions (Isen, Johnson, Mertz, & Robinson, 1985). One study in that series, which included word valence (determined by pretests) as a second variable, also found that control subjects gave more unusual first associates to positive stimulus words than to other words. This means that both a positive affect *state* and positive *words* as stimuli produced a broader range of first associates or a more complex associative context than normally.

These findings suggest that patterns of association are changed by positive affect, and they are compatible with the idea that positive affect influences the organization of cognitive material so that information is more integrated and interrelated. Again, the concepts of differentiation and integration both appear to be involved. Considering the stimulus word, it is clear that positive affect results in more different associates to it; but from the perspective of the body of material generated, that material is more interrelated than normally, because it has all been generated in response to the same word and is present in mind at the same time.

    c. Memory.   Studies of memory might also lend support to the idea that positive affect influences the way in which cognitive material is organized. This suggestion is based on the principle that chunking of material into larger groupings of related ideas tends to improve memory for the material organized in that way (e.g., Miller, 1956; Mandler, 1967). If positive affect facilitates the perception of relatedness among ideas, it might also promote the organization or chunking of those ideas; and this might improve memory for that material. Thus, if people who are feeling happy see relationships that are usually unnoticed, or create more inclusive categories, then one might expect their memory for items in these relatively unusual categories to be enhanced.

A recent study has found superior memory in positive-affect subjects, relative to controls, for material that can be grouped together but that usually is not grouped together. Subjects in either positive-affect or control conditions were given a list of 30 words to memorize. Spaced throughout the 30-word list there were 10 words relating to the American Revolution (e.g., doodle, stripes, stars). Half of the subjects in each group were given a cue that would prime the "category" of the American Revolution. Results of this study indicated that, without the cue, persons in whom happiness had been induced had better recall of the organizable 10-word subset within the longer list than did control group members. This advantage disappeared when the control group was given a cue which suggested the otherwise rather obscure theme, around which the 10-word subset was organizable (Isen, Daubman, & Gorgoglione, 1987).

d.   *Creative Problem Solving.*   Finally, the idea that positive affect may influence cognitive organization is supported by the studies mentioned above that suggest improved creative problem solving among persons in a positive state. If persons who are happy organize material more integratively or see relationships that are not ordinarily seen among items, they should put elements together differently from the usual way and be better able to come up with solutions to problems requiring creative ingenuity. Most current conceptualizations of the creative process suggest that an essential component of it is the bringing together of apparently disparate material in a useful or reasonable, if unusual, way (Koestler, 1964; Mednick, 1962).

Studies indicate that those in whom positive affect has been induced, either by means of a free gift or a comedy film, perform better than control subjects on tasks requiring creativity or innovation (Isen, Daubman, & Nowicki, 1987). In two studies, for example, subjects in positive-affect conditions were more likely to solve Duncker's candle task; and in two other studies positive-affect subjects got more correct answers on a subset (composed of moderate difficulty items) of the Remote Associates Test.

These studies, together with others described above such as those demonstrating an effect of positive affect on categorization, word association, and organization in memory, provide converging evidence that positive affect influences cognitive organization. It appears to promote a more flexible, more integrated cognitive organization that results in ideas seeming not only more varied but also more related than they would under other circumstances.

2.   Possible Mechanisms Underlying the Impact of Affect on Organization

Thus, there is a growing body of evidence suggesting that positive affect influences the way in which ideas are organized or related to one another. However, it is not yet clear exactly how this happens. Several kinds of processes may be involved, and these will be discussed next.

a.   *An Increase in the Complexity of the Cognitive Context.*   One way in which a more integrated approach might result from positive affect might be through the creation, by positive affect, of a complex cognitive context. Where more ideas come to mind at the same time (complex context), it is reasonable to suppose that more relatedness may be seen among them. Moreover, there is some evidence that the presence of a complex cognitive context promotes, further, the integration of ideas. For example, such complexity is known to facilitate the production of unusual word associations (e.g., Cramer, 1968), which may be reflective of a person integrating material or perceiving relatedness among elements not normally associated.

The idea that a more complex context might influence the interpretation or organization of the ideas being considered is compatible with the contextualist position in cognitive psychology. This model suggests that cognition, rather than involving the passive "firing" of a set of nodes already aligned in a prearranged organization or structure, may involve an active process of idea formation and reformation (e.g., Bransford, 1979; Bransford, McCarrell, Franks, & Nitsch, 1977; Jenkins, 1974; Neisser, 1967, 1976). In such a situation, context may help determine meaning and may influence the way ideas are organized and related to one another. This suggestion is also compatible with recent data showing that context can influence the structure of categories (e.g., Medin, 1983; Roth & Shoben, 1983).

Associative network theory would account for some of these data, such as the increase in unusual associates under conditions of positive affect, by postulating a deviation from the usual activation pattern, caused by the activation of the affect node. However, this would not account for that aspect of the word-association data that shows an interaction between positive affect and word type (it was only for neutral words that positive affect increased the number of unusual first associates).

Thus, a more complex context would be seen as capable of influencing cognitive organization, as ideas perhaps not normally associated are brought into contiguity with one another. This larger amount of material in mind might also result in defocusing of attention, a process thought to promote creativity and integration of ideas in a complex cognitive context (Martindale, 1981).

Positive affect may create this kind of complex cognitive context because it cues positive material in memory (e.g., Isen et al., 1978; Laird et al., 1982; Nasby & Yando, 1982; Teasdale & Fogarty, 1979), and positive material in memory is thought to be extensive (Boucher & Osgood, 1969; Bousfield, 1944, 1950; Matlin & Stang, 1979; White, 1936; White & Powell, 1936). Studies have shown, for example, that people give more associations to positive words than to other words and that the pool of cognitive material related to the positive appears larger than the pools of other material (see Boucher & Osgood, 1969; Matlin & Stang, 1979, for discussion of this issue). In addition, we know that both positive affect and positive material cue a wider range of associates than neutral material

(Isen, Johnson, Mertz, & Robinson, 1985). Thus, someone who is feeling good is more likely to think of more ideas and experience a complex cognitive context. This, then, may bring divergent material into mind at the same time, creating a complex cognitive context and creating the conditions that promote integration of ideas and the apparent changes in cognitive organization that have been observed.

    b.   Priming of Affective Features.   Some cognitions that are not primarily affective have affective components or affectively toned alternative meanings, and perceived relatedness among these ideas might be increased by the priming of such affect-related multiple or figurative meanings. That is, if the feeling tone that these words share is made salient, then the concepts might seem more similar than they would at another time. This idea would follow from a feature-based theory of similarity, which would suggest that making shared features salient should increase perceived similarity (e.g., Tversky, 1977). But it would also be compatible with network or contextualist accounts, such as we have been considering throughout this chapter.

    c.   Activation of Brain Regions that Promote Holistic Processing.   The phenomenon being proposed is one that characterizes holistic processing of information. Holistic processing has been found to be associated with activation of the right hemisphere of the brain. Some researchers (e.g., Tucker, 1981) have suggested that positive affect contributes to the activation of the posterior portion (but not the frontal lobe) of the right hemisphere, although there is some debate about this (e.g., Davidson, 1984; Tucker, 1981). Thus, perhaps the integration of ideas that has been hypothesized to result from positive affect occurs because of activation of brain regions that give rise to holistic processing. Work is continuing on localization of emotional functions, and this hypothesis is one that is also receiving attention.

3. An Alternative Interpretation: Are the Effects of Positive Affect Due to Simple Motivational Changes?

    One question that might be asked is whether these effects might be attributable to a change in motivation rather than in cognitive organization. Evidence is beginning to suggest that positive affect may have motivational consequences as well as cognitive ones. In particular, there seems to be evidence that positive affect gives rise to an inclination to maintain the positive feeling state. This suggestion is compatible with data reported earlier suggesting that people in whom positive affect has been induced are more cautious in risk situations and demonstrate greater sensitivity to potential loss in a utility-estimation task. It also fits with data indicating decreased preference for negative self-relevant information and decreased willingness to help another person where the helping task is depressing, on the part of those who are feeling happy. Thus, it appears that certain specific goals may be promoted by positive affect. These would not provide alternative interpretations of the phenomena described, however, and they are in no way incompatible with the cognitive interpretations offered.

Two rather general, simple, motivational hypotheses which have been suggested to explain the influence of affect on task performance appear less viable, however. These are "not trying as hard" and "trying harder." Both of these interpretations have been offered (separately, of course) to account for the findings described. For example, it has been suggested that the greater inclusiveness observed in the categorization studies or the use of intuition and heuristics that we have observed, as well as the simplification seen in the car-choice study, might have resulted from people in the positive-affect conditions not trying as hard as control subjects. In the car-choice study, positive affect was induced by means of report of success on an unrelated task; perhaps this report gives rise to increased confidence, and the latter results in successful subjects (positive-affect subjects) not trying as hard. (Of course, this reasoning would not apply as readily to the categorization and heuristics studies, which used different types of positive-affect induction not as likely to induce confidence.)

However, even in the car-choice study, the data do not suggest that subjects who had been given a report of success (positive affect) were trying less hard than controls. Although they took less time to reach a decision and eliminated some material from consideration, they tended to choose the same cars as the control group; and all of our analyses suggested that they used their strategies and information efficiently rather than carelessly. The only information to which they attended less than control subjects did was that which they had already considered or that which was judged uninformative by everyone (see Isen & Means, 1983, for a more detailed account of the process). The excellent performance of positive-affect subjects on some other tasks, the creativity tasks for example, also speaks against the interpretation of carelessness or lessened effort.

It is possible that positive affect produces a sense of relaxation, freedom from tension, which might be an important component of the positive affective state itself as well as a contributor to its effects on performance. This aspect of elation may play a role in the defocusing of attention and the integration of material that has been hypothesized. But this would be different from reduced motivation or carelessness, and it would seem a component of the affective state itself rather than an artifact of a particular means of affect induction.

It has also been suggested that positive-affect subjects may have been trying *harder* than control subjects. This interpretation has been offered for the results of the car-choice study, the creative problem-solving studies, and other studies in which positive affect has been found to facilitate performance. In the car-choice study, for example, where positive affect was induced by means of a report of success on a task, it might be argued that subjects in the positive (success) condition might have wanted to please the experimenter more than controls (out of a sense of thanks or obligation for the positive report, presumably) and might therefore have worked harder than controls on the task. Or it might be suggested that persons in the success condition tried harder because the report of success cued "achievement motivation" in them. However, these arguments would not seem to explain the entire phenomenon, since the positive affect group did not behave like especially "driven" people: they spent less time on the task and did less rechecking of information than the control group. In the creative problem-solving studies, likewise, the suggestion that the superior performance of the positive-affect groups should be attributed to greater effort on their part seems untenable. The nature of these tasks is such that simply trying harder would not seem to help. Indeed, there is a line of thinking that suggests that increased motivation should not facilitate (in fact, should impair) performance on these tasks, since they involve production of nondominant responses (e.g., Zajonc, 1965; see Isen, Johnson, Mertz, & Robinson, 1985, and Isen, Daubman, & Nowicki, 1987, for discussion of this issue applied to affect and creative problem solving).

Thus, it seems likely that if positive affect influences motivation, it is not via simply trying harder or less hard. Possibly, affect may influence the particular goals that subjects select for themselves, as for example, affect maintenance or as may have occurred in the study on negotiation, mentioned earlier. But this cannot account entirely for the observed effects of positive feelings on performance. If subjects were differentially motivated in the positive-affect vs. control groups, or differentially confident, still some other change may have occurred to enable them to work so efficiently and effectively. Cognitive material seems to be more flexibly organized and integrated when one feels happy.

4. Implications for Social Behavior

The points made thus far indicate that positive affect has a number of consequences for cognitive organization or processes related to organization. The idea that positive affect gives rise to a tendency to group more things together and to see more potential ways of organizing or grouping things together suggests that positive affect may influence social behavior and interpersonal interaction in ways not yet extensively explored. In this section, a few of these implications will be considered. Although the evidence is preliminary ragarding these topics, it suggests several interesting lines of investigation.

a. Interpersonal Problem-Solving and Negotiation. First, the increased flexibility in thinking and problem solving that has been observed in the non-social domain might be evident in interpersonal problem solving as well. People may be more able to come up with creative or integrative solutions to interpersonal disputes or other interpersonal "problem" situations (for example, a task such as how to make friends when moving to a new place).

As noted earlier, a recent study has reported that positive affect can facilitate finding integrative solutions and can improve the process of negotiation: whereas persons in a control condition who bargained face-to-face in an integrative bargaining task were most likely to break off negotiation without reaching agreement, those in whom positive affect had been induced were significantly more likely to reach agreement and to reach the optimal agreement possible for the two parties in the situation (Carnevale & Isen, 1986).

In addition, subjects in the positive-affect condition of this study engaged in less use of contentious tactics (i.e., tactics designed to get the other to concede— threats, ultimata, persuasive arguments, and put-downs) and greater use of problem-solving strategy (i.e., efforts apparently designed to find an alternative acceptable to both parties; these include exchange of truthful information about priorities, and "trial and error" tactics, such as changing one's offer, seeking the other's reaction to each offer, making larger concessions on items of lower priority, and systematic concession making), and they showed greater insight than control subjects into the other party's payoff matrix, a fact not given to them in the study. Apparently, positive-affect subjects went about the face-to-face negotiation task differently from the way in which control subjects approached it—with a more problem-solving orientation rather than one bent on contending for their own positions—and this may have helped them with the task. Pruitt (1981) has suggested, for example, that contentious tactics tend to interfere with the discovery of integrative solutions and that, if yielding can be prevented, problem-solving tactics can facilitate the discovery of integrative solutions.

Thus, these findings seem to confirm that the contribution that positive feelings can make to cognitive flexibility and integration of information in a nonsocial context applies as well to one involving interpersonal negotiation. In addition, they suggest that research on the link between positive affect, cooperativeness, and an integrative approach to problem solving might be useful to pursue.

Although it might seem, at first glance, that serious problem situations might arouse negative feelings and might therefore not be subject to the effect proposed here—that positive affect can facilitate a more task-oriented, productive approach and a more effective, successful solution—it may not be correct to think about problem-solving situations as necessarily negative. It is not clear that, in solving disputes or interpersonal problems, people focus on the fact that the situation is negative (problematic), nor that all of the material involved would necessarily be negative. Rather, effective problem solvers may focus on the desired end and work back to their present situation, looking for ways to link the present state of affairs to their objective. Thus, problem solving need not be conceptualized as residing in the affectively negative domain. In fact, perhaps persons who are happy might be better able to take this perspective, to view the problem as a challenge, or to think about the desired goal state and work from there. In this way, positive affect may help people obtain solutions to interpersonal problems other than in negotiations.

   b. Perception of Self and Other. i. Similarity between Self and Other. In view of the ideas put forth in this chapter involving integration of material and perception of relatedness not ordinarily noticed, together with findings suggesting a more cooperative orientation among those in a positive affect state, it is tempting to suggest that people who are happy may be more likely to integrate their view of themselves and others and perhaps see more overarching, unified goals for themselves and for people in general. That is, it may be that people who are happy see less distinction between themselves and others or see themselves and others in perspective as parts of a larger whole.

   This suggestion would be compatible not only with the data showing a more cooperative orientation in negotiation, but also with those indicating increased helpfulness and decreased aggression as a function of positive affect (e.g., Baron & Ball, 1974; Berkowitz, 1972; Isen, 1970; Isen & Levin, 1972). Likewise, it is compatible with data indicating greater sociability and improved conceptions of human nature on the part of persons who have been subject to positive-affect induction of the kind described in this chapter (e.g., Gouaux, 1971; Isen, 1970; Veitch & Griffitt, 1976). It would be interesting to see whether other behavior and conceptualizations reflective more specifically of the integrative process proposed here would also result from positive affect. For example, it would be of interest to know whether people see themselves as more similar to others or sharing more commonality with others when they are happy. This would seem to have important implications for social behavior and interpersonal relations.

   ii. Integration of Self Components. It is also possible, given this line of reasoning, that people see *themselves* as more integrated (for example, see more unity in their various roles or aspects of self) when they are happy. This would seem an important aspect of self-perception, relevant to both personal well-being and interpersonal functioning.

   Studies of both of these types are currently under way, and preliminary results are suggesting that both of these kinds of effects may occur. That is, people seem to view themselves more integratedly, see more relatedness between their various roles and ways of being when they are happy; in addition, there is some evidence that people may see more similarity between themselves and other people (at least some types of others) when they are happy than at another time. One of these studies also suggests that positive-affect subjects may tend less than others to make themselves the focus of comparison. These results are preliminary, but they indicate that these topics might be worth pursuing.

   c. Intergroup Relations: Ingroup–Outgroup Definition and Stereotyping. i. Ingroup–Outgroup Definition. If positive affect induces a perception or feeling of greater unity with others, one might expect improved intergroup relations. On the other hand, if the greater integration that occurs applies only to oneself or people very like oneself, then perhaps intergroup relations might be unaffected or might even worsen. Determinants of perception of ingroup–outgroup boundaries would seem very important to study, and the current work on the influence of positive affect on perception of relatedness suggests that positive affect may play a role in this process.

Social psychologists have written about the concept of "we-ness" (e.g., Piliavin, Dovidio, Gaertner, & Clark, 1982), giving this name to the sense of being bound together with others. Those authors use the idea in discussing the fact that helping behavior has been found to be more likely where perceived similarity or empathy is higher (e.g., Aderman & Berkowitz, 1970; Hornstein, Masor, Sole, & Heilman, 1971) and also in discussing the presence of more positive ingroup behaviors. If positive affect (which, as noted earlier, has also been found to promote helping) increases one's sense of connection to others or similarity to others, then one might perceive a larger ingroup for oneself in times of happiness.

However, the alternative conceptualization, that positive affect would promote self-orientation or even selfishness, is also possible, since ideas of self may be closely linked to feelings of happiness. Moreover, data show not only that people in positive affect states are more likely to help others, but that they are also more likely to reward themselves (e.g., Mischel, Coates & Raskoff, 1968) and are also more likely to do as they please (e.g., Isen & Simmonds, 1978; Forest et al., 1979).

Although it is thus plausible that people might become more self-centered when happy, it seems more likely that they will become more socially oriented, more outgoing, and more inclusive. Even studies showing increased willingness to behave as one pleases when happy also seem to reflect a greater sense of interpersonal responsibility (e.g., Berkowitz & Connor, 1966; Isen & Levin, 1972). For example, in one study, subjects in whom positive affect had been induced showed greater willingness to help another, but less willingness to annoy another, than those in a control condition (Isen & Levin, 1972).

Also, it should be noted that studies showing increased benefit of ingroup members as a function of factors such as similarity do not find a concomitant increase in harm to, or rejection of, outgroup members (e.g., Billig & Tajfel, 1973; Hornstein et al., 1971). Thus, neither would it be expected that happiness should lead to increased rejection of outgroup members. It might lead to closer feelings toward ingroup members and might also result in that ingroup being defined more broadly. Thus, studies designed to determine how people in positive affective states view themselves in relation to others and how they relate to groups other than their own would especially be of interest.

ii. Stereotyping. These processes that have been discussed may have relevance for important social phenomena such as stereotyping. It is possible that positive affect may reduce the tendency to stereotype or may influence some of the processes involved in stereotyping, through the impact on cognitive integration that we have been considering. First, if stereotyping relies on the existence of an outgroup, then positive affect may make the process less likely if it results in larger ingroups and fewer or smaller outgroups, as discussed above.

Second, another way in which improved integrative ability might help to reduce stereotyping, aside from reducing the likelihood of the construction of "outgroups" (or reducing the number and size of such groups), has been suggested in recent research reported by Rothbart and John (1985). This work indicated that the reason that evidence that would tend to disconfirm stereotypes does not often do so is that that disconfirming evidence is not easily integrated into a person's views of the stereotyped group. Thus, if positive affect improves ability to integrate diverse material, then it is possible that positive feelings might result in greater ability to see how disconfirming examples relate to the stereotype. Thus, in another way, the greater tendency toward cognitive integration that accompanies positive affect may serve to mitigate usual processes associated with stereotyping.

A word of caution is needed here, however, before drawing conclusions about, in general, how affect would influence stereotyping. We need to know more about the processes by which stereotyping occurs in order to make accurate predictions regarding affect's influence on it. If stereotyping is a way of summarizing a lot of information, similar to heuristic processing, then there might be some circumstances under which positive affect might *promote* the use of stereotypes (just as we have seen that sometimes it can promote simplifying strategies). If, on the other hand, stereotyping relies on the existence of discrimination and perception of separateness, then that may be less likely. If both are true of the process of stereotyping, that might suggest still another situation—that among happy people fewer occasions for stereotyping may exist, but that those groups which do remain defined as outgroups will be readily stereotyped (but perhaps only under certain circumstances, such as lack of feedback regarding consequences, as was observed for use of simplifying strategies in nonsocial domains). Much more work needs to be done on this important topic.

IV. Concluding Comments

A. IMPLICATIONS OF THE THEORETICAL CONSIDERATIONS

The material presented in this chapter suggests that affect influences both social behavior and cognitive processes significantly. Thus, it indicates that feelings serve as important ways by which we organize our thoughts and experiences.

The data also indicate that modifications in existing cognitive models may be necessary if they are to account for the effects of feelings. The memory data, as well as the more recent work indicating an impact of positive affect on cognitive organization, suggest that the influence of affect on cognition cannot be understood readily in terms of an associative-network and spreading-activation model of cognition alone. Affect itself appears to be processed more in terms of meaning or schematically than as a simple stimulus, and it also appears to promote schematic processing or integrated processing of other material. In addition, the effects of specific motivations (directing thought and behavior in particular ways) induced by the positive affect state are evident in various of the results. The associative-network model does not handle these kinds of phenomena easily. In contrast, schematic–contextualist–constructivist models can account for many of these data more readily. For example, they begin with the assumption that cognition is an active process rather than a passive or automatic one, that meaning, interpretation, motives, and goals of the person will play a role in the thought process. Thus, they can accommodate findings such as the influence of affect on apparent cognitive organization of other material; and it is possible that they may contribute to our understanding of the way in which affect influences cognition. But it would not be wise to argue that simple, associative learning never occurs with affective material. Perhaps this suggests that our current models of cognition are incomplete. We will need to use all of them in order to account for the data, and we may need to develop new ones in addition in order to understand cognition fully. In a sense, we already knew this, but the influence of affect on cognition reminds us of it.

The data on the cognitive effects of feelings suggest some things about affect, as well as cognition. It seems likely that affect has both stimulus properties and meaning properties and that both of these aspects of feelings can serve to organize material for encoding, memory storage, and retrieval of information. As suggested in an earlier paper (Isen, 1984), the data suggest that affect may operate in several ways, and on several levels, simultaneously.

B. IMPLICATIONS OF THE ASYMMETRY BETWEEN POSITIVE
    AND NEGATIVE AFFECT

We have not thought much about negative affect in this chapter, but we have noted the fact that negative and positive feelings often appear to have effects that are independent of one another, rather than identical or inverse. This point merits some consideration here, because it may tell us something about the nature of affect. If affect were simply arousal (as has been proposed, for example, by Duffy, 1934), one might expect similar effects of positive and negative affect inductions. On the other hand, if positive and negative affect were opposite ends of one single continuum, one would expect their effects to be inverse. In fact, however, neither of these results has consistently been obtained, and sometimes the effects of positive and negative affect inductions bear no apparent relationship to one another.

Research is beginning to suggest some ways of addressing this puzzle. First, it is likely that distinction must be made among negative affects. Anger, fear, and sadness may not all have similar effects. Likewise, different positive states may also produce different effects, although in the case of positive affect, the distinctions seem less clear. For example, in one series of studies, Nasby and Yando (1982) found that sadness failed to facilitate the recall of negative material but that, under some conditions, anger did result in improved memory for negative material. (In the same studies, and in others using a wide variety of affect-induction techniques, positive affect consistently facilitated the recall of positive material.) Somewhat similarly, Fried and Berkowitz (1979) found an influence of relaxing but not of otherwise pleasant music on helping (although, as reported earlier, other studies using several affect-induction techniques that might be expected to induce a state closer to elation than relaxation also reported an effect on helping). Recent work on brain and emotion is now beginning to address these questions and may prove helpful in understanding the relationship between positive and negative affect (e.g., Tucker, 1981).

Second, as suggested earlier, the cognitive schemata or patterns of material existent for different types of affective material may be different. The work on the influence of positive affect on cognitive organization suggests that positive material is extensive, elaborated, and well interconnected. For example, the results of the studies mentioned earlier, on unusualness of word association, suggest that positive words cue a broader range of associates than either neutral or negative words. In contrast, sad material may be less elaborated or less well interconnected in memory than positive material. Results of a wide range of studies suggest that for normal persons there is a smaller pool of negative material than positive. In addition, earlier literature suggests that negative affect tends to focus or restrict attention and categorization (e.g., Bruner, Matter, & Papanek, 1955; Easterbrook, 1959), whereas we have seen that positive affect produces effects that appear to correspond with defocused or broadened attention. Thus, there is evidence consistent with the suggestion that negative and positive affect may be differently organized in mind, with positive more global and interrelated, and negative more specific and insular. Further research on these proposals seems warranted.

In summary, then, we have seen that positive affect can influence cognitive processes and social behavior in diverse ways. The impact of positive affect on processes related to the organization of cognitive material suggests that affect may influence social behavior in still other ways, as yet relatively unexplored. In addition, there may be cognitive theoretical implications of these findings. The contextualist position in cognitive psychology appears capable of accommodating some of the findings of affect's influence on cognition a bit more easily than the associative-network view. Yet the latter is more precise in the predictions that it makes. Finally, these findings may hold implications regarding the nature of affect and the relationship among affective states. Hopefully, further research on the impact of affect on cognitive processes and social behavior will continue to contribute to our understanding of cognitive theory, social processes, and affect itself.

The answer to the Remote Associate item on p. 231 is "power."

ACKNOWLEDGMENTS

The author wishes to express appreciation to Robert A. Baron, C. Daniel Batson, Leonard Berkowitz, Gregory Diamond, and Mark Young for their helpful comments on the manuscript, and to Madelon Kellough and Terri Harold for their help in typing it. This work was supported in part by Research Grant BNS 8406352 from the National Science Foundation to the author.

REFERENCES

Adamson, R. E. (1952). Functional fixedness as related to problem solving. *Journal of Experimental Psychology*, **44**, 288–291.

Aderman, D. (1972). Elation, depression and helping behavior. *Journal of Personality and Social Psychology*, **24**, 91–101.

Aderman, D., & Berkowitz, L. (1970). Observational set, empathy, and helping. *Journal of Personality and Social Psychology*, **14**, 141–148.

Anderson, J. R. (1983). *The architecture of cognition*. Cambridge, MA: Harvard University.

Anderson, J. R., & Bower, G. H. (1973). *Human associative memory*. Washington, D.C.: Winston.

Arkes, H., Herren, L. T., & Isen, A. M. (1987). The role of potential loss in the influence of affect on risk-taking behavior. *Organizational Behavior and Human Decision Processes*, in press.

Arnold, M. B. (1970). Perennial problems in the field of emotion. In M. B. Arnold (Ed.), *Feelings and emotion*. New York: Academic Press.

Baron, R. A. (1984). Reducing organizational conflict: An incompatible response approach. *Journal of Applied Psychology*, **69**, 272–279.

Baron, R. A., & Ball, R. L. (1974). The aggression-inhibiting influence of non-hostile humor. *Journal of Experimental Social Psychology*, **10**, 23–33.

Bartlett, J. C., Burleson, G., & Santrock, J. W. (1982). Emotional mood and memory in young children. *Journal of Experimental Child Psychology*, **34**, 59–76.

Bartlett, J. C., & Santrock, J. W. (1979). Affect-dependent episodic memory in young children. *Child Development*, **50**, 513–518.

Batson, C. D., Coke, J. S., Chard, F., Smith, D., & Taliaferro, A. (1979). Generality of the "Glow of goodwill": Effects of mood on helping and information acquisition. *Social Psychology Quarterly*, **42**, 176–179.

Batson, C. D., Duncan, D. B., Ackerman, P., Buckley, T., & Birch, K. (1981). Is empathic emotion a source of altruistic motivation? *Journal of Personality and Social Psychology*, **40**, 290–302.

Batson, C. D., O'Quin, K., Fultz, J., Vanderplas, M., & Isen, A. M. (1983). Self-reported distress and empathy, and egoistic versus altruistic motivation for helping. *Journal of Personality and Social Psychology, 45,* 706–718.

Berkowitz, L. (1972). Social norms, feelings, and other factors affecting helping and altruism. In L. Berkowitz (Ed.), *Advances in experimental social psychology* (Vol. 6, pp. 63–108). New York: Academic Press.

Berkowitz, L., & Connor, W. (1966). Increasing the salience of the norm of social responsibility. *Journal of Personality and Social Psychology, 4,* 664–669.

Billig, N., & Tajfel, H. (1973). Social categorization and similarity in intergroup behavior. *European Journal of Social Psychology, 3,* 27–52.

Boucher, J., & Osgood, C. E. (1969). The pollyanna hypothesis. *Journal of Verbal Learning and Verbal Behavior, 8,* 1–8.

Bousfield, W. A. (1944). An empirical study of the production of affectively toned items. *Journal of General Psychology, 30,* 205–215.

Bousfield, W. A. (1950). The relationship between mood and the production of affectively toned associates. *Journal of General Psychology, 42,* 67–85.

Bower, G. H. (1981). Mood and memory. *American Psychologist, 36,* 129–148.

Bower, G. H., Gilligan, S. G., & Montiero, K. P. (1981). Selectivity of learning caused by affective states. *Journal of Experimental Psychology: General, 110,* 451–473.

Bower, G. H., & Mayer, D. (1985). Failure to replicate mood-dependent retrieval. *Bulletin of the Psychonomic Society, 23,* 39–42.

Bower, G. H., Montiero, K. P., & Gilligan, S. G. (1978). Emotional mood as a context for learning and recall. *Journal of Verbal Learning and Verbal Behavior, 17,* 573–585.

Bransford, J. D. (1979). *Human cognition.* Belmont, CA: Wadsworth.

Bransford, J. D., McCarrell, N. S., Franks, J. J., & Nitsch, K. E. (1977). Toward unexplaining memory. In R. E. Shaw & J. D. Bransford (Eds.), *Perceiving, acting and knowing.* Hillsdale, NJ: Erlbaum.

Brown, A. (1979). Priming effects in semantic memory retrieval processes. *Journal of Experimental Psychology: Human Learning and Memory, 5,* 65–77.

Bruner, J. S., Matter, J., & Papanek, M. L. (1955). Breadth of learning as a function of drive-level and maintenance. *Psychological Review, 62,* 1–10.

Carnevale, P. J. D., & Isen, A. M. (1986). The influence of positive affect and visual access on the discovery of integrative solutions in bilateral negotiation. *Organizational Behavior and Human Decision Processes, 37,* 1–13.

Craik, F. I. M., & Lockhart, R. S. (1972). Levels of processing. A framework for memory research. *Journal of Verbal Learning and Verbal Behavior, 11,* 671–684.

Craik, F. I. M., & Tulving, E. (1975). Depth of processing and the retention of words in episodic memory. *Journal of Experimental Psychology: General, 104,* 268–294.

Cramer, P. (1968). *Word association.* New York: Academic Press.

Cunningham, M. R. (1979). Weather, mood, and helping behavior: Quasi-experiments in the sunshine Samaritan. *Journal of Personality and Social Psychology, 37,* 1947–1956.

Davidson, D., Suppes, P., & Siegel, S. (1956). *Decision making: An experimental approach.* Stanford, CA: Stanford University Press.

Davidson, R. J. (1984). Affect, cognition, and hemispheric specialization. In C. E. Izard, J. Kagan, & R. B. Zajonc (Eds.), *Emotions, cognition, and behavior.* New York: Cambridge University Press.

Duffy, E. (1934). Emotion: An example of the need for reorientation in psychology. *Psychological Review, 41,* 184–198.

Duncker, K. (1945). On problem-solving. *Psychological Monographs, 58,* Whole No. 5.

Easterbrook, J. A. (1959). The effect of emotion of cue utilization and the organization of behavior. *Psychological Review,* **66,** 183–201.

Eich, J. E., & Birnbaum, I. M. (1982). Repetition, cueing and state-dependent memory. *Memory and Cognition,* **10,** 103–114.

Fisher, R. P., & Craik, F. I. M. (1977). The interaction between encoding and retrieval operations in cued recall. *Journal of Experimental Psychology: Human Learning and Memory,* **3,** 701–711.

Forest, D., Clark, M. S., Mills, J., & Isen, A. M. (1979). Helping as a function of feeling state and nature of the helping behavior. *Motivation and Emotion,* **3,** 161–169.

Frey, P. S. (1975). Affect and resistance to temptation. *Developmental Psychology,* **11,** 466–472.

Fried, R., & Berkowitz, L. (1979). Music hath charms . . . and can influence helpfulness. *Journal of Applied Social Psychology,* **9,** 199–208.

Galizio, M., & Hendrick, C. (1972). Effect of musical accompaniment on attitude: The guitar as a prop for persuasion. *Journal of Applied Social Psychology,* **2,** 350–359.

Goldstein, K. M., & Blackman, S. (1978). *Cognitive style.* New York: Wiley.

Gouaux, C. (1971). Induced affective states and interpersonal attraction. *Journal of Personality and Social Psychology,* **20,** 37–43.

Griffitt, W. B. (1970). Environmental effects on interpersonal affective behavior: Ambient effective temperature and attraction. *Journal of Personality and Social Psychology,* **15,** 240–244.

Harvey, O. J., Hunt, D. E., & Schroder, H. M. (1961). *Conceptual systems and personality organization.* New York: Wiley.

Hasher, L., & Zacks, R. T. (1979). Automatic and effortful processes in memory. *Journal of Experimental Psychology: General,* **108,** 356–388.

Higgins, E. T., & King, G. (1981). Accessibility of social constructs: Information processing consequences of individual contextual variability. In N. Cantor & J. F. Kihlstrom (Eds.), *Personality, cognition, and social interaction.* Hillsdale, NJ: Erlbaum.

Hornstein, H. A., Masor, H. N., Sole, K., & Heilman, M. (1971). Effects of sentiment and completion of a helping act on observer helping: A case for socially mediated Zeigarnik effects. *Journal of Personality and Social Psychology,* **17,** 107–112.

Isen, A. M. (1970). Success, failure, attention and reactions to others: The warm glow of success. *Journal of Personality and Social Psychology,* **15,** 294–301.

Isen, A. M. (1975). Positive affect, accessibility of cognitions, and helping. Paper presented as part of the symposium, ''Directions in theory on helping behavior'' (J. Piliavin, Chair), Eastern Psychological Association Convention, New York.

Isen, A. M. (1984). Toward understanding the role of affect in cognition. In R. Wyer & T. Srull (Eds.), *Handbook of social cognition.* Hillsdale. NJ: Erlbaum.

Isen, A. M. (1985). The asymmetry of happiness and sadness in effects on memory in normal college students. *Journal of Experimental Psychology: General,* **114,** 388–391.

Isen, A. M., Clark, M. S., & Schwartz, M. F. (1976). Duration of the effect of good mood on helping: ''Footprints on the sands of time.'' *Journal of Personality and Social Psychology,* **34,** 385–393.

Isen, A. M., & Daubman, K. A. (1984). The influence of affect on categorization. *Journal of Personality and Social Psychology,* **47,** 1206–1217.

Isen, A. M., & Daubman, K. A. (1986). *The influence of positive affect on the perceived organization of components of self.* Unpublished manuscript, University of Maryland, Catonsville, MD.

Isen, A. M., Daubman, K. A., & Gorgoglione, J. M. (1987). The influence of positive affect on cognitive organization: Implications for education. In R. Snow & M. Farr (Eds.), *Aptitude, learning, and instruction: Affective and conative factors.* Hillsdale, NJ: Erlbaum, in press.

Isen, A. M., Daubman, K. A., & Nowicki, G. P. (1987). Positive affect facilitates creative problem solving. *Journal of Personality and Social Psychology,* in press.

Isen, A. M., & Geva, N. (1987). The influence of positive affect on acceptable level of risk: The person with a large canoe has a large worry. *Organizational Behavior and Human Decision Processes, 39*, 145–154.

Isen, A. M., & Gorgoglione, J. M. (1983). Some specific effects of four affect-induction procedures. *Personality and Social Psychology Bulletin, 9*, 136–143.

Isen, A. M., Horn, N., & Rosenhan, D. (1973). Effects of success and failure on children's generosity. *Journal of Personality and Social Psychology, 27*, 239–247.

Isen, A. M., Johnson, M. M. S., Mertz, E., & Robinson, G. (1985). The influence of positive affect on the unusualness of word association. *Journal of Personality and Social Psychology. 48*, 1413–1426.

Isen, A. M., & Levin, P. F. (1972). The effect of feeling good on helping: Cookies and kindness. *Journal of Personality and Social Psychology, 21*, 384–388.

Isen, A. M., & Means, B. (1983). The influence of positive affect on decision-making strategy. *Social Cognition, 2*, 18–31.

Isen, A. M., Means, B., Patrick, R., & Nowicki, G. (1982). Some factors influencing decision-making strategy and risk-taking. In M. S. Clark & S. T. Fiske (Eds.), *Affect and cognition: The 17th Annual Carnegie Symposium on Cognition* (pp. 243–261). Hillsdale, NJ: Erlbaum.

Isen, A. M., & Nowicki, G. P. (1983). *The influence of affective state on the rating of familiar and unfamiliar words.* Unpublished manuscript, University of Maryland, Catonsville, MD.

Isen, A. M., Nygren, T. E., & Ashby, F. G. (1985). The influence of positive affect on the subjective utility of gains and losses: It's not worth the risk. Paper presented at the meeting of the Psychonomic Society, Boston, MA.

Isen, A. M., & Patrick, R. (1983). The effect of positive feelings on risk-taking: When the chips are down. *Organizational Behavior and Human Performance, 31*, 194–202.

Isen, A. M., & Shalker, T. E. (1982). Do you "accentuate the positive, eliminate the negative" when you are in a good mood? *Social Psychology Quarterly, 45*, 58–63.

Isen, A. M., Shalker, T., Clark, M., & Karp, L. (1978). Affect, accessibility of material in memory and behavior: A cognitive loop? *Journal of Personality and Social Psychology, 36*, 1–12.

Isen, A. M., & Simmonds, S. F. (1978). The effect of feeling good on a helping task that is incompatible with good mood. *Social Psychology Quarterly, 41*, 345–349.

Jacobson, J. Z. (1973). Effects of association upon masing and reading latency. *Canadian Journal of Psychology, 27*, 58–69.

Janis, I. L., Kaye, D., & Kirschner, P. (1965). Facilitating effects of "eating while reading" on responsiveness to persuasive communications. *Journal of Personality and Social Psychology, 11*, 181–186.

Jenkins, J. J. (1974). Remember that old theory of memory? Well, forget it! *American Psychologist, 29*, 785–795.

Johnson, E., & Tversky, A. (1983). Affect, generalization and the perception of risk. *Journal of Personality and Social Psychology, 45*, 20–31.

Kelly, G. A. (1955). *The psychology of personal constructs.* New York: Norton.

Koestler, A. (1964). *The act of creation.* New York: Macmillan.

Laird, J. D., Wagener, J. J., Halal, M., & Szegda, M. (1982). Remembering what you feel: The effects of emotion on memory. *Journal of Personality and Social Psychology, 42*, 646–657.

Leeper, R. W. (1948). A motivational theory of emotion to replace "emotion as disorganized response." *Psychological Review, 55*, 5–21.

Leeper, R. W. (1970). The motivational and perceptual properties of emotions indicating their fundamental character and role. In M. B. Arnold (Ed.), *Feelings and emotions.* New York: Academic Press.

Levin, P. F., & Isen, A. M. (1975). Something you can still get for a dime: Further studies on the effect of feeling good on helping. *Sociometry, 38*, 141–147.

Loftus, E. F. (1973). Activation of semantic memory. *American Journal of Psychology,* **86,** 331–337.

Loftus, G. R., & Loftus, E. F. (1974). The influence of one memory retrieval on a subsequent memory retrieval. *Memory and Cognition,* **2,** 467–471.

Mandler, G. (1967). Organization and memory. In K. W. Spence & J. T. Spence (Eds.), *The psychology of learning and motivation: Advances in research and theory* (Vol. 1). New York: Academic Press.

Manucia, G. K., Bauman, D. J., & Cialdini, R. B. (1984). Mood influences on helping: Direct effects or side effects? *Journal of Personality and Social Psychology,* **46,** 357–364.

Martindale, C. (1981). *Cognition and consciousness.* Homewood, IL: Dorsey.

Matlin, M. W., & Stang, D. (1979). *The Pollyanna Principle: Selectivity in language, memory and thought.* Cambridge, MA: Schenkman.

Medin, D. L. (1983). Structural principles in categorization. In T. J. Tighe & B. E. Shepp (Eds.), *Perception, cognition and development: Interactional analyses* (pp. 203–230). Hillsdale, NJ: Erlbaum.

Mednick, M. T., Mednick, S. A., & Mednick, E. V. (1964). Incubation of creative performance and specific associative priming. *Journal of Abnormal and Social Psychology,* **69,** 84–88.

Mednick, S. A. (1962). The associative basis of the creative process. *Psychological Review,* **69,** 220–232.

Meyer, D. W., & Schvaneveldt, R. W. (1971). Facilitation in recognizing pairs of words: Evidence of a dependence between retrieval operations. *Journal of Experimental Psychology,* **90,** 227–234.

Miller, G. (1956). The magical number seven, plus or minus two: Some limits on our capacity for processing information. *Psychological Review,* **63,** 81–97.

Mischel, W., Coates, B., & Raskoff, A. (1968). Effects of success and failure on self-gratification. *Journal of Personality and Social Psychology,* **10,** 381–390.

Mischel, W., Ebbesen, E., & Zeiss, A. (1973). Selective attention to the self: Situational and dispositional determinants. *Journal of Personality and Social Psychology,* **27,** 129–142.

Mischel, W., Ebbesen, E., & Zeiss, A. (1976). Determinants of selective memory about the self. *Journal of Consulting and Clinical Psychology,* **44,** 92–103.

Moore, B. S., Underwood, W., & Rosenhan, D. L. (1973). Affect and altruism. *Developmental Psychology,* **8,** 99–104.

Morris, C. D., Bransford, J. D., & Franks, J. J. (1977). Levels of processing versus transfer appropriate processing. *Journal of Verbal Learning and Verbal Behavior,* **16,** 519–533.

Murphy, G. L., & Medin, D. L. (1985). The role of theories in conceptual coherence. *Psychological Review,* **92,** 289–316.

Nasby, W., & Yando, R. (1982). Selective encoding and retrieval of affectively valent information. *Journal of Personality and Social Psychology,* **43,** 1244–1255.

Natale, M., & Hantas, M. (1982). Effects of temporary mood states on memory about the self. *Journal of Personality and Social Psychology,* **42,** 927–934.

Neely, J. H. (1976). Semantic priming and retrieval from lexical memory: Evidence for facilitatory and inhibitory processes. *Memory and Cognition,* **4,** 648–654.

Neely, J. H. (1977). Semantic priming and retrieval from lexical memory: Roles of inhibitionless spreading and activation and limited-capacity attention. *Journal of Experimental Psychology: General,* **106,** 226–254.

Neisser, U. (1967). *Cognitive psychology.* New York: Appleton.

Neisser, U. (1976). *Cognition and reality.* San Francisco: Freeman.

Palermo, D. S., & Jenkins, J. J. (1964). *Word association norms: Grade school through college.* Minneapolis: University of Minnesota Press.

Piliavin, J. A., Dovidio, J. F., Gaertner, S. L., & Clark, R. D. (1982). Responsive bystanders: The process of intervention. In V. J. Derlaga & J. Grzelak (Eds.), *Cooperation and helping behavior*. New York: Academic Press.

Pollio, H. R. (1964). Some semantic relations among word-associates. *American Journal of Psychology*, **77**, 249–256.

Posner, M. I., & Snyder, C. R. R. (1975). Attention and cognitive control. In R. L. Solso (Ed.), *Information processing and cognition: The Loyola symposium*. Hillsdale, NJ: Erlbaum.

Pruitt, D. G. (1981). *Negotiation behavior*. New York: Academic Press.

Pruitt, D. G. (1983). Strategic choice in negotiation. *American Behavioral Scientist*, **27**, 167–194.

Riskind, J. H. (1983). Nonverbal expressions and the accessibility of life experience memories: A congruence hypothesis. *Social Cognition*, **2**, 62–86.

Rosch, E. (1975). Cognitive representations of semantic categories. *Journal of Experimental Psychology: General*, **104**(3), 192–233.

Roth, E. M., & Shoben, E. J. (1983). The effect of content on the structure of categories. *Cognitive Psychology*, **15**, 346–378.

Rothbart, M., & John, O. P. (1985). Social categorization and behavioral episodes: A cognitive analysis of the effects of intergroup contact. *Journal of Social Issues*, **41**, 81–104.

Schiffenbauer, A. (1974). Effects of observer's emotional state on judgments of the emotional state of others. *Journal of Personality and Social Psychology*, **30**(1), 31–36.

Schwartz, J. C., & Pollack, P. R. (1977). Affect and delay of gratification. *Journal of Research in Personality*, **11**, 147–164.

Seeman, G., & Schwartz, J. C. (1974). Affective state and preferences for immediate versus delayed reward. *Journal of Research in Personality*, **7**, 384–394.

Shaffer, D. R., & Graziano, W. G. (1983). Effects of positive and negative moods on helping tasks having pleasant and unpleasant consequences. *Motivation and Emotion*, **7**, 269–276.

Sherman, S. J., & Corty, E. (1984). Cognitive heuristics. In R. S. Wyer & T. S. Srull (Eds.), *Handbook of social cognition* (Vol. 1). Hillsdale, NJ: Erlbaum.

Simon, H. (1967). Motivational and emotional controls of cognition. *Psychological Review*, **74**, 29–39.

Smith, E. E., & Medin, D. L. (1981). *Categories and concepts*. Cambridge, MA: Harvard University Press.

Snyder, M., & White, E. (1982). Moods and memories: Elation, depression, and remembering the events of one's life. *Journal of Personality*, **50**, 149–167.

Srull, T. K., & Wyer, R. S. (1979). The role of category accessibility in the interpretation of information about persons: Some determinants and implications. *Journal of Personality and Social Psychology*, **37**, 1660–1672.

Teasdale, J. D., & Fogarty, S. J. (1979). Differential effects of induced mood on retrieval of pleasant and unpleasant events from episodic memory. *Journal of Abnormal Psychology*, **88**, 248–257.

Teasdale, J. D., & Russell, M. L. (1983). Differential aspects of induced mood on the recall of positive, negative and neutral words. *British Journal of Clinical Psychology*, **22**, 163–171.

Teasdale, J. D., Taylor, R., & Fogarty, S. J. (1980). Effects of induced elation-depression on the accessibility of memories of happy and unhappy experiences. *Behavior Research and Therapy*, **18**, 339–346.

Thomson, D. M., & Tulving, E. (1970). Associative encoding and retrieval: Weak and strong cues. *Journal of Experimental Psychology*, **86**, 255–262.

Toi, M., & Batson, C. (1982). More evidence that empathy is a source of altruistic motivation. *Journal of Personality and Social Psychology*, **43**, 281–292.

Tucker, D. M. (1981). Lateral brain function, emotion, and conceptualization. *Psychological Bulletin*, **89**, 19–46.

Tulving, E. (1979). Relation between encoding specificity and levels of processing. In L. S. Cermak & F. I. M. Craik (Eds.), *Levels of processing in human memory*. Hillsdale, NJ: Erlbaum.

Tulving, E., & Osler, S. (1968). Effectiveness of retrieval cues in memory for words. *Journal of Experimental Psychology, 77,* 593–601.

Tulving, E., & Pearlstone, Z. (1966). Availability versus accessibility of information in memory for words. *Journal of Verbal Learning and Verbal Behavior, 5,* 381–391.

Tulving, E., & Thomson, D. M. (1973). Encoding specificity and retrieval processes in episodic memory. *Psychological Review, 80,* 352–373.

Tversky, A. (1972). Elimination by aspects. *Psychological Review, 72,* 281–299.

Tversky, A. (1977). Features of similarity. *Psychological Review, 84,* 327–352.

Tversky, A., & Gati, I. (1978). Studies of similarity. In E. Rosch and B. B. Lloyd (Eds.), *Cognition and categorization.* Hillsdale, NJ: Erlbaum.

Tversky, A., & Kahneman, D. (1973). Availability: A heuristic for judging frequency and probability. *Cognitive Psychology, 5,* 207–232.

Tversky, A., & Kahneman, D. (1974). Judgments under uncertainty: Heuristics and biases. *Science, 185,* 1124–1131.

Veitch, R., & Griffitt, W. (1976). Good news—bad news: Affective and interpersonal effects. *Journal of Applied Social Psychology, 6,* 69–75.

Warren, R. E. (1977). Time and the spread of activation in memory. *Journal of Experimental Psychology: Human Learning and Memory, 4,* 458–466.

Watkins, M. J. (1979). Engrams as cuegrams and forgetting as cue overload. In C. R. Puff (Ed.), *Memory organization and structure.* New York: Academic Press.

Weingartner, H., & Faillace, L. A. (1971). Alcohol state-dependent learning in man. *Journal of Nervous and Mental Disease, 153,* 395–406.

Weiss, R. F., Buchanan, W., Alstatt, L., & Lombardo, J. P. (1971). Altruism is rewarding. *Science, 26,* 1262–1263.

Weyant, J. M. (1978). Effects of mood states, costs, and benefits of helping. *Journal of Personality and Social Psychology, 36,* 1169–1176.

White, M. M. (1936). Some factors influencing the recall of pleasant and unpleasant words. *American Journal of Psychology, 48,* 134–139.

White, M. M., & Powell, M. (1936). The differential reaction time for pleasant and unpleasant words. *American Journal of Psychology, 48,* 126–133.

Young, P. T. (1943). *Emotions in man and animal.* New York: Wiley.

Young, P. T. (1961). *Motivation and emotion.* New York: Wiley.

Zajonc, R. B. (1965). Social facilitation. *Science, 149,* 269–274.

BETWEEN HOPE AND FEAR: THE PSYCHOLOGY OF RISK

Lola L. Lopes

DEPARTMENT OF PSYCHOLOGY
UNIVERSITY OF WISCONSIN
MADISON, WISCONSIN 53706

I. INTRODUCTION

Most things begin to look a little funny if you stare at them long enough. So too the psychology of risk. What is most disconcerting is that there is so much theory for so little substance. Countless hours have been spent by psychologists and economists alike in trying to explain theoretically why people buy both lottery tickets and insurance. Lottery tickets cost a dollar. One. We buy insurance (when we can afford it) so that we can sleep better. Is it really so strange that we should want to buy both?

This chapter is about risk: what risk is (if it is any *thing* at all), how people think about it, what they feel about it, and what they do about it. The chapter is also about how *psychologists* think about risk: how they study it, what tasks they use, what factors they vary, and what models they build (or borrow) to describe risk-taking behavior.

Technically, the word *risk* refers to situations in which a decision is made whose consequences depend on the outcomes of future events having known probabilities. Choices among the different kinds of bets in games like roulette and craps are good examples of choices made under risk. Insurance companies also operate under risk when they set the premiums for ordinary life insurance. But most of the time our knowledge of probabilities is not so exact. Sometimes it's pretty good (as with the weather tomorrow or the going rates for auto loans just now); other times it's pretty awful (as with whether a wedding reception should be held indoors or outdoors several months hence or whether the fixed-rate mortgage that's offered today is going to feel like a bargain or a burden 10

ADVANCES IN EXPERIMENTAL
SOCIAL PSYCHOLOGY, VOL. 20

years down the road). When our knowledge of probabilities is very inexact (or lacking entirely) we say that decisions are made under uncertainty or ignorance. Obviously, risk shades into ignorance and most important decisions are made part way between the poles.

Psychological studies of risky choice (which is the term used conventionally to refer to all but the most extreme instances of ignorance or ambiguity) fall into two groups. At one extreme are the studies run by mathematically inclined experimental psychologists in which subjects make decisions about gambles described in terms of amounts and probabilities. At the other extreme are studies run by personality psychologists who are mostly interested in individual differences in risk taking. Their tasks tend to be closer to everyday experience and they often involve elements both of chance and skill.

A. THE EXPERIMENTALISTS' VIEW

A good example of an experimental task comes from Kahneman and Tversky (1979), who asked subjects questions similar to this: which would you rather have, $3000 for sure or an 80% chance of winning $4000? Most subjects prefer the $3000 for sure even though the expected value of the gamble is higher, $.80 \times \$4000 = \$3200$. Such preferences are conventionally labeled "risk averse," as are preferences favoring a 90% chance of winning $3000 over a 45% chance of winning $6000.

Experimental psychologists tend to explain risk-averse behavior in one of two ways. Some theories of risky choice see the subject as trading off potential return with "risk," a construct that is most often identified with variability in the outcome distribution. For example, Coombs's (1975) "portfolio theory" is based on the premise that choices among risks reflect a compromise between maximizing expected value and achieving an individually determined ideal level of risk. Thus, investors who prefer low risk must accept the lower but safer returns associated with bonds, whereas investors who prefer more risk can opt for the higher but less safe returns of stocks and commodities.

Theories that consider risk to be a function of the variability among potential outcomes are intuitively appealing, but they are less commonly held than alternative theories based on weighted-value models, the best known of which is expected utility theory. In expected utility theory, subjects are assumed to "compute" something similar to an expected value, but instead of using the objective dollar amounts, they operate on subjective amounts (or utilities) which are usually nonlinearly related to dollar amounts.

The first use of the utility concept was made by Daniel Bernoulli in 1738. He argued that the value of money is not absolute, but depends on how much one has already: "Any increase in wealth, no matter how insignificant, will always result in an increase in utility which is inversely proportionate to the quantity of goods already possessed'' (Bernoulli, 1967, p. 25). This view implies that a constant gain, say $1000, will be worth more subjectively to a poor person than a rich person. It also implies that subjective differences between amounts of money that differ by a constant get smaller as the absolute magnitudes of the amounts get larger. In other words, there's more difference psychologically between $1000 and $2000, say, than between $10,000 and $11,000. In Bernoullian terms, money has *marginally decreasing utility* (which is short for saying that the subjective value of constant increments gets smaller and smaller). In mathematical terms, the utility function (which relates the objective value of money to its subjective value) is negatively accelerated. An example of a negatively accelerated utility function is shown in the upper left quadrant of Fig. 1.

Bernoulli's utility theory predicts risk aversion. This is easy to understand intuitively. Consider a gamble that offers a .5 chance of winning $2000 and a .5

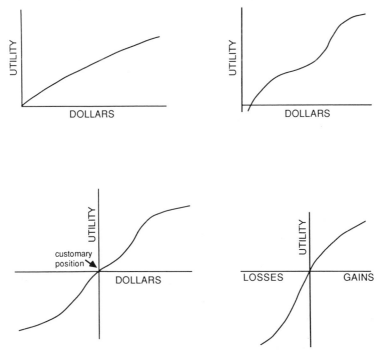

Fig. 1. Examples of utility functions with four different shapes. The Bernoullian function (upper left) is uniformly risk averse (negatively accelerated). The functions in the upper right, lower left, and lower right (suggested by Friedman & Savage, 1948; Markowitz, 1952; and Kahneman & Tversky, 1979, respectively) have regions of risk aversion (negative acceleration) and risk seeking (positive acceleration). The upper two functions range from zero assets to large positive assets. The lower two functions range about a customary asset level (e.g., the status quo).

chance of winning nothing. The expected value of the gamble is $1000, but it is worth less subjectively to anyone having a Bernoullian utility function. This is because the subjective value of $1000 is more than half the distance between nothing and $2000. Thus, the utility of $1000 for sure must be greater than the *average* of the utility of nothing and the utility of $2000 (which is all that the expected utility is—an average in which utilities are weighted by their probability of occurrence).

A problem, however, is that people are not always risk averse. For example, they buy lottery tickets even though it is well known that, on average, lotteries are mathematically unfair (which doesn't mean, of course, that they are crooked, but only that the price of the ticket is more than the expected value). People are also sometimes "risk seeking" (as it is conventional to say) when choosing among risks that have negative consequences (Markowitz, 1959; Williams, 1966; Kahneman & Tversky, 1979). For example, many people would prefer to face an 80% chance of losing $4000 than to lose $3000 for sure even though the expected value of the risky loss ($3200) is greater than the sure loss.

Risk-seeking choices can be explained by weighted-value theories in two different ways. One way is to say that the utility function is not always negatively accelerated, but instead has one or more regions of positive acceleration. Three examples of such kinky utility functions are shown in Fig. 1. The function in the upper right quadrant was proposed by Friedman and Savage (1948), that in the lower left by Markowitz (1952), and that in the lower right by Kahneman and Tversky (1979).[1] Each of these functions has one or more regions of negative acceleration (which predict risk-averse behavior such as the purchase of insurance and the rejection of gambles) and one or more regions of positive acceleration (which predict risk-seeking behavior such as the purchase of gambles, notably long shots that offer very large prizes at very small probabilities).

Another way to explain risk-seeking choices is to suppose that the weights people use in evaluating gambles are not identical to the objective probabilities. Thus, people may purchase lottery tickets because they (optimistically) assign more weight to the probability of winning than is justified objectively. This notion that subjective probabilities may differ from stated probabilities is consistent with subjectively expected utility theory (Savage, 1954). It is also consistent with more general weighted utility models (Edwards, 1962; Karmarkar, 1978; Kahneman & Tversky, 1979) in which the subjective values attached to probabilities do not even act like probabilities mathematically.

To sum up, then, most experimentalists explain risky choice by positing an

[1]Kahneman and Tversky (1979) call their function a "value function" to distinguish it from the utility function of modern expected utility theory (von Neumann & Morgenstern, 1947). Because this article deals primarily with the psychophysical or classical interpretation of utility, the single word "utility" is used throughout to refer to the subjective value of money or other commodities.

internal process for evaluating gambles that is structurally similar to computing expected values. However, the objective values are replaced by subjective values such as utilities and probability weights that differ quantitatively from their objective counterparts.

B.   THE PERSONOLOGISTS' VIEW

A good example of a task used by personality psychologists is the "ring toss" game originally used by McClelland (1958) in his studies of achievement motivation. In this task, subjects throw rings onto a peg from a distance that they are allowed to choose themselves. At one extreme, they can stand so near the peg that success is virtually certain. At the other extreme, they can stand so far away that success is virtually impossible. The variable of interest, therefore, is not how well they do objectively, but rather where they stand.

This is a task in risky choice (even though the probabilities are only roughly known) because subjects are choosing among alternative actions that have the character of gambles. One can choose (and some do) to stand near the peg, in which case the probability of success is high, but the personal satisfaction in getting the ring over the peg is small. Alternatively, one can stand further back, in which case the probability of success is smaller, but the satisfaction is greater. One can even choose a long shot (literally), in which the probability of success is virtually nil, but the potential satisfaction is enormous. (Consider the heady burst of satisfaction that comes in basketball when a desperation shot, tossed the full length of the court, drops neatly through the net. It helps, of course, if it is one's own team that has made the shot.)

Personologists explain people's choices in the ring toss game in terms of their motivations (McClelland, 1961; J. Atkinson, 1983). People who have high motivation to succeed (M_s) tend to pick intermediate distances (particularly if they are also low in the motive to avoid failure, M_{af}). The theoretical rationale for this is that there is a three-way multiplicative relation between motivation, probability, and incentive (J. Atkinson, 1957). Since probability of success (closeness to the peg) and incentive value (anticipated satisfaction from making the particular shot) are inversely related to one another, the attractiveness of the task for the person with high M_s and low M_{af} is least when the probability of succeeding is either very small or very large, and it is maximum when probability is at an intermediate value.[2]

People who are low in M_s, however, especially if they are also high in M_{af}, more often stand either very near or very far from the peg. Either way, these

[2]Originally the value was assumed to be .50, but now it is believed to be nearer .35 (J. Atkinson, 1983).

people reduce their performance anxiety by virtually guaranteeing that they will experience either the tepid success of a trivial accomplishment or the denatured failure of not doing something that cannot be done anyway except by sheer good luck.

Thus, personologists focus on the similarities and differences between different people's needs and on the various options that people pursue for meeting their needs. They also stress the often competitive nature of needs and the resulting compromises that must be made between certainty and incentive, for instance, or between the motive to achieve success and the motive to avoid failure (both of which can exist in the same person at the same time.)

II. PSYCHOPHYSICAL VERSUS MOTIVATIONAL THEORIES OF RISK

The gamble task and the ring toss task appear to have little in common, but they are alike structurally. In each case the subject chooses among alternative options, each of which can be characterized by the probabilities and values that are attached to uncertain outcomes. In fact, one can with some justice interpret subjects' choices in the ring-toss task as maximizing expected utility (cf. J. Atkinson, 1958). But there are profound differences in the theoretical mechanisms that have been used to explain subjects' choices in these two tasks.

Bernoullian explanations are *psychophysical* in exactly the sense of ordinary sensory psychophysics. In fact, the quantitative function that Bernoulli suggested for utility reappeared more than 100 years later as Fechner's general psychophysical law. But this means that in Bernoullian theory risk-averse *behavior* has neither to do with *risk* nor with *aversion*. Instead, it has only to do with the way we experience quantity. The person who turns down an 80% chance of winning $4000 in favor of a sure $3000 is *not*, therefore, avoiding risk, nor even experiencing risk in any theoretically relevant way, but is only responding to the same sorts of factors that make the difference in heaviness between 1 pound and 2 pounds seem greater than the difference between 10 pounds and 11 pounds.

The same can be said for explanations in which objective probabilities are replaced by subjective probabilities or by probability weights. In fact, Kahneman and Tversky (1984) have referred to their decision-weight function as reflecting the "psychophysics of chances" (p. 344). Their decision weights are assumed to differ from objective probabilities due to factors that are like those found in perception. For example, category-boundary effects make a change from impossibility to possibility (or from possibility to certainty) seem larger than a comparable change in the middle of the scale. This is the same sort of thing that happens in the "categorical perception" of human speech. Sounds that actually change in equal acoustic increments from an ideal "ba" to an ideal "da" are perceived to shift abruptly from sounding like clear ba's to sounding like clear da's (Liberman, Harris, Hoffman, & Griffith, 1957).

Motivational explanations, on the other hand, construe the decision maker as analyzing possible outcomes and assessing risks (by which is usually meant simply the probability of achieving some goal). For example, McClelland (1961) gave the following account of how children who are high in achievement motivation decide where to stand:

> If they stand too close to the peg, they are much more likely to throw the ring on . . . but they are less likely to get any feelings of achievement satisfaction from doing so. If they stand too far away, they are both much less likely to succeed and more likely to regard success as "luck," than if they stand a moderate distance from the peg. In fact, they are behaving like the businessman who acts neither traditionally (no risk) nor like a gambler (extreme risk), but who chooses to operate in a way in which he is most likely to get achievement satisfaction (moderate risk, in this case about one chance in three of succeeding). (p. 212)

There are many places in McClelland's account where one could evoke psychophysical mechanisms to explain why different children make different choices: they might attach different subjective values to success at different distances; or they might assign different probabilities to succeeding at a given distance; they might even differ in the way they perceive distances. But this is not how achievement theorists explain things. McClelland is careful to rule out such factors. For example, he acknowledges that children who are high in achievement motivation tend to perceive their probability of success more favorably than children with low achievement motivation, particularly when there is no evidence one way or the other. However, when they have reasonable knowledge based on past performance, they use that knowledge appropriately and do not display a greater perceived probability of success than children who are low in achievement motivation. In his words, achievement-motivated children "are not impractical 'dreamers' overestimating their success at everything; instead they rely on facts so far as they are available, and then fall back on generalized self-confidence" (McClelland, 1961, p. 223).

One can also examine the possibility that achievement-motivated children simply place higher subjective value on success by looking at their preferences in games of pure chance. In this situation they clearly prefer the shortest odds they can get (the safest bets) followed by intermediate values. Children with low achievement motivation, on the other hand, tend to like long shots that offer large prizes, but at small probability (McClelland, 1961).

A. THE ROLE OF COGNITION

We have, then, two different approaches to explaining risky choice, one primarily psychophysical and the other primarily motivational. The theories differ also in the degree to which they are *cognitive*. The motivational theories have strong cognitive components. In order to choose appropriately, task difficulty must be analyzed for the relative contributions of skill and chance, past experience must be marshalled and used to assess probabilities, goals must be set and future feelings predicted about what will be satisfying and what not. Thus, it is motivation that incites action and gives it direction (i.e., approach or avoidance), but it is cognition that guides action to its intended goal.

Psychophysical theories, on the other hand, have not been couched in cognitive terms, although they certainly might be. One could, for example, justify a Bernoullian utility function in terms of Maslow's (1954) notion of a need hierarchy. On this view, $1000 really *is* worth more to a poor person than to a rich person because the poor person will spend the money to satisfy more basic needs (food, shelter) whereas the rich person will spend it on more transcendent needs (operas, electronic running shoes). Likewise, people's tendency to treat small probabilities as zero might be justified cognitively in terms of the degree to which small probabilities can be expected to produce discernible impacts on how we choose to live our daily lives. This was done, in fact, by the early probabilist, Buffon, who urged that all probabilities less than .0001 be treated as "morally" (which is to say, psychologically) equal to zero (Daston, 1980).

This is not, however, how psychophysical theories are justified. Indeed, they tend most often not to be justified at all. But Kahneman and Tversky (1979) have been refreshingly clear about their theoretical foundations. They say of their value (or utility) function,

> Our perceptual apparatus is attuned to the evaluation of changes or differences rather than to the evaluation of absolute magnitudes. When we respond to attributes such as brightness, loudness, or temperature, the past and present context of experience defines an adaptation level, or reference point, and stimuli are perceived in relation to this reference point. . . . Many sensory and perceptual dimensions share the property that the psychological response is a concave function of the magnitude of physical change. . . . We propose that this principle applies in particular to the evaluation of monetary changes. (pp. 278–279)

Likewise, their description of probability weighting, while less clearly articulated, seems to rest primarily on perceptual and attentional metaphors.

B. RISK-TAKING RECONSIDERED

Personality psychologists and experimental psychologists tend to have very different goals. Personologists, at least traditionally (i.e., pre-Mischel, 1968) have taken an idiographic approach to explaining behavior. Thus, they have been concerned with the things that make us *different* from one another. Since these are necessarily attached to the individual and not to the situation (which is held constant), the theoretical emphasis has fallen on the structures and dynamics of the inner person. Experimentalists, on the other hand, have typically taken the nomothetic approach, which is aimed at understanding Everyman and the ways in which we are all alike. This approach puts the emphasis on the commonly experienced environment which, in the context of the laboratory, reduces to the *stimulus*. Experimental theories, whether they are behavioral or cognitive, tend to revolve around the transformation of the stimulus into the response. If this can be done without invoking individual differences or higher-level cognition, all the better. Hence the appeal of the psychophysical metaphor for explaining risky choice (or more properly, for explaining the most common choice pattern while ignoring entirely the patterns of a substantial minority of subjects).

When the scientific paths of personologists and experimentalists cross as they have in the area of risky choice, the weaknesses of each tradition are illuminated by the strengths of the other. Personality theorists paint with a broad brush and a richly hued palette, at least compared to their monochromatic experimental colleagues. McClelland's (1961) *The Achieving Society* is breathtaking in its scope and intent, ranging methodologically from the laboratory to the field and substantively from history to economics and from psychology to sociology. But the experimental evidence tends to be unsystematic and unconvincing, at least for the experimentalist schooled in the parametric (if you can vary it, vary it) tradition. Thus, although the motivational approach is appealing for its whole-person flavor (with motivation and emotion and cognition all having their place), the actual experiments are scattered far too sparingly over the conceptual domain. In particular, the motivational treatment of risk taking in the domain of pure chance is disappointing, especially when one considers that we regularly deal with risks (e.g., farmers planting crops, investors choosing a stock) whose outcomes are largely out of our personal control.

Experimentalists, on the other hand, tend to explore their domain more thoroughly, not necessarily because they are better scientists, but because the tradition of looking for "critical tests" keeps the experimental stimulus changing in interesting ways. Thus, the history of thought in risky choice has proceeded in relatively discrete steps as paradoxical results posed initially as challenges to the theory eventually became accommodated via theoretical elaboration. (A comparison with Ptolemaic astronomy would not be unwarranted after 250 years of elaboration on a theory that has remained essentially unchanged structurally). But in the service of the detailed view, the big picture tends to be lost. So it is with risky choice; after all the study and all the clever theorizing, we are left with a theory of risk taking that fails to mention risk. It also fails to consider (much less explain) the motivational and emotional factors that give risky choice its experiential texture: the hopes and fears that give us in due measure both purpose and pause.

In the remainder of this chapter, I present a theory of risky choice that

attempts to meld the strengths of both approaches. Empirically and methodologically it is tied to the experimental approach to risky choice. But theoretically it is more strongly tied to motivational approaches, particularly those
of McClelland (1961) and J. Atkinson (1983). Nevertheless, the theory was
developed independently of the latter theories and has at least some formal roots
in economics (see Lopes, 1984). Although the basic theoretical constructs of the
new theory are quite similar to those found in the achievement literature, I will
make no particular attempt to bring the two approaches into tighter theoretical
alignment since that could (and probably would) do disservice to the fact that the
task domains have important differences, particularly those involving the
skill/chance dimension. However, the strong theoretical similarities increase my
confidence in both approaches.

III. The Task and the Representation of the Stimulus

The term "risky choice" can be read two ways. Risky choices are choices
that have an element of danger. They are risky and may come to a bad end.
Losses may be sustained, hopes may be shattered, or opportunities wasted. Risky
choices are also choices among risks or between risks and sure things. In this
sense, risks are gambles. Most research on risk has concentrated on gambles in
which there are only two possible outcomes. In fact, a not inconsiderable part of
this research has dealt with what might be called one-outcome gambles, in which
one outcome represents a change (e.g., winning $4000) and the other represents
the *status quo*. The focus on two-outcome gambles seems reasonable to most
researchers in part because such gambles lend themselves well to parametric
manipulation in the laboratory. In addition, two-outcome gambles are conceptually simple, a fact of at least some consequence given the known limitations in
human beings' ability to process information.[3]

Real-world risks, on the other hand, hardly ever have just two outcomes.
More often they range essentially continuously over the outcome variable. (Consider interest rates on Individual Retirement Accounts. As I write, they are
averaging from around 7.5% for short-term investments up to around 9.5% for
long-term investments. Is 9.5% enough to tie up funds for a long period, or will
we have another bout of high interest rates? And if so, how high will they go?) In
fact, two-outcome gambles occur mostly in the context of formal gambling (and
psychology experiments). A $2 bet on red in roulette, for example, will either
win $2 or lose $2. Likewise, a horse player betting $2 at odds of 5 to 1 will either

---

[3]Researchers presumably also have limitations in their ability to process information. This might
be an additional reason for preferring two-outcome gambles, though it does not get mentioned.

win $8 or lose $2. In either case, it seems unlikely that players will make a separate decision each time they place a bet. Instead, the decision to play usually entails placing a series of bets, with resulting net outcomes that range in principle from all losses to all wins.

The experiments described in this chapter have investigated how people chose among multioutcome gambles (or "lotteries" as we refer to them with subjects). Figure 2 gives six examples of these lotteries listed in the order in which they are preferred by risk-averse subjects (Schneider & Lopes, 1986):

RISKLESS

Prize	Tickets
$200	I
$187	II
$172	III
$157	IIII
$143	IIIII
$129	IIIIII
$114	IIIIIIII
$ 99	IIIIIIIIIIII
$ 85	IIIIIIIIIIIIIIIII
$ 70	IIIIIIIIIIIIIIIIIIIIIIIIII

SHORT SHOT

Prize	Tickets
$130	IIIIIIIIIIIIIIIIIIIIIIIIIIIII
$115	IIIIIIIIIIIIIIIIIII
$101	IIIIIIIIIIIII
$ 86	IIIIIIIIII
$ 71	IIIIIII
$ 57	IIIII
$ 43	IIII
$ 28	III
$ 13	II
ZERO	I

PEAKED

Prize	Tickets
$200	I
$186	I
$172	III
$159	IIIII
$146	IIIIIII
$132	IIIIIIIII
$119	IIIIIIIIII
$106	IIIIIIIIIII
$ 93	IIIIIIIIIIII
$ 80	IIIIIIIIII
$ 66	IIIIIIIII
$ 53	IIIIIII
$ 40	IIIII
$ 26	III
$ 13	I
ZERO	I

RECTANGULAR

Prize	Tickets
$200	IIIII
$189	IIIII
$178	IIIII
$168	IIIII
$158	IIIII
$147	IIIII
$136	IIIII
$126	IIIII
$116	IIIII
$105	IIIII
$ 94	IIIII
$ 84	IIIII
$ 74	IIIII
$ 63	IIIII
$ 52	IIIII
$ 42	IIIII
$ 32	IIIII
$ 21	IIIII
$ 10	IIIII
ZERO	IIIII

BIMODAL

Prize	Tickets
$200	IIIIIIIIIIII
$186	IIIIIIIIII
$172	IIIIIIIII
$159	IIIIIII
$146	IIIII
$132	III
$119	I
$106	I
$ 93	I
$ 80	I
$ 66	III
$ 53	IIIII
$ 40	IIIIIII
$ 26	IIIIIIIII
$ 13	IIIIIIIIII
ZERO	IIIIIIIIIIII

LONG SHOT

Prize	Tickets
$439	I
$390	II
$341	III
$292	IIII
$244	IIIII
$195	IIIIII
$146	IIIIIIIII
$ 98	IIIIIIIIIIII
$ 49	IIIIIIIIIIIIIIIIII
ZERO	IIIIIIIIIIIIIIIIIIIIIIIIIIIIIIII

Fig. 2. Examples of stimulus lotteries for gains. Each lottery has 100 tickets (represented by tally marks) and each has an expected value of approximately $100. The values at the left give the prizes that are won by tickets in that row. The lotteries are ordered from the upper left to the lower right in the order that they are preferred by risk-averse subjects.

riskless > short shot > peaked > rectangular > bimodal > long shot. Each of the lotteries has 100 lottery tickets (represented by tally marks) and each has an expected value of approximately $100. The lotteries differ, however, in how the prizes are distributed. The long shot, for example, has 31 tickets that each win nothing, 22 tickets that each win $49, and so forth up to a single ticket that wins $439. In contrast, the short shot has only 1 ticket that wins nothing, 2 tickets that each win $13, and so forth up to 31 tickets that each win $130. (Note that the riskless lottery is so named because it has a riskless, i.e., sure, component that guarantees, in this case, a minimum win of $70.)

All the lotteries in the figure are "gain" lotteries, which means that their prizes are all ≥ 0. Loss lotteries were also used in some of the experiments. Loss lotteries are just like gain lotteries except that their outcomes are negative. Thus, for example, the long shot for losses has 31 tickets that each lose zero, 22 tickets that each lose $49, and so forth down to 1 ticket that loses $439. Likewise, the riskless loss lottery guarantees a riskless (sure) loss of at least $70.

Three kinds of task have been used. In the most common task subjects were shown pairs of lotteries in all possible combinations and asked which they would prefer if they were allowed a free draw from either (Lopes, 1984, Experiments 1 and 2; Schneider & Lopes, 1986). Pair-preference data can be used to infer preference orders over the entire set of stimuli. The second kind of task involved judgments of riskiness also expressed in pair-choices (Lopes, 1984, Experiments 3 through 6). These can be used to infer risk orders (which are not the same as preference orders except for risk-averse people). The third kind of task (Lopes, 1987) was embedded in a standard pair-preference task. Subjects were shown pairs of lotteries and asked to express their preferences for each. For a subset, however, they were also asked to explain their preferences in writing. These written protocols were collected for a group of 14 graduate students from a variety of departments. In order to avoid the known pitfalls of retrospective reports (Ericsson & Simon, 1980), the protocols were obtained directly at the point of choice.

This chapter focuses primarily on preference data from Lopes (1984) and Schneider and Lopes (1986). Examples of the verbal protocols are used throughout, however, for illustration. In the protocols, lotteries are referenced by the names listed in Fig. 2. These names were not, however, used by the subjects.

A. HOW CAN WE REPRESENT RISKS?

One of the most important steps in psychological theorizing is to find a representation of the stimulus that has psychological fidelity, by which I mean a representation that highlights the stimulus features that actually affect behavior. For the most part, two-outcome gambles have been treated as though the functional stimulus is identical with the presented stimulus: a pair of outcomes each associated with a probability of occurrence. For lotteries like those in Fig. 2, however, we seem to respond more to the *shapes* of lotteries than to the amounts and probabilities of individual outcomes.

The idea that risk is a function of shape has been proposed both for theories of risk perception (Luce, 1980; Pollatsek & Tversky, 1970) and for theories of risk preference (Allais, 1979; Coombs, 1975; Hagen, 1969; Markowitz, 1959). In these theories, shape is identified with the statistical moments of the distribution, particularly mean, variance, and skewness.[4] Variance is generally considered to be bad (i.e., risky), whereas positive skewness (a predominance of low outcomes with a few high outcomes) has been identified with hope and negative skewness (a predominance of high outcomes with a few low outcomes) has been identified with fear (Hagen, 1969). In this view preference for the short shot over the long shot would be interpreted as due to the short shot's much lower variance. Likewise, preference for the riskless lottery over the short shot would be interpreted as a preference for positive skewness since these lotteries have equal variance.

Moments models have several virtues, not the least of which is that any distribution can be described, in principle, to any desired level of precision by a sufficiently large set of its moments. But they also have major difficulties. Some of these are technical as, for instance, the fact that, subjectively speaking, risk does not really act like variance.[5] More serious, however, is the fact that such theories implicitly assume that moments have independent psychological reality. That seems doubtful except for the simplest comparisons. It is not all that easy to intuit the relative variance of lotteries that differ in skewness (e.g., the peaked lottery versus the short shot) except when the differences are very great (e.g., the peaked lottery versus the long shot).

In the present theory, lotteries are represented by cumulative graphs called Lorenz curves that are used in economics to show how wealth is distributed among people. Welfare economists find them useful for saying things like "The poorest 20% of the population in Country X have less of their country's wealth than the poorest 20% in Country Y." What is relevant for us is that subjects tend to talk as though they also view lotteries in cumulative terms. Here, for example, are reasons given by three typically risk-averse subjects for why, in a forced

[4]Hagen's (1969) theory is expressed in terms of the moments of the distribution of psychological or subjective values. In the present case, however, the relations among the moments of the objective distributions are similar to those that would obtain for the subjective distributions.

[5]The variance is unchanged when a positive constant is added to each outcome in the distribution. Risk, however, decreases (Keller, Sarin, & Weber, 1986). For example, if $1,000,000 were added to each of the outcomes in the various lotteries in Fig. 2, their variances would be unchanged, but they would have become much more similar in terms of perceived riskiness.

choice between the short shot and the long shot. they prefer the short shot (Lopes, 1987).

> I'd rather have greater chances of winning a little something than greater chances for nothing. The triple jackpot [in the long shot] doesn't make me want to go for it cuz the odds are too great. (Subject #10)

> I choose the [short shot] because there is only one chance of me losing and the best odds indicate a good chance of winning $71 or more. The [long shot] has too many opportunities to lose—it is too risky. (Subject #7)

> In the [long shot], 32% do better than the best in the [short shot], but 31% get nothing at all. The [short shot] is the better risk. (Subject #14)

Notice the inequalities: the keynote of these protocols is the cumulative likelihood of meeting or exceeding a goal (e.g., "greater chances of winning a little something," "a good chance of winning $71 or more," "do better than the best"). The protocols also suggest that the subjects are mostly concerned about doing badly (getting zero or a small amount).

Here for comparison are protocols from three subjects who chose the long shot. These subjects were among the most risk seeking of the group. Note their clear focus on the long shot's large prizes.

> The chance for winning nothing is small with the [short shot] but since the dollar amount in the [long shot] is attractive I run the risk of losing and go for the [long shot]. (Subject #12)

> The top prize money of the [long shot] is better. You still have a good chance of winning some money in the [long shot] as well as having a shot at the top prize money. The in-between prize money in the [long shot] is not all that bad, and is greater than the top prize money of the [short shot]. (Subject #9)

> I'll take the added risks of losing it all or getting a lower number for the chance of the higher prizes. Therefore I'll pick the [long shot]. (Subject #11)

B.   HOW TO DRAW A LORENZ CURVE (AND WHY)

Lorenz curves are convenient for looking at lotteries cumulatively and for comparing lotteries selectively on either low outcomes or high outcomes. They also highlight differences and similarities among lotteries that are not immediately apparent by direct inspection of the lotteries. Figure 3 shows how a Lorenz curve is graphed. Column 1 at the left shows the prizes for the peaked lottery ordered from the least (at the top) to the most (at the bottom). Column 2 gives the number of tickets at each level and column 3 converts these into probabilities.

PRIZES (P)	TICKETS (T)	PROB (PR)	P x T	CUM PR.	CUM P x T	CUM P x T / TOT P x T
0	1	.01	0	.01	0	.000
13	1	.01	13	.02	13	.001
26	3	.03	78	.05	91	.009
40	5	.05	200	.10	291	.029
53	7	.07	371	.17	662	.067
66	9	.09	594	.26	1256	.126
80	11	.11	880	.37	2136	.215
93	13	.13	1209	.50	3345	.337
106	13	.13	1378	.63	4723	.475
119	11	.11	1309	.74	6032	.607
132	9	.09	1188	.83	7220	.726
146	7	.07	1022	.90	8242	.829
159	5	.05	795	.95	9037	.909
172	3	.03	516	.98	9553	.961
186	1	.01	186	.99	9739	.980
200	1	.01	200	1.00	9939	1.000

Fig. 3. Demonstration of how to draw the Lorenz curve for a lottery. The left part of the figure shows how probabilities and relative gains can be cumulated for the peaked lottery. The graph on the right gives the Lorenz curve. This plots the cumulative probability on the abscissa and the cumulative proportion of the winnings on the ordinate.

Column 4 is the product of columns 1 and 2 (which is the total prize money at each level). Columns 5 and 6 are running sums of columns 3 and 4, respectively, and column 7 is column 6 divided by the total prize money. This gives the cumulative proportion of prize money at each level.[6]

The Lorenz curve is plotted at the right. The abscissa gives the cumulative probability (column 5) and the ordinate gives the cumulative proportion of prize money (column 7). Notice that the Lorenz curve runs from the lower left (the low or "bad" end of the curve representing tickets with small prizes) to the upper right (the high or "good" end of the curve representing tickets with big prizes). If every ticket in the lottery were a $100 sure thing, the Lorenz curve would fall on the diagonal. To the extent that the tickets have unequal prizes, the Lorenz curve bows away from the diagonal.

Figure 4 gives the Lorenz curves for the long shot and the short shot. Notice that the curve for the long shot lies everywhere *below* the curve for the short shot. This is the sign of large relative dispersion. The long shot's several large outcomes (indicated by the steepness of the curve at the upper end) must be paid for by its many zero and small outcomes (indicated by the flatness of the curve at the lower end). The Lorenz curve for the short shot, on the other hand, lies nearer the diagonal since it has no really large outcomes and only a few small outcomes. These considerations lead directly to a simple rule for choosing between lotteries:

[6]The graphical analyses that are used in this chapter apply only to lotteries having equal expected value. Although Lorenz curves can be drawn for lotteries that differ in expected value (by omitting the normalization step in column 7), comparisons of such Lorenz curves would need to take this into account. In such cases, comparison by means of a mathematical index of security or potential would probably be preferable (see Section IV,A).

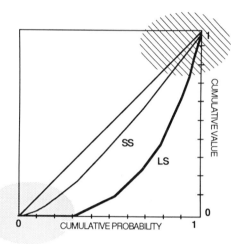

Fig. 4.   Comparison of the Lorenz curves of the long shot (LS) and the short shot (SS) Lorenz curves that lie near the diagonal at the low end (stippled area) have relatively few small outcomes. Lorenz curves that lie far from the diagonal at the high end (striped area) have a few extremely large outcomes or relatively many moderately large outcomes.

people who want to avoid the *worst* outcomes should prefer lotteries whose Lorenz curves lie *near* the diagonal at the *low* end (stippled area at lower left), and people who want to have a go at the *best* outcomes (at least as good a go as can be gotten) should prefer lotteries whose Lorenz curves lie *far* from the diagonal at the *high* end (striped area at upper right).

Figure 5 shows the Lorenz curves for the short shot and the riskless lottery. These make an interesting comparison because their Lorenz curves cross one another: the curve for the riskless lottery is nearer the diagonal at the low end (stippled area lower left) but further away at the high end (striped area upper right). Thus, the riskless lottery offers both higher minima *and* higher maxima. Not surprisingly, it appeals to both kinds of subjects. Here are Subject #10 (risk averse) and Subject #11 (risk seeking) from Lopes (1987) explaining why they chose the riskless lottery.

> The [riskless lottery] has (1) a higher jackpot (2) greater chance of winning a larger amount *under* $100. I look at the highest amount I could lose rather than the highest amount I could win. (Subject #10)

> I picked the [riskless lottery] because both the minimum and the maximum amounts are more, and because for both there's a good chance of getting around $100. (Subject #11)

Figure 6 gives Lorenz curves for the bimodal lottery and the long shot. These lotteries (which look very different superficially) are similar at their low

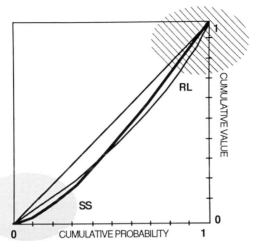

Fig. 5. Comparison of the Lorenz curves for the riskless lottery (RL) and the short shot (SS). The fact that the curves cross one another indicates that RL is good both for avoiding small outcomes (stippled area) and for approaching large outcomes (striped area).

ends (lots of small outcomes) but differ markedly at their high ends (lots of moderately large outcomes versus a few *really* large outcomes). People who want to avoid low outcomes should have a mild preference for the bimodal lottery since it lies a little nearer to the diagonal at the low end. People who want

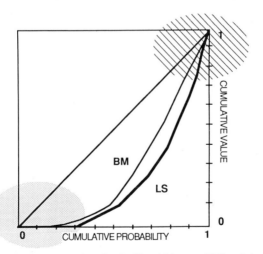

Fig. 6. Comparison of Lorenz curves for the bimodal lottery (BM) and the long shot (LS). These lotteries are very similar at their low ends (stippled area) but very different at their high ends (striped area).

to win large outcomes, however, should have a relatively strong preference for the long shot since its Lorenz curve lies quite a bit further from the diagonal at the high end. This is exactly what happens (Lopes, 1984; Schneider, & Lopes, 1986). The pattern is illustrated by the following two protocols from Lopes (1987), the former expressing a mild preference for the bimodal lottery and the latter expressing a stronger preference for the long shot.

> I chose the [bimodal lottery], because there seems to be twice as much chance to get nothing in the [long shot]. Unfortunately, there's a 50% chance of getting less than $100 in the [bimodal lottery]. The [long shot] also has higher stakes. However, all those zeros worry me. (Subject #5)

> [Took long shot] because (1) very hi win possible, (2) chance of winning ⩾ $100 about same as for other distribution. [The bimodal lottery] has too little possible gain for the hi risk of winning nothing. (Subject #6)

Lorenz curves can also be used to describe loss lotteries. The only thing that needs to be remembered is that for losses, the *best* (biggest) outcome is zero. (Not hard to remember when real losses are being considered!) Figure 7 gives the Lorenz curves for the bimodal loss lottery and the long-shot loss lottery. Although they look a little different than Lorenz curves for gain lotteries (the curves now being *above* the diagonal), they are read in exactly the same way. Cumulative probability still runs from 0 at the left to 1 at the right and cumulative proportion of value still runs from the smallest value at the bottom (*minus* 1) to the largest value at the top (zero). The worst outcomes are still in the lower left

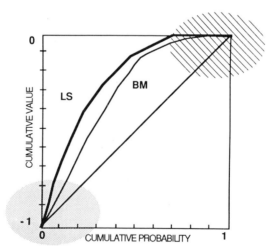

Fig. 7. Comparison of Lorenz curves for the bimodal (BM) and long-shot (LS) *loss* lotteries. These lotteries are very different at their low ends (stippled area) but very similar at their high ends (striped area).

corner and the best outcomes are still in the upper right corner. If all the tickets were for a $100 loss, the Lorenz curve would fall on the diagonal.

The rule for choosing also stays the same: people who want to avoid the worst outcomes (big losses) should prefer lotteries whose Lorenz curves lie *near* the diagonal at the low (bad) end (stippled area); people who want to obtain the best outcomes (small losses) should prefer lotteries whose Lorenz curves lie *far* from the diagonal at the high (good) end (striped area).

These different reasoning patterns can be seen clearly in subjects' protocols. Here, for example, are two typically risk-averse subjects from Lopes (1987) explaining why they prefer the bimodal loss lottery to the long-shot loss lottery:

> With the [bimodal lottery], the most that I can lose is $200. With the [long shot], I could lose $439. (Subject #2)

> I would not risk losing $439, or even $292 and up. (Subject #3)

In contrast, here is a subject who chooses the long shot:

> I choose the [long shot] because there is a preponderance of tickets that can incur no loss, and a fair number of other tickets that could lose less than $98. In the [bimodal lottery] 50% of the tickets do stand to lose $93 or less but there are fewer that can promise to cause no financial loss. I notice that there are large amounts to be lost if one is unlucky, but the chances of being unlucky are somewhat slimmer in the [long shot]. (Subject #1)

Negative lotteries are particularly interesting because they often present difficult choices. Here, for example, is a subject who has chosen the peaked loss lottery over the rectangular loss lottery:

> I go back and forth on this, the gain on improving the chances on a low loss increases the chance of a higher loss. I pick the [peaked lottery] to try to reduce the higher loss. (Subject #11)

Another subject, however, chooses to gamble on the long shot rather than take a sure $100 loss.

> In the [sure thing] no way could I lose more than $100. But no way could I lose less, either. In the [long shot] there are enough chances to lose less than $100 to justify losing a lot more. I'll go ahead and see if I can get less than $100 loss—maybe even zero loss—rather than accept a sure loss of $100. If I lose $100 I might as well lose $439. I don't like it either way. However, the [chances] of losing $439 or $390 or $341—etc. down to $146 are quite high. But so are zero, $49, or $98 or $146. So I'll take the chance. I don't feel great about it, though. (Subject #13)

Conflicts such as these are relatively common for loss lotteries. This is important because it suggests the existence of an additional factor in risky choice that is not captured by the Lorenz curve analysis. This factor will be discussed below.

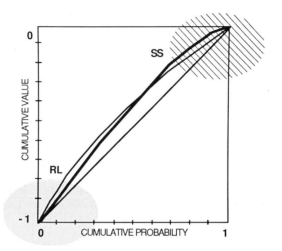

Fig. 8. Comparison of Lorenz curves for the riskless (RL) and the short-shot (SS) *loss* lot-teries. The fact that the curves cross one another indicates that SS is good both for avoiding large losses (stippled area) and for approaching small or zero losses (striped area).

Finally, Lorenz curves for loss lotteries can also cross one another, produc-ing agreement in choice between risk-averse and risk-seeking individuals. Figure 8 shows the Lorenz curves for the riskless loss lottery and the short-shot loss lottery. Below are protocols from the same two subjects (the former risk averse and the latter risk seeking) who previously defended their choice of the riskless lottery over the short shot for gains. Below they tell why they *reject* the riskless lottery for losses.

> [Took short shot because] (1) there is a greater chance of losing $130 or more with the [riskless lottery]. (2) There is a greater chance of losing less than $70 in the [short shot]. (Subject #10)

> I pick the [short shot] because the maximum loss is less and because you may be able to hit as low as zero loss. No matter what, you lose $70 and possibly $200 in the [riskless lottery]—too much risk. (Subject #11)

To sum up, Lorenz curves have at least four virtues for representing lot-teries. First, being cumulative, they reflect the fact that subjects tend to evaluate lotteries in terms of inequalities. Second, they facilitate comparison of the partic-ular regions in lotteries that appear to be salient to people with different goals. Third, they suggest similarities and differences among lotteries that, although they may seem obvious in retrospect, do not easily come to mind from inspection of the lotteries themselves. Fourth, they predict when people having different goals will agree (or disagree) about lotteries and when differences will be relatively large (or small). These are no small virtues for a stimulus representation. But that is all that Lorenz curves are: a way of representing lotteries. It is not to be supposed that people convert risks into "mental Lorenz curves." Clearly, they do not. The purpose of the Lorenz curve representation is to deepen understanding of the functional stimulus and to help us psychologists see (literally) what it is that people focus on when they compare lotteries.

IV. A Two-Factor Theory for Risky Choice

Until fairly recently, personologists focused largely on variables inside the skin, leaving experimentalists to deal with situational variables. Lately, however, personologists have come to agree with Mischel's judgment that "traditional trait-state conceptualizations of personality, while often paying lip service to man's complexity and to the uniqueness of each person, in fact lead to a grossly oversimplified view that misses both the richness and the uniqueness of individual lives" (Mischel, 1968, p. 301). Nevertheless, it is clear that "while stimuli or situations come to evoke and maintain behavior patterns, they do not respond by themselves" (Mischel, 1968, p. 295). Behavior has sources, both inner and outer. We are disposed by our unique constitutions and histories to behave in certain ways, but it is "situational stimuli that evoke [our responses], and it is changes in conditions that alter them" (Mischel, 1968, p. 296).

The present theory uses both a dispositional factor and a situational factor to explain risky choice. The dispositional factor describes the underlying motives that dispose people to be generally oriented to achieving security (i.e., risk averse in conventional terminology) or to exploiting potential (i.e., risk seeking in conventional terminology). The situational factor describes people's responses to immediate needs and opportunities. As will be shown, these factors are sometimes in conflict and sometimes in concert, producing complex patterns of behavior in which risk-averse choices and risk-seeking choices exist side by side in the same individual's behavior.

A. FACTOR 1: SECURITY VERSUS POTENTIAL

In an earlier article (Lopes, 1984), I argued that risk-averse and risk-seeking individuals differ in whether they pay most attention to the worst outcomes in a distribution or the best outcomes. Risk-averse people appear to be motivated by a desire for *security,* whereas risk-seeking people appear to be motivated by a desire for *potential.* The former motive values safety and the latter, opportunity.

In mathematical terms, security motivation corresponds to weighting the worst outcomes in a lottery more heavily than the best outcomes, and potential motivation corresponds to the opposite. Such processes could be modeled mathematically by applying appropriate weights to the cumulative functions that constitute the data for Lorenz curves. Indeed, there are several functions currently in use by welfare economists that could be used to quantify risk-averse and risk-seeking preferences (A. Atkinson, 1970; Dahlby, 1985). Describing these functions will not be necessary at present, however, since raw Lorenz curves show all we need to know.

There are, however, two general points that should be made about weighting. First, weights in the theory are joint functions of the magnitudes of probabilities *and* the magnitudes of the outcomes to which they are attached. This is a fundamental departure from the family of weighted-value models since, in those models, probability and value are independent. Second, weights reflect individuals' *goals* and not their perception of probabilities or values. Thus, the fact that a person chooses, for example, to minimize the likelihood of a bad outcome does not imply either that (subjectively) he underestimates the value of good outcomes or that he overestimates the probability of bad outcomes. Although psychophysical effects may occur in either the money or the probability domain, these are considered to be of secondary importance in determining risky choice.

The security/potential factor is conceived to be a dispositional variable, reflecting the way individuals typically respond to risks. Not surprisingly, security motivation (risk aversion) is the far more common pattern (see Lopes, 1984; Schneider & Lopes, 1986), so common, in fact, that economists have considered it to be the pattern for Everyman (Arrow, 1971; Pratt, 1964). This is probably not due to chance. Standards of prudence are passed from parent to child in the normal course of growing up. If that is not enough, hard experience informs us in no uncertain terms that, as Damon Runyan said, "the race is not always to the swift nor the battle to the strong, but that's the way to bet" (cited in Ellsberg, 1961, p. 644). Risk seekers, on the other hand, may dog the long shots, waiting (as a famous risk seeker once said) for "that one streak of luck, properly ridden and encouraged," to compensate them for all the bad times (Thackrey, 1968, p. 67, quoting Nick the Greek).

It should also be noted that the fact that someone is primarily motivated by one of the poles of the security/potential factor does not imply that he or she is unaware of the other pole. It is better to think of these opposing tendencies as existing in some strength in everyone (as do M_s and M_{af} in Atkinson's 1983, theory), but with potential much less important than security and aspiration for risk-averse people and security much less important than potential and aspiration for risk-seeking people. Such weak motives would tend to come into play primarily when the stronger motives are insufficient to determine choice.

B. FACTOR 2: ASPIRATION LEVEL

The security/potential factor reflects the way that a person usually looks at risks. Risk-averse people look more at the downside and risk seekers more at the upside. But risk seekers may play it safe from time to time, and even the most risk-averse person will take chances—even big chances—when necessary. Aspiration level (Lopes, 1983; Siegel, 1957; Simon, 1955) is a situational variable that reflects the opportunities at hand ("What can I get?") as well as the constraints imposed by the environment ("What do I need?").

The aspiration level that functions in any given situation (including the present task situation) can reflect at least three different sources. The first is the direct assessment of what is reasonable or safe to hope for. For illustration, here is a subject from Lopes (1987) who has rejected the short shot in favor of the peaked lottery:

> The chances are in the [peaked] lottery that I will get something close to $100, and I might get much more. I don't know why [I should] let $130 be the top limit when there's a reasonable chance of nearing $100 and a possibility for more. (Subject #3)

The next subject has chosen the riskless lottery in preference to a $100 sure thing.

> Since I am assured of winning something I am willing to risk a moderate amount for the possibility of a substantially greater amount. (Subject #4)

In both these cases, the subjects have taken the riskier option, but not before assuring themselves that it is prudent to shoot for its somewhat higher prizes.

The second source of aspiration levels is the direct contextual influence of the other alternatives in the choice set. Here, for example, is a subject choosing between the short shot and the riskless lottery:

> I chose the [riskless lottery] because I am assured of winning at least $70. In addition, I have a better than even chance of winning more than $70. It is the assurance of winning $70 that appeals to me. (Subject #7)

Based on this rationale, the subject's aspiration level appears to be no higher than $70. However, when the same subject is given a choice between a sure $100 (the sure thing) and the riskless lottery, she says,

> I chose the [sure thing] because I would rather take the $100 as a sure thing than risk winning less. The other lottery also offers a sure thing ($70 at the least), however, the chances of winning less than $100 are about 50-50 in that lottery, so I opt for the safe bet of $100, a sure thing. (Subject #7)

The same shifting of aspiration level also occurs for losses. Here are two more protocols from the previous subject. In the first she rejects the long-shot loss lottery in favor of the short shot. In the second she accepts the long shot in favor of a sure $100 loss.

> I chose the [short shot] because the most I could lose would be $130 and that seems safer than the [long shot]. Also the odds in both lotteries seem to favor a loss of between $50–$150, so I figure the lottery which has the lowest ceiling on a possible loss is the safest risk. (Subject #7)

> A $100 loss up front is too hard for me to swallow—I chose the [long shot] as it allows for many chances to lose *less* than $100. True, the maximum loss could be as high as $439, but it is still a risk I am willing to take. (Subject #7)

Notice that the subject seems to switch from considering a $130 loss to be acceptable to considering a $100 loss to be unacceptable. Statements like these make it clear that sure things have a powerful influence in organizing choice, and the same seems to be true of values that are highly likely, though not certain.

The seemingly special status of certainty in risky choice has received a prominent role in several theories (Allais, 1979; Kahneman & Tversky, 1979; Machina, 1982), but the mechanism through which certainty effects operate is as yet unclear. One possibility (Kahneman & Tversky, 1979) is that they are instances of subjective category-boundary effects in the perception of probability (see Section II). Another possibility, however, is that certainty *is* objectively special since it permits planning to proceed unimpeded by uncertainty about outcomes that may not be resolved in the near future (see Section VI,C).

The third way that aspiration levels get set is by outside influence. For example, a recent study by Lopes and Casey (1987) looked at the role of necessity in a competitive game in which players attempted to take or defend territory on a game board by choosing among moves having distributions of possible outcomes similar to the lotteries in Fig. 2. The data revealed a tendency for subjects to prefer riskier moves when they were in a bad position near the end of a round. This is quite sensible: if there is little or no chance that the safer option will yield sufficient territory for a win within the number of moves remaining, the riskier option may be the probabilistically better choice (i.e., more likely to yield a winning outcome).[7]

---

[7]It is worth noting that strategies that involve maximizing the probability of meeting a goal or aspiration level are fundamentally different from strategies of maximizing expected utility. In the utility formulation, necessity can only be captured by assuming that the utility function temporarily becomes positively accelerated in the region of the target value (see, e.g., Kahneman & Tversky, 1979, p. 279). Such explanations are obviously ad hoc since they can be called into play anytime the standard psychophysics of the situation cannot explain the preference. The alternative view that subjects sometimes attempt to maximize the probability of achieving aspiration levels has been taken

Finally, it should be noted that, although aspiration level is situational, it probably interacts with the security/potential factor, with security-motivated people tending to set more modest aspiration levels than potential-motivated people for both gains and losses. This possible interaction necessarily complicates the independent assessment of the contributions of security/potential and aspiration to risky choice. Nevertheless, support for the conceptual distinction between the two factors exists in the fact that, as will be seen, the factors often act in opposition to one another.

C. CONFLICT BETWEEN SECURITY/POTENTIAL AND ASPIRATION

Conflict arises in two places in the present theory. One, obviously, is the conflict between security and potential. It is a truism in the investment world that risk and return go together. If you want safety, you pay for it in yield; if you want yield, you pay for it in worry. To say that security/potential defines a dispositional variable is to say that people typically choose one way or the other between avoiding bad outcomes and approaching good outcomes. But this does not mean that people do not *see* what they do not *choose*. In making a clear decision for, say, security, a person may acknowledge regretfully the loss of opportunity. People also are quick to notice the special benefits of choices such as the riskless lottery that allow them to have their cake and eat it too.[8]

The second form of conflict is both more interesting and less obvious. These are the conflicts that can be created as different situations induce different patterns of agreement and disagreement between dispositional motives toward security or potential and the immediate needs and opportunities affecting aspiration level.

Consider someone who is dispositionally motivated to achieve security and suppose that, in the present task situation, the person has a modest aspiration level, say $50. Faced with the choice between the short shot and the long shot,

---

by Allais (1979) and by Lopes (1981). Although this view seems to make intuitive sense, it violates the axioms of expected utility theory and has been considered to be irrational for that reason (see, e.g., Samuelson, 1977, p. 48).

[8]In cases of strong conflict involving extremely important outcomes (e.g., health issues, large financial transactions, career changes, etc.) conflict may be reduced by various psychological bolstering processes (Festinger, 1957; Janis & Mann, 1977). Whether these entail distortion of values and probabilities during the choice process or selectional mechanisms operating in the construction of a postdecisional rationalization for the chosen alternative is an important question, but not one to which the present experiments can speak. Nevertheless, even if there is considerable distortion predecisionally, security/potential and aspiration level would still function in people's deliberations about the presumably distorted distributions.

the person would tend to reject the long shot on both counts: it is clearly less secure in Lorenz curve terms and it is also less likely to satisfy the aspiration level. The same would be true for almost any pair of gain lotteries. This is because there is a positive correlation between the ordering of the lotteries in terms of security and the ordering of the lotteries in terms of the probability that they will achieve the aspiration level.

For losses, however, there is a conflict between security and aspiration. Consider the same person choosing between the same two lotteries, but this time for losses, and suppose that the aspiration level is to lose no more than $50. The short shot is obviously more secure since its losses are capped at $130, but it is much less likely to yield a loss of $50 or less. This would be true for almost any pair of loss lotteries: the ordering on security runs essentially opposite to the ordering on aspiration level.

For a potential-motivated person, the situation would be just reversed. For losses, potential and aspiration level are positively correlated, but for gains they are quite likely to be negatively correlated.

Conflict between security/potential and aspiration can produce quite complex patterns of data (see Coombs & Avrunin, 1983, for a general discussion of data patterns produced by conflict). Table I gives some values for illustration. The top of the table is for a risk-averse individual and the bottom is for a risk seeker. Gain choices are on the left and loss choices on the right. The aspiration level of the risk-averse person is assumed to be $50 for both gains and losses, whereas the aspiration level of the risk seeker is assumed to be $80 for gains and $20 for losses. These values are purely hypothetical, but they accord with our intuition that risk-averse people probably have more modest aspiration levels than risk seekers.

Let's begin with the risk-averse person. Column 1 lists the six lotteries from Fig. 2 plus a $100 sure thing. Columns 2 and 6 (AL) give the probabilities that the lotteries will yield the aspiration level: $50 or more for gains and $50 or less for losses. Columns 3 and 7 (SEC) give hypothetical values on security. (Keep in mind that the riskless lottery and the short shot change places as one goes from gains to losses.) These values range evenly between 1 for the sure thing and 0 for the long shot except for a tie in each ordering. (For gains, the worst outcomes in the short shot and the peaked lottery are almost identical in probability and value. Their Lorenz curves would be essentially superimposed at the low end. In the same way, for losses, the worst outcomes for the riskless lottery and the peaked lottery are almost identical. Their Lorenz curves would also be superimposed at the low end.)

Columns 4 and 8 (SEC × AL) show how security and aspiration are integrated. A multiplying rule is used because the choice is *conjunctive*. A lottery lacking good values on either security or aspiration will be rejected. The final two columns (REL PREF) simply normalize the products to a common base (by

TABLE I

Hypothetical Preferences for Risk-Averse and Risk-Seeking Individuals for Gain
and Loss Lotteries

Risk-averse individual

LOT[a]	Gain lotteries				Loss lotteries			
	AL	SEC	SEC × AL	REL PREF	AL	SEC	SEC × AL	REL PREF
ST	1.00	1.00	1.000	.310	0.00	1.00	.000	.000
RL	1.00	0.83	0.830	.257	0.00	0.58	.000	.000
SS	0.90	0.58	0.522	.162	0.10	0.83	.083	.284
PK	0.90	0.58	0.522	.162	0.10	0.58	.058	.199
RC	0.75	0.33	0.248	.077	0.25	0.33	.083	.284
BM	0.60	0.17	0.102	.032	0.40	0.17	.068	.233
LS	0.47	0.00	0.000	.000	0.53	0.00	.000	.000

Risk-seeking individual

LOT	Gain lotteries				Loss lotteries			
	AL	POT	POT × AL	REL PREF	AL	POT	POT × AL	REL PREF
ST	1.00	0.00	0.000	.000	0.00	0.00	.000	.000
RL	0.69	0.42	0.290	.143	0.00	0.17	.000	.000
SS	0.78	0.17	0.133	.065	0.03	0.42	.013	.022
PK	0.74	0.42	0.311	.153	0.02	0.42	.008	.013
RC	0.60	0.66	0.396	.195	0.10	0.66	.066	.111
BM	0.52	0.83	0.432	.213	0.24	0.83	.199	.333
LS	0.47	1.00	0.470	.231	0.31	1.00	.310	.520

[a]Abbreviations: ST, sure thing; RL, riskless lottery; SS, short shot; PK, peaked lottery;
RC, rectangular lottery; BM, bimodal lottery; and LS, long shot. AL is probability of achieving the
aspiration level. SEC is security and POT is potential. REL PREF is relative preference.

dividing by the sum of products) in order to allow an easier comparison of
relative preference.

A similar anaylsis is given in the bottom of the table for the risk-seeking
person. Values for potential (POT) have replaced values for security, and the
aspiration levels are now $80 or more for gains and $20 or less for losses. Note
here that the ties in potential are now between the riskless lottery and the peaked
lottery for gains and the short shot and the peaked lottery for losses.

Starting first with the risk-averse person, note that relative preferences for
gain lotteries tend to decrease from the sure thing to the long shot. This reflects
the strong positive correlation between SEC and AL for gains ($r = .97$). For
losses, however, there is an inverse U pattern: preferences are low at the extremes but higher in the middle. This reflects the strong negative correlation
between AL and SEC for losses ($r = -.91$).

For the risk seeker, the simple pattern occurs for losses: preferences tend to increase from the sure thing to the long shot, reflecting the strong positive correlation between POT and AL for losses ($r = .92$). For gains, however, the pattern is complex. The least preferred lotteries are the sure thing and the short shot, and the most preferred are the bimodal, the rectangular, and the long shot. This complexity reflects the negative correlation between POT and AL for gains ($r = -.97$).

To sum up, the present two-factor theory integrates a dispositional tendency to seek either security or potential with situationally driven aspiration levels. Security motivation captures the Bernoullian (1967) intuition that people are generally disposed to prefer sure things and gambles without large chances of bad outcomes. However, the theory handles equally directly the less prevalent tendency of some people to approach long shots and other gambles offering the unlikely possibility of large outcomes. In addition, the theory deals directly with situational circumstances that may cause a person to experience conflict between dispositionally driven preferences and externally driven goals. Thus, the theory explains how the person can be risk averse in the economic sense (i.e., typically preferring sure things) but sometimes make the same choices as someone who is ordinarily risk seeking.

V. Evidence for the Two-Factor Theory

A. RISKINESS IS THE ABSENCE OF SECURITY

The first bit of support for the present theory comes from judgments of riskiness. In Experiments 3 and 4 of Lopes (1984), subjects were shown pairs of gain lotteries and were asked to say which was the riskier. In virtually every case, the lottery judged to be the riskier was the one whose Lorenz curve lay further from the diagonal at the low end. The only exceptions involved the relative riskiness of riskless lotteries and short shots. (There were three examples of each.) About half the subjects judged the riskless lotteries to be the riskier (contrary to the original expectation) and about half judged the opposite.

Experiments 5 and 6 of the same study suggested why this was so. In the former experiments, the term "risk" was left vague so that subjects could supply their own meanings. In the latter experiments, however, subjects were asked to select the lottery for which it would be riskier to pay $100. Under this condition, judgments for the other lotteries were virtually unchanged, but subjects were now nearly unanimous that the (so-called) riskless lotteries were the risker, a judgment that makes objective sense because there is a good chance that riskless lotteries will yield substantially less than $100 (e.g., $70). Apparently in the original experiment subjects adopted different aspiration levels. For most lotteries, riskiness does not depend on whether the aspiration level is low ($50) or high ($100), but for the riskless lotteries the shift in aspiration is crucial.

The ability of the present theory to account for judgments of riskiness is a point in its favor, particularly as contrasted with psychophysical models. In the latter models, there is no such thing as risk. Although they predict risky choice, they are silent on judgments of risk. Intuitively, however, risk plays a role in risky choice. Risk is the absence of security; security is the absence of risk. Seems simple enough.

B. RISK ATTITUDE IS MORE THAN THE PSYCHOPHYSICS OF MONEY

The second bit of support for the theory is that it can predict the preferences of both risk-averse and risk-seeking people. In experiments 1 and 2 of Lopes (1984), subjects were shown various pairs of lotteries and asked to say which they would prefer to play. The subjects were then divided according to whether or not they tended to take the sure thing when it was offered. Risk-averse subjects (i.e., those subjects who took the sure thing 8 or more times out of 10) had preferences that were essentially perfectly predicted by security motivation (i.e., they preferred lotteries whose Lorenz curves lay near the diagonal at the low end). Risk-seeking subjects (i.e., those who took the sure thing 3 or fewer times out of 10) had preferences that were for the most part predicted by potential motivation (i.e., they preferred lotteries whose Lorenz curves lay far from the diagonal at the high end).

The ability to account for people whose choices are primarily risk seeking is another benefit of the present theory. Psychophysical theories and moments theories are theories of Everyman because they are based mechanistically on principles that should hold for us all: "our perceptual apparatus is attuned to the evaluation of changes or differences" (Kahneman & Tversky, 1979, p. 278); "uncertainty . . . has a disutility growing worse with increasing speed when [the] standard deviation [of utilities] increases" (Hagen, 1979, p. 274). But Everyman is risk averse for gains even though every man (or woman) is not.[9] The two-factor theory puts risk seekers and risk-averse people on equal footing. Although their choices may differ profoundly, their choice *processes* have more

[9]One could, of course, explain individual differences within a psychophysical theory by supposing that people with different preferences have different utility and probability functions. This would, however, vitiate the claim that risky choices can be explained by basic perceptual processes. At the limit, the functions would become a means for summarizing preferences after the fact (as is the case for the von Neumann & Morgenstern, 1947, utility function), but such functions would lack predictive and explanatory power.

similarities than differences. They understand risks in the same way (cumulatively) and they trade off the same factors. Their goals may differ, but they have the
same conceptual equipment.

C. RISKY CHOICE IS NOT CONFLICT FREE

The best evidence for the two-factor theory comes from a recent study of the
preferences of preselected risk-averse and risk-seeking subjects for gain and loss
lotteries (Schneider & Lopes, 1986). Subjects were selected from a large group
of undergraduates who had filled out a brief questionaire asking for their preferences in five choice pairs. Each pair contained a positive two-outcome gamble
and a sure thing of equal expected value. In accord with conventional usage,
risk-averse subjects were defined as those who selected the sure thing every time,
and risk-seeking subjects were defined as those who selected the gamble at least
four times. Thirty subjects were selected from each group.

The 10 stimuli in the experiment included the 6 stimuli in Fig. 2 plus a $100
sure thing. Subjects were given the stimuli in all possible pairs and asked for
their preferences. The pooled data are in Figs. 9 and 10 for risk-averse and risk-

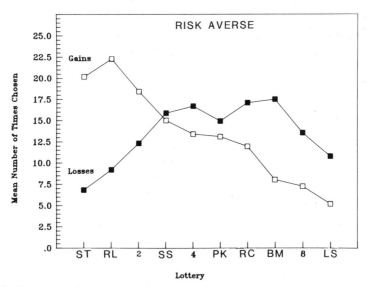

Fig. 9.   Mean preference data for risk-averse subjects for gain lotteries (open symbols) and loss
lotteries (filled symbols). Data are the number of times a subject chose a lottery out of the total
number of times the lottery was available for choice. (From ''Reflection in preferences under risk:
Who and when may suggest why'' by S. L. Schneider and L. L. Lopes, *Journal of Experimental
Psychology: Human Perception and Performance,* 1986. Copyright 1986 by The American Psychological Association. Reprinted by permission.)

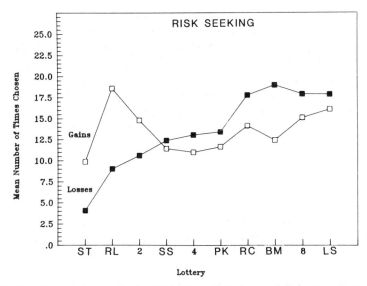

Fig. 10.   Mean preference data for risk-seeking subjects for gain lotteries (open symbols) and loss lotteries (filled symbols). Data are the number of times a subject chose a lottery out of the total number of times the lottery was available for choice. (From "Reflection in preferences under risk: Who and when may suggest why" by S. L. Schneider and L. L. Lopes, *Journal of Experimental Psychology: Human Perception and Performance,* 1986. Copyright 1986 by The American Psychological Association. Reprinted by permission.)

seeking subjects, respectively. The stimuli from Fig. 2 and the sure thing are listed on the abscissa by letter codes (ST = sure thing, RL = riskless, SS = short shot, PK = peaked, RC = rectangular, BM = bimodal, LS = long shot). The lotteries identified by number were an additional riskless lottery (2), an additional short shot (4), and an additional long shot (8). The open symbols are for gain lotteries and the filled symbols are for loss lotteries.

Looking first at the risk-averse subjects, it is clear that their preferences for gains decrease essentially monotonically from the sure thing to the long shot. Their preferences for losses, however, have an inverse U pattern, being low for the sure thing and the riskless lotteries (at the left) as well as for the long shots (at the right). These qualitative patterns (which were highly reliable statistically) are exactly what the present theory predicts (cf. Table I). For gain lotteries, security and aspiration support the same choices, producing monotonicity. For losses, however, security and aspiration conflict, producing nonmonotonicity.

The risk-seeking subjects also follow the pattern predicted by the two-factor theory. Their preferences are essentially monotonically increasing from the sure thing to the long shot for losses, but vary complexly for gains. Worst liked are the sure thing, the short shots, and the peaked lottery; long shots and riskless lotteries are better liked. These patterns were also highly reliable statistically.

Considering the crudeness of the estimates used in Table I, the fit is remarkably good. Both groups like RL a little better than they should for gains, and risk seekers like long shots a little less well than they should for losses, but the overall picture is as it should be. The presence of nonmonotonicity in both data sets confirms the existence of conflicting factors in risky choice. And the mirror symmetry between the two subject groups confirms their structural similarity. They are basically doing the same thing, but their values differ at least on the security/potential factor, and probably on aspiration level as well.

VI.   The Things We Don't Talk About

Psychologists who study risky choice *don't* talk about a surprisingly large number of factors that are psychologically relevant in choosing among risks. Given the poverty of our theoretical language, it is, perhaps, surprising that we manage to talk at all. Here are some words that are not to be found in the theoretical vocabulary: fear, hope, safety, danger, fun, plan, conflict, time, duty, custom. Nor can these words be given meaning in psychophysical theories. The language of psychophysics is the language of perceptual distortion. It has room neither for the experience of emotion (fear, hope, fun), nor for the physical context in which risks occur (safety, danger), nor for the social constraints on individual action (custom, duty), nor for the cognitive activity of the chooser (plan, conflict).

Distributional theories, on the other hand, can express these meanings easily. Oddly, however, it was an economist (Hagen, 1969) who identified skewness with hope and fear, whereas psychologists working with similar theories (Coombs, 1975; Coombs, & Lehner, 1981; Luce, 1980; Pollatsek & Tversky, 1970) have shied away from using such language.

Queasiness about the ordinary language of emotion and intention goes back in psychology at least to Watson's behaviorist manifesto and in the area of risky choice has been amplified by exposure to a similar movement in economics termed *positive economics* (Friedman, 1953). In fact, modern economic expected utility theory (von Neumann and Morgenstern, 1947) has relegated even the classical psychophysical concept of utility to the status of an epiphenomenon. In the modern view, utility does not precede and cause preferences; it is, instead, merely a convenient fiction that can be used by the practitioner to summarize the preferences of those who, by choice or chance, follow the dictates of the von Neumann and Morgenstern axiom system.

If, however, hope and fear and plans are necessary ingredients in risky choice, then it is not unscientific to talk about them. Many social scientists working outside the narrow confines of the laboratory or the mathematical proof treat these terms casually, like old friends. In the remainder of this chapter I draw on these broader approaches to risk and show their relation to the present theory.

A.   FEAR AND THE SAFETY-FIRST PRINCIPLE

Psychophysical theories of risky choice do without a psychological concept of risk, but people cannot. Risk is a fact of our physical and social environments. This is nowhere more clear than in agriculture, particularly subsistence agriculture in which one's livelihood can be literally threatened from all sides (by floods, by pests, by invading armies). Agricultural economists look at risk quite differently than the axiomatically minded economists who have influenced psychology most strongly in recent years. For the agricultural economist, both risk and risk aversion are real, with behavior connected to need by a simple rule called the safety-first principle.

The subsistence farmer is in a difficult position. Food crops provide food for the table and have low variance of return, but their expected return is also low. Cash crops are more variable but have higher expected return. The problem is how much of each crop to plant. Although many different models of farmers' choice processes have been developed (Anderson, 1979), they all boil down to a simple rule: first take care of subsistence needs (food for the larder and seed for the coming season) and then plant cash crops. Although the farmer's world may be risky, the farmer does not view himself as gambling. In Ortiz's (1979) words, "The peasant's preference for subsistence over starvation cannot be rephrased into a preference for X chance of Y income over $X - n$ chance of $Y - m$ income; such paraphrasing totally misrepresents his options and it is unnecessary" (p. 235).

It should also be noted that, although fear feeds risk aversion, risk taking can be fed either by hope or by necessity (see Section IV,B). Conventional economic theory treats risk taking as a luxury. Neither individuals nor firms are supposed to indulge in it unless they can afford it. Kunreuther and Wright (1979), however, have pointed out that sometimes the poorest farmers devote as large a proportion of their land to cash crops as the richest farmers. Likewise, Bowman (1982) has demonstrated that economically troubled firms often engage in riskier behavior than economically sound firms. In both these cases, risk-seeking behavior is interpreted as arising from necessity. If there is not enough safety even when safety is put first, the risky choice may be the only choice.

The connections between the safety-first principle and the two-factor theory are obvious. The safety-first principle aims at security. A target level is set and choices are made so as to maximize the probability of achieving the target. The resulting choices are "cautiously suboptimal" (Day, 1979). However, risk-taking behavior may predominate when the aspiration level cannot be achieved safely. In neither case do the choices reflect the psychophysics of money or of chances. Nor are they merely the signs of pessimistic or optimistic world views. Farmers who follow the principle want (and need) to accept the risks of cash cropping, but they can do so only up to a point. Their choices reflect the planful activities of intelligent, though unsophisticated, people who know the odds and bet that way.

B. PLANNING IS APPLIED HOPING

The flip side of the safety-first principle is entrepreneurship, in which safety takes second place to opportunity. McClelland (1961) described entrepreneurs as people who display a willingness to take risks in situations in which their skills and effort can make a difference. The issue of control appears to be particularly important. Although spectators may judge that entrepreneurs take more risks than the average person, entrepreneurs see themselves as not being particularly risk prone (Keyes, 1985, pp. 207–209; McClelland, 1961, p. 222). This is also true of people who engage in physically risky professions or hobbies: "First they challenge fate, and then they try to bullwhip fate to its knees by making their adventure as predictable as possible. In fact, it's not adventure they're after. It's mastery" (Keyes, 1985, p. 115). Even in casino gambling, where outcomes cannot be controlled, high-stakes gamblers take pride in the control of their emotions (see for example, Alvarez, 1983, pp. 47, 169; Thackrey, 1968, pp. 62–63).

A lot has been written about control in recent years. Langer (1977) has synthesized an impressive body of experimental evidence documenting the fact that people behave as though they believe that chance events can be controlled. In her view, the illusion of control comes about for several good reasons: (1) people are motivated to master their environment; (2) it is unpleasant to believe that one has no control; (3) chance and skill elements coexist in many situations; and (4) the illusion can help us emotionally more than it can harm us practically.

One might suppose (as Langer has *not*) that risk-taking behavior is caused by the optimistic illusion that outcomes are more controllable than they really are. McClelland (1961), however, has argued that entrepreneurship is independent of optimism. He presents evidence from four different countries that school boys who are high in optimism are "conscientious, efficient, forward-looking, *managerial* types [who work] hard and efficiently at everything more or less indiscriminately" (pp. 227–228), but they are not necessarily high in achievement motivation. A student who is high in achievement motivation works hard only on those things that can give a sense of personal responsibility. "If there is no challenge, he doesn't work so hard: in this sense he would make a poor bureaucrat" (p. 228).

The belief that one can control one's fate appears to be necessary to good mental health (Abramson, Seligman, & Teasdale, 1978). When highly desired outcomes are believed to be unlikely or when highly undesirable outcomes are believed to be likely, and when the individual believes that nothing can be done to change these likelihoods, depression results, causing attendant motivational and affective deficits.

Beliefs about control and motivation feed back on one another. When aversive events occur despite one's efforts to prevent them, motivation to control events is reduced both in animals (Maier & Seligman, 1976) and in humans (Hiroto, 1974; Hiroto & Seligman, 1975). When control is later made possible, the motivational deficit prevents learning from occurring. Responses that are not made cannot be reinforced. A vicious cycle results.

Feedback between control and motivation can also be positive. Sawyer (cited in McClelland, 1961, p. 222) has argued that self-confidence in individuals can lead to the very circumstances that are necessary to achieve success. He gives as an example the settling of the American West in the 19th century. Had not so many people behaved as though it was possible, it would *not* have been possible. Although individuals failed in large numbers, sufficiently many survived that settlement was collectively accomplished.

In the present theory, people may be motivated by achievement (potential) as well as by security. McClelland (1961) stressed in his work that people who are high in achievement motivation do not like to gamble. That may be so in the narrow confines of two-outcome gambles presented in the laboratory. In the real world it seems unlikely that achievement-motivated people could be obsessed by security. Although one cannot control the actual outcome in chance situations, one can control the likely outcome. This is what portfolio managers do in the investment field. Maximum return and maximum safety cannot both be had, but one can assemble portfolios that trade a little risk for an acceptable return. Balancing the unavoidable risks in one's personal portfolio is a skillful activity that should appeal to achievement-motivated individuals.

C. ANTICIPATION AND IMAGINATION

Uncertainty is embedded in time. There is a now in which some things are true, a future in which other things may be true, and a still farther future in which we may reflect on the past. At the point of choice we look forward along this track, and we also anticipate looking back. The temporal element is what gives risk both savor and sting.

Pope (1983) has criticized expected utility theory for having ignored the time between the decision and the resolution of the uncertainty, what she calls the pre-outcome period, during which fear and hope operate. She points out that the period can be long not only for long-term decisions such as individuals choosing careers, governments embarking on social programs, and businesses making major capital investments, but also for repeat short-term decisions: "after deciding to devote a fraction of the housekeeping funds to a weekly lottery ticket, housekeepers can dream from age nineteen to ninety-nine that they will become millionaires after the next drawing" (p. 156).

Uncertainty in the pre-outcome period can be pleasurable or unpleasurable. A traveler to Las Vegas may pay an extra fee to avoid the worrisome uncertainty of the $1000 deductible on a rental car and then proceed at all speed to a casino in order to purchase the delightful uncertainty of gambling. Insurance cannot stop disaster from happening, but it can stop worry. Gambling cannot guarantee future bliss, but it can give hope. For small amounts of money we can enjoy the current psychological benefits of either in the same way that we enjoy other psychological commodities such as entertainment and convenience.

Decisions involving larger amounts of money and other sorts of serious consequences require us to extend our analysis beyond the time in which the uncertainty is resolved. Fears and hopes are then no longer relevant, but regret and disappointment are. Bell (1982, 1985) has argued that if we experience regret over decisions that turned out badly or disappointment over outcomes that fail to match up to expectations, these factors are as important to consider as more tangible monetary benefits and losses. "Psychological satisfaction, as opposed to the satisfaction derived from consumption, is an appropriate objective that should be included in any decision analysis if the decision maker regards it as a criterion for decision" (Bell, 1985, p. 26).

Decision makers also look to a future in which their preferences may change (March, 1978) and in which options not currently imagined may have become possible. Day (1979) has pointed out that farmers and business managers alike resist procedural changes that put them too far from current practice. This is a sensible rule for adapting to dynamic environments (both internal and external) since it leaves the old practice available as a fallback position should the new policy not produce the expected effects.

The importance of having safe fallback positions in real life may account for the fact that the perceived riskiness of technological hazards is not solely related to estimates of annual fatalities but also reflects dread of outcomes that are perceived to be uncontrollable, catastrophic, not easily reversed, and of high risk to future generations. Thus, intelligent but technically unsophisticated raters (students and members of the League of Women Voters) estimate fewer annual deaths from nuclear power than from home appliances but nevertheless consider nuclear power to be much more risky (Slovic, Fischhoff, & Lichtenstein, 1980, Tables 2 and 3).

Psychophysical theories of risk do not consider time, although one might conceive a psychophysics of future events. Economists use a similar notion (time preference rates) to handle the fact that money now is generally worth more than money later. But as Pope (1983) has argued, such a concept would deal only with changes in the worth of the final outcomes and not with the emotions that one experiences in the interim. Theories (such as the present theory) that recognize planning and conflict resolution as an integral part of risky choice can deal more naturally with such temporal factors both as they affect changes in the aspiration level and as they affect position on the security/potential dimension.

D. SHERPAS AND OTHER HIGH ROLLERS

All life chooses among risks, though we do not ordinarily think of trees choosing how to gamble their seed or amoebas choosing whether to approach or avoid possible prey. For the lowest organisms, evolution has done the choosing and equipped them with prewired choices. For higher organisms, however, cognition increasingly intervenes, allowing learning and reason to override rote instinct. Humans are the most complex cognitively and exhibit responses to risk that sometimes have little to do with the satisfaction of immediate wants or needs. Among these are the responses of our social selves.

High-standard mountaineering is incredibly risky. The chances of being killed on a Himalayan climb are about 1 in 10. Why is it done? What is there on the top of such mountains that anyone might want? Obviously, the answer is aesthetic, not practical, at least for the recreational climber (if such a word can be applied to so hazardous an avocation), who must expend considerable personal resources and obtain even more considerable institutional resources just to make the attempt.

But the Sherpas who carry the loads also share in the risks. Why do the Sherpas climb? The conventional view is that they climb out of economic necessity. Michael Thompson (1980), however, himself an Everest climber, disputes this distinction between Sherpa and non-Sherpa. In Thompson's view, risks that are pursued for practical purposes become tame in the process as has commercial air travel. But risks that are pursued for themselves do not become tame. Thus, for aesthetic purposes a proposed Everest route "is only felt to be worthwhile if there is considerable uncertainty as to its outcome" (p. 278). Sherpas also take this view and refer scornfully to the route that Hillary and Tenzing followed, the easiest of the routes for obvious reasons, as "the Yak route"—a small joke among those who share a common aesthetic.

Risk taking is one of the ways we define ourselves psychologically and socially (Douglas and Wildavsky, 1982). It is a mistake to suppose even in the realm of financial risks that choice is a purely monetary matter. For entrepreneurs and high-stakes gamblers alike, money is not the main thing. It is a way of measuring results, a way of keeping score (cf. Alvarez, 1983, p. 42; Mc-

Clelland, 1961, p. 237; Thackrey, 1968, pp. 57–58). In the same way, many currently well-to-do people who grew up in the Great Depression continue to value security in a way that their more fortunate children cannot understand. A penny saved is not a penny saved; it is security in the bank.

Nor should custom and duty be forgotten in their effects on risk taking. Consider the story of the *Reindeer* and the *Montcalm* (Mowat, 1982). In March of 1932 the salvage tug *Reindeer* set to sea carrying 28 men in a furious storm to rescue a damaged freighter. *Reindeer* was not designed for such work and was old and ill-equipped. Within hours the tug was foundering 60 miles from land. The vessel *Montcalm,* meanwhile, had been damaged also by the storm and was running for harbor. When it became clear that no other ship could reach *Reindeer* in time, the master of *Montcalm,* Captain Rothwell, turned his ship back to sea. "It had been no easy decision. *Montcalm* carried sixty passengers and a crew of fifty, and their lives were all in Rothwell's care. The risk to them was real enough, but the death of *Reindeer's* men was sure unless that risk was taken" (Mowat, 1982, p. 46). Although *Reindeer* sank, all were saved, even the ship's dog.

To understand such events requires a more comprehensive view than can be provided by the simple psychophysics of lives saved or lives lost (cf. Tversky & Kahneman, 1981) or even by the machinery of hope and fear. *Reindeer* was there because risk is the essence of salvage work. Rothwell was captain of *Montcalm* because he was capable of exercising the traditional duty that sailors bear to other sailors. Theories that attempt to explain all of risky choice in the narrow terms of purely perceptual or purely cognitive or purely motivational mechanisms will necessarily miss much of what impels people toward or away from particular risks. The factors that influence human risk taking range from psychophysics to society and from fear to fun. So too should the psychology of risk.

ACKNOWLEDGMENTS

The writing of this article and the research reported in it were facilitated by Office of Naval Research contract N00014-84-K-0065, NR 197-079. I am grateful to Leonard Berkowitz, Patricia Devine, Mary Douglas, Robin Keller, David Messick, Gregg Oden, Sandra Schneider, and Alex Wearing for their helpful criticism and comments and (again) to Gregg Oden for his MacWonderful help with the graphics.

REFERENCES

Abramson, L. Y., Seligman, M. P., & Teasdale, J. D. (1978). Learned helplessness in humans: Critique and reformulation. *Journal of Abnormal Psychology,* **87,** 49–74.
Allais, M. (1979). The foundations of a positive theory of choice involving risk and a criticism of the

postulates and axioms of the American School. In M. Allais & O. Hagen (Eds.), *Expected utility hypotheses and the Allais Paradox* (pp. 27–145). Dordrecht: Reidel (original work published 1952).

Alvarez, A. (1983). *The biggest game in town*. Boston: Houghton Mifflin.

Anderson, J. R. (1979). Perspective on models of uncertain decisions. In J. A. Roumasset, J.-M. Boussard, & I. Singh (Eds.), *Risk, uncertainty, and agricultural development* (pp. 39–62). New York: Agricultural Development Council.

Arrow, K. J. (1971). *Essays in the theory of risk-bearing*. Chicago: Markham.

Atkinson, A. B. (1970). On the measurement of inequality. *Journal of Economic Theory, 2,* 244–263.

Atkinson, J. W. (1957). Motivational determinants of risk-taking behavior. *Psychological Review, 64,* 359–372.

Atkinson, J. W. (1958). Towards experimental analysis of human motivation in terms of motives, expectancies, and incentives. In J. W. Atkinson (Ed.), *Motives in fantasy, action, and society* (pp. 288–305). Princeton NJ: Van Nostrand.

Atkinson, J. W. (1983). *Personality, motivation, and action*. New York: Praeger.

Bell, D. E. (1982). Regret in decision making under uncertainty. *Operations Research, 30,* 961–981.

Bell, D. E. (1985). Disappointment in decision making under uncertainty. *Operations Research, 33,* 1–27.

Bernoulli, D. (1967). *Exposition of a new theory on the measurement of risk*. Farnsborough Hants, England: Gregg Press (original work published in 1738).

Bowman, E. H. (1982). Risk seeking by troubled firms. *Sloan Management Review, 23,* 33–42.

Coombs, C. H. (1975). Portfolio theory and the measurement of risk. In M. F. Kaplan & S. Schwartz (Eds.), *Human judgment and decision processes*. New York: Academic Press.

Coombs, C. H., & Avrunin, G. S. (1983). Single-peaked functions and the theory of preference. *Psychological Review, 84,* 216–230.

Coombs, C. H., & Lehner, P. E. (1981). Evaluation of two alternative models of a theory of risk: I. Are moments of distributions useful in assessing risk? *Journal of Experimental Psychology: Human Perception and Performance, 7,* 1110–1123.

Dahlby, B. G. (1985). *Ranking income distributions in a Harsanyi framework*. Research paper 85-12, Department of Economics, University of Alberta.

Daston, L. J. (1980). Probabilistic expectation and rationality in classical probability theory. *Historia Mathematica, 7,* 234–260.

Day, R. H. (1979). Cautious suboptimizing. In J. A. Roumasset, J.-M. Boussard, & I. Singh (Eds.), *Risk, uncertainty, and agricultural development* (pp. 115–130). New York: Agricultural Development Council.

Douglas, M., & Wildavsky, A. (1982). *Risk and culture*. Berkeley CA: University of California.

Edwards, W. (1962). Subjective probabilities inferred from decisions. *Psychological Review, 69,* 109–135.

Ellsberg, D. (1961). Risk, ambiguity, and the Savage axioms. *Quarterly Journal of Economics, 75,* 643–669.

Ericsson, K. A., & Simon, H. A. (1980). Verbal reports as data. *Psychological Review, 87,* 215–251.

Festinger, L. (1957). *A theory of cognitive dissonance*. Evanston, IL: Row Peterson.

Friedman, M. (1953). *Essays in positive economics*. Chicago: University of Chicago.

Friedman, M., & Savage, L. J. (1948). The utility analysis of choices involving risk. *Journal of Political Economy, 56,* 279–304.

Hagen, O. (1969). Separation of cardinal utility and specific utility of risk in theory of choices under uncertainty. *Saertrykk av Statsokonomisk Tidsskrift, 3,* 81–107.

Hagen, O. (1979). Towards a positive theory of preferences under risk. In M. Allais & O. Hagen (Eds), *Expected utility hypotheses and the Allais Paradox* (pp. 271–302). Dordrecht: Reidel.

Hiroto, D. S. (1974). Locus of control and learned helplessness. *Journal of Experimental Psychology,* **102,** 187–193.

Hiroto, D. S., & Seligman, M. E. P. (1975). Generality of learned helplessness in man. *Journal of Personality and Social Psychology,* **31,** 311–327.

Janis, I. L., & Mann, L. (1977). *Decision making: A psychological analysis of conflict, choice, and commitment.* New York: Free Press.

Kahneman, D., & Tversky, A. (1979). Prospect theory: An analysis of decision under risk. *Econometrica,* **47,** 263–291.

Kahneman, D., & Tversky, A. (1984). Choices, values, and frames. *American Psychologist,* **39,** 341–350.

Karmarkar, U. S. (1978). Subjectively weighted utility: A descriptive extension of the expected utility model. *Organizational Behavior and Human Performance,* **21,** 61–82.

Keller, L. R., Sarin, R. K., & Weber, M. (1986). Empirical investigation of some properties of the perceived riskiness of gambles. *Organizational Behavior and Human Decision Processes,* **38,** 114–130.

Keyes, R. (1985). *Chancing it.* Boston: Little, Brown.

Kunreuther, H., & Wright, G. (1979). Safety-first, gambling, and the subsistence farmer. In J. A. Roumasset, J.-M. Boussard, & I. Singh (Eds.), *Risk, uncertainty, and agricultural development* (pp. 213–230). New York: Agricultural Development Council.

Langer, E. J. (1977). The psychology of chance. *Journal for the Theory of Social Behavior,* **7,** 185–207.

Liberman, A. M., Harris, K. S., Hoffman, H. S., & Griffith, B. C. (1957). The discrimination of speech sounds within and across phoneme boundaries. *Journal of Experimental Psychology,* **54,** 358–368.

Lopes, L. L. (1981). Decision making in the short run. *Journal of Experimental Psychology: Human Learning and Memory,* **7,** 377–385.

Lopes, L. L. (1983). Some thoughts on the psychological concept of risk. *Journal of Experimental Psychology: Human Perception and Performance,* **9,** 137–144.

Lopes, L. L. (1984). Risk and distributional inequality. *Journal of Experimental Psychology: Human Perception and Performance,* **10,** 465–485.

Lopes, L. L. (1987). *Reasoning and risk aversion.* In preparation.

Lopes, L. L., & Casey, J. (1986). *Tactical and strategic responsiveness in a competitive risk-taking game* (Technical Report WHIPP 28). Madison, WI: Human Information Processing Program.

Luce, R. D. (1980). Several possible measures of risk. *Theory and Decision,* **12,** 217–228.

Machina, M. J. (1982). "Expected utility" analysis without the independence axiom. *Econometrica,* **50,** 277–323.

Maier, S. F., & Seligman, M. E. P. (1976). Learned helplessness: Theory and evidence. *Journal of Experimental Psychology: General,* **105,** 3–46.

March, J. G. (1978). Bounded rationality, ambiguity, and the engineering of choice. *Bell Journal of Economics,* **9,** 587–608.

Markowitz, H. (1952). The utility of wealth. *Journal of Political Economy,* **60,** 151–158.

Markowitz, H. M. (1959). *Portfolio selection: Efficient diversification of investments.* New York: Wiley.

Maslow, A. H. (1954). *Motivation and personality.* New York: Harper.

McClelland, D. C. (1958). Risk-taking in children with high and low need for achievement. In J. W. Atkinson (Ed.) *Motives in fantasy, action, and society* (pp. 306–321). Princeton NJ: Van Nostrand.

McClelland, D. C. (1961). *The achieving society.* Princeton NJ: Van Nostrand.

Mischel, W. (1968). *Personality and assessment.* New York: Wiley.

Mowat, F. (1982). *Grey seas under.* New York: Bantam.

Ortiz, S. (1979). The effect of risk aversion strategies on subsistence and cash crop decisions. In J. A. Roumasset, J.-M. Boussard, & I. Singh (Eds.), *Risk, uncertainty, and agricultural development* (pp. 231–246). New York: Agricultural Development Council.

Pollatsek, A., & Tversky, A. (1970). A theory of risk. *Journal of Mathematical Psychology, 7,* 540–553.

Pope, R. (1983). The pre-outcome period and the utility of gambling. In B. P. Stigum & F. Wenstøp (Eds.), *Foundations of utility and risk theory with applications* (pp. 137–177). Dordrecht: Reidel.

Pratt, J. W. (1964). Risk aversion in the small and in the large. *Econometrica, 32,* 122–135.

Samuelson, P. A. (1977). St. Petersburg paradoxes: Defanged, dissected, and historically described. *Journal of Economic Literature, 15,* 24–55.

Savage, L. J. (1954). *The foundations of statistics.* New York: Wiley.

Schneider, S. L., & Lopes, L. L. (1986). Reflection in preferences under risk: Who and when may suggest why. *Journal of Experimental Psychology: Human Perception and Performance, 12,* 535–548.

Siegel, S. (1957). Level of aspiration and decision making. *Psychological Review, 64,* 253–262.

Simon, H. A. (1955). A behavioral model of rational choice. *Quarterly Journal of Economics, 69,* 99–118.

Slovic, P., Fischhoff, B., & Lichtenstein, S. (1980). Facts and fears: Understanding perceived risk. In R. C. Schwing & W. A. Albers, Jr. (Eds.), *Societal risk assessment: How safe is safe enough?.* New York: Plenum.

Thackrey, T. (1968). *Gambling secrets of Nick the Greek.* Chicago: Rand McNally.

Thompson, M. (1980). Aesthetics of risk: Culture or context. In R. C. Schwing & W. A. Albers, Jr. (Eds.), *Societal risk assessment: How safe is safe enough?.* New York: Plenum.

Tversky, A., & Kahneman, D. (1981). The framing of decisions and the psychology of choice. *Science, 211,* 453–458.

von Neumann, J., & Morgenstern, O. (1947). *Theory of games and economic behavior.* Princeton NJ: Princeton University (2nd ed.).

Williams, A. C. (1966). Attitudes toward speculative risks as an indicator of attitudes toward pure risks. *Journal of Risk and Insurance, 33,* 577–586.

TOWARD AN INTEGRATION OF COGNITIVE AND MOTIVATIONAL PERSPECTIVES ON SOCIAL INFERENCE: A BIASED HYPOTHESIS-TESTING MODEL

Tom Pyszczynski

DEPARTMENT OF PSYCHOLOGY
UNIVERSITY OF COLORADO AT COLORADO
SPRINGS
COLORADO SPRINGS, COLORADO 80933

Jeff Greenberg

DEPARTMENT OF PSYCHOLOGY
UNIVERSITY OF ARIZONA
TUCSON, ARIZONA 85721

I. Introduction

Although virtually all psychologists agree that cognitions are often subject to bias, there is very little agreement concerning the mechanisms responsible for such bias. One group of theorists, those espousing a motivational position, argue that cognitions are biased to meet the needs or desires of the individual. Influenced by the psychodynamic theories of Freud and others, these theorists maintain that cognitive biases result from powerful drives, internal conflicts, and affective states. They posit a variety of motives, such as needs for self-esteem, cognitive consistency, and a belief in a just world, that lead to inferences other than those which would result from a purely logical consideration of evidence. The other group of theorists, those espousing a purely cognitive perspective, view cognitive biases as the result of rational, albeit imperfect, inferential processes. Influenced by recent developments in cognitive psychology and information processing, these theorists focus on the way people encode, organize, the retrieve information and on the knowledge structures, transformation rules, and heuristics that are used to make inferences of various kinds. Rather than viewing cognitive bias as a result of the affective consequences of various cognitive

ADVANCES IN EXPERIMENTAL
SOCIAL PSYCHOLOGY, VOL. 20

configurations, they view it as a consequence of the dispassionate workings of the cognitive system.

This pervasive theoretical conflict can be seen in the debates waged between proponents of cognitive dissonance (e.g., Festinger, 1957; Wicklund & Brehm, 1976) and self-perception (Bem, 1967, 1972) theories of postdecisional attitude change; egotism (e.g., Bowerman, 1978; Heider, 1958; Snyder, Stephan, & Rosenfield, 1976) and information-processing (e.g., Miller & Ross, 1975; Nisbett & Ross, 1980) analyses of the self-serving attributional bias; and motivational (e.g., Allport, 1954; Greenberg & Rosenfield, 1979; Katz & Glass, 1979) and cognitive (e.g., Allport, 1954; Hamilton, 1979, 1981; Linville & Jones, 1980) perspectives on ethnocentric bias. The purpose of this chapter is to attempt an integration of these seemingly contradictory perspectives by proposing a model which specifies (1) the conditions under which affective and motivational factors do and do not influence inferential processes, and (2) the mechanisms through which affective and motivational processes influence inferential processes to produce biased conclusions. We focus our presentation on the role of a self-esteem motive in producing the self-serving attributional bias. We have chosen this particular motive because a wide variety of theorists throughout the history of psychology have suggested that the need for self-esteem exerts a poweful influence on people's cognitions and behavior (e.g., Allport, 1961; Aronson, 1969; Becker, 1962; Bowerman, 1978; Greenberg, Pyszczynski, & Solomon, 1986; Horney, 1937; James, 1890; Tesser & Campbell, 1983). It should be pointed out, however, that our model is quite general and applicable to the mechanisms through which other motives influence inferences as well.

II. The Self-Serving Attributional Bias

A. THE THEORETICAL DEBATE: COGNITIVE VERSUS MOTIVATIONAL PERSPECTIVES

The self-serving attributional bias refers to the well-replicated finding that people tend to make dispositional attributions for their successes and situational attributions for their failures. Thus, whereas a high grade on a test is likely to be attributed by an actor to a high level of ability, a low grade is likely to be attributed to bad luck, unfair questions, or a lack of effort. Early demonstrations of this phenomenon (e.g., Beckman, 1970; Johnson, Feigenbaum, & Weiby, 1964; Streufert & Streufert, 1969) were generally viewed as evidence of the effect of a self-esteem motive on the attribution process. However, Miller and

Ross (1975) and Kelley (1971) have argued that the findings from these studies could be more parsimoniously accounted for as the dispassionate consequences of the manner in which people process information. Specifically, Miller and Ross proposed that asymmetrical attributions for success and failure may result from "the tendency for people to (a) expect their behavior to produce success, (b) discern a closer covariation between behavior and outcomes in the case of increasing success than in the case of constant failure, and (c) to misconstrue the meaning of contingency" (1975, p. 213). It has also been suggested that if a person believes he/she has a high level of ability in a given area and then receives a low score on a test of that ability, it is quite rational for him/her to conclude that the failure was caused by external factors, such as flaws in the test itself. On the other hand, if this same person receives a high score on the test, it is quite reasonable for him/her to conclude that the success was caused by internal factors, such as his/her high level of the ability in question. Since he/she knows he/she possesses the ability, it is only reasonable for him/her to conclude that this ability was responsible for the success.

Since other writers have reviewed the merits of these alternate perspectives (e.g., Miller, 1978; Miller & Ross, 1975; Nisbett & Ross, 1980; Snyder *et al.*, 1976; Weary-Bradley, 1978; Zuckerman, 1979), we will not attempt a thorough discussion of these issues here. We suggest that under different circumstances each position is correct. Furthermore, we agree, for the most part, with Tetlock and Levi's (1982) contention that since both positions can be stretched to fit most available data, further refinement or integration of the two perspectives is urgently needed. Indeed, the goal of our model is to provide such an integration.

However, inherent in such an effort is the assumption that both cognitive and motivational factors play a role in producing the self-serving bias. Self-esteem theorists do not argue that cognitive processes play no role in the self-serving bias; thus, although they have not previously attempted to specify the cognitive mechanisms through which a self-esteem motive might influence such inferential processes, they would have no qualms about such an integration. On the other hand, some cognitively oriented theorists have implied that since the bias can be explained without positing a self-esteem motive, the integration of such a motive into a theory of attribution processes is unnecessary. The present integrative model is in conflict with such a position. Indeed, we believe that this latter position is untenable in light of several recent findings that cannot be accounted for without resorting to motivational constructs. Specifically, recent research has supported the role of a self-esteem motive in producing asymmetrical attributions by showing that (1) a self-serving pattern of attributions does indeed produce the affective consequences that are hypothesized to mediate the bias; (2) the self-serving bias can be increased or decreased through the use of misattribution of arousal procedures; and (3) individuals sometimes go so far as to create barriers to their own success if by so doing they are able to avoid a dispositional attribution for an anticipated failure.

B. RECENT EVIDENCE FOR MOTIVATIONAL MEDIATION
    OF THE SELF-SERVING BIAS

McFarland and Ross (1982) have provided evidence supporting the first point in a study in which subjects were induced to attribute their success or failure on a test of social sensitivity to either their level of the ability in question or to characteristics of the test. As predicted, success-internal subjects reported more positive affect, less negative affect, and higher feelings of self-esteem than did success-external subjects; failure-internal subjects, on the other hand, reported less positive affect, more negative affect, and lower self-esteem than did failure-external subjects. A number of correlational studies (e.g., Arkin & Maryuma, 1979; Covington & Omelich, 1979; Feather, 1969) and studies using hypothetical outcomes (e.g., Nichols, 1976; Weiner, Russell, & Lerman, 1978, 1979) have yielded similar findings. In addition, Mehlman and Snyder (1985) have shown that subjects report less anxiety and hostility after failure when they are given the opportunity to make an excuse for the failure than when they are not. Also relevant to this issue are our own recent findings (Pyszczynski & Greenberg, 1985) which suggest that the absence of self-serving distortions among depressed individuals may be associated with their tendency to show a decrease in self-esteem after failures. Whereas nondepressed subjects exhibited the usual self-serving bias and did not decrease in self-esteem after failure, depressed subjects did not show the self-serving bias and did decrease in self-esteem after failure.

Taken together, these studies provide clear evidence that the attributions people make for performance outcomes do indeed influence their self-esteem and affective states after such outcomes. To the extent that people are motivated to seek positive affect and avoid negative affect, the affective consequences of attributions for success and failure would be expected to encourage them to make self-serving attributions for their performance outcomes. Such hedonistic tendencies are especially likely to influence attributions in situations in which causality is ambiguous, as is generally the case when making attributions for performance on achievement-oriented tasks.

Also consistent with a self-esteem maintenance interpretation of asymmetric attributions for performance outcomes is recent research using misattribution of arousal procedures which suggests that the perception of arousal plays a central role in producing such bias. Stephan and Gollwitzer (1981) found that subjects who were led to believe that a placebo pill they had taken would produce autonomic arousal were less prone to make self-serving attributions for a prior success or failure than were no-placebo control subjects. In a similar vein, Fries and Frey (1980) found that subjects were less likely to derogate a test after failure if they could attribute arousal caused by the failure to a nonthreatening source. Presumably, the self-serving bias is weakened when arousal generated by a failure is misattributed to a nonthreatening source because if the failure is not perceived to be the cause of intensive negative affect it is experienced as much less of a threat to self-esteem.

In another study, Stephan and Gollwitzer (1981) provided subjects with false feedback concerning their levels of physiological arousal after a success or failure experience. Subjects who were led to believe they were highly aroused were more self-serving in their performance attributions than were low-arousal feedback and subjects. Finally, Gollwitzer, Earle, and Stephan (1982) demonstrated that unlabeled residual arousal from physical exercise also increased the self-serving nature of subjects' attributions. Gollwitzer *et al.* interpreted these findings as support for the idea that the residual arousal intensified subjects' perceptions of outcome-related affect and thus motivated them to become more self-serving in their attributions to minimize this affect after failure and to maximize it after success.

Research on self-handicapping and related anticipatory attributional defenses also supports a self-esteem maintenance explanation of the self-serving bias. These studies have shown that people sometimes choose to take performance-inhibiting drugs, make negative self-disclosures, avoid social interactions, report test anxiety, report hypochondrical symptoms, or reduce effort on an important test in order to provide themselves with nonthreatening attributions for possible future failures (e.g., Berglas & Jones, 1978; Frankel & Snyder, 1978; Greenberg, Pyszczynski, & Paisley, 1984; Pyszczynski & Greenberg, 1983; Smith, Snyder, & Handelsman, 1982; Smith, Snyder, & Perkins, 1983; Tucker, Vuchinich, & Sobell, 1981). If people are actually willing to hinder their own chances for success in order to avoid the loss of self-esteem that would follow from a dispositional attribution for a possible failure, it is at least as likely that they bias their attributions for threatening outcomes *after* they have occurred.

C. INTEGRATING THE TWO PERSPECTIVES: HOW DO
    MOTIVES AFFECT COGNITIONS?

Taken together, these lines of research clearly indicate that a self-esteem motive can play an important role in producing asymmetrical attributions for success and failure. Given that there is an element of guesswork in any causal inference, it is not surprising that people tend to give themselves the benefit of the doubt. However, there has been no prior attempt to specify the mechanisms through which such a self-serving tendency influences the processes through which self-serving attributions are produced. The major purpose of this chapter is to provide a model that gives some tentative answers to the question of *how* motives affect cognitions.

It is possible that when a clear threat to self-esteem is involved, normal attributional processing is simply bypassed. Rather than attempting to logically analyze the available data, the individual may simply select an attribution that suits his/her needs without considering how that attribution fits the available data. However, it seems highly unlikely that attributional egotism occurs in such an informational vacuum. Such a data-free approach would be extremely tenuous and vulnerable to falsification by others or by further data. In order for a defensive attribution to be effective in protecting self-esteem, it seems desirable that it appear, at least to oneself, to be logically derived from available evidence. McFarland and Ross' (1982) finding that subjects' exhibited higher self-esteem when the information provided to them by the experimenter suggested an internal attribution for their successes and an external attribution for their failures is consistent with this assumption. Although a data-free approach may be used in certain extreme situations (to be discussed later in this chapter), it is probably more often the case that data supporting the self-serving conclusion must be made available. The fact that people sometimes go so far as to create self-handicaps (cf. Jones & Berglas, 1978) documents the strength of the need for a seemingly rational basis from which to derive one's self-serving attributions. As Heider (1958) has noted, attributions must fit both the needs of the perceiver *and* the available data.

We suggest, then, that self-serving attributions are usually the result of a self-esteem motive's influence on the same processes that produce attributions when such a motive is not exerting an influence. The present analysis suggests that even when attributions are biased to meet the individual's needs, the attributor perceives logically consistent data patterns from which his/her attributions can be derived. Indeed, attributions for which a seemingly logically consistent data pattern could not be produced might threaten the person's conception of him/herself as a reasonable, rational individual (cf. Aronson, 1969; Festinger, 1957). Of course, a dispassionate observer, or an observer with other vested interests, might perceive a contradictory pattern from which the opposite conclusion could be derived. Thus, we argue that when self-esteem or other motives influence one's attributions, they do so in ways that enable one to maintain an *illusion of objectivity* concerning the manner in which these inferences were derived. To maintain such an illusion, the perceiver must control the information that he or she brings to bear on the inference in question. We turn now to a general model of attributional processing to be used in our analysis of the mechanisms which produce biased inferences.

III. The Hypothesis-Testing Model
of Attributional Processing

Before proceeding to a discussion of mechanisms through which motives influence attributions, we must first specify a model of the cognitive processes through which such inferences are derived when such forces are minimal. Unfortunately, although a great deal of progress has been made in the last 20 years toward specifying the processes through which attributions are generated, there is still no general all-encompassing theory of attribution processes. For the most part, theory and research on inference processes have been dominated by two approaches: the normative theories of Kelley (1967, 1971, 1972) and Jones and Davis (1965; Jones & McGillis, 1976), which specify a variety of complex logical inference rules that are applied to available data to derive conclusions, and the cognitive heuristic approaches of Tversky & Kahneman (1974, 1978) and Nisbett and Ross (1980), which specify a series of short-cut rules that are used to simplify inferential problems.

The model of attributional processing proposed here attempts to integrate these two general approaches to social inference with a general hypothesis-testing approach to cognitive processes, similar to those proposed by Bruner, Goodnow, and Austin (1956), Restle (1962), and Levine (1971). The hypothesis-testing perspective employs the "naive scientist" metaphor of social inference (cf. Heider, 1958; Kelley, 1967; Kelly, 1955; Ross, 1977; Snyder & Gangestad, 1981) and posits that, rather than being purely data-driven empiricists, persons approach inferential tasks with hypotheses which are then evaluated in light of available data (cf. Bruner, 1957). The normative and heuristic rules are used at particular stages of the hypothesis-testing process. However, the model specifies other stages of the attribution process that also exert an influence on its outcome. Similar applications of a hypothesis-testing approach to social inference have recently been proposed by Kruglanski (1980), Hastie (1983), and Snyder and Gangestad (1981).

From this perspective, the difference between normative and heuristic approaches to inference-making is quantitative rather than qualitative. The thorough causal analysis that seems to be implied by Kelley's covariation model involves a relatively thorough and exhaustive execution of a hypothesis-testing sequence in which a variety of sources of information are brought to bear on the problem; on the other hand, when one employs a heuristic, one is testing one's hypothesis in a simple, straightforward manner in which only one type of information is used. Much of the research on heuristics involves demonstrations of the failure to use relatively abstract and remote normative information when other more vivid or obvious sources of information upon which to base one's inferences are available. From the present perspective, these studies are viewed as demonstrating that, in instances in which simple, intuitively reasonable bases for inference are available, hypothesis-testing activities are terminated after a relatively small amount of information relevant to the hypothesis is accessed. The present model specifies a variety of factors that influence how thorough one's hypothesis-testing activities are likely to be.

A. PREEXISTING CAUSAL THEORIES
    AND ACTIVE HYPOTHESIS TESTING

The present model makes a distinction between two qualitatively distinct modes of attributional processing. We propose that when events occur that are consistent with expectancies, the individual relies on *preexisting causal theories* to make his or her attribution. However, when novel or unexpected events occur, the individual engages in a process we refer to as *active hypothesis testing*.

Ajzen (1977) has suggested that the expectancies that individuals hold regarding the occurrence of various events are determined largely by the intuitive causal theories they use to explain such events. In general, expectancies are generated by using a causal schema (Kelley, 1972) and reasoning from knowledge of the presence of one or more given causal factor(s) to the expectation that a consequent event will occur. For example, a person's expectancies regarding the occurrence of aggressive behavior in a given situation are likely to be strongly influenced by his/her intuitive theories about the causes of aggression. If a person believes that frustration causes people to become aggressive, his/her subjective probability estimate of a friend becoming aggressive would increase if he/she knew that the friend had recently lost his/her job. Similarly, people have prior beliefs and expectancies about the specific actors and entities involved in an event. If a person believes that his or her friend generally becomes violent when he drinks, observing the friend drinking will lead to the expectation of aggression.

When an event occurs that confirms one's causal theory-based expectancy, the theory which gave rise to that expectancy is used for causal explanation, without consideration of other possible explanations or a search for other attribution-relevant information. In such instances, the individual may not even make an attribution unless asked to do so (Enzle & Shopflocher, 1978) and, if asked, will produce an attribution by retrieving a ready-made explanation from memory without invoking an active inferential process. Lingle, Geva, Ostrom, Leippe, and Baumgardner's (1979) finding that memory-based judgments involve retrieval of the outcome of prior inferential processes rather than the intitial information upon which the previous inference was based is generally consistent with this proposition. We suggest then, that the active inferential processing positied by many attribution theorists does not take place when expected events are observed.

However, when novel or unexpected events occur, especially events of potential affective significance to the perceiver, epistemic curiosity (Berlyne, 1960) is aroused, and the individual engages in a process of active hypothesis testing. In such instances, the individual often, though not always, becomes aware that he or she does not presently understand why the event occurred and begins to actively seek a solution to the problem. Consistent with the above distinction, research suggests that people seek more attribution-relevant information and are more likely to spontaneously offer causal attributions after unexpected events than after expected events (e.g., Hastie, 1984; Pyszczynski & Greenberg, 1981; Swann, Stephenson, & Pittman, 1981; Wong & Weiner, 1981). Also consistent with this proposition is research demonstrating superior recall for expectancy-disconfirming information (e.g., Hastie, 1980, 1984; Pyszczynski, LaPrelle, & Greenberg, 1987. This greater recall presumably reflects more thorough processing of inconsistent information.

Active hypothesis-testing consists of several sequential phases: selection of a hypothesis for testing, generation of one or more inference rule(s) to be used to test the hypothesis, search for information relevant to the hypothesis, assessment of the fit between the pattern of information implicated by the inference rule and that accessed during the information search phase, evaluation of the validity of the accessed information for testing the hypothesis, acceptance or rejection of the hypothesis, and finally, verbalization of the attribution and/or action based on the attribution. When application of an inference rule leads to the conclusion that the available evidence is inconsistent with the hypothesis, the individual can either continue with the same inference rule and seek additional information, continue with the same hypothesis but generate a new inference rule to guide further hypothesis-testing activities, or discard the original hypothesis and generate a new one. A diagram depicting the sequence of stages in the hypothesis-testing process is presented in Fig. 1.

The individual may or may not be consciously aware of the execution of the various stages in the hypothesis-testing sequence. As Nisbett and Wilson (1977) and others have pointed out, a great deal of information processing occurs at a level beneath conscious awareness; we suggest that hypothesis-testing activities are certainly no exception. In many instances, the attributions we make seem to simply "pop into our heads" without any conscious effort being directed to the problem. Even in such instances, however, a considerable amount of inferential processing takes place before our conclusion is known to us. Of course in other instances, we are painfully aware of the deliberations and weighing of evidence that go into the making of an attributional inference. The present model assumes that, although the process is likely to be somewhat more extensive when it is

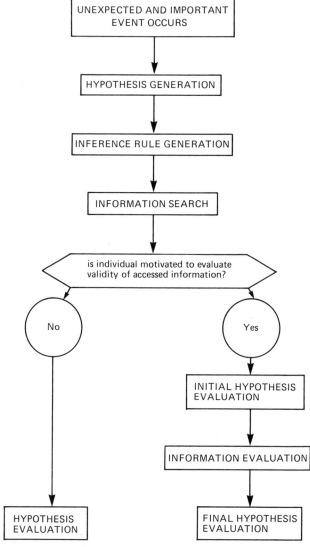

Fig. 1.   Sequence of stages in active hypothesis testing.

consciously attended to, it is essentially the same regardless of whether attention is or is not focused on it.

Before discussing the ways in which motivational factors affect the hypothesis-testing process, we will briefly discuss some of the major influences on various steps in the sequence when the only goal of the process is to arrive at an accurate attribution for the observed event.

B. GENERATION OF HYPOTHESES FOR TESTING

We suspect that in most cases, if you asked a person to describe how they choose hypotheses for testing, they would respond by saying they select hypotheses that seem to "make the most sense" in the situation at hand. That is, they select hypotheses for testing that are subjectively perceived as plausible explanations for the event in question. But what determines what is plausible? Following Tversky and Kahneman's (1974) analysis of the availability heuristic, we suggest that perceptions of plausibility among potential attributional hypotheses are determined largely by the ease with which the individual can imagine the potential cause producing the effect in question. The ease of imagining a given causal sequence is determined by individual differences in intuitive causal theories, recent activation of the causal theory or related information, and the perceptual salience of the various potential causal factors.

Clearly, individuals differ in the intuitive causal theories that they use to generate expectancies and explain events. It also seems likely that, to some extent, these intuitive causal theories are culturally transmitted; thus, causal attributions for a given occurrence may be fairly similar within members of a given culture but differ between members of different cultures (e.g., Albert, 1983; Albert & Adamopolous, 1976; Triandis, 1975). However, as a result of variations in socialization experiences within a culture, there may also be substantial within-culture variability in the causal theories that individuals routinely use to explain social events. Research has shown that individual differences on a variety of dimensions, including achievement motivation (e.g., Bar-Tal, 1978), locus of control (e.g., Phares, 1976), self-esteem (e.g., Fitch, 1970), and depression (e.g., Kuiper, 1978; Pyszczynski & Greenberg, 1985; Rizley, 1978), influence the attributions that are made in a variety of situations; it seems likely that these dimensions reflect differences in the intuitive causal theories used by various types of individuals to explain events. These intuitive theories influence attributions both by serving as ready-made explanations for occurrences that are consistent with the theories and by influencing the availability of alternative hypotheses when unexpected events occur.

In addition to the influence of individual differences, the availability of hypotheses may also be influenced by situational factors, such as recent "priming'' by environmental events. Indeed, a substantial body of literature exists suggesting that recently primed material in memory exerts a powerful influence on later recall, inferences, and attributions (e.g., Higgins, Rholes, & Jones, 1977; Srull & Wyer, 1979; Wyer & Hartwick, 1980; Wyer & Srull, 1981). Although these findings are usually interpreted as the result of a schematic influence on the interpretation of ambiguous material, such an analysis is not inconsistent with the possibility that primed materials influence the hypotheses that are selected for testing as part of a more extensive hypothesis validation process. We suggest, therefore, that the greater the availability of a given bit of information in memory, the more likely it is to be selected as a causal hypothesis to be subjected to further testing.

Finally, the hypothesis selection phase may also be affected by one's focus of attention and the perceptual salience of objects in the environment (e.g., Duval & Hensley, 1976; McArthur, 1981; Smith & Miller, 1979; Storms, 1973; Taylor & Fiske, 1975, 1978). Objects that are perceptually salient or upon which attention is focused may be especially likely to be selected as part of a causal hypothesis to be validated with further processing. From this perspective, salience, availability, and self-focused attention are seen as influencing which of a variety of possible hypotheses are selected for further analysis.

C. GENERATION OF AN INFERENCE RULE TO BE USED
TO TEST THE HYPOTHESIS

Once a hypothesis is selected as a potential explanation for the event in question, an inference rule must then be generated to be used to test the hypothesis. As a result of implicit and explicit socialization experiences, individuals have access to a variety of inference rules that can be applied in various situations. To continue with the "naive scientist" metaphor, the individual generates simple intuitive research designs that are then used to evaluate the correctness of the hypothesis under consideration. These inference rules are simple, "if-then" statements that are implied by the hypothesis under consideration.[1] If the hypothesis is correct, then x, y, and z should be true. By comparing available data with that implicated by the inference rule, the individual tests the viability of the hypothesized attribution.

Much of the prior theoretical work on attribution theory has been concerned with specifying the various inferential rules that people use to test attributional hypotheses (e.g., Jones & Davis, 1965; Kelley, 1967, 1971, 1972). Presumably

---

[1]Of course we do not wish to imply that these inference rules necessarily follow the dictates of formal deductive logic; rather, we suggest that the rules *appear* to be logical to the person testing the hypothesis. Indeed, a great deal of literature exists documenting the shortcomings of the logical activities of the lay epistemologist (for a review, see Nisbett & Ross, 1980).

people have access to a wide range of rules that can be used for this purpose. We suggest that there are two general types of rules that people generate. As Kelley (1967) suggested, people often look for evidence that the hypothesized cause covaries with the effect in question. Thus, as Kelley suggested, people may attempt to ascertain whether the effect covaries with the person or the situation by accessing distinctiveness, consensus, and consistency information. For example, after generating the hypothesis that one's low score on an important exam was externally determined by the difficult nature of the questions, an individual may reason that, if his or her hypothesis is correct, then most other students would have also performed poorly.

We suggest that there is also a second broad class of inferential rules that are often used for testing attributional hypotheses. When an a priori causal theory clearly links a given causal factor with the effect in question, the person may focus on determining whether the causal factor was, in fact, present when the effect occurred. For example, since it is generally agreed that difficult, ambiguous, or poorly written exam questions cause poor performance, an individual attempting to test the hypothesis that his or her poor exam performance was due to the poor quality of the test may attempt to determine whether the questions were, in fact, overly difficult, ambiguous, and poorly written. In such instances the person may access inference rules that state that, if the exam was indeed faulty, then the questions would be laden with polysyllabic words, he or she would be able to easily generate alternative interpretations of the wording of the questions, and other students in the class would agree that it was an unfair test. Given that the student accepts the preexisting causal theory linking faulty exams to poor performance, demonstrating that the exam was of poor quality would seem to intuitively imply to the individual that his or her poor performance was externally determined. Thus when a preexisting causal theory clearly links a potential cause with the given effect, *rather than assessing the covariation between a potential causal factor known to be present and the effect in question, the individual attempts to determine whether a factor known to covary with the effect is present or absent.*

We suspect that given the high level of knowledge people have concerning most of the domains in which they typically behave, this latter mode of causal analysis is quite common, perhaps even more common than the covariation analysis. To the extent that people know (or think they know) what causes covary with what effects, their attributional hypotheses are likely to be concerned with whether known causal factors are present or absent. However, regardless of whether the individual is attempting to ascertain whether a factor known to be present covaries with the effect or whether a factor known to covary with the effect is present, the individual tests the hypothesis by generating an "if-then" inference rule and seeking the information required by that rule to test the hypothesis.

However, this does not necessarily imply that people extend their analysis to all possible "logical" implications of the hypothesis under consideration. The individual accesses a finite number of "if-then" rules that provide a basis for evaluating the hypothesis and seeks the information implicated by these rules to test the hypothesis. As Kruglanski and colleagues (Kruglanski, 1980; Kruglanski & Ajzen, 1983) have suggested, the extensiveness of the hypothesis-testing sequence depends on the individual's epistemic needs at the time. The greater the need for structure or a fast answer to guide subsequent thought and action, the fewer the inferential rules that are likely to be brought to bear on the hypothesis. On the other hand, the greater the need for accuracy (or fear of invalidity in Kruglanski's terms), the more thorough the hypothesis-testing sequence and the more inferential rules that are likely to be brought to bear. Use of multiple inferential rules is also likely when the initially gathered data is inconsistent and unclear with respect to its fit with the pattern implicated by the initial inference rule. Thus people are likely to perseverate in their hypothesis-testing activities when the outcomes of their initial tests are ambiguous.

What determines which of the many inference rules that *could* be generated is (are) actually used by the individual to test the hypothesis? Smith (1984) argued that the more accessible a given inference rule, the more likely it is to be activated for use in inferential processing. Accessibility of inference rules may be determined by recent priming for use in other inferential problems and by association with other information that is salient at the time. For example, if other people are readily available for social comparison, the individual may be especially likely to generate an inference rule involving the use of consensus information. Clearly, the question of which of the many possible inference rules an individual actually applies when testing causal hypotheses is an important area for further research.

D.　INFORMATION SEARCH

Once a hypothesis is selected for testing and an inference rule has been generated, the individual is assumed to search both the external environment and his or her memory for information potentially relevant to an evaluation of that hypothesis. Research has shown that information search is both more extensive and more likely to be directed at attribution-relevant information when novel or unexpected events occur than when expected events occur (cf. Lau & Russell, 1980; Pyszczynski & Greenberg, 1981; Swann *et al.*, 1981; Wong & Weiner, 1981). In addition, it seems likely that the specific type of information that is sought will be determined largely by the specific inference rule that is being used to test the hypothesis. Thus if one's inference rule states that if a hypothesis is correct certain propositions must be true, the individual would be especially prone to search for information relevant to those propositions and overlook other information that is equally relevant to the question of why the event occurred but not implicated by that particular inference rule.

Research on the effect of processing objectives (e.g., Anderson & Pichert, 1978; Wyer, Srull, Gordon, & Hartwick, 1982; Zadny & Gerard, 1974) indicates that specific inferential goals exert a strong influence on both the information that is retrieved from memory and the inferences that are ultimately made. From the perspective of the present model, processing objectives are the equivalent of hypotheses currently under consideration, and they exert their influence by affecting the inference rules that are generated to test the hypothesis, which in turn affect the type of information that is sought. Research on judgmental heuristics and the underutilization of base rate information shows that when one source of evidence is used for testing a hypothesis, other information that is also logically relevant to the issue is often ignored (e.g., Ajzen, 1977; Tversky & Kahneman, 1978).

Interestingly, Snyder and colleagues (Snyder, 1984; Snyder & Gangestad, 1981) have suggested that people are generally prone to a confirmatory bias in their hypothesis-testing activities; once a hypothesis is selected for testing, people tend to seek and thus find evidence that could confirm the hypothesis rather than evidence that could disconfirm it. From their perspective, this confirmatory bias arises because of a pervasive tendency for people to find feature-positive or confirmatory instances of phenomena more informative than disconfirmatory or negative instances; consequently, information capable of confirming a hypothesis is more likely to be sought than information capable of disconfirming a hypothesis. From the present perspective, we suggest that people seem especially prone to influence by feature-positive information because such information is more strongly associated with the hypotheses that they consider. Thus when a person tests the hypothesis that he/she could not correctly answer the exam questions because they were ambiguous, the first inference rules likely to enter his or her mind are likely to center around ascertaining whether or not the questions were, in fact, ambiguous. It is actually quite reasonable for him/her to first look for instances of such feature-positive information (i.e., questions that he/she answered wrong that were ambiguous). If he/she cannot find any, the hypothesis is readily disconfirmed; only if he/she finds some such feature-positive instances does it make sense to look for ambiguous questions that he/she answered correctly or unambiguous questions that he/she answered incorrectly. Clearly, if people tend to find some evidence for whatever they search for, and if they tended to be cognitively lazy, the primacy of searching for feature-positive information may lead to a tendency to confirm the hypothesis under consideration.

Snyder further argues that, given the wide cross-situational variability in any individual's behavior, virtually any hypothesis that is tested is likely to find at least some support from prior instances of that person's behavior. If this is true, then all one would have to do to arrive at a desirable attribution is to select the preferred hypothesis for initial testing. Once chosen for testing, the initial hypothesis would guide information search in such a way as to ensure its confirmation.

Although there is considerable evidence that people are indeed more prone to use feature-positive information in a variety of inferential tasks (e.g., Fazio, Sherman, & Herr, 1982; Jenkins & Ward, 1965), the evidence for a confirmatory bias in information search is less conclusive. In support of such a bias, Snyder & Swann (1978) demonstrated that, when asked to test the hypothesis that another person is an extrovert, people preferred to ask questions with the potential to confirm the hypothesis (e.g., "What would you do if you wanted to liven things up at a party?") over questions that could disconfirm the hypothesis (e.g., "What factors make it hard for you to really open up to people?"). Likewise, Snyder and Campbell (1980), Snyder and Cantor (1979), and others have reported evidence consistent with such a bias (for a review, see Snyder, 1984).

However, Trope and Bassok (1982) have reported evidence that severely challenges the validity of the previous confirmatory bias findings. They argue that in previous studies, subjects were never given the option of asking questions that were diagnostic in the sense that different answers would imply different conclusions about the validity of the hypothesis. Rather, the questions used in these studies assumed either introversion or extraversion and would thus be appropriate to ask persons for whom a conclusion about the hypothesis has already been made. Answers to questions about what one would do to liven up a party may be useful in making a judgment about the *extent* of a person's extraversion, but would not be useful in determining whether the person is an introvert or extrovert, unless the respondent answered by saying that he or she would never do such a thing. Given the rather restricted choice of obtaining information relevant to one hypothesis or the other, it is not surprising that subjects chose information relevant to the hypothesis they were attempting to test. Trope and Bassok provide evidence that when truly diagnostic information is made available it is strongly preferred and little interest in information biased toward either confirming or disconfirming the hypothesis is exhibited.

Thus although it is probably true that people are better able to make use of feature-positive information, this does not necessarily imply that they are inevitably prone to a confirmatory bias when seeking information to test hypotheses. Although the greater ease of using confirmatory or feature-positive information may sometimes confer a certain advantage to the hypothesis under consideration, particularly when the need for structure is high and the need for accuracy is low, the hypotheses we choose to test (in experiments as well as in everyday life) are certainly not always confirmed. As Trope and Bassok have demonstrated, when truly diagnostic information is available, subjects clearly prefer it to purely confirmatory information. However, as we will argue later in the chapter, when the outcome of a hypothesis-testing sequence has strong affective implications, this even-handed preference for diagnostic information is often abandoned.

E. HYPOTHESIS EVALUATION

As information is accessed, it is immediately evaluated for what it implies regarding the acceptance or rejection of that hypothesis. As information is transferred from perceptual buffers or long-term memory to working memory, it is compared with the pattern implied by the deductive inference rule being used to test the hypothesis. This search-and-evaluate process continues until sufficient hypothesis-consistent data has been processed for the hypothesis to be accepted or sufficient hypothesis-inconsistent data has been encountered for the hypothesis to be rejected. Note, however, that the search-and-evaluate process is sometimes interrupted by an assessment of the validity of the incoming information. Conditions under which this occurs are discussed in the following section on information evaluation.

As suggested by research on the feature-positive effect (e.g., Fazio *et al.*, 1982; Jenkins & Ward, 1965; Snyder, 1984), people are generally better able to make use of information that suggests that the hypothesis is correct than information that suggests that it is not. This creates an asymmetry in the evidential requirements for bringing the hypothesis-testing sequence to a halt and drawing a conclusion. Generally, people will require less hypothesis-consistent evidence to accept a hypothesis than hypothesis-inconsistent information to reject a hypothesis. However, we propose that a variety of factors determines the extent of this asymmetry. Specifically, the needs for accuracy and structure, along with the initial confidence with which the hypothesis is held, influence the relative amount of hypothesis-consistent and hypothesis-inconsistent information that an individual requires before drawing a conclusion. The more concerned the individual is with drawing an accurate inference, the more consistent data will be required to accept the hypothesis and the less inconsistent data will be required to reject the hypothesis. In a related vein, in discussing factors that lead to the freezing of hypothesis generation, Kruglanski and Freund (1983) have noted that the greater the fear of invalidity (i.e., the greater the concern about drawing a correct conclusion), the less quickly a given hypothesis will be accepted without further processing. Similarly, they pointed out that the greater the need for structure (i.e., the greater the need for an immediate inference to guide subsequent thought and behavior), the less consistent data are required to accept a given hypothesis and the more inconsistent data are required to reject it. The amount of evidence that is required before the hypothesis is either accepted or rejected is also partly determined by the confidence with which the hypothesis was held before the testing process was initiated (cf. Chapman & Chapman, 1967, 1982). Specifically, the greater the confidence with which the hypothesis is held, the less consistent and the more inconsistent information is required before a decision regarding the truth of the hypothesis is made.

F. INFORMATION EVALUATION

In many instances, incoming information is simply taken at face value and it is either immediately used as a basis for the acceptance or rejection of the hypothesis or it is stored for later combination with other sources of information for use in evaluating the hypothesis. However, if, for one of a variety of reasons the individual is motivated to subject the incoming information to further scrutiny, the search process is interrupted and an evaluation of the incoming information takes place. This evaluation of incoming information is likely to occur either when the person has an especially strong need for an accurate inference or when there is a discrepancy between the incoming information and what the person expected the information to show.

In such cases, the individual assesses the validity of the information by generating a hypothesis concerning the validity or trustworthiness of the information in question and testing that hypothesis, just as he or she would test any other hypothesis. Information concerning the validity of the questioned evidence is accessed and compared with that implicated by the inference rule activated to test this second-order hypothesis. In most cases, this secondary evaluation of the validity of the incoming information is less extensive than the evaluation of the hypothesis itself. Because the individual's attention is focused on the validity of the hypothesis itself, he or she is less likely to closely scrutinize these secondary judgments. Nonetheless, in some cases, even these secondary judgments are very carefully weighed, using a variety of inference rules and sources of information.

If this information evaluation process finds the information invalid, it is discarded and further information search is conducted; if subsequent search is unlikely to be fruitful, a different inference rule is generated, thus directing the search to other types of information. If the information is judged valid, it is eventually used in a final hypothesis evaluation.

If the information is judged consistent with the hypothesis, the person continues with the hypothesis-testing sequence and either makes a final hypothesis evaluation and accepts the hypothesis, seeks additional information, or accesses an additional inference rule. The greater the need for structure and the greater the a priori confidence in the hypothesis, the more likely the individual is to accept the hypothesis on the basis of minimal confirming evidence and the sooner the final hypothesis evaluation. The greater the need for accuracy and the less the information conforms to what the individual expected, the more additional processing is required before final hypothesis evaluation.

If the information is judged inconsistent with the hypothesis, the person continues to sample information of that type until sufficient information has been sampled to render a judgment on the basis of that rule. When sufficient information inconsistent with the pattern implied by the current inference rule has been gathered, the individual then either accesses another inference rule and continues to test that same hypothesis or selects an alternate hypothesis and repeats the process. The greater the confidence in the original hypothesis, the more likely the individual is to access alternative inference rules and seek information of other kinds before discarding the hypothesis. This hypothesis-testing cycle continues through various alternative hypotheses until an inference is made.[2] Each successive choice of hypotheses is determined by the same factors that determine initial hypothesis selection. If the hypothesis is accepted, the individual then either overtly or covertly verbalizes the inference and encodes it in memory along with other aspects of the event. The attribution may then influence affective linkages to and schematic representations of the event and the actors and entities involved.

IV. Motivational Influences on the
Hypothesis-Testing Process

Up until this point, our discussion of the hypothesis-testing model has assumed that the only motives impinging on the process were those of attaining an accurate and efficient understanding of the cause of the event in question. However, a variety of other motives, such as needs for self-esteem, faith in the cultural world-view, ethnocentrism, control, cognitive consistency, equity, and a belief in a just world, can also influence the inferential process. In fact, our conceptualization does not view a need for accuracy as necessarily the primary motive directing the inference process. Accuracy is certainly one very important goal that affects the nature of attributional processing (cf. Swann, 1984); however, the desire for this goal varies, just as the desire for other goals varies.

---

[2]It is likely that in some instances people withhold judgment on a given hypothesis until alternative hypotheses are also evaluated. In such cases, the inference that is ultimately accepted would presumably depend on the relative strength of the evidence brought to bear on the various alternative hypotheses. Although the model could be expanded to consider such cases of consideration of alternatives, in the interest of simplicity and heuristic utility, we have chosen to limit the current model to cases in which hypotheses are tested sequentially until one is accepted. Such consideration of alternative hypotheses is most likely to occur when there is a relatively high need for a valid inference and a relatively low need for structure (cf. Kruglanski & Ajzen, 1983).

Sometimes it is extremely important to arrive at an accurate attribution; other times the need for accuracy is markedly less important or overwhelmed by other more powerful needs and desires. For example, although most jurors who serve in actual trials are undoubtedly highly motivated to arrive at accurate attributions for a defendant's behavior, these same individuals would probably be much less concerned about accuracy when participating in a mock trial. Likewise, the anger and outrage of a relative of a victim of a serious crime may interfere with or overwhelm the juror's desire to draw objective conclusions about the incident in question. The stronger the accuracy motive, the more thorough the execution of the various components of the hypothesis-testing sequence. Similarly, other goals will have a large or small impact on inferential processes, depending on their value and salience at the time the inference is being made.

These other goals often involve a desire on the part of the individual to arrive at particular attributional conclusions (cf. Kruglanski, 1980; Kruglanski & Ajzen, 1983).[3] For example, after poor performance on an ego-relevant task, a person may be motivated to arrive at an external attribution because of a desire to maintain a positive self-image. Specific attributional conclusions acquire their motivational properties by virtue of their association with particular affective consequences (cf. McFarland & Ross, 1982; Weiner *et al.,* 1978). Attributions that help the individual attain a particular goal (e.g., a positive self-image) generate positive affect or minimize negative affect; attributions that hinder the individual from attaining the goal generate negative affect or minimize positive affect. Consequently, the hypothesis-testing process may be biased by such motives to produce attributions of maximal hedonic value.

Of course, such additional motives are often in conflict with the accuracy motive. When such conflicts occur, the manner in which hypothesis-testing proceeds will depend on the relative strengths of the motives involved. The motive that is strongest or most salient at the time an inference is needed will have the greatest effect on the manner in which hypotheses are tested and, ultimately, on the conclusion that is reached. Thus, the accuracy motive is often overwhelmed by the more immediate anticipated affective consequences of the desired conclusion. However, as we will argue in the following sections, the

---

[3]It should be noted that our analysis of motivational influences on social inferences is similar in some ways to that offered by Kruglanski and colleagues (e.g., Kruglanski, 1980; Kruglanski & Ajzen, 1983; Kruglanski & Freund, 1983). According to their perspective, inferences are affected by three general forces: the need for structure, the fear of invalidity, and the need for specific conclusional contents. These forces influence the process of generating and testing hypotheses and, consequently, the inferences that are made. We believe that our model is quite compatible with Kruglanski's lay epistemological perspective. While their model is a broader, more molar level analysis of the inference process in general, ours is a ''finer-grained'' analysis of the influence of motives on various specific components of the hypothesis-testing sequence. Thus, we view the two models as somewhat complementary.

need for accuracy is not simply ignored when other motives impinge on the hypothesis-testing process. Rather, when other motives are involved, the process through which attributions are derived is essentially a compromise between one directed by the individual's preferred conclusions and the individual's need to perceive the world as accurately as possible. The question then becomes how do these other motives influence the hypothesis-testing process to produce biased attributions?

The present model is certainly not the first to consider the question of how an individual's needs influence his or her inferences and beliefs. Perhaps the most important, and certainly the most thoroughly researched, theory of motivated cognitive change is Leon Festinger's (1957) theory of cognitive dissonance. According to this theory, the perception of inconsistent cognitions gives rise to cognitive dissonance, an aversive tension state that the individual is motived to reduce. Dissonance can be reduced by altering cognitions, adding new cognitions, or altering the perceived importance of cognitions. Festinger further posited that situations that would increase the magnitude of one's dissonance are actively avoided. More recently, Wicklund & Brehm (1976) reviewed a wide body of literature and concluded that dissonance is aroused only when a person perceives that he or she has freely chosen a course of behavior that produces foreseeable aversive consequences.

The majority of the research stimulated by cognitive dissonance theory has been concerned with the determinants of the arousal of dissonance (e.g., choice, commitment) and the effects of dissonance arousal on subsequent attitudes and behavior (e.g., spreading of choice alternatives, attitude change in the direction of counterattitudinal behavior) rather than with the cognitive mechanisms through which dissonance is reduced. Nonetheless, theory and research in the dissonance tradition provides some very useful insights into these processes. Inherent in cognitive dissonance theory, as well as in all other cognitive consistency theories (e.g., Heider, 1958; Osgood & Tannabaum, 1955), is the notion that one's inferences and the available data must fit together in what appears to be a logically consistent manner. Thus inferences that do not appear to follow logically from available data are posited to produce considerable discomfort for the individual. The present model is an attempt to specify the ways in which available data are processed so as to preserve this consistency between available data and desired conclusions. We argue, then, that in order to best meet one's needs, people seek to maintain an illusion of objectivity concerning the manner in which their beliefs and inferences are formed.

In discussing the ways in which dissonance is reduced, Festinger pointed out that the responsiveness of cognitions to reality places a limitation on people's abilities to alter their beliefs. That is, because our perceptions are generally firmly grounded in reality, we cannot simply believe anything we so desire (e.g., if one receives an F on an exam, it is virtually certain that, at least at some level, this fact will be cognitively represented). Thus Festinger argues that efforts at dissonance reduction are focused on the cognitive element that is least resistant to change. Occasionally this amounts to changing the reality upon which one's cognition is based (i.e., changing one's behavior or the environment); more commonly, it involves changing the element for which the correspondence to reality is least clear and unambiguous, usually one's attitudes and evaluations.

Festinger also posited that to facilitate one's attempts to keep dissonance at a minimal level, information that is expected to reduce dissonance will be actively sought and information that is expected to increase dissonance will be actively avoided. This "selective exposure" hypothesis has had a long and checkered history. In a review of the literature available at that time, Freedman and Sears (1965) concluded that there was little evidence available supporting the existence of such tendencies. However, Wicklund and Brehm (1976) took issue with this conclusion and argued that the equivocal nature of the support for selctive exposure may be the result of a variety of extratheoretical factors, including self-presentational efforts to appear objective, norms of intellectual honesty, and greater curiosity about and utility of attitude-discrepant information.

In addition, Festinger's (1964) later analysis suggested that, in some instances, individuals could more effectively reduce dissonance by exposing themselves to nonsupportive information and refuting it than by selectively exposing themselves to only consonant information. Consistent with this argument, Lowin (1967) assessed subjects' interest in receiving strong or weak information about political candidates whom they either supported or opposed and found that, although people were generally more likely to choose consonant information, dissonant information that was easy to refute was chosen just as often as strong consonant information. More recent research by Frey (1981a) also produced findings consistent with this analysis, demonstrating that consonant information is preferred when the source of that information is high in credibility but that dissonant information is preferred when its source is low in credibility.

Indeed, in a recent extensive review of the selective exposure literature, Frey (1986) concluded that there is now substantial support for the existence of such tendencies. Selective exposure to consonant information appears most likely to occur when subjects freely choose to engage in dissonant behavior (Frey & Wicklund, 1980) or are highly committed to their decision (Frey & Stahlberg, 1984; Schwarz, Frey, & Kumpf, 1980; Sweeney & Gruber, 1984), when there is a relatively large amount of information available (Frey, 1985), when the available information is strong, highly reliable and/or difficult to refute (Frey, 1981a, 1985; Frey & Stahlberg, 1986; Lowin, 1967), when the decision is irreversible (Frey, 1981b; Frey & Rosch, 1984), and when the magnitude of dissonance arousal is moderate (Frey, 1981c). These more recent studies suggest that the early pessimism about the selective exposure hypothesis was premature. Individuals do indeed selectively expose themselves to decision-consistent information, but the extent of this effect depends on a variety of other factors that also influence information search. As will be seen below, selective exposure to information consistent with a self-serving conclusion is one important means through which individuals maintain an illusion of objectivity concerning their attributions.

The biased hypothesis-testing model builds on the earlier theoretical and empirical work on cognitive dissonance processes in an attempt to provide a general model of the ways in which motives bias the processing of information. In general, we attempt to merge recent theoretical and empirical work from the social-cognitive perspective with the insights derived from theory and research within the cognitive dissonance and self-esteem maintenance traditions.[4] Given the previously described general hypothesis-testing model, such motives could produce biased conclusions by influencing any or all stages in the hypothesis-testing sequence. To illustrate, the following sections consider the nature of these influences on the generation of self-serving attributions.

A. ACTIVATION OF THE HYPOTHESIS-TESTING SEQUENCE

According to the biased hypothesis-testing model, attributions for events that are consistent with expectations are formed by relying on the preexisting causal theory upon which the expectations were based; in such instances, the hypothesis-testing sequence is not activated. When expected outcomes occur, very little inferential activity is instigated, regardless of the implications of the event for self-esteem. Instead, when an attribution for such an event is required, the individual simply retrieves a ready-made attribution from memory. Thus when expectations for positive or negative outcomes are confirmed, attributions are made by resorting to preexisting causal theories. If the expectancy was based on a dispositional causal theory, a dispositional attribution will be made; if the expectation was based on a situational causal theory, a situational attribution will be made.

---

[4]Indeed, some theorists have argued that, to the extent that dissonance is most likely to be aroused when people feel responsible for producing a foreseeable aversive consequence (cf. Wicklund & Brehm, 1976), dissonance theory can be subsumed with a more general self-esteem maintenance framework (e.g., Aronson, 1969; Bowerman, 1978; Greenwald & Ronis, 1978). The basic idea is that all evidence of dissonance reduction can be interpreted as evidence that individuals alter their beliefs to deny that they have done something stupid, incompetent, or immoral. From this perspective, believing that one is responsible for producing a foreseeable aversive outcome constitutes a threat to self-esteem and thus leads to attitude change in an attempt to reduce this threat. Thus, the arousal of cognitive dissonance can be viewed as a specific type of threat to self-esteem and dissonance-reducing attitude change can be viewed as a strategy to reduce the threat to self-esteem produced by the individuals' previous behavior.

In cases where a dispositional causal theory gives rise to an expectation of success, and this expectation is subsequently confirmed, our analysis of the process through which a dispositional attribution for the success is derived is quite consistent with those offered by the purely cognitive perspectives on attributional bias (e.g., Miller & Ross, 1975; Nisbett & Ross, 1980). The hypothesis-testing sequence is not instigated and an attribution is made by relying on the causal theory that gave rise to the expectancy. Although the person's expectancies and preexisting causal theories may be biased by a self-esteem motive, the actual inferential process by which the attribution is generated is not. Likewise, in cases where a situational causal theory gives rise to an expectation of failure (e.g., a person fails an extremely difficult task), and that expectation is subsequently confirmed, a similar process is likely to lead to a seemingly self-serving situational attribution. In both instances, the person retrieves a ready-made attribution from memory and motivational factors are relatively unlikely to impinge on the process.

Only when an event is novel or unexpected does active hypothesis testing occur. This type of inferential process is more susceptible to motivated bias because in such cases the appropriate attribution is unclear and ambiguous; the event does not follow from the person's preexisting theories, so these prior theories appear unable to provide an adequate explanation. Indeed, this ambiguity is the very reason the active hypothesis-testing process is initiated. Given the wide variety of potential causal hypotheses that could be tested, the diverse sources of information that can be brought to bear on the issue, and the component judgments of the validity and applicability of the various bits of information that one has gathered, active hypothesis-testing provides a multitude of opportunities for motivated biases to influence one's ultimate conclusion. A recent study of the search for attribution-relevant information among depressed and nondepressed individuals (Pinkley, LaPrelle, Pyszczynski, & Greenberg, 1987), to be described below, provided evidence generally consistent with the proposition that motivated bias is most likely to occur when relatively unexpected events occur.

B. GENERATION OF HYPOTHESES FOR TESTING

The first step in an active hypothesis-testing sequence is the selection of a hypothesis for further testing. When the to-be-explained outcome is high in ego relevance, the implications of the hypothesis that is being considered arouse affect (cf. Fries & Frey, 1980; Gollwitzer et al., 1982; McFarland & Ross, 1982; Stephan & Gollwitzer, 1981). But how does this affect influence the processing of information? It seems likely that before a self-esteem motive can influence processing, the person must first consider the possibility that he/she actually *is* responsible for a failure or *is not* responsible for a success. This rather threatening possibility produces negative affect, which then motivates the individual to process information in a way that would refute this possibility and provide evidence for a more satisfactory alternative hypothesis. Indeed, in studies in which nonthreatening explanations for failure are made readily available (e.g., the test was poorly constructed), egotistic biases are greatly reduced or eliminated (e.g., Frey & Stahlberg, 1986; Miller, 1978). Therefore, we argue that consideration of a self-threatening hypothesis produces an aversive state of arousal, which motivates the individual to rather quickly select a less threatening hypothesis for testing. For example, if a student fails an important exam, he or she will bias the process by which an attribution is generated only if he/she first briefly considers the possibility that his/her poor performance was caused by a lack of ability (or some other ego-threatening entity), in which case he/she will very quickly select a less threatening hypothesis for further consideration. Of course, in most situations, people do consider the possibility that they are responsible for their outcomes; consequently, affective factors often exert an influence on the manner in which hypothesis-testing is conducted. By choosing self-serving hypotheses to test, the production of self-serving conclusions is set in motion.

C. GENERATION OF INFERENCE RULES
AND THE INFORMATION SEARCH

Once a hypothesis is selected, the individual generates an inference rule to be used in testing the hypothesis and searches both the environment and his/her memory for evidence relevant to that rule. We discuss both steps in the same section because they are mutually interdependent and their motivational influences are quite similar. The inference rule that is accessed determines the specific type of information that is sought. However, according to the present model, the individual's expectancy about what a given category of information will reveal influences both the specific inference rule that is accessed to test the hypothesis (and therefore the specific type of information that is sought) and the extensiveness of the search for information of that type. A diagram of motivational influences on the generation of inference rules and information search is provided in Fig. 2. In general, people's hypothesis-testing activities are biased toward sources of evidence likely to confirm one's desired conclusion. Thus people are especially likely to access inference rules and seek information when they expect that they will support a self-serving hypothesis; conversely, people are most likely to avoid inference rules and sources of information when they expect that they will refute a self-serving hypothesis.

Once an inference rule is selected, how vigorously the individual persists in

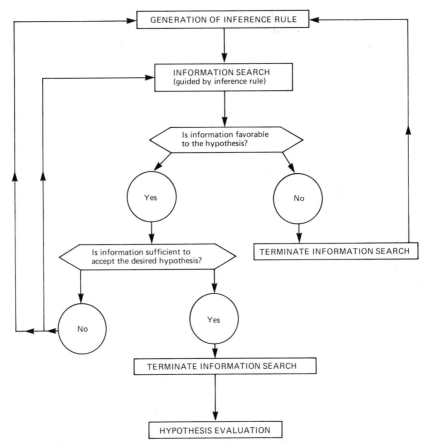

Fig. 2.   Diagram of motivational influences on the generation of inference rules and information search.

his/her search for the information implicated by that rule depends on what the
initially gathered information reveals. If this information has favorable implications, he/she will continue to search for information of that type and show little
interest in information of other types, unless the other types of information are
sufficiently similar to lead to an expectation that they too will yield supportive
information; if the initially gathered data have unfavorable implications, he/she
will terminate the search for that class of evidence, generate a new inference
rule, and search especially vigorously for information with more favorable implications for the hypothesis.

The findings from the selective exposure literature discussed above are
generally consistent with this model (for a review, see Frey, 1986). These studies

TABLE I
AMOUNT OF INFORMATION REQUESTED AS A FUNCTION
OF OUTCOME AND INFORMATION EXPECTANCY[a]

| | Outcome | |
Information expectancy	Success	Failure
High scores	(N = 11)	(N = 10)
Number of answer sheets	2.73	1.00
Proportion requesting any	.18	.10
Low scores	(N = 10)	(N = 10)
Number of answer sheets	1.00	9.10
Proportion requesting any	.10	.70

[a]From Pyszczynski, Greenberg, and LaPrelle (1985).

show that, at least when it is feasible to do so, people selectively seek information that facilitates their efforts to avoid aversive states of arousal. However, most of these prior studies are only indirectly relevant to a specification of how people derive self-serving attributions because they deal with how people respond to information relevant to their attitudes or prior behavioral commitments rather than information relevant to the attributions they are in the process of making for ego-relevant outcomes.

In two studies of subjects' inclination to seek information directly relevant to performance attributions, Pyszczynski, Greenberg, and LaPrelle (1985b) demonstrated a particularly extensive search for consensus information after failure, but only among subjects who expected this information to be consistent with self-serving hypothesis. In the first study, subjects were given either success or failure feedback on a supposedly valid (but actually bogus) social sensitivity test and then led to expect that available information would reveal that most other students performed either well or poorly on the test. As may be seen in Table I, failure subjects who expected that most others also obtained low scores sought more information than did subjects in any other condition. Finding that most others also received low scores provides high consensus (Kelley, 1967) for the failure and thus implies that the failure was situationally determined. Consequently, failure subjects sought more information when they expected high consensus than when they expected low consensus for the outcome.

Also consistent with the model, success subjects showed little interest in the additional consensus information, regardless of what they expected it to reveal. Since before taking the test subjects were told that it was a very good measure of social sensitivity, it seems unlikely that they would have considered the possibility that their performance was externally determined (by a dubious test). Of course, entertaining the hypothesis that the success was externally determined would be necessary in order for a bias in information search to occur. Alternately, it may have been that before taking it subjects expected to do well on the test; thus, their success may have been explained via the preexisting causal theory that generated their expectations. Our model predicts biased hypothesis testing after success only when an individual considers the possibility, even very briefly, that an affectively undesirable attribution may be appropriate.

Such a situation occurred in a second study reported by Pyszczynski *et al.* (1985b), in which subjects were led to expect that others scored higher, lower, or the same as themselves. Although the effects were stronger in the failure condition, both success and failure subjects showed a linear trend in information search as a function of expectancies about what the information about others' performance would reveal. High-score-expectancy subjects showed relatively little interest in the information, and low-score-expectancy subjects showed a great deal of interest. A number of factors may have contributed to the self-serving bias in information search exhibited by the success subjects in this study. Unlike the first study, success subjects in one condition were confronted with the possibility that others scored higher than they did. This expectation is likely to produce negative arousal; consequently, success subjects in this condition avoided such threatening social comparison information. In addition, the outcome manipulation was weaker and more ambiguous than that employed in the first study; therefore, success subjects may have been less certain that their performance was actually superior. If these subjects were insecure about the meaning of the positive outcome (i.e., they considered a threatening interpretation), the model predicts an aversive state of arousal, which would exert a bias on the manner in which they searched for evidence.

Frey (1981c) and Frey and Stahlberg (1986) demonstrated a biased search for information about the validity of intelligence tests after subjects received negative feedback about their performance on such tests. In these studies, negative feedback subjects showed a marked preference for test-disparaging over test-supporting information. Frey and Stahlberg's (1986) finding that when an external attribution for failure was made available to subjects (by telling them that the tests may have been incorrectly scored) the search for information about the validity of the test became substantially less biased is also consistent with the model. Providing subjects with an external attribution for their poor performance may have made it less likely that they would have seriously considered the possibility that they were responsible for the failure. If this were the case, less negative affect would be generated and the search would be less likely to be biased. These studies also demonstrate that the information search bias after performance outcomes generalizes to types of attribution-relevant information other than consensus.

Biased search tendencies have also recently been demonstrated within an interpersonal context (Holton & Pyszczynski, 1986). Given the importance of interactions with others in the development and maintenance of one's self-concept, it seemed likely that people would be strongly motivated to positively evaluate another person who complimented them and negatively evaluate another person who insulted them (cf., Byrne & Rhamey, 1965; Greenberg *et al.*, 1986). By so doing, the boost to self-esteem of the other's compliment is increased but the threat to self-esteem of the other's insult is diminished. Thus we hypothesized that people would selectively seek favorable information about another who had complimented them but unfavorable information about another who had insulted them.

Subjects received a favorable or unfavorable evaluation of their responses to a choice dilemma problem from a confederate posing as another subject and were subsequently asked to evaluate that other person's competence as an evaluator. Because of the implications of the confederate's evaluations for subjects' self-esteem, we assumed that subjects who had received a favorable evaluation would be motivated to support the hypothesis that the confederate was a competent evaluator and that subjects who had received an unfavorable evaluation would be motivated to support the hypothesis that the confederate was an incompetent evaluator. Data from this study may be found in Table II. When later given an opportunity to inspect the evaluations the confederate had received from people he had supposedly interacted with in previous sessions, subjects who received a positive evaluation from the confederate requested more information if they had been led to expect that the evaluations of the confederate would be mostly positive than if they had been led to expect that they would be mostly negative, subjects who received a negative evaluation from the confederate requested more information if they were led to expect that the evaluations of the confederate would be mostly negative than if they were led to expect that they would be mostly positive.

Furthermore, observer subjects, who merely witnessed the confederate's positive or negative evaluation of the actor subjects, showed no hint of such a

TABLE II

AMOUNT OF INFORMATION REQUESTED AS A FUNCTION OF SUBJECT'S PERSPECTIVE, FEEDBACK, AND INFORMATION EXPECTANCY[a]

Information expectancy	Actor's perspective		Observer's perspective	
	Positive feedback	Negative feedback	Positive feedback	Negative feedback
Positive	5.13	3.13	2.94	2.67
Negative	2.43	5.31	3.06	2.50

[a]From Holton and Pyszczynski (1986).

bias. This absence of biased search on the part of observers occurred in spite of the fact that their evaluations of the confederate did not differ from those made by the actively involved subjects; both actively involved and observer subjects evaluated the confederate more favorably when he praised subjects than when he criticized them. This suggests that the bias in information search exhibited by actively involved subjects is not simply the result of a general tendency to seek hypothesis-confirming information (cf., Snyder & Swann, 1978). Rather it appears that, at least in this study, it was emotional involvement with the other's evaluation that led to biased search.

Recent research comparing the information search activities of depressed and nondepressed persons (Pinkley, LaPrelle et al., 1986) is also consistent with the model. The procedures for this study were modeled after those used by Pyszczynski et al. (1985b, Study 1), described above. Data are displayed in Table III. Consistent with previous research, nondepressed subjects sought more consensus information when they expected that it would support a self-serving attribution for prior failure, i.e., they sought more information when they expected it to reveal that most other subjects performed poorly on the test than when they expected it to reveal that most other subjects performed well. Also consistent with previous findings, this bias did not emerge after success. Depressed subjects, however, showed no evidence of a self-serving bias after failure; sought the same amount of information regardless of their expectancies as to what it would reveal about other subjects' scores. To the extent that these subjects expected to perform poorly on the test (premanipulation checks on subjects' expectancies confirmed this assumption), their failures would not be expected to instigate active hypothesis testing and, consequently, they would be expected to derive their attributions from the preexisting causal theory that gave rise to their expectancies. However, after success, the depressed subjects showed a strong self-serving bias in the information they sought; that is, they sought more information when they expected it to reveal that most other subjects performed poorly than when they expected it to reveal that most other subjects performed well.

TABLE III

AMOUNT OF INFORMATION REQUESTED AS A FUNCTION OF DEPRESSION, PERFORMANCE OUTCOME, AND INFORMATION EXPECTANCY[a]

Information expectancy	Nondepressed		Depressed	
	Success	Failure	Success	Failure
High scores	5.47	1.59	4.60	2.63
Low scores	7.86	6.38	12.82	3.11

[a]From Pinkley, LaPrelle, Pyszczynski, and Greenberg (1986).

Given arguments that depressed persons are particularly realistic and free from bias in their self-relevant judgments (e.g., Alloy & Abramson, 1981; Lewinsohn, Mischel, Chaplin, & Barton, 1980), this latter finding may seem somewhat surprising. However, to the extent that these subjects expected to do poorly on the test, their successful performance would be expected to instigate a hypothesis-testing sequence and lead them to seek information. When they learned that the available information supported an internal attribution for their success, they showed a great deal of interest in this information. Thus it may be that the usual pattern of realistic attributions among depressed persons is the result of their pessimistic expectations about being able to support a more self-serving conclusion. The breakdown in defensiveness among the depressed may thus represent a general belief that available evidence will not support self-serving inferences. However, when such persons are confronted with a high probability of information consistent with a self-serving conclusion, as was the case in the Pinkley *et al.* study, they apparently show a great deal of interest in it and bias their attributions accordingly. By providing insights into the mechanisms responsible for the oft-found absence of self-serving distortions among depressed individuals, this research may provide information useful to the development of therapies aimed at helping depressives make more beneficial attributions for their outcomes. The findings from this study thus highlight the importance of developing process-oriented models of the manner in which biased attributions are derived.

Taken together, these studies clearly demonstrate a self-serving bias in the search for attribution-relevant information after performance outcomes. They also suggest that this bias is most likely to occur after unexpected outcomes or when individuals are likely to at least briefly entertain the possibility of a self-threatening hypothesis. It appears, then, that one way that people generate self-serving attributions is by controlling the information upon which their attributions are based.

In the studies reviewed above, cues to the likely content of a set of information were shown to affect subjects' tendencies to sample information from that category. However, the model also makes predictions about the effects of exposure to information from one category on interest in information from other categories. The model suggests that when the initially processed information is unsupportive, people terminate their hypothesis-testing activities with that particular inference rule and quickly access a different rule with a better chance of yielding supportive information. For example, when testing the hypothesis that his low exam score was due to the ambiguity of the questions, the fewer technical words the student can find in the text of the exam, the more likely he is to generate alternative rules for testing the hypothesis. He might then reason that if the questions are ambiguous, he will be able to easily generate alternative interpretations for the intended meaning of the question, or, if the questions are ambiguous, he will be able to elicit agreement about their ambiguity from his fellow students. Once such alternative inference rules are generated, the student would then use them to guide his search for different types of information.

Similarly, when at the outset of the hypothesis-testing sequence one believes that the likelihood of finding supporting evidence is low, one may be especially likely to terminate the search-and-evaluate process after uncovering a small amount of supportive evidence. Thus, when confidence in the hypothesis is low, the greater the support for the self-serving hypothesis provided by information from one category, the less likely the person is to generate additional inference rules for further testing of the hypothesis, and the lower the interest in information from other categories. These latter two implications of the model have yet to be tested.

D. INFORMATION EVALUATION
    AND HYPOTHESIS EVALUATION

The biases we have discussed up to this point tend to lead the individual to access hypothesis-supporting information. Given that such information serves the individual's purposes, in many cases it is simply used to test the hypothesis without any evaluation of its validity. In many instances, however, individuals are unable to control the information to which they are exposed. In other cases, public or private concerns about appearing to be objective may inhibit such selective exposure (cf. Wicklund & Brehm, 1976). Either way, individuals are, in fact, often exposed to information inconsistent with self-serving hypotheses. The present model suggests that such information produces negative affect, which motivates the individual to become actively engaged in attempting to refute the implications of the threatening information. As suggested above, such efforts sometimes center on accessing other information more favorable to the hypothesis. Threatening information may also be dealt with directly, by attempting to refute it. Thus, when threatening evidence is encountered, it would be expected that (1) greater processing capacity would be devoted to evaluating that evidence and, consequently, (2) such hypothesis-inconsistent information would be viewed as less valid or relevant to the hypothesis than would hypothesis-consistent information.

Indirect evidence for the more extensive processing prediction comes from a recent study by Wyer and Frey (1983) in which subjects exhibited better recall for arguments supporting the validity of intelligence tests after performing poorly than after performing well on such a test; observer subjects who did not themselves take the test showed no such bias. Wyer and Frey (1983) interpreted these findings as indicating that failure subjects were especially thorough in their processing of the test-supporting information in an attempt to undermine its

TABLE IV

EVALUATIONS OF RESEARCH REPORTS AS A
FUNCTION OF PERFORMANCE OUTCOME AND
RESEARCH CONCLUSIONS[a]

Research conclusions	Performance outcome	
	Success	Failure
ISSS high validity		
Well conducted	6.14	5.44
Convincing	5.77	4.72
ISSS low validity		
Well conducted	5.09	6.22
Convincing	4.36	6.33

[a]From Pyszczynski, Greenberg, and Holt (1985).
Higher values reflected positive ratings of the studies.

validity. Consistent with this interpretation, failure subjects judged the information to be less favorable to intelligence tests and intelligence tests to be generally less valid than did success subjects. Of course, more direct evidence of such especially thorough processing of hypothesis-inconsistent information is needed.

Also consistent with the notion that individuals attempt to undermine the validity of hypothesis-threatening information are findings from a recent study by Pyszczynski, Greenberg, and Holt (1985a). In this study, subjects were asked to evaluate two research reports concerning the validity of a social sensitivity test shortly after receiving feedback indicating that they had performed either well or poorly on that test. One of the reports concluded that the social sensitivity test was high in validity and the other that it was low in validity. As predicted, success subjects rated the high-validity-conclusion study as more convincing and better conducted than did failure subjects, and failure subjects rated the low-validity-conclusion study as more convincing and better conducted than did success subjects. Relevant means are shown in Table IV. Thus, subjects evaluated the quality of the evidence concerning the validity of the social sensitivity test in a way that supported a self-serving conclusion.

It also appears that this biased evaluation of attribution-relevant information influences the inferences that are subsequently made. Before exposure to the information, subjects' self-evaluations of social sensitivity were unaffected by their scores on the test. However, exposure to the mixed test validity evidence led to an increase in self-ratings of social sensitivity after success (compared to ratings before exposure to the studies) but had no effect on subjects' self-ratings after failure. Given that success subjects viewed the high-validity-conclusion study as more convincing than the low-validity-conclusion study, it follows that their self-ratings of social sensitivity would increase. Likewise, given that failure subjects viewed the low-validity-conclusion study as the more convincing of the two, it follows that their self-ratings would be unaffected by the information.

After a given bit of evidence is evaluated for its validity for testing the hypothesis, it is either used to support or refute the hypothesis or discarded, thus initiating additional search and/or generation of additional inference rules. As demonstrated in the Pyszczynski *et al.* (1985a) study, evaluations of the validity of information and its implications for the hypothesis are interrelated. Only if information is not invalidated during the information evaluation phase is it used as evidence in testing the hypothesis. However, information with desirable implications for the hypothesis is evaluated as being more valid and thus is more likely to be used as a basis for the inference.

The information evaluation phase produces considerable flexibility for the hypothesis tester in his or her covert attempts to ensure that his or her self-serving hypotheses are supported. Clearly not all information that one encounters is equally valid or relevant for hypothesis-testing purposes, and thus decisions need to be made about what information to use. The sometimes elaborate maneuvers of researchers to "explain away" data inconsistent with their findings are a particularly striking example of this bias in information evaluation (cf. Mahoney, 1977).

Finally, besides a bias in judgments of the relevance or utility of information, it is also possible that people are biased in their evidential requirements when assessing the fit between the data pattern implicated by the inference rule and that gathered during the information search phase of the sequence. It seems likely that the greater the affect associated with a favored conclusion, the less hypothesis-consistent information is required to accept it and the more hypothesis-inconsistent information is required to reject it. Note, however, that in most cases, threatening information will be defused before it must be used for drawing an inference, and thus greater tolerance for hypothesis-disconfirming information may not be necessary in order to arrive at conclusions that fit one's needs.

V. Responses to the Disconfirmation of Self-Serving Hypotheses

As should be evident by now, the present model suggests that hypothesis-testing processes are biased such that favored hypotheses are likely to be "supported" by available data. A self-serving bias is likely to intrude on the selection of hypotheses for testing, the generation of inference rules, the search for attribution-relevant information, the evaluation of the information that one accesses, and the amount of confirmatory and disconfirmatory evidence that is required before an inference is made. In this way, the individual is able to maintain an "illusion of objectivity" concerning the way he/she thinks about him/herself and the social world.

However, in some instances, the available evidence against a self-serving hypothesis may be simply so strong, abundant, or salient that the self-serving hypothesis must be rejected. In such cases, three outcomes are possible. One possibility is that the individual will test and, if the evidence is very strong, accept a self-threatening hypothesis and experience the resulting negative affect and loss of self-esteem. Such an outcome is especially likely when the motive for accuracy is very strong. For example, it has been shown that self-serving attributions are less likely to occur when one's inferences are subject to public scrutiny or when one anticipates a future performance for which an accurate assessment of one's capabilities would be beneficial (e.g., Greenberg, Pyszczynski & Solomon, 1982; Rosenfeld, Melburg, & Tedeschi, 1981; Weary, Harvey, Schwieger, Olson, Perloff, & Pritchard, 1982; Wortman, Costanzo & Witt, 1973). These studies show that, although the self-serving bias is a generally pervasive phenomena, there are situations in which other motives overwhelm the need for a positive self-evaluation. Repeated experiences in situations in which one is unable to derive a self-serving attribution could eventually lead to a loss of motivation to defend self-esteem (cf. Abramson, Seligman, & Teasdale, 1978; Alloy & Abramson, 1981; Brehm, Wright, Solomon, Silka, & Greenberg, 1983; Pyszczynski & Greenberg, 1985) and the development of a chronically negative self-image.

Alternately, the person could accept a self-serving conclusion without supporting data by bypassing the hypothesis-testing cycle altogether. After assessing that the available evidence is too strong to be refuted, the person may nonetheless accept a self-serving conclusion, but without subjecting it to the scrutiny that is normally involved when hypotheses are tested. Such a data-free approach is likely to occur only when the self-esteem motive is very strong, the person expects that a more rational approach would not be successful, and the accuracy motive is relatively weak. In order for such a strategy to be effective, the person must abandon normal information processing and avoid confrontation with evidence of any kind. Tesser and colleagues (Tesser & Blusiewicz, 1987; Tesser, Moore, & Lorden, 1985) have recently investigated such "defensive self-beliefs" and found evidence generally consistent with the notion that people avoid confrontation with outside information when they have committed themselves to beliefs about themselves that are discrepant with other available information. In such cases, attention may be diverted from the issue, and distractions of various kinds may be sought.

Such strategies may play a role in obsessional neuroses and perhaps even schizophrenia, in which the individual may abandon logical thought completely. The more the person bypasses rational thought processes to arrive at desired conclusions, the further removed from shared social reality he or she becomes. Perhaps we all do this in small ways on occasion, but individuals who are confronted with circumstances that require them to frequently do so may eventually abandon rational thought processes altogether. Of course such an outcome will occur only when hypothesis-testing processes reveal evidence that undeniably supports a conclusion so terrifying that its acceptance is more adversive than the abandonment of reason (cf., Greenberg et al., 1986).

A related possibility is that the person might simply divert attention from the threatening issue altogether and not make an attribution for the outcome. Rather than suffering the pain inherent in acceptance of a self-threatening hypothesis or engaging in the break with social reality necessary for a hypothesis to be accepted without supporting evidence, he or she may avoid the issue by diverting attention from the threatening outcome. Such avoidance responses are likely when the self-esteem motive is strong, the person perceives a low probability of successfully using the available information to support a self-serving hypothesis, and the accuracy motive is also very strong. Research on the avoidance of self-focused attention is indirectly supportive of this proposition. This research shows that attention is diverted from the self when a negative discrepancy between one's current and desired state exists and there are no means available to successfully reduce that discrepancy (e.g., Gibbons & Wicklund, 1976; Steenbarger & Aderman, 1979). In these studies people avoid self-focus so as to avoid confrontation with their shortcomings. The present model of biased hypothesis testing posits that people divert attention from information relevant to their negative outcomes when they believe they will be unable to generate a seemingly rational nonthreatening attribution for such outcomes.

We should point out that given the rather ambiguous nature of social reality, situations in which people are confronted with an abundance of clear unassailable information supporting a self-threatening hypothesis are probably relatively rare. As others have suggested (cf. Nisbett & Ross, 1980; Snyder & Gangestad, 1981), in most situations, information supportive of a variety of plausible hypotheses is readily available. Thus, instances of breaks with social reality are probably rather infrequent. Instances in which attention is diverted from the issue altogether are probably somewhat more common, given the existence of alternate sources upon which one's self-esteem may be based. However, as we have suggested elsewhere (Pyszczynski & Greenberg, 1987), the fewer the alternative sources of self-worth, the more difficult it may be to avoid focusing on an important shortcoming.

VI. Summary and Conclusion

We have argued that attributional processing is influenced by a variety of motives. Although the need for accuracy is often very strong, it is sometimes outweighed by other motives that have more powerful and immediate implications for one's affective state. Likewise, although we believe that the need for self-esteem plays a central role in a wide range of social behavior (cf. Greenberg *et al.*, 1986), other needs or motives may sometimes inhibit the operation of self-serving tendencies. For example, Greenberg *et al.* (1984) have shown that the presence of large extrinsic incentives for success reduces the tendency to erect anticipatory attributional defenses before undertaking a self-esteem threatening task.

In most cases, a person's needs and motives influence inferential processes in a way that enables him or her to maintain an illusion of objectivity concerning the manner in which his/her inferences are derived; such an ostensibly rational process has adaptive value, both for the person's interactions with others and for his/her private self-concept. Consideration of an undesirable hypothesis produces an aversive state of arousal that influences which hypotheses are selected for further testing, which inference rules are generated to test one's hypotheses, the type of information that is sought to evaluate the hypothesis, the extensiveness of the search, and the manner in which information that has already been accessed is evaluated. Of course at its present stage of development, the model probably oversimplifies the processes through which biased inferences are derived. However, for present purposes, we believe that a relatively simple model is most likely to be useful in directing attention to the questions of interest concerning these issues. The model is consistent with the existing literature on self-serving biases and can be used to generate a variety of new testable hypotheses. Although further research on various aspects of the model is needed, those studies that have been conducted as tests of the model have been generally supportive

Although we have focused largely on the role of a self-esteem motive in the generation self-serving attributions for performance outcomes, the model can be readily generalized, both to other types of motives (e.g., the needs to perceive control, to believe in a just world, or to believe in the superiority of one's ingroup) and other types of cognitive tasks (e.g., belief formation and change, predictions). Regardless of the particular motive or resulting cognition, the affective consequences of a given cognitive configuration are posited to influence the manner in which information relevant to that configuration is processed. Thus, the products of people's inferential activities reflect a compromise between conclusions that may satisfy a variety of motives and those that can be supported by the information that is available.

In conclusion, we would like to suggest that cognitive, motivational, and affective processes simply cannot be understood in conceptual isolation from each other. Although such distinctions have been somewhat useful in helping to frame various approaches to understanding the mental life and behavior of the individual, they necessarily lead to a distorted depiction of the individual and an incomplete explanation of the phenomena of interest.

ACKNOWLEDGMENTS

The authors wish to thank Robert Arkin, Jurgen Beckman, Leonard Berkowitz, Jack Brehm, Shelly Duval, Peter Gollwitzer, Arie Kruglanski, John LaPrelle, Lynne Steinberg, Challenger Vought and two anonymous reviewers for their helpful comments on an earlier version of this chapter.

REFERENCES

Abramson, L. Y., Seligman, M. E. P., & Teasdale, J. D. (1978). Learned helplessness in humans: Critique and reformulation. *Journal of Abnormal Psychology, 87,* 49–74.

Ajzen, I. (1977). Intuitive theories of events and the effects of baserates on prediction. *Journal of Personality and Social Psychology, 35,* 303–314.

Albert, R. D. (1983). *Communications across cultures: A guide to Latin-American culture for North Americans.* Raleigh, MA: Newbury House.

Albert, R. D., & Adamopolous, J. (1976). An attributional approach to cultural learning: The cultural assimilator. *Topics in Culture Learning, 4,* 53–60.

Alloy, L., & Abramson, L. (1979). Judgments of contingency in depressed students: Sadder but wiser? *Journal of Experimental Psychology: General, 108,* 441–445.

Allport, G. W. (1954). *The nature of prejudice.* Garden City, NY: Doubleday.

Allport, G. W. (1961). *Pattern and growth in personality.* New York: Holt.

Anderson, R. C., & Pichert, J. W. (1978). Recall of preciously unrecallable information after a change in perspective. *Journal of Verbal Learning and Verbal Behavior, 17,* 1–12.

Arkin, R. M., & Maryuma, G. M. (1979). Attribution, affect, and college exam performance. *Journal of Educational Psychology, 21,* 85–93.

Aronson, E. (1969). The theory of cognitive dissonance: A current perspective. In L. Berkowitz (Ed.), *Advances in experimental social psychology,* (Vol. 4, pp. 1–34). New York: Academic Press.

Bar-Tal, D. (1978). Attributional analysis of achievement-related behavior. *Review of Educational Research, 48,* 259–271.

Becker, E. (1962). *The birth and death of meaning.* New York: Free Press.

Beckman, L. (1970). Teachers' and observers' perceptions of causality for a child's performance. *Journal of Educatioal Psychology, 65,* 198–204.

Bem, D. (1967). Self-perception: An alternative interpretation of cognitive dissonance phenomena. *Psychological Review, 74,* 183–200.

Bem, D. (1972). Self-perception theory. In L. Berkowitz (Ed), *Advances in experimental social psychology* (Vol. 6). New York: Academic Press.

Berglas, S., & Jones, E. E. (1978). Drug choice as a self-handicapping strategy in response to noncontingent success. *Journal of Personality and Social Psychology, 36,* 405–417.

Berlyne, D. E. (1960). *Conflict, arousal, and curiosity.* New York: McGraw-Hill.

Bowerman, W. R. (1978). Subjective competence: The structure, process, and function of self-referent causal attributions. *Journal for the Theory of Social Behavior, 8,* 45–75.

Brehm, J. W., Wright, R., Solomon, S., Silka, L., & Greenberg, J. (1983). Perceived difficulty, energization, and goal attractiveness. *Journal of Experimental Social Psychology, 19,* 21–48.

Bruner, J. S. (1957). Going beyond the information given. In H. Gruber, G. Terrell, & M. Wertheimer (Eds.), *Contemporary approaches to cognition.* Cambridge, Mass.: Harvard University Press.

Bruner, J. S., Goodnow, J. J., & Austin, G. A. (1956). *A study of thinking.* New York: Wiley.

Byrne, D., & Rhamey, R. (1965). Magnitude of positive and negative reinforcement as determinants of attraction. *Journal of Personality and Social Psychology,* **2,** 884–889.

Chapman, L. J., & Chapman, J. P. (1967). Genesis of popular but erroneous diagnostic observations. *Journal of Abnormal Psychology,* **72,** 193–204.

Chapman, L. J., & Chapman, J. P. (1982). Test results are what you think they are. In D. Kahneman, P. Slovic, & A. Tversky (Eds.), *Judgments under uncertainty: Heuristics and biases.* New York: Cambridge University Press.

Covington, M. V., & Omelich, C. L. (1979). Are causal attributions causal? A path analyses of the cognitive model of achievement motivation. *Journal of Personality and Social Psychology,* **37,** 1487–1504.

Duval, S., & Hensley, V. (1976). Extensions of objective self-awareness theory: The focus of attention-causal attribution hypothesis. In J. Harvey, W. Ickes, & R. Kidd (Eds.), *New directions in attribution research.* Hillsdale, NJ: Erlbaum.

Enzle, M. E., & Shopflocher, D. (1978). Instigation of attribution processes by attributional questions. *Personality and Social Psychology Bulletin,* **4,** 595–599.

Fazio, R. H., Sherman, S. J., & Herr, P. M. (1982). The feature positive effect: Does not doing matter as much as doing? *Journal of Personality and Social Psychology,* **42,** 404411.

Feather, N. T. (1969). Attribution of responsibility and valence of outcome in relation of initial confidence and success and failure of self and other. *Journal of Personality and Social Psychology,* **18,** 173–188.

Festinger, L. (1957). *A theory of cognitive dissonance.* Stanford, CA: Stanford University Press.

Festinger, L. (1964). *Conflict, decision, and dissonance.* Stanford, CA: Stanford University Press.

Fitch, G. (1970). Effects of self-esteem, perceived performance, and choice on causal attributions. *Journal of Personality and Social Psychology,* **16,** 311–315.

Frankel, A., & Snyder, M. L. (1978). Poor performance following unsolvable problems: Learned helplessness or egotism? *Journal of Personality and Social Psychology,* **36,** 1415–1423.

Freedman, J. L., & Sears, D. O. (1965). Selective exposure. In L. Berkowitz, (Ed.), *Advances in experimental social psychology* (Vol. 2). New York: Academic Press.

Frey, D. (1981a). Postdecisional preferences for decision-relevant information as a function of the competence of its source and the degree of familiarity with this information. *Journal of Experimental Social Psychology,* **17,** 621–626.

Frey, D. (1981b). Reversible and irreversible decisions: Preference for consonant information as a function of attractiveness of decision alternatives. *Personality and Social Psychology Bulletin,* **7,** 621–626.

Frey, D. (1981c). The effect of negative feedback about oneself and cost of information on preferences for information about the source of this feedback. *Journal of Experimental Social Psychology,* **17,** 42–50.

Frey, D. (1985). *Amount of available information and selective exposure.* Unpublished manuscript, Christian-Albrechts-University, Kiel, Federal Republic of Germany.

Frey, D. (1986). Recent research on selective exposure. In L. Berkowitz (Ed.), *Advances in experimental social psychology* (Vol. 19). New York: Academic Press.

Frey, D., & Rosch, M. (1984). Information seeking after decisions. The roles of novalty of information and decision reversibility. *Personality and Social Psychology Bulletin,* **10,** 91–98.

Frey, D., & Stahlberg, D. (1984). *Information-seeking and attitude change after attitude-discrepant behavior.* Unpublished Manuscript, Christian-Albrechts-University, Kiel, Federal Republic of Germany.

Frey, D., & Stahlberg, D. (1986). Selection of information after receiving more or less reliable self-threatening information. *Personality and Social Psychology Bulletin.*

Frey, D., & Wicklund, R. (1980). A clarification of selective exposure: The impact of choice. *Journal of Experimental Social Psychology,* **16,** 405–416.

Fries, A., & Frey, D. (1980). Misattribution of arousal and the effects of self-threatening information. *Journal of Experimental Social Psychology, 16,* 405–416.

Gibbons, F. X., & Wicklund, R. (1976). Selective exposure to self. *Journal of Research in Personality, 10,* 98–106.

Gollwitzer, P. M., Earle, W. B., & Stephan, W. G. (1982). Affect as a determinant of egotism: Residual excitation and performance attributions. *Journal of Personality and Social Psychology, 43,* 702–709.

Greenberg, J., Pyszczynski, T., & Paisley, C. (1984). Extrinsic incentives and the use of test anxiety as an anticipatory attributional defense: Playing it cool when the stakes are high. *Journal of Personality and Social Psychology, 47,* 1136–1145.

Greenberg, J., Pyszczynski, T., & Solomon, S. (1982). The self-serving attributional bias: Beyond self-presentation. *Journal of Experimental Social Psychology, 18,* 56–67.

Greenberg, J., Pyszczynski, T., & Solomon, S. (1986). The causes and consequences of a need for self-esteem: A terror-management theory. In R. Baumeister (Ed.), *Public self and private self.* New York: Springer-Verlag.

Greenberg, J., & Rosenfield, D. (1979). White's ethnocentrism and their attributions for the behavior of blacks: A motivational bias. *Journal of Personality, 47,* 643–657.

Greenwald, A. G., & Ronis, D. L. (1978). Twenty years of cognitive dissonance: Case study in the evolution of a theory. *Psychological Review, 85,* 53–57.

Hamilton, D. L. (1979). A cognitive-attributional analysis of stereotyping. In L. Berkowitz (Ed.), *Advances in experimental social psychology,* (Vol. 12). New York: Academic Press.

Hamilton, D. L. (1981). *Cognitive processes in stereotyping and intergroup behavior.* Hillsdale, NJ: Erlbaum.

Hastie, R. (1980). Memory for behavioral information that confirms or contradicts a personality impression. In R. Hastie, T. M. Ostrom, E. B. Ebbesson, R. S. Wyer, D. L. Hamilton, & D. E. Carlston (Eds.), *Person memory: The cognitive basis of perception.* Hillsdale, NJ: Erlbaum.

Hastie, R. (1983). Social inference. *Annual Review of Psychology, 34,* 511–542.

Hastie, R. (1984). Causes and effects of causal attribution. *Journal of Personality and Social Psychology, 46,* 44–56.

Heider, F. (1958). *The psychology of interpersonal relations.* New York: Wiley.

Higgins, E. T., Rholes, W. S., & Jones, C. R. (1977). Category accessibility and impression formation. *Journal of Experimental Social Psychology, 13,* 141–154.

Holton, B., & Pyszczynski, T. (1986). *Biased information search in the interpersonal domain.* Submitted for publication, University of North Carolina, Chapel Hill, NC.

Horney, K. (1937). *The neurotic personality of our times.* New York: Norton.

James, W. (1890). *The principles of psychology.* New York: Dover.

Jenkins, H. M. & Ward, W. C. (1965). Judgments of contingency between response and outcomes. *Psychological Monographs: General and Applied, 79* (Whole No. 594).

Johnson, T. J., Feigenbaum, R., & Weiby, M. (1964). Some determinants and consequences of teachers' perceptions of causation. *Journal of Educational Psychology, 55,* 237–246.

Jones, E. E., & Berglas, S. (1978). Control of attributions about the self through self-handicapping strategies: The appeal of alcohol and the role of underachievement. *Personality and Social Psychology Bulletin, 4,* 200–206.

Jones, E. E., & Davis, K. (1965). From acts to dispositions: A theory of correspondent inferences. In L. Berkowitz (Ed.), *Advances in experimental social psychology.* (Vol. 2). New York: Academic Press.

Jones, E. E., & McGillis, D. (1976). Correspondent inferences and the attribution cube: A comparative reappraisal. In J. H. Harvey, W. J. Ickes, & R. F. Kidd (Eds.), *New directions in attribution research,* (Vol. 1). Hillsdale, NJ: Erlbaum.

Katz, I. & Glass, D. C. (1979). An ambivalence-amplification theory of behavior toward the stigmatized. In W. G. Austin & S. Worchel (Eds.), *The social psychology of intergroup relations.* Monterey, CA: Brooks/Cole.

Kelley, H. H. (1967). Attribution theory in social psychology. In D. Levine (Ed.), *Nebraska symposium on motivation.* Lincoln: University of Nebraska Press.

Kelley, H. H. (1971). *Attribution in social interaction.* Morristown, NJ: General Learning Press.

Kelley, H. H. (1972). Causal schemata and the attribution process. In E. E. Jones, D. E. Kanouse, H. H. Kelley, R. E. Nisbett, S. Valins, & B. Weiner (Eds.), *Attribution: Perceiving the causes of behavior.* Morristown, NJ: General Learning Press.

Kelly, G. A. (1955). *The psychology of personal constructs.* New York: Norton.

Kruglanski, A. W. (1980). Lay epistemology process and contents. *Psychological Review,* **87,** 70–87.

Kruglanski, A., & Ajzen, I. (1983). Bias and error in human judgment. *European Journal of Social Psychology,* **13,** 1–44.

Kruglanski, A., & Freund, T. (1983). The freezing and unfreezing of lay-inferences: Effects on impressional primacy, ethnic stereotyping, and numerical anchoring. *Journal of Experimental Social Psychology,* **19,** 448–468.

Kuiper, N. (1978). Depression and causal attribution for success and failure. *Journal of Personality and Social Psychology,* **36,** 236–246.

Lau, R. R., & Russell, D. (1980). Attributions in the sports pages. *Journal of Personality and Social Psychology,* **39,** 29–38.

Levine, M. (1971). Hypothesis theory and non-learning despite ideal S-R reinforcement contingencies. *Psychological Review,* **78,** 130–140.

Lewinsohn, P., Mischel, W., Chaplin, W., & Barton, R. (1980). Social competence and depression: The role of illusory self-perceptions. *Journal of Abnormal Psychology,* **89,** 203–212.

Lingle, J. H., Geva, N., Ostrom, T. M., Leippe, M. R., & Baumgardner, M. H. (1979). Thematic effects of person judgments on impression organization. *Journal of Personality and Social Psychology,* **37,** 674–687.

Linville, P. W., & Jones, E. E. (1980). Polarized appraisals of out-group member. *Journal of Personality and Social Psychology,* **38,** 689–703.

Lowin, A. (1967). Approach and avoidance: Alternate modes of selective exposure to information. *Journal of Personality and Social Psychology,* **6,** 1–9.

Mahoney, M. J. (1977). Publication prejudices: An experimental study of confirmatory bias in the peer review system. *Cognitive Therapy and Research,* **1,** 161–175.

McArthur, L. Z. (1981). What grabs you? The role of attention in impression formation and attribution. In E. T. Higgins, C. P. Herman, & M. P. Zanna (Eds.), *Social cognition: The Ontario symposium* (Vol. 1). Hillsdale NJ: Erlbaum.

McFarland, C., & Ross, M. (1982). Impact of causal attributions on affective reactions to success and failure. *Journal of Personality and Social Psychology,* **43,** 937–946.

Mehlman, R. C., & Snyder, C. R. (1985). Excuse theory: A test of the self-protective role of attributions. *Journal of Personality and Social Psychology,* **49,** 994–1001.

Miller, D. T. (1978). Ego-involvement and attributions for success and failure. *Journal of Personality and Social Psychology,* **34,** 901–906.

Miller, D. T., & Ross, M. (1975). Self-serving biases in the attribution of causality: Fact or fiction? *Psychological Bulletin,* **82,** 213–225.

Nicholls, J. G. (1976). Effort is virtuous but it's better to have ability: Evaluative responses to perceptions of effort and ability. *Research in Personality,* **10,** 306–315.

Nisbett, R. & Ross, L. (1980). *Human Inference: Strategies and shortcomings of social judgement.* Englewood Cliffs, NJ: Prentice-Hall.

Nisbett, R., & Wilson, T. D. (1977). Telling more than we can know: Verbal reports on mental processes. *Psychological Review,* **84,** 231–259.

Osgood, C. E., & Tannebaum, P. H. (1955). The principle of congruity in the prediction of attitude change. *Psychological Review, 62,* 42–55.

Phares, E. D. (1976). *Locus of control in personality.* Morristown, NJ: General Learning Press.

Pinkley, R., LaPrelle, J., Pyszczynski, T., & Greenberg, J. (1987). Depression and the biased search for information consistent with a self-serving attribution. *Journal of Social and Clinical Psychology,* in press.

Pyszczynski, T. A., & Greenberg, J. (1981). Role of disconfirmed expectancies in the instigation of attributional processing. *Journal of Personality and Social Psychology, 40,* 31–38.

Pyszczynski, T., & Greenberg, J. (1983). Determinants of reduction in intended effort as a strategy for coping with anticipated failure. *Journal of Research in Personality, 17,* 412–422.

Pyszczynski, T., & Greenberg, J. (1985). Depression and preference for self-focusing stimuli following success and failure. *Journal of Personality and Social Psychology, 49,* 1066–1075.

Pyszczynski, T., & Greenberg, J. (1987). Depression, self-focused attention and self-regulatory preservation. In C. R. Snyder & C. E. Ford (Eds.), *Coping with negative life events: Clinical and social psychological perspectives.* New York: Plenum, in press.

Pyszczynski, T., Greenberg, J., & Holt, K. (1985a). Maintaining consistency between self-serving beliefs and available data: A bias in information evaluation following success and failure. *Personality and Social Psychology Bulletin, 11,* 179–190.

Pyszczynski, T., Greenberg, J., & LaPrelle, J. (1985b). Social comparison after success and failure: Biased search for information consistent with a self-serving conclusion. *Journal of Experimental Social Psychology, 21,* 195–211.

Pyszczynski, T., LaPrelle, J., & Greenberg, J. (1987). Encoding and retrieval effects of general person characterizations on memory for incongruent and congruent information. *Personality and Social Psychology Bulletin,* in press.

Restle, F. (1962). The selection of strategies in cue learning. *Psychological Review, 69,* 329–343.

Rizley, R. (1978). Depression and distortion in the attribution of causality *Journal of Abnormal Psychology, 87,* 32–48.

Rosenfeld, P., Melburg, V., & Tedeschi, J. T. (1981). Self-serving attributions: Biased private perceptions and distorted public descriptions. *Journal of Personality and Social Psychology, 41,* 224–231.

Ross, L. (1977). The intuitive psychologist and his shortcomings: Distortions in the attribution process: In L. Berkowitz (Ed.), *Advances in experimental social psychology,* (Vol. 10). New York: Academic Press.

Schwarz, N., Frey, D., & Kumpf, M. (1980). Interactive effects of writing and reading a persuasive essay on attitude change and selective exposure. *Journal of Experimental Social Psychology, 16,* 1–17.

Smith, E. (1984). Model of social inference processes. *Psychological Review, 91,* 392–413.

Smith, E. R., & Miller, F. D. (1979). Atributional information processing: A reaction time model of causal subtraction. *Journal of Personality and Social Psychology, 37,* 1723–1731.

Smith, T. W., Snyder, C. R., & Handelsman, M. M. (1982). On the self-serving if an academic wooden leg: Test anxiety as a self-handicapping strategy. *Journal of Personality and Social Psychology, 42,* 314–321.

Smith, T. W., Snyder, C. R., & Perkins, S. C. (1983). On the self-serving function of hypochondriacal complaints: Physical symptoms as self-handicapping strategies. *Journal of Personality and Social Psychology, 44,* 787–797.

Snyder, M. (1984). When belief creates reality. In L. Berkowitz (Ed.), *Advances in experimental social psychology* (Vol. 18). New York: Academic Press.

Snyder, M., & Campbell, B. H. (1980). Testing hypotheses about other people: The role of the hypothesis. *Personality and Social Psychology Bulletin, 6,* 421–426.

Snyder, M., & Cantor, N. (1979). Testing hypotheses about other people: The use of historical knowledge. *Journal of Experimental Social Psychology,* **15,** 330–342.

Snyder, M., & Gangestad, S. (1981). Hypothesis-testing processes. In J. W. Harvey, W. J. Ickes, & R. F. Kidd (Eds.), *New directions in attribution research,* (Vol. 3). Hillsdale, NJ: Erlbaum.

Snyder, M., & Swann, W. B., Jr. (1978). Behavioral confirmation in social interaction: From social perception to social reality. *Journal of Experimental Social Psychology,* **14,** 148–162.

Snyder, M. L., Stephan, W. G., & Rosenfield, D. (1976). Egotism and attribution. *Journal of Personality and Social Psychology,* **33,** 435–441.

Srull, T. K., & Wyer, R. S. (1979). The role of category accessibility in the interpretation of information about people: Some determinants and implications. *Journal of Personality and Social Psychology,* **37,** 1660–1672.

Steenbarger, B., & Aderman, D. (1979). Objective self-awareness as a non-aversive state: Effect of anticipating discrepancy reduction. *Journal of Personality,* **47,** 330–339.

Stephan, W. F., & Gollwitzer, P. (1981). Affect as a mediator of attributional egotism. *Journal of Experimental Social Psychology,* **17,** 443–458.

Storms, M. D. (1973). Videotape and the attribution process: Reversing actors' and observers' points of view. *Journal of Personality and Social Psychology,* **27,** 165–175.

Streufert, S., & Streufert, S. C. (1969). Effects of conceptual structure, failure, and success on attribution of causality and interpersonal attitudes. *Journal of Personality and Social Psychology,* **11,** 138–147.

Swann, W. B. (1984). Quest for accuracy in person perception: A matter of prgamatics. *Psychological Review,* **91,** 457–477.

Swann, W. G., Stephenson, B., & Pittman, T. S. (1981). Curiosity and control: On the determinants of the search for social knowledge. *Journal of Personality and Social Psychology,* **40,** 635–642.

Sweeney, P. D., & Gruber, K. L. (1984). Selective exposure: Voter information preferences and the Watergate Affair. *Journal of Personality and Social Psychology,* **46,** 1208–1221.

Taylor, S. E., & Fiske, S. T. (1975). Point of view and perceptions of causality. *Journal of Personality and Social Psychology,* **32,** 439–445.

Taylor, S. E., & Fiske, S. T. (1978). Salience, attention, and attribution: Top of the head phenomena. In L. Berkowitz (Ed.), *Advances in experimental and social psychology* (Vol. 11). New York: Academic Press.

Tesser, A., & Blusiewicz, C. (1987). Dependency, conflict, and underachievement. *Journal of Social and Clinical Psychology,* in press.

Tesser, A., & Campbell, J. (1983). Self-definition and self-evaluation maintenance. In J. Suls & A. Greenwald (Eds.), *Social Psychological perspectives on the self* (Vol. 2). Hillsdale, NJ: Erlbaum.

Tessor, A., Moore, J., & Lorden, R. (1985). *The functioning of defensive self-beliefs.* Unpublished manuscript. University of Georgia.

Tetlock, P. E., & Levi, A. (1982). Attribution bias: On the inconclusiveness of the cognition-motivation debate. *Journal of Experimental Social Psychology,* **18,** 68–88.

Triandis, H. C. (1975). Culture learning, cognitive complexity, and interpersonal attitudes. In R. Brislin, S. Bochner, & W. Looner (Eds.), *Cross-cultural perspectives on learning.* Beverly Hills and New York: Sage and Wiley/Halstead.

Trope, Y., & Bassok, M. (1982). Confirmatory and diagnosing strategies in social information gathering. *Journal of Personality and Social Psychology,* **43,** 22–34.

Tucker, J. A., Vuchinich, R. E., & Sobell, M. B. (1981). Alcohol consumption as a self-handicapping strategy. *Journal of Abnormal Psychology,* **90,** 220–230.

Tversky, A., & Kahneman, D. (1974). Judgment under uncertainty: Heuristics and biases. *Science,* 185, 1124–1131.

Tversky, A., and Kahneman, D. (1978). Causal schemata in judgments under uncertainty. In M. Fishbein (Ed.), *Progress in social psychology*. Hillsdale, N.J.: Erlbaum.

Weary-Bradley, G. (1978). Self-serving biases in the attribution process: A reexamination of the fact or fiction problem. *Journal of Personality and Social Psychology*, **36**, 56–71.

Weary, G., Havey, J., Schwieger, P., Olson, C., Perloff, R., & Pritchard, S. (1982). Self-presentation and the moderation of self-serving attributional biases. *Social Cognition*, **1**, 140–159.

Weiner, B., Russell, D., & Lerman, D. (1978). Affective consequences of causal attribution. In J. H. Harvey, W. J. Ickes, & R. F. Kidd (Eds.), *New directions in attribution research*, (Vol. 2). Hillsdale: NJ: Erlbaum.

Weiner, B., Russell, D., & Lerman, D. (1979). The cognition-emotion process in achievement-related contexts. *Journal of Personality and Social Psychology*, **37**, 1211–1220.

Wicklund, R., & Brehm, J. (1976). *Perspectives on cognitive dissonance*. Hillsdale, NJ: Erlbaum.

Wong, P. T., & Weiner, B. (1981). When people ask "why" questions, and the heuristics of attributional search. *Journal of Personality and Social Psychology*, **40**, 650–663.

Wortman, C.B., Costanzo, P. R., & Witt, T. R. (1973). Effects of anticipated performance on the attribution of causality to self and others. *Journal of Personality and Social Psychology*, **27**, 372–381.

Wyer, R. S., & Frey, D. (1983). The effects of feedback about self and others on the recall and judgments of feedback-relevant information. *Journal of Experimental Social Psychology*, **19**, 540–559.

Wyer, R. S., & Hartwick, J. (1980). The role of information retrieval and conditional retrieval processes in belief formation and change. In L. Berkowitz (Ed.), *Advances in experimental social psychology* (Vol. 13). New York: Academic Press.

Wyer, R. S., & Srull, T. K. (1981). Category accessibility: Some theoretical and empirical issues concerning the processing of social stimulus information. In E. T. Higgins, C. P. Herman, & M. P. Zanna (Eds.), *Social cognition: The Ontario symposium* (Vol. 1). Hillsdale, N.J.: Erlbaum.

Wyer, R. S., Srull, T. K., Gordon, S. E., & Hartwick, J. (1982). Effects of processing objectives on the recall of prose material. *Journal of Personality and Social Psychology*, **43**, 674–688.

Zadny, J., & Gerard, H. B. (1974). Atttributed intentions and information selectivity. *Journal of Experimental Social Psychology*, **10**, 34–52.

Zuckerman, M. (1979). Attribution of success and failure revisited, or: The motivational bias is alive and well in attribution theory. *Journal of Personality*, **47**, 245–287.

INDEX

A

Accessibility, positive affect and, 214
Achievement
  biased hypothesis testing and, 300, 307
  disposition and, 9, 39
  positive affect and, 240
  risk and, 259, 261, 288, 289
Affirmative action, disposition and, 21, 29, 32, 33
Aggregation, disposition and
  consistency, 4–7, 53
  correspondence, 40
  moderating variables, 25
  solution, 10–13
    consistency, 13, 14, 16–19
    global dispositions, 14–16
  specific actions, 42
Aggression
  attitudes and, 2
    aggregation solution, 12, 17
    moderating variables, 22, 23, 30
  biased hypothesis-testing and, 304
  positive affect and
    cognitive organization, 242
    cooperativeness, 210
    risk preference, 213
Alternation, group process and, 133, 136
Altruism, positive affect and, 208
Altruistic motivation, see Prosocial motivation
Ambivalence, opinion formation and, 171, 175, 180–184, 186
Anger
  biased hypothesis-testing and, 316
  positive affect and, 246
Anxiety
  biased hypothesis-testing and, 300, 301

disposition and, 8, 9
group process and, 130, 131
prosocial motivation and, 76, 81, 83
Approach-avoidance conflict, opinion formation and, 176–180, 183, 187
Arousal, biased hypothesis-testing and, 300, 301, 321, 323, 324, 333
Aspiration, risk and, 276–283, 285–287
Associative memory, positive affect and, 231
Associative network, positive affect and, 223–225, 245, 247
Asymmetry
  biased hypothesis-testing and, 301, 313
  positive affect and, 216–218, 223, 225, 226, 245
Attachment, prosocial motivation and, 91–93, 95, 96
Attention
  biased hypothesis-testing and, 307, 308, 332
  positive affect and, 237, 239, 246
  prosocial motivation and, 84
    altruistic views, 77
    empathy, 91, 102
Attitude, 1–3, 10, 52–55
  aggregation solution, 10–13
    consistency, 6, 7
    specific actions, 8, 10
  biased hypothesis-testing and, 298, 318
  correspondence and, 35–38
    consistency, 41, 42
  disposition and, 3
    consistency, 6, 7
    specific actions, 8, 10
  group process and, 130
  moderating-variables solution, 19
    behavioral factors, 31, 32
    consistency, 32–35